This is not just a textbook . . . it is a rural development resource that can be used in a multitude of ways, both in academic and non-academic circles.

Cheryl Burkhart-Kriesel, University of Nebraska-Lincoln, USA

Rural Wealth Creation

This book investigates the role of wealth in achieving sustainable rural economic development. The authors define wealth as all assets net of liabilities that can contribute to well-being, and they provide examples of many forms of capital – physical, financial, human, natural, social, and others. They propose a conceptual framework for rural wealth creation that considers how multiple forms of wealth provide opportunities for rural development, and how development strategies affect the dynamics of wealth. They also provide a new accounting framework for measuring wealth stocks and flows. These conceptual frameworks are employed in case study chapters on measuring rural wealth and on rural wealth creation strategies.

Rural Wealth Creation makes numerous contributions to research on sustainable rural development. Important distinctions are drawn to help guide wealth measurement, such as the difference between the wealth located within a region and the wealth owned by residents of a region, and privately owned versus publicly owned wealth. Case study chapters illustrate these distinctions and demonstrate how different forms of wealth can be measured. Several key hypotheses are proposed about the process of rural wealth creation, and these are investigated by case study chapters assessing common rural development strategies, such as promoting rural energy industries and amenity-based development. Based on these case studies, a typology of rural wealth creation strategies is proposed and an approach to mapping the potential of such strategies in different contexts is demonstrated.

This book will be relevant to students, researchers, and policy makers looking at rural community development, sustainable economic development, and wealth measurement.

John L. Pender is an economist at the US Department of Agriculture's Economic Research Service, USA.

Bruce A. Weber is Professor of Applied Economics and Director of the Rural Studies Program at Oregon State University, USA.

Thomas G. Johnson is Professor of Applied Economics and Public Affairs at the University of Missouri, USA.

J. Matthew Fannin is Associate Professor in the Department of Agricultural Economics and Agribusiness at Louisiana State University, USA.

Routledge Textbooks in Environmental and Agricultural Economics

Rural Wealth Creation

Edited by
John L. Pender, Bruce A. Weber,
Thomas G. Johnson, and
J. Matthew Fannin

Routledge
Taylor & Francis Group

LONDON AND NEW YORK

First published 2014
by Routledge
2 Park Square, Milton Park, Abingdon, Oxon OX14 4RN

and by Routledge
711 Third Avenue, New York, NY 10017

Routledge is an imprint of the Taylor & Francis Group, an informa business

© 2014 selection and editorial material, Bruce A. Weber, Thomas G.
Johnson, and J. Matthew Fannin; individual chapters, the contributors

British Library Cataloguing in Publication Data
A catalogue record for this book is available from the British Library

Library of Congress Cataloging in Publication Data
Rural wealth creation / edited by John L. Pender, Bruce A. Weber,
Thomas G. Johnson and J. Matthew Fannin.
        pages cm
  Includes bibliographical references and index.
  1. Wealth. 2. Rural development. I. Pender, J.
  HB251.R87 2014
  338.9009173'4–dc23   2013040859

ISBN: 978-0-415-85897-7 (hbk)
ISBN: 978-0-415-85898-4 (pbk)
ISBN: 978-0-203-79762-4 (ebk)

Typeset in Times New Roman
by Sunrise Setting Ltd, Paignton, UK

Printed and bound in the United States of America by
Edwards Brothers Malloy on sustainably sourced paper.

Contents

Figures

Tables

Contributors

Faqir S. Bagi is an economist with the Economic Research Service of the US Department of Agriculture. His research includes estimation of technical efficiency of various types of farms, adoption of farm technologies, and rural economic development, and has appeared in journals and ERS publications.

Conner Bailey is a professor of Rural Sociology at Auburn University. His primary research interests are in the sociology of natural resources as they relate to rural and community development. He received his PhD from Cornell University in 1980 and is a past President of the Rural Sociological Society.

Jason P. Brown is an economist in the Regional Affairs Department of the Federal Reserve Bank of Kansas City. He conducts research on issues related to regional economic growth, emerging industries, and structural change in regional industry and labor markets. His research has been published in regional science, energy, and agricultural economic journals. Prior to joining the Federal Reserve Bank of Kansas City, Jason was an economist at the USDA Economic Research Service in Washington, DC.

Yong Chen is an assistant professor of Applied Economics at Oregon State University. His research efforts are focused on rural development, in particular the interactions between human and natural systems, land use change, and economic resilience to natural disasters.

Steven C. Deller is a professor of Agricultural and Applied Economics with the University of Wisconsin-Madison and a Community Economic Development Specialist with the University of Wisconsin-Extension. His research and extension programs focus on rural economic development policy including modeling rural economic growth and development processes and local public finance issues related to community economic growth and development.

Robert Dinterman is a PhD graduate student in the Department of Agriculture and Resource Economics at North Carolina State University. His areas of research interest are regional economics and spatial econometrics.

J. Matthew Fannin is Associate Professor in the Department of Agricultural Economics and Agribusiness at Louisiana State University. His primary areas of research and teaching include rural economic development, public sector fiscal health, and community resiliency. His research has appeared in agricultural economics, regional science, and policy journals. He serves as Associate Director of Analytic and Academic Programs with the Rural Policy Research Institute.

Hodjat Ghadimi is Assistant Professor with a joint appointment in the Division of Design and Merchandising and Division of Resource Management at West Virginia University. He is also a Faculty Research Associate Professor in the Regional Research Institute. His primary fields of interests are in development planning, economic development patterns of energy-rich regions around the world, and the transition of exhaustible natural capital-based economies to a sustainable and diversified economy. He is also interested in the interface between the rigor of the social sciences and the creativity of design.

Trevor M. Harris is Eberly Distinguished Professor in the Department of Geology and Geography and Associate of the Regional Research Institute at West Virginia University. He specializes in Geographic Information Science with a current focus on 3D immersive geographies, qualitative GIS, critical GIS, and the spatial humanities. Harris co-directs the West Virginia State GIS Technical Center and the Virtual Center for Spatial Humanities.

Beth Walter Honadle is Director of the Program Monitoring and Research Division in the Office of Policy Development and Research at the US Department of Housing and Urban Development in Washington, DC. Honadle has been a Professor at the University of Minnesota, Bowling Green State University, and the University of Cincinnati. In the 1980s she was National Program Leader for Economic Development for the Cooperative Extension System and an Economist in the Economic Research Service at the US Department of Agriculture. Her research has focused on program evaluation, workforce development, the fiscal health and condition of local governments, economic development, and intergovernmental relations. Any views in the chapter she co-authored are her own and not official positions of HUD.

Becca B.R. Jablonski is a PhD candidate in the Department of City and Regional Planning at Cornell University and a predoctoral fellow with the US Department of Agriculture's National Institute of Food and Agriculture. Her primary areas of research include rural economic development and regional food system planning. She is also involved in several extension programs focused on project evaluation, distribution, and marketing.

Thomas G. Johnson is Professor of Applied Economics and Public Affairs at the University of Missouri. His primary area of research and teaching is rural economic development. Johnson's research has appeared in agricultural economics, regional science, and other social science journals. Johnson directs the Rural Policy Research Institute's Analytic and Academic Programs.

Melissa Levy is a senior associate at Yellow Wood Associates, a consulting firm focused on rural community and economic development. She is the co-author of a paper on community wealth indicators, 'Measuring Community Wealth'. Her other work includes measurement coaching, and research and facilitation for diverse natural resource-based rural economic development initiatives.

Sarah A. Low is an economist for the Economic Research Service, US Department of Agriculture. Her research interests revolve around rural economic development, in particular how entrepreneurship, manufacturing, land use, and amenities affect the rural economy. She previously worked at the Federal Reserve Bank of Kansas City's Center for the Study of Rural America and completed her PhD at the University of Illinois, Urbana-Champaign.

Mahua Majumdar received her MS in Rural Sociology from Auburn University in 2011. Her research interests include rural development and social stratification.

Alexander W. Marré is a research economist with the US Department of Agriculture's Economic Research Service. His primary area of research is in the area of rural and community economic development, especially education, human capital, and migration.

John L. Pender is an economist at the US Department of Agriculture's Economic Research Service. His current research focuses on concepts and measurement of rural wealth and well-being, and impacts of economic development programs and other policies on the US rural economy. Prior to joining ERS in 2009, he led research on rural development and natural resource management in developing countries at the International Food Policy Research Institute. He is the author of numerous research monographs, journal articles, and book chapters, and has co-edited two peer-reviewed books on rural development and natural resource issues in developing countries.

Neus Raines is Postdoctoral Fellow at the Agricultural and Applied Economics Department at the University of Missouri-Columbia. She is an online Professor at the European University, Business School MBA program. Raines' primary areas of research and teaching are organizational learning, strategic management, regional economics, and rural development.

Shanna Ratner is the Principal and Founder of Yellow Wood Associates, a consulting firm focused on rural community and economic development in the United States. Shanna was one of a dozen members of the Aspen Institute's Learning Cluster on Rural Community Capacity Building, a member of the first class of Donella Meadows Fellows in Systems Thinking, and a Mel King Fellow class of 2012–2013 at MIT. Shanna developed You Get What You Measure®, a values-based process for measuring progress toward shared goals.

Richard J. Reeder, now retired, was a researcher for the US Department of Agriculture, Economic Research Service from 1980 to 2013. His research covers a wide range of rural economic development policies and strategies, and has been published as book chapters, journal articles, and government research reports.

Timothy A. Warner is Professor of Geology and Geography at West Virginia University. His research focuses on terrestrial remote sensing, including biogeographical, geological, and urban land use applications, as well as the spatial properties of images. He is an editor of *Remote Sensing Letters*, and the Progress Reports Editor of *Progress in Physical Geography*. Starting in 2014, he will serve as Editor in Chief of the *International Journal of Remote Sensing*.

Bruce A. Weber is Professor of Applied Economics at Oregon State University. His teaching, research, and outreach efforts are focused on rural community economic vitality; hunger, poverty, and the social safety net in rural areas; and rural–urban interdependence. He is Director of the Oregon State University Rural Studies Program.

Jeremy G. Weber is an economist at the Resource and Rural Economics Division of the USDA Economic Research Service. His research covers issues involving energy development, farms, and land, and his work has been published in a variety of academic journals. Jeremy earned his PhD from the Agricultural and Applied Economics Department at the University of Wisconsin-Madison.

Acknowledgments

The idea for this book grew out of discussions among the co-editors and others involved in planning and conducting the National Conference on Rural Wealth Creation and Livelihoods; held in Washington, DC in October, 2011, and co-convened by the US Department of Agriculture (USDA) Economic Research Service (ERS) and the Ford Foundation. The conference was financially supported by the USDA National Institute for Food and Agriculture (NIFA) Agriculture and Food Research Initiative (NIFA grant number 2011-67023-30087) and by the Ford Foundation. We thank these organizations for their support. We are also grateful to Wayne Fawbush, Program Officer of the Ford Foundation, and Secretary of Agriculture Thomas Vilsack, whose leadership on the issue of rural wealth creation has inspired this work. The opinions discussed in this book are solely the authors' and do not necessarily represent the position of any of the afore-mentioned organizations or individuals, or the US Department of Agriculture.

We would like to thank the authors who contributed to this effort as reviewers as well as authors. We would also like to thank two anonymous reviewers of the book proposal and first two chapters, and John Cromartie, Colleen Heflin, and Deborah Markley, who reviewed particular chapters. Any errors are solely the responsibility of the authors and editors.

John L. Pender, Bruce A. Weber,
Thomas G. Johnson, and J. Matthew Fannin

Part I
Conceptual foundations

1 Rural wealth creation

Introduction and overview

John L. Pender, Thomas G. Johnson,
Bruce A. Weber, and
J. Matthew Fannin[1]

In August, 1992, Hurricane Andrew hit south Florida and inflicted tremendous damage, including twenty-six deaths and more than $26 billion in total property losses – making it the most expensive natural disaster in United States history at that time (Baade et al. 2007). Despite the large negative impact on local lives and physical wealth, economic activity was only temporarily reduced, and within one month after the storm taxable sales revenue in Miami was more than 5 percent higher than its usual level, and above normal spending continued for eighteen months after the storm. Although far from universal, such post-disaster economic "booms" have occurred in many cases, due to reconstruction-related expenditures largely financed by external insurance claim payments and Federal disaster funds (Burrus et al. 2002).

This example illustrates the importance of distinguishing between flows of economic activity, such as sales, income or employment, and changes in wealth, if one is concerned about the well-being of people. Although a disaster may generate economic activity, possibly even increasing employment and income for some time, few would argue that this means that the residents of the affected region or the nation as a whole are better off as a result. Apart from the people who died or otherwise suffered physical or emotional losses, many people lost a substantial amount of wealth. To understand how people's well-being was affected, one therefore needs to understand how their wealth was affected, in addition to impacts on economic activity.

The importance of understanding wealth and changes in wealth is fairly well understood when it comes to assessing the impacts of natural disasters. However, the importance of wealth for well-being is not always adequately recognized in other areas of public concern and policy debate. For example, during the recent recession and its aftermath, many policy makers have understandably put a high priority on the near-term employment and income impacts of any policy or program under consideration; such as how many jobs have been created or saved by the American Recovery and Reinvestment Act (ARRA). The longer-term benefits of ARRA and many other policies will depend on their effectiveness in creating new wealth – whether improvements in physical infrastructure, human capital, or other forms of wealth – and the economic and social returns that will accrue to those investments. Yet little attention has been paid so far to the impacts of that policy (and most other policies) on wealth.

Wealth, as we define and use the term in this book, includes all types of assets (net of liabilities) that can contribute to the well-being of people. This includes not only financial assets such as money, stocks, and bonds, and physical assets such as infrastructure, buildings, and equipment. It also includes natural capital such as renewable and non-renewable natural resources and natural amenities; human capital embodied in the education, skills, and health of people; social capital inherent in social networks and norms; and other intangible assets.[2] Although some forms of intangible capital have long been recognized as important contributors to economic performance and well-being – e.g., human capital – the idea that wealth includes much more than tangible assets has gained stature in recent years due to efforts by prominent scholars such as Nobel laureate Kenneth Arrow and his colleagues (Arrow et al. 2004, 2012) and development organizations such as the World Bank (World Bank 2006, 2011) and the United Nations (UNU-IHDP and UNEP 2012) to define and measure broader conceptions of wealth and savings.

It has been argued that intangible wealth is like the concept of "dark matter" used by astrophysicists to explain cosmological phenomena.[3] Intangible wealth plays a similar role in understanding economic phenomena: although not easily observed, it may play a dominant role in determining differences in economic performance. For example, the World Bank (2006) has estimated that intangible capital accounts for most of the differences in wealth and consumption among nations. Arrow et al. (2012) estimated that human capital accounts for more than 90 percent of the comprehensive wealth of several countries, including the US, China, Brazil, India, and Venezuela.

Investing in multiple forms of wealth is necessary if economic development efforts are to be sustainable. For example, a nation or region may increase income in the near term by depleting its natural resources, but this growth will not be sustainable unless some of the proceeds are invested in other forms of reproducible capital yielding a sufficiently high return (Hartwick 1977). Even without depletion of natural capital, economic growth theory has shown that economic growth eventually stagnates as a result of diminishing returns to produced capital (Solow 1956), unless investments are made in a broader set of types of capital, such as human capital and knowledge (Barro and Sala-i-Martin 1995).

Wealth matters not only for the economic performance of nations, but also for economic, social, and environmental outcomes within nations. For example, people with low wealth may get trapped in poverty because of their inability to cope with risks or to invest in high-return activities (Carter and Barrett 2006). Unfortunately, many social policies in the US have ignored the importance of wealth, instead subsidizing the income or consumption of the poor, and in some cases inhibiting their ability to accumulate wealth (Sherraden 1991). Without income support, poor people would undoubtedly be worse off, but wealth accumulation remains critical to achieving long-term reductions in poverty.

The distribution of wealth is a critical determinant of the distribution of poverty and well-being within the United States and other nations. The measured tangible wealth (net worth of physical and financial assets) of households in the United States is even more unequally distributed than income. In 2007, the top quintile of households owned 85 percent of total household tangible net worth, while the top quintile of income recipients in 2006 received 61 percent of total income (Wolff 2010, p. 44). Among countries for which household net worth distribution data are available, the United States has among the most unequal net worth distributions. For example, the Luxembourg Wealth Study, which has compiled wealth distribution data for several industrialized countries, found that the share of household net worth owned by the top 1 percent, 5 percent, and 10 percent of households was greater in the United States than in the six other countries studied (Canada, Finland, Germany, Italy, Sweden, and the United Kingdom) (Sierminska et al. 2006).[4] In a larger study of international household wealth distribution, Davies et al. (2009) estimated that the US had among the most unequal distributions of household net worth among twenty countries, although the top 10 percent of families held a somewhat larger share of household net worth in Denmark and Switzerland than in the United States.

Little is known about the distribution of other forms of wealth besides household wealth (such as public wealth) or of less tangible forms of wealth, which also influence the distribution of poverty and well-being. Very little is known about the distribution of wealth in subnational regions, such as the distribution of wealth in rural vs. urban areas. The available evidence on wealth in rural areas of the United States is limited mainly to data on the marketable net worth (physical and financial assets) of farm operator households (Wye City Group 2012), with little evidence yet on non-farm rural households or on other types of rural wealth.

Rural development policy makers, funders, and practitioners in the United States have begun to focus on rural wealth creation as the key to achieving lasting rural prosperity. Secretary of Agriculture Thomas Vilsack has argued that the US Department of Agriculture (USDA) "must help rural communities create wealth so they are self-sustaining, repopulating and thriving economically".[5] The Appalachian Regional Commission has embraced an "asset-based development" approach, emphasizing investment strategies that build upon the cultural, natural, physical, and leadership assets of Appalachian communities. In 2008, the Ford Foundation launched a program to promote wealth creation in poor rural communities in rural Appalachia, the South, and the Rio Grande Valley, and asks grantees to measure impacts of projects on seven forms of wealth.

Despite the increased attention being paid to wealth and wealth creation by scholars, international development organizations, and rural development policy makers and practitioners, solid empirical research on this topic is still quite limited. There are large and growing literatures on some types of assets and their relationship to economic development, such as human, natural, and social capital. However, there has been much less research investigating the interactions and dynamics of investments in these different types of assets, and how these concepts can be measured. This book seeks to begin to address these knowledge gaps, focusing on rural wealth creation in the United States.

Objectives and intended audience

This book seeks to synthesize and contribute to knowledge about the concept of rural wealth creation, how rural wealth can be measured, and strategies for creating and maintaining rural wealth that contribute to lasting and broadly shared rural prosperity. The empirical focus is on approaches to create and measure rural wealth in the United States. This is not to assert that wealth creation is important only in rural areas and only in the United States. Rather, this focus grows out of the research experience and emphasis of the editors and authors of this book, and reflects the need to keep our task manageable.

There are many researchers, practitioners, and others working on community and economic development issues in other countries and in urban environments of the United States for whom the concepts and empirical methods presented in this book are likely to be useful, even if the empirical contexts in which they work are different. Conversely, we draw upon concepts, frameworks, and methods that have been developed and applied in many other contexts.[6] For example, the conceptual framework for rural wealth creation presented by Pender and Ratner in Chapter 2 draws heavily upon the Sustainable Livelihoods Framework (Carney 1998) developed by the Department for International Development of the United Kingdom (and other frameworks proposed in the literature), which has been applied in many developing country contexts.

Although our focus on rural wealth creation in the United States is primarily for practical reasons, this context is a useful focus in its own right. Rural areas generally face different opportunities and constraints to achieving sustained prosperity than urban areas, largely due to different wealth endowments. For example, natural resources and amenities usually play a greater role in economic development strategies in rural areas, whether as the basis for agriculture, forestry, or mining activities, or as a key factor attracting residents and tourists. By contrast, many forms of physical and human capital are often more scarce in rural areas, due to their low population density, distance from population centers, and the fixed costs of acquiring and maintaining such assets. Rural wealth creation opportunities in more developed countries such as the United States are likely to differ from those in developing countries, where rural communities tend to be much more dependent upon agriculture for economic subsistence and opportunities for amenity-based rural development are likely to be more limited.

Despite these general patterns, rural areas of the United States are highly diverse, with large variations in the extent of their dependence on agriculture or other natural-resource-based industries, access to infrastructure and services, demographic characteristics, social and political relationships, poverty, and other characteristics. Thus, although lessons about wealth creation opportunities in the rural United States may not be directly applicable in other countries or in urban contexts, the rural United States provides a valuable "laboratory" within which the challenges and opportunities of creating and measuring wealth in diverse contexts can be investigated. Furthermore, several of the chapters of the book investigate differences in wealth or wealth creation strategies between urban and rural areas, broadening the set of contexts addressed in the book.

This book is intended to be a foundation for further research on wealth and wealth creation, rather than a distillation of key messages and best practices learned from a completed program of research. Hence, two of the main objectives are to demonstrate a framework and approach to conducting useful research on this topic, and to identify critical knowledge gaps and priorities for future research. Implications for rural development policy and practice are drawn when these are well supported by the available theory and evidence, but drawing such implications is not the primary objective of this book.

The primary audience for this book is expected to be applied researchers and students of sustainable rural economic development, community development, regional science, and rural sociology. Although the focus is on rural areas of the United States, researchers working on such issues in more urban contexts or in other countries should find the concepts, frameworks, and methods applied in this book to be useful, even if some adaptation to other contexts may be required. Comparison of development strategies being pursued in particular rural contexts of the United States with similar contexts in other countries may be especially useful. Policy makers and development funders and practitioners may also find these concepts, methods, and comparisons useful.

Contributions to the literature

The book makes several important contributions to the rural economic and community development literature. In Chapter 2, Pender and Ratner review and define the different kinds of wealth discussed in various literatures, and propose a conceptual framework for rural wealth creation that incorporates the wealth types, their interactions and dynamics, key contextual factors, and the decision makers, decisions, and outcomes influenced by and influencing wealth. The conceptual framework draws and builds upon the literature on rural development in developing countries as well as the North American literature, a link that has been largely absent in previous studies of US rural development. As argued by Steven Deller in Chapter 10, this framework represents an evolution of thinking about community economic development, elaborating and emphasizing particular features of community economic development analysis related to multiple types of wealth. The framework is used to guide the case studies of wealth creation strategies presented in Part III, and to develop several general hypotheses about the process of rural wealth creation that the case studies shed light upon. The lessons that the case studies provide with respect to these hypotheses are summarized in Chapter 18.

Among the hypotheses addressed in the book is the importance of accounting for local context and wealth endowments when considering strategies for sustainable rural development and wealth creation. The case studies in Part III illustrate the importance of various contextual factors in determining the potential for particular wealth creation strategies. Chapter 17 goes beyond identifying lists of important contextual factors, demonstrating an approach to mapping the locations that have potential (in some cases apparently underexploited potential) to pursue a particular strategy (attracting retirees in this case). Such an approach has been little used in the research literature, but could be of value to policy makers and other decision makers considering strategy options in particular regions or communities.

The volume also advances the literature by demonstrating approaches to measure multiple types of rural wealth at different scales. In Chapter 3, Johnson et al. propose an accounting framework for measuring wealth, incorporating capital accounts into an extended social accounting matrix (SAM) framework. Their framework builds upon the System of Environmental and Economic Accounts proposed by the United Nations et al. (2003); and highlights four key issues related to wealth measurement: (1) the scope of wealth, (2) stocks vs. flows, (3) people vs. place wealth, and (4) public vs. private wealth. We believe that the book contributes to an understanding of each of these issues.

Scope of wealth

While the book draws on the popular "community capitals" paradigm (e.g., Emery and Flora 2006), it provides alternative ways of characterizing them. For example, financial wealth is often viewed as being in the same class as other forms of wealth. However, as argued by Johnson et al., financial wealth is different in kind from many other forms of wealth, since it is not a direct input in a production process or a direct contributor to well-being, as are many other forms of wealth. Rather, financial assets and liabilities contribute instrumentally to well-being, by facilitating economic transactions, liquidity, risk management, savings, and investments in other types of assets; and by reflecting the complex patterns of ownership of other types of assets. The particular characteristics of other types of wealth are considered as well.

Stocks vs. flows

Johnson et al. clarify that wealth is comprised of *stocks* of assets contributing to well-being. These stocks are accumulations of the *flows* that are typically used as measures of economic performance. The wealth accounting framework proposed by Johnson et al. conceptualizes wealth as accumulated stocks of all types of capital. While the traditional SAM framework measures the flows of current account resources between institutions (households, governments, enterprises), Johnson et al.'s wealth-accounting framework allows for the interactions between capital account stocks of institutions. Flows to and from these stocks of assets, and the ownership of these assets by households, governments, and enterprises provide the conceptual basis for measuring changes in net wealth of regions and/or the residents of regions, thus providing a basis for both place-based and people-based measures of wealth.

People- vs. place-based wealth

Johnson et al. distinguish between ownership and geographic location of wealth (*people- vs. place*-based wealth). In some cases, the two forms of wealth intersect; for example, human capital can be assigned to both the individual person in whom this capital is embodied as well as the place that the individual resides. By contrast, the owners of natural or physical capital may not reside where these assets are located, so there is an important distinction between where such wealth is located and who owns it. This book makes clear that only people-based wealth can have liabilities held against it. A place cannot have liabilities held against its assets since the place does not "own" the asset. The distinction between these concepts is illustrated in a case study of people- vs. place-based wealth by Fannin and Honadle in Chapter 7.

Public vs. private wealth

Johnson et al. distinguish private and public sector wealth, and Fannin and Honadle provide an example illustrating measurement of some components of public wealth for the State of Louisiana and a particular parish in the state.

Although this book contributes to knowledge about rural wealth in several ways, it is important to emphasize that it represents only a starting point for research on rural wealth and wealth creation. As is emphasized throughout the book, there is a lack of data and research that measures rural wealth of different kinds, the interactions among different types of rural wealth, the distribution of rural wealth, or the dynamics of rural wealth. We hope that this book will help to stimulate much more research on this topic.

Overview of the book

The book consists of four parts. Part I provides the conceptual foundations for the book, including two chapters discussing the basic concepts and frameworks. Part II includes six chapters on measuring multiple types of wealth at different scales. Part III includes seven chapters on wealth creation strategies, including an initial chapter on rural economic development approaches that have been used in the past and their relationship to wealth creation, and six chapters on particular wealth creation opportunities and strategies. Part IV includes two chapters – one developing a typology of wealth creation approaches and contexts, drawing from the case studies in Part III, and a final chapter that draws conclusions and implications from all of the material in the book. A brief synopsis of each chapter follows.

In Chapter 2, "Wealth concepts", John L. Pender and Shanna Ratner define wealth and explain that wealth includes a broader set of assets than is commonly understood. They discuss several types of wealth that have been discussed in the literature (including physical, financial, natural, human, intellectual, social, political, and cultural capitals), key characteristics of all forms of wealth, and distinguish wealth from other related concepts. They present a conceptual framework for rural wealth creation, drawing upon frameworks in the domestic and international literature, and explain the purposes of the framework. They conclude with a discussion of how this framework guided the case studies in the book, and provide several general hypotheses about rural wealth creation strategies based on the framework.

In Chapter 3, "Comprehensive wealth accounting: bridging place-based and people-based measures of wealth", Thomas G. Johnson, Neus Raines, and John L. Pender describe the principles upon which a comprehensive wealth-accounting system must be based. They then develop a conceptual wealth-accounting framework that accommodates all types of capital, including market and non-market and publicly and privately owned capital. The resulting conceptual framework is related to the concept of sustainability. These concepts are then used to describe an extended current social-accounting matrix and a linked capital account. Finally, the framework is used to demonstrate how place-based and people-based measures of comprehensive wealth could be calculated.

In Chapter 4, "Measuring rural wealth: valuing human and built capital at the community level", Alexander W. Marré and John L. Pender focus on valuing two major components of comprehensive wealth – property values and human capital – for municipalities in Oregon between 1990 and 2010. This period of time includes the implementation of the Northwest Forest Plan (NWFP). They show how the value of human capital can be estimated for rural places in the United States using publicly available data. They build on theoretical work by Arrow et al. (2012) and empirical work by Mumford (2012) and are the first to measure human capital at the sub-state level. Human capital and property values for NWFP-adjacent and non-adjacent municipalities are compared.

In Chapter 5, "The net worth of households: is there a rural difference?", Alexander W. Marré compares the dynamics of household wealth for residents in urban and rural areas between 1999 and 2009 using data from the Panel Study of Income Dynamics. Rural and urban differences in household net worth were found only in two of four subcategories of net worth – financial capital and home equity – driven by demographic characteristics, initial wealth, and wages. Results from this study suggest that improving educational attainment in rural areas would increase wages and reduce the rural and urban gap in financial capital and home equity.

In Chapter 6, "The role of wealth measurements in improving practice: lessons from the field", Shanna Ratner and Melissa Levy argue that measurement provides information that improves decision making for practitioners/policy makers and generates insight for researchers. Existing literature offers limited lessons on how best to measure stocks of wealth. In 2008, the Ford Foundation began the program Wealth Creation in Rural Communities – Building Sustainable Livelihoods. This chapter explains how a wealth matrix based on seven forms of wealth is used by program grantees to plan and adjust interventions, engage partners in wealth creation value chains, and assess progress in order to improve wealth creation and livelihood outcomes in real time. The chapter provides examples of indicators of the different forms of wealth being measured by four development networks in central Appalachia.

In Chapter 7, "Defining and measuring public sector wealth: how much control does the public have over public wealth in a fiscally stressed world?", J. Matthew Fannin and Beth Walter Honadle identify public wealth as a subset of overall regional wealth. They divide public wealth into people- and place-based dimensions. Through an example using financial statement data of an individual Louisiana parish, they show how to distribute ownership of state government assets to individual parish (county) geographies. They discuss liquidity as a special subset of financial wealth that provides returns to organizing public transactions. They also show how local governments are constrained by state governments in generating revenues or making strategic investments that improve long-run fiscal health and sustainability.

In Chapter 8, "Measuring the wealth of regions: geospatial approaches to empirical capital estimation", Hodjat Ghadimi, Trevor M. Harris, and Timothy A. Warner argue that measuring wealth through empirical metrics is challenging; particularly at subnational scales necessary for advancing regional sustainable development and evaluating development policy impacts. In conjunction with rapid innovations in geographical information systems (GIS) and remote sensing technologies, spatial data infrastructures at regional, national, and global scales have been developed that contain authenticated and well-attributed spatial data. These spatial data resources provide a rich reservoir of information from which to generate empirical wealth estimates at subnational scales. In this chapter they examine how geospatial technologies and associated spatial data infrastructures can be used to generate metrics or proxies for multi-scalar wealth estimation.

In Chapter 9, "Absentee forest and farm land ownership in Alabama: capturing benefits from natural capital controlled by non-residents", Conner Bailey and Mahua Majumdar examine ownership of forest and farmland in Alabama using county tax records from fifty of sixty-seven counties. These data show that absentee owners, defined as people who do not live in the county where their land is located, own more than half of all land in Alabama. They find that absentee ownership is negatively correlated with per capita income and educational attainment, and is positively correlated with the percentage of children receiving free or reduced-cost meals in public schools. They conclude that the absentee ownership of land is a constraint to wealth generation in Alabama.

In Chapter 10, "Strategies for rural wealth creation: a progression of thinking through ideas and concepts", Steven C. Deller argues that the idea of rural wealth creation is rooted in the foundations of decades of rural economic growth and development thinking, research, and policies. A review of those historical foundations is provided in this chapter. The progression of thinking about economic development, community development, and rural development over time is outlined. As our theoretical and empirical understanding of the growth process has progressed over time, our thinking about strategies has also been refined. He argues that the rural wealth creation framework as a systems-thinking approach to rural economic growth and development can broaden our thinking about rural development strategies.

In Chapter 11, "Rural wealth creation and emerging energy industries: lease and royalty payments to farm households and businesses", Jeremy G. Weber, Jason P. Brown, and John L. Pender observe that new technologies, changes in global energy markets, and government policies encouraged growth in the natural gas and wind industries in the 2000s, and that this growth has offered new opportunities for wealth creation in many rural areas. They explore several salient issues for rural wealth and energy development, providing concrete examples of the wealth-related ideas discussed throughout the book. Locally, households owning land or mineral rights can benefit from energy development through lease and royalty payments. Using nationally representative data on US farms from 2011, they assess the consumption, investment, and wealth implications of the $2.3 billion in lease and royalty payments that energy companies paid to farm businesses. They estimate that the savings of current energy payments combined with the effect of payments on land values added $104,000 in wealth for the average recipient farm.

In Chapter 12, "Natural capital and rural wealth creation: a case study of Federal forest policy and community vitality in the Pacific Northwest", Yong Chen and Bruce A. Weber show how Federal policy about federally owned natural capital (forests) creates winners and losers for owners of other forms of capital in nearby communities. When the NWFP reduced Federal timber harvests by 90 percent during the 1990s, many Oregon timber towns saw mill closures and loss of wood products jobs. They found that in the short run, mill closures reduced growth in population and the value of real property wealth, and loss of logging jobs reduced community median income (returns to job-specific human capital). At the same time, however, communities close to NWFP-protected forests had enhanced amenities and grew faster in population and community real property value. Real property values continued to grow faster in the NWFP-adjacent communities in the subsequent decade but the detrimental effects of the NWFP in nearby logging and mill towns disappeared after 2000.

In Chapter 13, "Entrepreneurship and rural wealth creation", Sarah A. Low focuses on the relationship between the wealth a rural community has, or could invest in, and entrepreneurship as an economic livelihood strategy. Specifically, the chapter delves into the relationship between county levels of financial, physical, human, intellectual, and natural capital and entrepreneurship, using insights from the literature and original empirical analysis. The chapter also includes discussion of the various motivations for entrepreneurship and proxies for measuring entrepreneurship that work for US regions and across time, including self-employment and establishment births.

In Chapter 14, "Evaluating the impact of farmers' markets using a rural wealth creation approach", Becca B.R. Jablonski uses the literature on farmers' markets as a lens to evaluate the potential for local food systems to enhance asset building and capital creation in rural communities. With a focus on financial, social, human, and natural capitals, and particularly on their interrelationships, she demonstrates that using a wealth creation approach to measuring the impacts of local food initiatives paints a far different picture than evaluating the same strategy by its economic impact alone. The chapter concludes with key areas for future research.

In Chapter 15, "Attracting retirees as a rural wealth creation strategy", Richard J. Reeder and Faqir S. Bagi examine how retiree attraction fits into the wealth creation framework and how communities can avoid potential pitfalls. Research suggests that natural and/or man-made amenities and other characteristics can attract retirees. During the 1990s and 2000s, rural American communities attracting retirees generally added significantly to their financial, physical, and human capital, even during the more recent and difficult economic times. However, these communities might benefit more by using the wealth creation framework when designing their retiree attraction strategies.

In Chapter 16, "Casino development as a rural wealth creation strategy", John L. Pender reviews the literature on casinos and finds that casino development has been most affected by changes in the legal and regulatory context and in social norms and consumer preferences, technological change, access to markets and infrastructure, proximity to urban markets and large local populations, and local institutions. There is substantial evidence of positive economic impacts of casinos, particularly on employment, population, earnings and income per capita, and property values. Impacts on tax revenues are more uncertain. There are many social costs of casino development, due largely to impacts on problem and pathological gambling. Casinos can have social benefits as well as costs, resulting from improvements in economic opportunities. Some studies suggest that casinos may be having substantial impacts on several types of wealth, including financial wealth, property values, social capital, and others. Many of the costs, benefits, and wealth impacts are likely to be context dependent, though few studies have investigated this.

In Chapter 17, "Developing a typology of wealth creation approaches and contexts: hypotheses and an example for the case of attracting retirees", John L. Pender and Robert Dinterman develop a typology of rural wealth creation strategies and hypotheses about the key contextual factors and assets affecting the potential of these strategies, drawing upon the conceptual framework presented in Chapter 2 and the case studies in Part III. They demonstrate an approach to mapping the places in which one particular strategy – attracting retirees – has potential. They conclude with some observations about how this approach could be extended and used to guide a program of applied research on rural wealth creation.

In Chapter 18, "Rural wealth creation: conclusions and implications", John L. Pender, Bruce A. Weber, Thomas G. Johnson, and J. Matthew Fannin synthesize the major findings of the book and discuss implications. They argue that the book has provided a foundation for understanding rural wealth creation, and that more data collection and research are needed on this topic. Although existing data sources limit research on rural wealth, much can be accomplished with available data. The foundational chapters of the book provide frameworks to guide further research on key issues such as how to distinguish people-based from place-based wealth, the importance of contextual factors in determining wealth creation opportunities, and how the multiple types of wealth interact and change over time as rural communities pursue such opportunities. The empirical chapters provide examples of research that can be conducted on these topics using available data sources.

Notes

1   The views expressed are those of the authors and should not be attributed to the US Department of Agriculture or to the Economic Research Service.
2   In Chapter 2, Pender and Ratner define and provide examples of eight forms of wealth.
3   <http://blogs.worldbank.org/developmenttalk/of-dark-matter-and-domesday>.
4   However, the Gini index for net worth distribution was larger for Sweden than for the United States (Sierminska et al. 2006).
5   From a speech by Secretary Vilsack on the El Reno, Oklahoma Tour Stop, 23 September 2009.
6   Linkages of this research to such concepts, frameworks, and methods are discussed in Chapters 2 and 3, and in Pender et al. (2012).

References

Arrow, K., Dasgupta, P., Goulder, L., Daily, G., Ehrlich, P., et al. (2004) "Are we consuming too much?", *Journal of Economic Perspectives*, 18(3): 147–72.
Arrow, K.J., Dasgupta, P., Goulder, L.H., Mumford, K.J., and Oleson, K. (2012) "Sustainability and the measurement of wealth", *Environment and Development Economics*, 17: 317–53.
Baade, R.A., Baumann, R., and Matheson, V. (2007) "Estimating the economic impact of natural and social disasters, with an application to Hurricane Katrina", *Urban Studies*, 44(11): 2061–76.
Barro, R. and Sala-i-Martin, X. (1995) *Economic Growth*, New York: McGraw-Hill.
Burrus, R., Dumas, C., Farrell, C., and Hall, W. (2002) "Impact of low-intensity hurricanes on regional economic activity", *Natural Hazards Review*, August, pp. 118–25.
Carney, D. (1998) "Implementing the sustainable livelihoods approach", in D. Carney (ed.), *Sustainable Rural Livelihoods: What Contribution Can We Make?* London: Department for International Development.
Carter, M.R. and Barrett, C.B. (2006) "The economics of poverty traps and persistent poverty: an asset-based approach", *Journal of Development Studies*, 42(2): 178–99.
Davies, J.B., Sandström, S., Shorrocks, A., and Wolff, E. (2009) "The global pattern of household wealth", *Journal of International Development*, 21: 1111–24.
Emery, M. and Flora, C. (2006) "Spiraling-up: mapping community transformation with community capitals framework", *Community Development*, 37(1): 19–35.
Hartwick, J. (1977) "Intergenerational equity and the investing of rents from exhaustible resources", *American Economic Review*, 66: 972–74.
Mumford, K.J. (2012) "Measuring inclusive wealth at the state level in the United States", in UNU-IHDP and UNEP, *Inclusive Wealth Report 2012: Measuring Progress toward Sustainability*, Cambridge: Cambridge University Press.
Pender, J., Marré, A., and Reeder, R. (2012) Rural Wealth Creation: Concepts, Strategies, and Measures, Economic Research Report No. 131, Washington, DC: US Department of Agriculture Economic Research Service.

Sherraden, M. (1991) *Assets and the Poor: A New American Welfare Policy*, London: M.E. Sharpe.

Sierminska, E., Brandolini, A., and Smeeding, T.M. (2006) "Comparing wealth distribution across rich countries: first results from the Luxembourg Wealth Study". Online. Available at: <http://papers.ssrn.com/sol3/Papers.cfm?abstract_id=927402> (accessed 25 August 2010).

Solow, R.M. (1956) "A contribution to the theory of economic growth", *Quarterly Journal of Economics*, 70(1): 65–94.

United Nations, European Commission, International Monetary Fund, Organisation for Economic Co-operation and Development, and World Bank (2003) *Integrated Environmental and Economic Accounting 2003. Handbook of National Accounting, Studies in Methods*, New York: United Nations.

United Nations University International Human Dimensions Programme on Global Environmental Change (UNU-IHDP) and United Nations Environment Programme (UNEP) (2012) *Inclusive Wealth Report 2012: Measuring Progress Toward Sustainability*, Cambridge: Cambridge University Press.

Wolff, E.N. (2010) "Recent trends in household wealth in the United States: rising debt and the middle-class squeeze – an update to 2007", Working Paper No. 589, Annandale-on-Hudson, NY: Levy Economics Institute of Bard College.

World Bank (2006) *Where is the Wealth of Nations? Measuring Capital for the 21st Century*, Washington, DC: World Bank.

World Bank (2011) *The Changing Wealth of Nations. Measuring Sustainable Development in the New Millennium*, Washington, DC: World Bank.

Wye City Group (2012) *The Wye Group Handbook. Statistics on Rural Development and Agricultural Household Income*, Food and Agricultural Organization of the United Nations. Online. Available at: <http://www.fao.org/fileadmin/templates/ess/pages/rural/wye_city_group/index.htm> (accessed 25 February 2012).

2 Wealth concepts[1]

John L. Pender and Shanna Ratner[2]

If we are to make progress in pursuing and measuring rural wealth creation, we need a clear understanding of wealth concepts and how wealth creation can be achieved. Discussions of wealth and wealth distribution typically focus on households' or businesses' ownership of physical assets such as land, buildings, and equipment, and financial assets such as currency, stocks, and bonds, net of liabilities (Wye City Group 2012). More recently, some prominent scholars and development organizations have sought to define and measure broader conceptions of wealth, incorporating other assets that contribute to human well-being, such as wealth embodied in natural resources (natural capital), in human beings (human capital), in social relationships (social capital), and other intangible forms of wealth (Arrow et al. 2010; World Bank 2006, 2011).

In this chapter, we discuss what is meant by "wealth" and present a conceptual framework for wealth creation, which will be applied throughout this book.

What is "wealth"?

Many people think of wealth in terms of money. A Google search on "wealth" turns up numerous websites devoted to the accumulation of financial assets. A wealthy person is commonly thought of as a person with a lot of money and other financial assets, and a wealthy community as a community where a lot of wealthy individuals live. Wealth is less commonly thought of as a shared asset, or as including assets that cannot be reduced to a monetary value.

In our society, if you have financial wealth, you have choices. If you are sufficiently wealthy, you have the choice of living off the income stream from your financial wealth without having to work. If you steward your accumulated financial assets well, they can provide you and even future generations with a relatively steady stream of returns. However, if you deplete your wealth, the income it earns will dry up, and your financial well-being will decline. This provides a clue to how to achieve a sustainable society, but only if we broaden our definition of wealth to include all of the types of wealth needed for well-being.

Society's focus on accumulation of financial wealth has led us to undervalue the impact of financial wealth accumulation on other essential assets such as workers, natural resources, ideas, power, and relationships. Financial wealth has often been accumulated over time through the exploitation of these other assets. We see these depreciated assets all around us in polluted water, air, and soil, deteriorated infrastructure, and political gridlock. At the same time, progress has been made in many aspects of well-being through investments in health, education, environmental restoration, and more. If we can learn to recognize and limit the negative tradeoffs inherent in many approaches to wealth accumulation and learn to live off the "income" provided by multiple forms of wealth, while maintaining the underlying assets through ongoing investments in stewardship, we will come closer to realizing a sustainable society.

A first step toward a more sustainable society is to redefine the meaning of "wealth". Many thinkers have been at the forefront of expanding our definition of wealth in pursuit of sustainability.[3] The World Bank has redefined wealth to include three broad categories of assets: produced (e.g., buildings, machines, roads, etc.), natural, and intangible capital. In rich countries like the United States, intangible wealth, which includes technological change, institutional innovation, learning by doing, and social capital, along with other factors, is a fundamental driver of the economy.

We define wealth broadly to include all assets, net of liabilities, that can contribute to the well-being of an individual or group. This definition is similar in some respects to the definition provided by Arrow et al. (2010, p. 2), who defined comprehensive wealth as "the social worth of an economy's entire productive base", which "consists of the entire range of factors that determine intergenerational well-being". However, unlike Arrow et al., we do not use the term "social worth", which suggests that all types of wealth can be measured using a single metric of social worth. We think it is useful to consider many different types of assets as wealth, even if they cannot all be aggregated into a single monetary measure. Also, although we indicate that wealth *can* contribute to well-being, wealth doesn't necessarily determine well-being, since well-being depends upon how wealth and the costs and benefits of investing in wealth are distributed, and on how wealth is used.[4]

This broad definition lets us think creatively about how best to invest limited resources to create the best future for the most people. It indicates that not all wealth is financial wealth or private wealth that privileges some and excludes others. In fact, much of our wealth is shared, and investing in our shared wealth can benefit us all.

Toward a broader definition of wealth

Eight forms of wealth have been identified in the literature as different types of capital, which, taken together, form the basis for a systems approach to sustainable development. Much has been written about each. Some rural development frameworks focus on four capitals, some on five, or six or seven or eight.[5] The specific number is not as important as recognition that we need a broader definition of wealth to achieve inclusive and sustainable development. We have chosen to discuss these eight forms of wealth because we believe there is value in specificity, and because each of these has been discussed to a significant extent in the literature. The definitions used here are designed to contribute to an actionable framework for sustainable development. By considering the impact of development activities on each of the forms of wealth, and crafting interventions that result in strengthening the underlying capitals and increasing their capacity to generate "income" (here we consider a broad notion of income to reflect well-being, including non-monetary aspects of well-being) both individually and synergistically, practitioners can discover new opportunities to enhance rural livelihoods and well-being.

Physical, produced or built capital includes the stock of produced capital goods (i.e., buildings and equipment) used by firms to produce outputs; infrastructure used to reduce costs of commerce (e.g., roads, bridges, waterways, telecommunication networks) or provide public services (e.g., water and sewer treatment plants); and durable goods used by households for either production or consumption purposes (e.g., houses, vehicles, household equipment). Physical capital depreciates over time and with use and requires ongoing investment to maintain its value. Depreciated physical capital may not be wealth at all; in fact it may be detrimental to well-being. Like all forms of capital, physical capital can contribute to well-being by contributing to other forms of wealth. For example, sewer and water treatment plants contribute to human capital (health). Schools contribute to human capital (skill development) and social capital (if they are used as community gathering places) and may contribute to natural capital (if they include natural areas that are maintained or protected by the school).

Financial capital is the stock of money and other liquid financial assets, such as stocks, bonds, and letters of credit – net of financial liabilities – that can be readily converted to money. Financial capital includes claims of rights to flows of income or services from other forms of capital. For example, owners of stock shares of a corporation own rights to earnings that flow from the use of the corporation's full set of assets. For many forms of financial capital, such as bonds and other forms of credit, one person's asset is someone else's liability, so these do not contribute directly to the net wealth of society as a whole, although they contribute positively to the wealth of some and negatively to others. Financial capital, if well-managed, generates monetary returns that can be used for further investment or consumption. Unlike some other forms of capital, financial capital does not contribute directly to production or well-being. Rather, its contribution is instrumental, by facilitating transactions in other forms of capital and in goods and services, providing liquidity and helping people to manage risk.

Natural capital is the stock of healthy environmental assets (e.g., air, water, land, flora, fauna, etc.) in a region, which are capable of producing returns in the form of flows of goods and services, including non-marketed ecosystems services. Natural capital includes: (1) non-renewable resources such as oil and minerals that are extracted from ecosystems,[6] and (2) renewable resources such as fish, wood, and drinking water that are produced and maintained by the processes and functions of ecosystems.[7] Investments in natural capital include restoration and maintenance. "Income" from natural capital includes a sustainable supply of raw materials and environmental services such as maintenance of the quality of the atmosphere, climate, operation of the hydrological cycle including flood controls and drinking water supply, waste assimilation, recycling of nutrients, generation of soils, pollination of crops, and the maintenance of a vast genetic library. Natural capital and its systems are essential for life. People can destroy, degrade, impair, and/or restore natural capital but cannot create it.

Human or individual capital is the stock of education, skills, and physical and mental health of people.[8] Investments in human capital include spending on skill development (e.g., literacy, numeracy, computer literacy, technical skills, etc.) and health maintenance and improvement. "Income" from investments in human capital includes wage and salary income, as well as psychic returns from the capacity to use and apply existing knowledge and internalize new knowledge.

Intellectual capital is the stock of knowledge, innovation, and ideas embodied not in individual minds – as human capital is – but instead in the enduring intellectual products those minds have created. Intellectual capital is thus dependent on the human capital involved in creating it, but exists separately from particular individuals.[9] Innovation involves creating new knowledge and discovering new products, ideas, or new ways of organizing human activities. Investment in intellectual capital is often through research and development and support for activities that engage the imagination, as well as diffusion of new knowledge and applications. Intellectual capital may be owned privately or in common by the public (e.g., common knowledge). Intellectual property rights, such as patents and copyright protections, are used to provide private rights to intellectual capital, to increase incentives for private individuals and firms to invest in creating it. "Income" from intellectual capital includes the economic and psychic returns from inventions, new discoveries, new knowledge, and new ways of seeing.

Social capital is the stock of trust, relationships, and networks that support civil society.[10] There are at least two forms of social capital: bridging and bonding (Gittell and Vidal 1998).[11] Investments in bridging social capital are those that lead to connections between otherwise unconnected individuals and groups. Investments in bonding social capital are those that strengthen relationships within groups. For example, sponsoring a town-wide festival could be seen as an investment in bonding social capital for town residents. As with other forms of capital, aspects of social capital may be owned by individuals (e.g., the social obligations that one friend "owes" to another, which are one person's asset and the other's liability), or by groups (e.g., a social network). "Income" from investment in social capital includes returns from improved coordination and collective action, such as improved health outcomes, educational outcomes, and reduced transaction costs, among others.

Political capital is the stock of power and goodwill held by individuals, groups, and organizations that can be held, spent, or shared to achieve desired ends.[12] Political capital is evidenced by the ability of an individual or a group to influence the distribution of resources within a social unit, including helping set the agenda of what resources are available. Investments in political capital are made through inclusive organizing that includes information gathering and dissemination, and increasing voice, access to and inclusion among decision makers. "Income" from investments in political capital includes increased influence in decision making, increased access to and control over other forms of capital, and the ability to engage in reciprocal relationships, among others.

Cultural capital is the stock of practices that reflect values and identity rooted in place, class, and/or ethnicity.[13] Cultural capital influences the ways in which individuals and groups access other forms of capital. Cultural capital includes the dynamics of who we know and feel comfortable with, what heritage is valued, collaboration across races, ethnicities, and generations, etc. Investments in cultural capital create or sustain the values, traditions, beliefs, and/or language that become the currency to leverage other types of capital. Investments in cultural capital could include support for venues to showcase cultural achievements, programs to preserve and pass on cultural knowledge and skills, and support for cultural transformations, among other things. "Income" from investments in cultural capital may include increased "buy in" to institutional rules and shared norms of behavior, strengthened social capital, and increased access to other capitals through increased visibility and appreciation of cultural attributes and through cultural transformation; for example acquisition of language skills (Bebbington 1999; Jeannotte 2003).

Key characteristics of wealth

As mentioned previously, we define wealth broadly as the stock of all assets, net of liabilities, which can contribute to the well-being of an individual or group. Investments in the different forms of wealth increase the stock of wealth, while depreciation reduces the stock. All forms of wealth have a tendency to depreciate over time; ongoing investment is required to maintain and grow stocks that will, in turn, generate increased flows of goods and services over time. Wealth-based development requires shifting focus from flows such as income to also paying attention to the quantity and quality of the underlying stocks of wealth.

As a stock of assets, wealth is durable and can be accumulated or depleted through investment and consumption decisions. As illustrated in our definitions of the different types of wealth, the nature of investment and of the "income" resulting from each type of wealth is distinct, though investments in one type of wealth often affect others, and investments in more than one type at a time may create positive synergies reflected in more positive and robust outcomes. Wealth stocks generate flows of goods and services ("income") that contribute to well-being, though not all of these stocks and flows can be monetized. Some forms of wealth, such as cultural capital, may be difficult to measure on any sort of cardinal or ordinal scale, let alone measure in monetary terms. Nevertheless, it is possible to ask about the impact on each form of wealth of any given intervention and to consider how interventions might be structured to add or, at least, do no harm to existing stocks of wealth.

How much an asset contributes to wealth depends on how much it has depreciated; that is, whether it is healthy enough to produce a positive flow of goods and services on a sustainable basis. A polluted wetland or a mountain decimated by mountain-top removal may, in fact, become so depreciated as to damage well-being (i.e., a negative form of wealth). Thus, investing in maintaining assets or restoring them to a fully functional state can be a crucial part of a wealth-based development approach.

Wealth is only actionable from a development perspective to the extent that it is owned or influenced by the individual or group benefitting from it. Therefore, understanding concepts of inclusive and exclusive ownership and control is critical to using wealth concepts to achieve the broadest possible impact on well-being.[14]

A conceptual framework for wealth creation

Understanding how wealth can be created and sustained in rural areas requires a conceptual framework that reflects the diverse contexts and complex set of factors influencing the process and its outcomes (Figure 2.1). Our framework for wealth creation draws upon other frameworks in the rural development literature,[15] and includes the eight types of wealth discussed above – physical, financial, natural, human, intellectual, social, cultural, and political capital – embedded

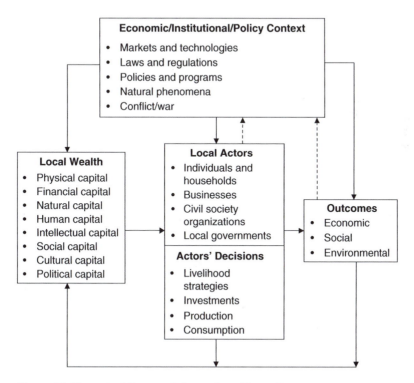

Figure 2.1 Conceptual framework for rural wealth creation

in a systems context. This framework is similar in structure and emphasis to the Sustainable Livelihoods Framework (SLF) developed by the Department for International Development of the United Kingdom (Carney 1998), which also emphasizes the role of local wealth endowments and contextual factors in influencing livelihood strategy decisions of local actors and their economic, social, and environmental outcomes. The SLF has been influential among rural development funders, practitioners, and researchers working in developing countries, but has not received much attention in the literature on rural or community development in the United States. Our framework incorporates additional types of wealth not included in the SLF but which have been highlighted in other frameworks and literature.

In our framework, we focus on assets that are (or could be) owned or controlled by actors in the rural community or region, including individuals, households, businesses, non-profit civic organizations, and local governments. Within a place, the assets controlled by these actors are "endogenous", meaning that decisions made by local actors directly affect the accumulation or depletion of the assets. Other assets that affect local decisions but that are owned or controlled by external actors – such as Federal and State lands and highways, externally owned corporations, land and mineral resources owned by absentee owners, electrical and telecommunications systems, and universities – are treated as part of the local economic, institutional, and policy context.

This framework emphasizes that place matters and that stocks of wealth both influence and are influenced by their location. It focuses on the decisions made by local actors. Key economic decisions include long-term choices about livelihood strategies, such as how to connect with market and non-market economies; whom to partner with; what business enterprises and occupations to pursue and where to live; what investments to make and how to protect them; how much of particular goods and services to produce or provide and what inputs to use in their production; how much of different goods and services to consume; how to handle the waste products of production and consumption; and what incentives, supports, or regulations may be used by local governments to influence public and private investments. Local actors must also make decisions about how to interface with the economic, institutional, and policy context in which they operate.

Local places' and actors' endowments of different types of wealth, combined with who owns and controls that wealth, determine what opportunities are available and the attendant costs, returns, risks, and constraints (indicated in Figure 2.1 by the arrow from the wealth box to the local actors and decisions box). These decisions are also affected by the economic, institutional, and policy context, such as the functioning of formal and informal markets and the prices determined for various goods and services; technological innovations affecting the feasibility of economic opportunities; local laws, regulations, and policies; Federal and State programs; and even natural phenomena such as natural disasters or climate change.

Conditional upon actors' endowments and the context of a given place, wealth creation decisions lead to outcomes such as changes in employment, income, property values, financial assets, infrastructure, and tax revenues (economic); changes in ideas, education, health, nutrition, and security (social); and changes in air and water quality, land quality, biodiversity, and carbon stocks (environmental).

These decisions and outcomes often change the level of capital stocks – like depletion of natural capital stocks resulting from water pollution or improvement in human capital stocks resulting from investments in education and health – with consequences for future wealth creation (indicated in Figure 2.1 by the arrows from the decisions and outcomes boxes to the local wealth box). Over a larger scale, local wealth decisions may also affect the community's economic, institutional, and policy context (indicated by the dashed arrows).

Purpose of the framework

This framework is not a theory of economic development; rather, it is an overarching framework that encompasses more specific theories. Such theories specify assumptions regarding who are the key local actors, what are their decision rules, and whether and how these decisions influence outcomes and changes in assets. For example, the standard neoclassical economic theory of competitive markets is one type of theory that addresses some of the relationships shown in Figure 2.1, based on a particular set of assumptions. In the static general equilibrium version of that theory, the key decision makers are business firms and households, who are assumed to make decisions based on profit maximization (firms) and utility maximization (households), subject to the technologies available to the firms, the prices determined in perfectly competitive markets, and the natural, human, physical, and financial capital endowments of the households.[16] The outcomes in the general equilibrium theory include the levels of utility or well-being achieved by the households as a result of their consumption decisions. In the dynamic version of the general equilibrium neoclassical economic theory, households and firms are assumed to maximize intertemporal objective functions and at least some of the capital endowments are treated as dynamic, evolving over time as a result of the consumption and savings decisions of households and investment decisions of the firms. Changes in capital endowments are thus part of the set of outcomes of household and business decisions in the dynamic theory.

Although it can be used to make predictions about the dynamics of multiple kinds of wealth, the dynamic general equilibrium neoclassical theory is restrictive in several ways that limit its ability to explain rural wealth dynamics. It usually does not incorporate other decision makers and decisions that are important in determining such dynamics, such as the decisions of local governments and civil society organizations affecting provision of collective goods, regulation of the uses of private assets, and other decisions influencing private market behavior. It usually does not incorporate non-market outcomes that influence well-being, such as changes in flows of environmental services (although work in environmental economics using neoclassical models does incorporate such outcomes) or social conflict, or levels and changes in intangible forms of wealth, such as social or cultural capital.

The conceptual framework that we propose brings attention to such issues, and to alternative theories that incorporate such elements. For example, political economy and public choice theory models may consider who makes or influences decisions at the local government level concerning levels of taxation and spending, public investment, regulations, and other decisions that affect local economic activity, and what decision rules are used. Such models may also seek to understand how the institutional and policy context is influenced by different local actors, and how this in turn affects local decisions and the dynamics of development.

The framework proposed here does not pre-specify assumptions concerning which actors are most influential, what decision rules they use, which outcomes are of greatest concern to these actors, or many other issues related to the components and linkages in the framework. Any such assumptions are unlikely to be universally valid, and are more usefully specified for particular contexts. The framework is offered as a more general way of thinking about possible dynamic relationships involved in rural wealth creation than a specific set of assumptions and relationships, and is intended to be useful as a guide to developing more specific research questions, theories, and hypotheses about the wealth creation process in particular contexts.

Applying the framework

One of the main objectives of this book is to apply this framework to the study of rural wealth creation opportunities and strategies. Several case studies of different opportunities and strategies are presented in Part III of the book, using this framework as a way of reviewing and synthesizing the lessons from the available literature on these issues, and identifying key research gaps.

The lessons from these case studies will be discussed in Parts III and IV. However, some preliminary hypotheses about wealth creation strategies can be suggested based upon consideration of this framework and the example of the recent ethanol boom in parts of rural America:

1   *Wealth creation is highly context dependent*, as the success of efforts to achieve it depends greatly upon the initial wealth endowments of (and distribution within) rural communities, and the local economic, institutional, and policy context. For example, policies to promote biofuel production have contributed to rapid growth in ethanol production in rural areas with access to high-quality cropland, water, and natural gas for refining, transportation infrastructure, financial services, and an entrepreneurial class of farmers (Low and Isserman 2009). Where these factors are not in place, investments in biofuel production may be unprofitable, and may deplete rather than increase rural financial wealth. Even where such conditions are initially present, changes in market conditions or policies can render biofuel investments unprofitable, as has been observed in some cases in recent years. And financial profitability is not sufficient to ensure that investments in new opportunities contribute to rural

wealth creation, broadly defined. For example, ethanol production increases demand on local water supplies, especially in locations where the feedstock is irrigated, and may increase demands on the soil, potentially depleting this form of natural capital. Other types of capital (such as human and social capital) may be affected positively or negatively by ethanol production, and such impacts also likely depend on the context in which this opportunity is pursued, and how it is pursued.

2   *It is important to take into account interrelationships among asset types.* Wealth creation can best be understood in a systems context, weighing investment consequences throughout the system, rather than by focusing on any one form of wealth in isolation. The example of ethanol production illustrates that different types of capital are often complementary: i.e., investment in one type of capital increases the returns to investing in another type. For example, among places otherwise suitable for ethanol production, those with prior investments in transportation infrastructure likely could earn greater returns from investing in ethanol facilities than those without such infrastructure. In other cases, different assets may be substitutes. For example, it might prove cheaper or more environmentally beneficial in some cases to reduce net greenhouse gas emissions by planting trees rather than by promoting ethanol production. Such interrelationships among different types of assets suggest that the process of planning and coordinating or selecting different types of investments is likely to be critical for success.

3   *Investments in any single form of rural wealth creation are generally risky, but investing in a portfolio of types of wealth may help to reduce risk.* This point is also illustrated by the biofuels example. Since the boom period for ethanol production in the mid-2000s, the profitability of ethanol plants has fallen dramatically as corn prices and competition in the industry increased, resulting in a significant number of failures. Portfolio diversification is one potential strategy to reduce such risk exposure, which could involve investing in different types of assets that have uncorrelated or negatively correlated risks. For example, communities that invest in livestock production as well as corn and ethanol production are protected to some extent from declines in corn and ethanol prices, since livestock producers can benefit from lower feed costs.

4   *Investments in locally owned assets can increase the long-term viability of rural communities, but this may involve tradeoffs and risks.* For example, locally owned ethanol plants led the expansion of the sector for several years, with high returns to local investors during the initial boom period when profit margins were high. This can lead to greater local economic impacts from locally owned plants than from plants owned by outside investors. But profit margins in ethanol production have since declined, as noted above. As a result, local investors are becoming less numerous in the industry and the local economic impacts of ethanol plants may be diminishing. More generally, investors who focus only on investing locally may miss opportunities to invest in assets elsewhere that offer higher returns, and may face greater risks than if their portfolio also included assets located outside of the community.

5   *Wealth creation is a dynamic process with multiple possible pathways.* Actors may save and invest in a broad range of assets, leading to increased income over time (sustainable development path); they may deplete multiple forms of wealth and suffer from declining income over time (poverty trap); they may maintain relative stability in wealth and income per capita (steady state); or they may accumulate some assets while others are depleted (transitional path). In the latter case, the growth and sustainability of income depends upon whether investments in new assets yield sufficient returns to offset the losses resulting from depleting other assets. Knowing which type of path a community is on is critical to be able to identify effective strategies to change or build on the path; yet data on wealth are rarely collected and used for this.

We return to these issues in Parts III and IV of the book.

Notes

1   This chapter adapts material from Pender et al. (2012a, 2012b) and Ratner (2010).
2   The views expressed are those of the authors and should not be attributed to the US Department of Agriculture or to the Economic Research Service.
3   See, for example, Serageldin and Steer (1994); Hamilton and Clemens (1999); Arrow et al. (2004); Boyd (2004); Atkisson (2005); World Bank (2006); Arrow et al. (2010); World Bank (2011).
4   Arrow et al. (2010) defined the value of comprehensive wealth using the concept of "shadow prices", which are defined to reflect the marginal contribution of each kind of wealth to intergenerational well-being, measured in monetary terms. As proven by Arrow et al., if such shadow prices were observable and all kinds of wealth that contribute to well-being were included in the measure, increases in comprehensive wealth would be necessary and sufficient to ensure improvement in intergenerational well-being (their definition of sustainability). However, measuring such shadow prices is fraught with major difficulties (if not impossibilities), as argued convincingly by the Commission on the Measurement of Economic Performance and Social Progress (Stiglitz et al. 2009). Using more feasible measures of wealth, such as the cumulated and depreciated value of investments (as usually used to value physical wealth), it is not the case that increases in such measures are necessary or sufficient for improvements in everyone's intergenerational well-being, since such investments may be inefficient or have adverse distributional consequences for some people even if they are efficient (Pritchett 2000; Pender et al. 2012b).
5   Examples of rural development frameworks that consider multiple forms of capital include Kretzmann and McKnight (1993); Carney (1998); Castle (1998); Bebbington (1999); Green and Haines (2002); de Janvry (2003); Flora and Flora (2004); Pender et al. (2006); Reimer (2006); and Ratner (2010). These frameworks are reviewed in Pender et al. (2012b).
6   Within a wealth creation context, withdrawal of non-renewable resources results in a net loss of wealth unless the financial returns from that withdrawal are invested in other stocks of wealth capable of producing sustainable "income" flows over time.
7   Costanza and Daly (1992).
8   Becker (1962) defined human capital as resources embedded in people, such as their education, skills, and health.
9   Romer (1990) distinguished knowledge and innovation from human capital, arguing that innovation, such as the design of a new good, is not tied to specific people and is therefore non-rival in nature (i.e., its use by one person does not reduce its availability

for use by someone else). Human capital, by contrast, is embedded in particular people and therefore rival in nature. This distinction is important because the non-rival nature of knowledge and innovation can lead to increasing returns to scale, which is a source of long-run growth in an economy (ibid.). Romer argued that human capital is an essential input to the production of innovations.

10 Putnam (1993, p. 35) defined social capital as "features of social organization, such as networks, norms and trust that facilitate coordination and cooperation for mutual benefit".

11 Some authors have defined a third type of social capital – "linking" social capital – as "norms of respect and networks of trusting relationships between people who are inter-acting across explicit, formal or institutionalized power or authority gradients in soci-ety" (Szreter and Woolcock 2004, p. 655). As defined, linking social capital is a subcategory of bridging social capital as originally conceived (relationships among people of different groups); but is distinct from bridging social capital involving rela-tionships among people having similar power or status, such as ethnic traders seeking similar partners in overseas markets.

12 Baumann and Sinha (2001, p. 1) defined political capital as "the ability to use power in support of political or economic positions and so enhance livelihoods". Flora and Flora (2004, p. 108) defined political capital as "the ability of a group to influence the distri-bution of resources within a social unit".

13 Flora and Flora (2004) defined cultural capital as people's understanding of society and their role in it, values, symbols, and rituals. An example is the "Protestant work ethic", which Weber (1905) argued was an important factor contributing to the rise of capital-ism in the West. Choby defined cultural capital as "the rules for engaging other types of capital (human, economic, social)", <http://pattichoby.wordpress.com/2010/06/05/what-is-cultural-capital/>.

14 See Kelly and Ratner (2009) for examples of approaches to foster local ownership and control of wealth.

15 Kretzmann and McKnight (1993); Carney (1998); Castle (1998); Bebbington (1999); Green and Haines (2002); de Janvry (2003); Flora and Flora (2004); Pender et al. (2006); Reimer (2006); Ratner (2010).

16 In the terminology of the neoclassical theory, these endowments are referred to as land, labor, capital, and the distribution of ownership of these factors of production.

References

Arrow, K., Dasgupta, P., Goulder, L., Daily, G., Ehrlich, P., et al. (2004) "Are we consuming too much?", *Journal of Economic Perspectives*, 18(3): 147–72.

Arrow, K.J., Dasgupta, P., Goulder, L.H., Mumford, K.J., and Oleson, K. (2010) "Sustainability and the measurement of wealth", NBER Working Paper 16599, Cambridge, MA: National Bureau of Economic Research.

Atkisson, A. (2005) "Introducing 'inclusive wealth': a new economic measure of sustain-ability". Online. Available at: <http://www.worldchanging.com/archives/003004.html> (accessed 1 May 2012).

Baumann, P. and Sinha, S. (2001) "Linking development with democratic processes in India: political capital and sustainable livelihoods analysis", *Natural Resource Perspectives*, 68, London: Overseas Development Institute.

Bebbington, A. (1999) "Capitals and capabilities: a framework for analyzing peasant via-bility, rural livelihoods and poverty", *World Development*, 27(12): 2021–44.

Becker, G.S. (1962) "Investment in human capital: a theoretical analysis", *Journal of Political Economy*, 70(5, pt 2): 9–49.

Boyd, D.R. (2004) *Sustainability within a Generation: A New Vision for Canada*, Vancouver, BC: Suzuki Foundation.

Carney, D. (1998) "Implementing the sustainable livelihoods approach", in D. Carney (ed.), *Sustainable Rural Livelihoods: What Contribution Can We Make?*, London: Department for International Development.

Castle, E.N. (1998) "A conceptual framework for the study of rural places", *American Journal of Agricultural Economics*, 80: 621–31.

Costanza, R. and Daly, H.E. (1992) "Natural capital and sustainable development", *Conservation Biology*, 6(1): 37–46.

Flora, C.B. and Flora, J.L. (2004) *Rural Communities: Legacy and Change*, 2nd edn, Boulder, CO: Westview Press.

Gittell, R. and Vidal, A. (1998) *Community Organizing: Building Social Capital as a Development Strategy*, Newbury Park, CA: Sage Publications.

Green, G. and Haines, A. (2002) *Asset Building and Community Development*, Thousand Oaks, CA: Sage.

Hamilton, K. and Clemens, M. (1999) "Genuine savings rates in developing countries", *World Bank Economic Review*, 13(2): 333–56.

de Janvry, A. (2003) "Achieving success in rural development: tools and approaches for implementation of an integral approach", unpublished manuscript, University of California, Berkeley, Department of Agricultural and Resource Economics.

Jeannotte, M.S. (2003) "Singing alone? The contribution of cultural capital to social cohesion and sustainable communities", *International Journal of Cultural Policy*, 9(1): 35–49.

Kelly, M. and Ratner, S. (2009) "Keeping wealth local: shared ownership and wealth control for rural communities", Wealth Creation in Rural Communities, Phase Two Report. Online. Available at: <http://www.yellowwood.org/assets/resource_library/resource_docs/keeping%20wealth%20local.pdf> (accessed 1 April 2014).

Kretzmann, J. and McKnight, J. (1993) *Building Communities from the Inside Out: A Path toward Finding and Mobilizing Community Assets*, Chicago: ACTA Publications.

Low, S. and Isserman, A. (2009) "Ethanol and the local economy: industry trends, location factors, economic impacts, and risks", *Economic Development Quarterly*, 23(1): 71–88.

Pender, J., Ehui, S., and Place, F. (2006) "Conceptual framework and hypotheses", in J. Pender, F. Place, and S. Ehui (eds.), *Strategies for Sustainable Land Management in the East African Highlands*, Washington, DC: International Food Policy Research Institute.

Pender, J., Marré, A., and Reeder, R. (2012a) "Rural wealth creation: concepts, measures, and strategies", *American Journal of Agricultural Economics*, 94(2): 535–41.

Pender, J., Marré, A., and Reeder, R. (2012b) *Rural Wealth Creation: Concepts, Strategies and Measures*, Economic Research Report No. 131, Washington, DC: US Department of Agriculture, Economic Research Service.

Pritchett, L. (2000) "The tyranny of concepts: CUDIE (cumulated, depreciated, investment effort) is not capital", *Journal of Economic Growth*, 5: 361–84.

Putnam, R. (1993) "The prosperous community: social capital and public life", *American Prospect*, 4(13): 35–42.

Ratner, S. (2010) "Formulating a sustainable economic development process for rural America: second interim report", Yellow Wood Associates, St. Albans, VT. Online. Available at: <http://www.yellowwood.org/wealthcreation.aspx> (accessed 1 March 2012).

Reimer, B. (2006) "The rural context of community development in Canada", *Journal of Rural and Community Development*, 1(2): 155–75.

Romer, P. (1990) "Endogenous technological change", *Journal of Political Economy*, 98(5, pt 2): S71–S102.

Serageldin, I. and Steer, A. (1994) "Epilogue: expanding the capital stock", in I. Serageldin and A. Steer (eds.), *Making Development Sustainable: From Concepts to Action*, Environmentally Sustainable Development Occasional Paper Series No. 2, Washington, DC: World Bank.

Stiglitz, J.E., Sen, A., and Fitoussi, J.-P. (2009) *Report by the Commission on the Measurement of Economic Performance and Social Progress*. Online. Available at: <http://www.stiglitz-sen-fitoussi.fr/en/index.htm> (accessed 1 March 2012).

Szreter, S. and Woolcock, M. (2004) "Health by association? Social capital, social theory, and the political economy of public health", *International Journal of Epidemiology*, 33: 650–67.

Weber, M. (1905) *The Protestant Ethic and 'The Spirit of Capitalism'*, trans. Stephen Kalberg, Los Angeles: Roxbury Publishing.

World Bank (2006) *Where is the Wealth of Nations? Measuring Capital for the 21st Century*, Washington, DC: World Bank.

World Bank (2011) *The Changing Wealth of Nations. Measuring Sustainable Development in the New Millennium*, Washington, DC: World Bank.

Wye City Group (2012) *The Wye Group Handbook. Statistics on Rural Development and Agricultural Household Income*, Food and Agricultural Organization of the United Nations. Online. Available at: <http://www.fao.org/fileadmin/templates/ess/pages/rural/wye_city_group/index.htm> (accessed 25 February 2012).

3   Comprehensive wealth accounting

Bridging place-based and people-based measures of wealth

Thomas G. Johnson, Neus Raines, and John L. Pender[1]

Introduction

Welfare economics (the branch of economics that studies the economic well-being of individuals and society) allows, and ideally includes, a comprehensive view of well-being. Welfare economics deals with the abstract concept of utility that conceptually includes all aspects of well-being, whether provided privately or publicly, or within or outside markets. It encompasses consumption, production, savings, investment, and wealth. It permits the consideration of place, risk and uncertainty, and dynamics.

In this chapter we examine the concept of wealth creation through this more comprehensive lens offered by welfare economics. We extend the conceptual basis somewhat by distinguishing and relating the wealth of a region's residents to the collective wealth of the region itself – that is, people-based wealth and place-based wealth.

Welfare and wealth

The neoclassical theory of welfare economics is based on the postulate that the well-being of each individual is determined by the consumption of all "goods and services", tangible and intangible, intended and unintended, earned and unearned, private and public. For convenience, the value of all these goods is combined into a utility-based metric referred to as Fisherian income (Nordhaus 2000).[2] Fisherian income differs in important ways from the production-based measures used in most systems of national accounts. Fisher describes this concept of income as follows: "The income from any instrument is thus the flow of services rendered by that instrument. The income of a community is the total flow of services from all its instruments" (Fisher 1906, p. 101, as quoted by Nordhaus 1995, p. 4). Nordhaus demonstrates that Fisherian income is equivalent to sustainable income because it is the annual yield (annuity) produced by society's wealth including all intangible capitals. If Fisherian income is constant or increasing then wealth is constant or increasing and is sustainable. Fisherian income equals consumption (including capital consumption) plus net investment in all types of capital.

Society's combined welfare is a weighted aggregate of all individuals' Fisherian income. Each individual's rate of income is determined by his or her initial endowment (wealth) of time and assets, including access to public goods (Samuelson 1954). Fisherian income considers income streams from both market and non-market capitals as well as the liabilities associated with the income generated, thus providing a comprehensive measure of people and regional welfare (net income). Fisherian wealth, then, is the present value of all future Fisherian income (estimated as annual Fisherian income divided by the real social discount rate). Furthermore, the Fisherian income approach provides a framework for sustainable wealth creation that goes hand in hand with a sustainable level of consumption, and indirectly with a sustainable level of investment. A sustainable level of consumption, as Nordhaus (1995, p. 4) posits, is "the maximum amount that a nation can consume while ensuring that members of all current and future generations can have expected lifetime consumption or utility that is at least as high as current consumption or utility". This corresponds to the concept of weak sustainability in ecological economics (Pearce and Atkinson 1993). We apply the concept of Fisherian income to people-based or place-based measures of wealth.

Macroeconomic accounting systems such as the US National Income and Product Accounts, the international System of National Accounts (United Nations et al. 2009) and typical regional social accounting matrices (SAM), calculate common indicators such as gross domestic product (GDP), net domestic product (NDP), gross national product (GNP), net national product (NNP), net national income (NNI), national savings, and a number of other related values. These indicators monitor annual flows of goods and services, but are related to stocks of various types of market-valued capitals. As Corrado et al. (2009) demonstrate, these measures of the economy give a distorted view of the economy because they overlook various types of capital. Expenditures on such things as education, information, intellectual assets, and social relationships are either excluded in these accounts or they are treated as consumption or as intermediate goods rather than as investments.[3] Since intermediate goods are not included in final demand, GDP is less than it would be otherwise. As a result, the rate of national savings and investment, and the total value of capital stocks, is also underestimated. Corrado et al. (2009) show that when investments in intangible capitals are correctly treated as final demand, some of the value added attributed to tangible capital and labour would be instead attributed to this intangible capital. As a result, the income attributed to tangibles and labour is overestimated but the growth rate of total income is underestimated. Since expenditures on intangibles would be considered savings and investment, rather than consumption, the true national saving rate would be greater. Of course the depreciation of these assets becomes important when measuring capital stocks and net domestic product (NDP).

During the last two decades there have been significant advances made in expanding national accounting systems to include various non-market and intangible capitals (especially natural capital) and their associated flows to estimate broader indicators of wealth (Nordhaus 1995, 2006; United Nations et al. 2003; Arrow et al. 2012; European Commission et al. 2012). One approach has been to develop satellite accounts that are then linked to the financial capital accounts. A second approach is that of building extended or augmented accounts. The primary difference between these two approaches is that the augmented accounts change the structure of the standard economic accounts, whereas the satellite accounts leave them unchanged. As Nordhaus (2006) explained, the addition of non-market elements to market-based accounts requires certain definitional changes and leads to different values in some sectors.

In this chapter we propose and describe an extension of the standard regional social accounts that incorporates stocks and flows, various types of capitals, and place-based and people-based measures. First we describe the basic concepts more fully.

Wealth accounting concepts

Below we offer several ideas for sharpening the conceptual foundations of regional wealth creation and for building the foundations of a more comprehensive accounting framework capable of measuring the level and rate of growth in regional wealth.

Stocks versus flows

Hoffer and Levy (2010) provide a very nice starting point for our discussion. They point out the importance of distinguishing stocks and flows. The change in wealth (a stock) over time is the cumulative effect of income and expenditures (flows). It is important to remember that the outflow of stocks (consumption) is the basis of our welfare and prosperity. Maintaining at least a minimum rate of consumption into the future is the definition of sustainability.

Our most widely used measure of economic performance, GDP is a gross flow measure that ignores changes in (investment in or depreciation of) assets. Net wealth is a stock measure that is solely focused on the changing stock of assets, net of liabilities. Like GDP, well-being is a flow, but one which depends critically on net wealth measured in a number of dimensions in addition to financial wealth (Arrow et al. 2012). Combining and linking our stock and flow accounting is essential if we hope to understand the process of wealth creation. For example, we should ask, "Are the flows into local stocks of wealth new wealth, or simply transfers from the stocks of other communities, or from other types of wealth?" Furthermore, "Who owns these stocks, and thus who receives the flow of returns generated by the stocks?"

Asset, liabilities, and wealth

The terms "wealth", "capital", and "assets" are often used interchangeably or indiscriminately. Wealth, of course, is a net indicator and is equal to assets less liabilities.[4] It is usually more useful, especially in a comprehensive accounting framework, to identify both assets and liabilities rather than net worth or wealth. Liabilities are frequently ignored in the discussions about wealth creation, but the concept is an important part of the wealth accounting process. Everyone's liability is someone else's asset. Liabilities are a key factor in distinguishing people-based from place-based wealth.

Place-based versus people-based assets and wealth

In national accounts, production and income produced within a geographic area (GDP and gross domestic income or GDI) are distinguished from production and income of people (GNP and Gross National Income or GNI). Similarly, employment reports are reported as employment by place of work or employment by place of residence. Here we distinguish between capital and wealth associated with place, and capital and wealth owned by people.[5]

People-based wealth

Personal financial wealth is familiar to most people. It is typically equated to net worth – the total value of one's assets less one's liabilities (Kennickell 2003). Typical assets included in personal wealth are owned real estate, personal property, stocks, bonds, automobiles, and similar marketable assets (regardless of the location of those investments). To calculate comprehensive wealth we must add one's human capital assets (such as education, work experience, and health), social capital assets (access to networks, for example), and so on for each of the types of capital identified in Chapter 2. As we will see below we must also value publicly provided assets. From this we subtract any liabilities attached to these assets such as social obligations, political obligations, etc. Care must be taken not to double-count any of these assets and liabilities. For example, student loans are liabilities incurred to acquire human capital but these are generally a part of one's typical net worth calculation and should not be subtracted again when the value of education is added to wealth. The sum of the people-based wealth of all residents is that region's people-based wealth and is analogous to people-based product, GNP. This should not be confused with place-based wealth.

Place-based wealth

In a closed system people-based and place-based wealth are equal. A place's assets are those that are located in the place regardless of the location of the assets' owners. Thus place-based wealth is equivalent to its assets. Place-based wealth includes the local assets of residents but also those assets owned by non-residents. Thus, place-based wealth indicators include housing stocks, fixed commercial and industrial capital, public infrastructure, environmental quality, and social networks. In order to generate indicators comparable to currently used place-based and people-based indicators of economic performance (GDP and GNP, respectively), a comprehensive regional wealth accounting system must accommodate both place-based and people-based concepts. Even more importantly, this dual approach to wealth measurement is needed in order to adequately assess the efficacy of place-based and people-based policies focused on everything from economic development to natural resource management to poverty alleviation.

The bridge between place-based and people-based wealth is the spatial distribution of asset ownership and the incidence of external benefits and costs flowing from these assets. For example, the place-based wealth of a mining community may be very large due to the value of minerals located there; yet the wealth of the residents of that community may be limited if the mineral rights are owned by non-residents. If mining activities in that community cause pollution or undermine scenic amenities, resulting in reduced property values, both the place-based and people-based wealth of that community and neighboring communities may be reduced.

Terms of trade and property rights

Wealth is the summation of net assets. Asset and liability values are determined by (1) the terms of trade upon which these assets and their services are valued, and (2) the property rights that individuals and communities have with respect to these assets. For tangible market assets in the absence of market failure, "terms of trade" is synonymous with price. For intangibles and non-market assets "terms of trade" instead refers to their relative worth. Arrow et al. (2012) suggest that in such cases the appropriate terms of trade are indicated by shadow prices. Several techniques have been suggested for estimating the "terms of trade" of intangible and non-market assets, including (1) analysing consumer behaviour and identifying underlying revealed valuation, (2) unbundling the commodities or inputs and valuing component parts using such techniques as hedonic analysis, and (3) contingent valuation and other hypothetical approaches. Higher accuracy comes from the first two techniques, since they are based on observed human behavior and market prices (Nordhaus 2006).

A proposed multi-capital wealth accounting system

GDP has a number of useful features such as relative ease of measurement, accounting rigor, and international comparability. However, the standard SAM accounts only for economic flows and contains very little capital account information. It captures only market activities, ignoring such activities as volunteerism, home production, non-market production and consumption, public goods production and consumption, environmental stocks and flows, investments in human and social capital, etc. It also ignores capital consumption (depreciation). However, it does provide a useful starting point for developing a performance system based on wealth. In order to develop a wealth accounting system from the standard SAM, we must disaggregate several existing accounts and add several new sub-accounts.

Capital accounts

The most fundamental adjustment to the standard SAM is to add capital accounts to the current accounts and link them. Wealth (broadly defined) is assets less liabilities. Wealth creation occurs when assets rise faster than liabilities. Assets rise when investments and acquisitions rise faster than depreciation, obsolescence, and dispositions. Liabilities decline as liens and mortgages are retired. Wealth rises when overall net savings are positive. Wealth rises fastest when the savings are reinvested in the most productive assets. Savings is net production (value-added) less consumption. Thus, in order to fully account for changes in people-based wealth, we would need a balanced capital account for residents of each region. We address this feature next.

Residence-based accounting

Standard SAMs and most data series indicate economic flows – production, employment, tax payments, and transfers to the capital account – by place of production. Some accounting systems show the flows of returns to owners of capital but the residence of workers is typically ignored. In order to link place-based and people-based accounts we must know where people live and where their assets are located or employed. Thus to calculate residence-based income and consumption, we must know the following: in-commuter and out-commuter income, local consumption by non-residents (tourists, for example), non-local consumption by residents, local assets owned by residents, non-local assets owned by residents, rates of return to these assets, debt of residents, rates of savings, rates of investment, and transfer income.

Non-financial accounts

Each type of capital – financial, physical, natural, human, intellectual, social, cultural, and political – has both current and capital accounts. For example, human capital (education, skills, and health) is a factor of production as well as a source of directly consumed services. It is produced through investment, owned by individuals, and generates rates of return depending on the market conditions. Publicly owned physical capital (infrastructure) is also a factor of production as well as a source of directly consumed services. Infrastructure is produced through investment, owned collectively by residents, and generates rates of return which are diffused and unrecorded. Both current and capital sub-accounts must be constructed for each of these capitals, and incorporated into a comprehensive SAM (assuming data are available).

Place-based versus people-based wealth

As with the distinction between GDP (place-based production) and GNP (people-based production) in the current account, one can distinguish between domestic wealth (place-based wealth) and national wealth (people-based wealth). Table 3.1 distinguishes the components of both definitions of wealth.

Here, A is capital assets, L is liabilities, and subscript r indicates residents of the region, p indicates public, and w is rest-of-world. Thus the double subscript rw indicates assets and liabilities of the region's residents which are located in the

Table 3.1 Framework for distinguishing public versus private and place versus people wealth

	Region		Rest-of-world	
	Assets	Liabilities	Assets	Liabilities
Residents' private	A_{rr}	L_{rr}	A_{rw}	L_{rw}
Regional public	A_{pr}	L_{pr}	A_{pw}	L_{pw}
Rest of the world	A_{wr}	L_{wr}	A_{ww}	L_{ww}

rest of the world. The subscript *pw* indicates assets and liabilities of the region's public sector located outside the region.

Using these values we can calculate four types of wealth measures – two people-based and two place-based wealth.

Measures of people-based wealth

Residents' private wealth is simply the assets less liabilities of all residents no matter where the assets are located. Residents' total wealth is this plus the public assets less liabilities of their region.[6]

$$\text{Residents' private wealth} = (A_{rr} + A_{rw}) - (L_{rr} + L_{rw})$$

$$\text{Residents' total wealth} = (A_{rr} + A_{rw} + A_{pr} + A_{pw}) - (L_{rr} + L_{rw} + L_{pr} + L_{pw})$$

Measures of place-based wealth

To calculate place-based wealth we ignore the ownership of the assets since we are concerned with the value of assets located in the region. Since liabilities are essentially ownership interests in an asset held by others, they are not included in the place's wealth. Thus to convert people-based wealth into place wealth we subtract residents' ownership of non-local assets (A_{rw}) and add back the value of non-residents' interests in local assets (L_{rw}). Thus regional private wealth is the sum of assets located within the region owned by residents and non-residents (that is, the value of all privately owned capital). Total regional wealth is the private assets plus public assets.

$$\text{Regional private wealth} = A_{rr} - L_{rr}$$

$$\text{Regional total wealth} = (A_{rr} + A_{pr}) - (L_{rr} + L_{pr})[7]$$

Using these definitions and expanding our definition to the eight capitals allows a comprehensive assessment of both regional domestic wealth and regional residents' wealth. It also facilitates a more complete understanding of the role of the public sector.

Public services, infrastructure, and taxation

The public sector plays a special role in regional wealth creation by influencing the terms of trade, allocating and strengthening property rights, and redistributing wealth. Asset values are usually determined by the forces of supply and demand, which in turn are influenced by taxes, subsidies, and regulation. Government programs may enhance wealth, especially for some, by strengthening property rights, thus reducing transaction costs and increasing the effective demand for assets.

In addition, governments directly provide a majority of public assets. Public assets provide services to residents just as their private assets do. The value of public assets, less liabilities (usually bonds), contributes to both the place-based wealth and the people-based wealth of the region.

Taxation has obvious effects on wealth but may be an overlooked variable in wealth creation. The right to tax is a type of property right held by the public on behalf of citizens. The taxes required to fund public programs and build public infrastructure reduce the flow of income or utility from the regions' private assets, thus reducing these assets' values to the individual since asset value is the present value of the stream of net earnings from the asset. The public services and infrastructure made possible by these taxes may increase productivity, thus increasing the value of the region's private assets. From the perspective of regions, local taxes are appropriations of local wealth since they are used either to create a flow of benefits to residents (services and amenities), or are invested in place-based assets (infrastructure, education, etc.). In either case, they convert private asset value into public asset value. The public assets may be of lesser or greater value than the private assets they displace, depending on the productivity of the assets. National and state taxes, on the other hand, are expropriations of regional wealth. Non-local taxes reduce regional asset values, but do not necessarily increase the public assets of the region. They may, however, increase the value of assets of residents if the state or national government invests in public assets that benefit the residents. Interestingly, many local taxes are paid by residents and non-residents alike. Thus, in terms of people-based wealth, local taxes replace some assets owned by non-residents with assets that are "owned" by residents. Who pays taxes and how the revenues are spent determine if local people-based wealth is increased or decreased by these local taxes.

Capital accounts

A typical capital account simply records the starting stock at the beginning of the year, adds increases to the stock during the year, subtracts reductions, and calculates end-of-year stocks. As an example, consider the United Nations et al.'s

(2003) proposed integrated environmental and economic accounting system. Their proposed accounting of natural capital is as follows:

Opening stock
+ Increases during the year, for example:
    New discoveries of minerals
    Natural growth of plants and animals
    Land reclamation
− Decreases during the year, for example:
    Extraction of minerals
    Soil erosion
    Loss of capacity of reservoirs due to silting
    Harvesting of plants and animals
    Natural death of plants and animals
= Closing stock

To estimate comprehensive wealth, we need something similar for each type of capital. Here we use the capital definitions from Chapter 2, and identify types of capital account entries in the literature (Hoffer and Levy 2010; Becker 1962; Romer 1990; Woolcock 1998; Putnam 1993; Gittell and Vidal 1998; Costanza and Daly 2003; Baumann and Sinha 2001).

Financial capital

Financial capital is the stock of money and other liquid financial assets such as stocks, bonds, and letters of credit – net of financial liabilities – that can be readily converted to money. Financial capital includes claims of rights to flows of income or services from other forms of capital. For example, owners of stocks of a corporation own rights to the earnings that flow from the use of the corporation's assets. For many forms of financial capital, such as bonds and other forms of credit, one person's asset is someone else's liability, so these do not contribute directly to the net wealth of society as a whole, although they contribute positively to the wealth of some and negatively to others. Financial capital, if well managed, generates monetary returns that can be used for further investment or consumption.

Financial capital is not capital in the same sense as physical and other types of capital that contribute directly to production or well-being. Financial capital is a vehicle for distributing and redistributing ownership (property rights) in other real capital. One possible exception is the productive value provided by liquidity. Financial capital is often more easily shifted from one use to another, thus facilitating transactions and helping people to manage risk. In the standard accounting framework, the financial capital row is the conduit for current funds to flow into capital stocks. Once in the financial capital stock account, it is allocated to consumption by others or to investment into one of the real capitals.

Physical capital

Physical capital is one of the most familiar types of capital. It includes the stock of built capital goods (i.e., buildings and equipment) used by firms to produce outputs; infrastructure used to reduce costs of commerce (e.g., roads, bridges, waterways, telecommunication networks) or provide public services (e.g., water and sewage treatment plants); and durable goods used by households for either production or consumption purposes (e.g., houses, vehicles, household equipment). Physical capital depreciates over time with use or obsolescence and requires additional investment and maintenance.

Physical capital is often valued at cost less depreciation. However, the best method of valuing physical (and other) capital is by calculating the net present value of all future benefits derived from the capital. This measure of value considers depreciation, obsolescence, the consequences of technological change, and changes in demand. Value should also include intangible benefits, and external costs and benefits associated with the capital. Thus a complete accounting of physical capital would start with the current value of physical capital and would adjust this estimate over time for depreciation, obsolescence, destruction and export of capital, new construction or import of capital, and renovations to existing capital. Accounts should include both privately owned and publicly owned assets.

Natural capital

Natural capital includes both non-renewable and renewable resources. Investments in natural capital include exploration and restoration. Natural capital provides benefits in the form of raw materials and ecosystems services (Costanza and Daly 2003) such as maintenance of the quality of the atmosphere, waste assimilation, recycling of nutrients, generation of soils, and pollination of crops.

A number of advances have been made in the construction of natural accounts (European Commission et al. 2012). These approaches generally include physical measures of supply and use of various types of natural capitals. These are rarely true capital accounts since they do not include estimates of stocks but simply annual flows.

Human or individual capital

The concept of human capital has been a key component of economic theory at least since the work of Theodore Schultz, Jacob Mincer, and Gary Becker in the 1950s and 1960s. Since that time economists have spent a great deal of effort on defining human capital and its various components such as formal and informal education, health, experience, and mobility. Recently, theorists have distinguished individual capital from intellectual capital, the former being capital that is inseparable from individuals whereas intellectual capital can be stored and communicated.

Human capital accounting is a more recent concept. It was first identified as a potential component in the financial statements of individual firms (Lev and

Schwartz 1971) and more recently extended to the public sector and nations (Arrow et al. 2012).

Human capital is typically measured as the current value of future income streams of an individual. These income streams imply expected rates of unemployment and underemployment, loss of work due to illness, rising levels of experience, obsolescence of skills, etc. An important distinction between human and physical capital is that the benefits of human capital can include non-market benefits related to non-employment personal consumption – enjoyment of learning, home production, social status, etc.

Based on these arguments, human capital accounts should reflect the following changes in the determinants of human capital: graduation rates from high school, trade schools, community colleges, literacy programs, and GED programs; improvements in health status in the population; and the human capital embodied in immigrants. Decreases in human capital should include declines in health status; the human capital embodied in emigrants; and death of residents.

Human capital is owned by individuals. However, some human capital generates external benefits that are enjoyed by others. Good governance and general economic progress are often attributed in part to the level of literacy in the population, for example. Our proposed accounting framework should reflect these public benefits of human capital by raising the value of property and productivity of the regional labour force.

Intellectual capital

As Chapter 2 explains, intellectual capital is the stock of codified knowledge. Our accounting framework should identify the stock of patents; copyrighted material (books, music, journal articles, etc.); copyrighted and open access computer programs and applications; games; photographs, and recordings; and websites and blogs. Intellectual capital is generally owned in common (i.e., common knowledge) but intellectual property rights, such as patents and copyright protections, create and strengthen private rights to intellectual capital, thus increasing incentives for individuals and firms to invest, innovate, and create new intellectual capital.

Intellectual capital increases with the discovery of new knowledge as a result of research, experimentation, and production of creative works. Indicators of intellectual capital include patents, copyrighted material and open access software. Intellectual capital depreciates because of obsolescence.

Intellectual capital may be either private or public depending on the nature and strength of the associated property rights. Patents and copyrights strengthen individual property rights and weaken common property rights. But whether open access or copyrighted, knowledge is considered intellectual capital if it is recorded. In contrast, tacit knowledge is human capital until it is codified and made transferable.

Intellectual capital has value to a place, if the private owner of the capital is a resident or if the capital has some particular relevance to the place. An innovation that has general applicability and is owned by a non-resident (a musical recording, for example) cannot be claimed as a place's asset. A patent held by a resident is both a place-based and people-based asset of the region. An open access website describing the history of a region, on the other hand, is a place-based intellectual asset because it adds value to residents of the region just as a road or public building would. Because copyrights are difficult to enforce in some cases (music sharing, for example) and because the value of most intellectual property is not limited to a particular place, the distinctions between private and public, and between people-based and place-based will not, in general, be absolute, but rather a matter of degree.

Social capital

Numerous attempts have been made to quantify social capital (Gittell and Vidal 1998). As with other forms of capital, aspects of social capital may be owned by individuals (e.g., the social obligations that one person "owes" to another person, which are the second person's asset and the first person's liability), or by groups (e.g., social networks). Returns on investment in social capital include such benefits as improved coordination and reduced transaction costs.

As in the case of other capitals, people-based social capital may differ from place-based social capital if a resident owes social obligations to non-residents or if residents are owed social obligations by non-residents. This is likely to be the case when residents are involved in non-local networks such as labour unions or professional associations. New residents will bring with them social assets and obligations from their previous region, but many of these will not be portable. For example, trust and social status acquired in the workplace may have little value when a person takes a new job in a different location.

A social capital account would include indicators of the strength and size of interpersonal networks in a region. It might count the membership of various groups and organizations – the level of volunteerism, for example. Over time social capital may change because of changes in organizational membership and volunteerism due to resignations and new enlistments, including changes due to in- and out-migration and death of residents.

Cultural capital

Cultural capital includes various tangible and intangible assets associated with the culture of a region (Throsby 1999). Tangible assets include works of art, architecture, and places of cultural significance such as monuments. Intangible cultural capital includes beliefs, traditions, and practices that distinguish and identify groups of people, usually from a particular region. Some tangible cultural capital artefacts are valued in the market while others, perhaps most, are not marketable.

An accounting of cultural capital would start with an inventory of tangible and intangible assets of a region. Changes in cultural capital would involve the production or identification, and the loss or destruction of culturally significant artefacts.

Political capital

In many respects, political capital is similar to social capital. Political capital is the stock of power and goodwill held by individuals, groups, and organizations that can be held, spent, or shared to achieve desired ends (Flora 1992; Baumann and Sinha 2001). Political capital also permits individuals or groups to influence the distribution of resources.

Individuals invest in political capital by acquiring information, and by establishing relationships with policy makers, not unlike social capital. The benefits that flow from investments in political capital include increased influence in policy making, which ultimately increases the individual's access to and control over other forms of capital.

A political capital account would establish the number of politically relevant interpersonal relationships. Examples would include the region's total capacity for lobbying, its system of political networks, etc. Change in political capital would be measured by increases or decreases in lobbying capacity, including the out-migration, retirement or death of key political operatives.

Incorporating the capitals into an extended social accounting matrix

As indicated above, SAMs record the flows of market transactions among the private, public, and household sectors of regional economies. These flows, referred to as "real economy" transactions, can serve as bases for a comprehensive wealth accounting framework.

Real economy transactions are flows of goods and services from sellers to buyers, and flows of money from buyers to sellers. The goods and services represent the products of productive assets of all types. Payments for these goods and services accrue to the owners of the physical, human, natural, and other capitals, and to governments (through taxes) to allow them to provide productive public capital. Payments represent the buyers' marginal willingness-to-pay for these services. Not all capitals are owned and not all owners are compensated for the capital involved in production. Nevertheless, the basic SAM can be extended to account for these non-market relationships.

The flows of services from the eight types of capital discussed above can be estimated in one of three ways depending on their relationship to the real economy transactions captured in the regional SAM. First, there are those capitals whose flows are directly related to the "real economy". These flows can be predicted directly from values in the current account SAM. An example of this first type of flow is the consumption of forest capital by the forestry industry. In the case of the forestry sector, the forest capital will change (in this case decline) in proportion to the level of the forestry sector output. Flows of this first type of capital can be incorporated directly into the SAMs and predicted using standard SAM or computable general equilibrium algorithms. Thus predicted changes in the demand and production of forest products will change the inventories of forest capital according to fixed coefficients. Other capitals of this type would include skilled labour (human capital), intellectual skills in the case of research expenditures, and cultural capital in the case of certain types of construction. We will refer to these as Δ coefficients in our accounting system.

The second category of flows includes those that are not directly related to the real economy flows but are predictable. As an example, consider the natural growth of forest capital. The regeneration of forests depends on the current stock and biological processes. Levels of production, consumption, and investment will influence growth rates but only indirectly through reductions in forest land, air pollution, and other intermediate factors. Capital accounts can include this second type of capital flow but the flows will not be directly and linearly related to real economy transactions in the current account SAM. Other examples of this type of capital include most biological assets, education, and mortality of residents. We will refer to these as R coefficients below.

The third type of flows includes those that are unrelated to the real economy and are predictable only in a probabilistic sense. An example is forest fires, which reduce the stock of forest capital but happen stochastically. These flows can be measured but predicted only over large areas and periods of time. Again, SAMs can also include this third type of capital flow but they will not be directly and linearly related to other economic flows. Their impact on wealth can be reported as an annual average and treated like depreciation, or as a probabilistic interval such as fifty- and a hundred-year floods. We will refer to these as K coefficients.

Note that flows of the second and third (R and K) types, while not directly related to the real economy, have significant impacts on the real economy. For example, forest fires, floods and storms reduce wealth but increase short-term economic activities related to mitigation and reconstruction. Thus, changes in capitals have real economy effects and may result in indirect changes in wealth.

To incorporate these capital stocks and flows into the accounting framework we must measure them. Many of these capitals are difficult to measure directly. Many types of capital have important qualitative characteristics that defy quantitative measurement. However, indicators can be developed for all of these stocks and flows. The wealth accounts described here can be populated with a mix of monetary and non-monetary indicators, and even with qualitative descriptions when quantitative indicators are insufficient.

Ideally, a comprehensive wealth accounting system would measure all capitals on a single monetary scale. Conceptually, willingness-to-pay captures the relative value of any good or service including intangibles. Ultimately, value indicators could be established using contingent valuation, hedonic analysis, or one of the other choice-modelling techniques (Hanley et al. 2001). However, as a first step, non-monetary indicators are more feasible in many cases. Thus social capital may be measured using indices of trust and reciprocity or as rates of volunteerism, for example. Note that while the monetary values of the various capitals are almost always subject to double-counting, the non-monetary indicators are not. If natural amenities rise and land values rise, both can be reported. It would be double-counting however to add the value of natural amenities to the land values because some of the increase in land values would be due to the rise in natural amenities. As the field of research advances, estimating people's willingness-to-pay for these assets may be possible. The remainder of this volume proposes a number of indicators of capital assets.

A conceptual extended SAM

The standard SAM

We begin with the standard definitions of GDP based on the expenditure identity, the income identity, and the value added identity.[8]

$$GDP = C + I + G + E - M$$
$$GDP = C + T + S$$
$$GDP = Y + T$$

Where

C = Consumption from domestically produced and imported sources

I = Purchases for investment purposes from domestically produced and imported sources

G = Purchases by government from domestically produced and imported sources

E = Exports

M = Imports

T = Payments to government (taxes)

S = Savings

Y = Payments to factors

Gross national product adjusts GDP for flow of factor payments into and out of the region.

$$GNP = GDP - F_{out} + F_{in}$$

Adding intermediate inputs (AX) to GDP equals gross regional production, X, which is the SAM's row identity.[9]

$$GDP + AX \equiv X \equiv AX + C + I + G + E^{10}$$

Where

A = Input-output coefficients

X = Gross regional production

In the typical rectangular SAM depicted in Table 3.2, both commodities and production activities are identified, and the simple A matrix is replaced by two matrices – the use commodity input coefficients matrix (U), which describes industry (activity) purchases of commodity inputs, and the make commodity coefficients matrix (B), which describes each industry's production of commodities.[11] Each row and column in Table 3.2 is a category that can contain as many rows as necessary adequately to represent the regional system but for simplicity

Table 3.2 Standard financial social accounting matrix

		Production activities	Commodities	Factors	Households	Enterprises	Regional governments	Combined capital accounts	Rest-of-world	Totals
Production	Production activities		Make matrix (production) BX							Total production X
	Commodities	Use matrix (inputs) UX			Household consumption C		Government purchases G	Fixed capital formation and change in inventories I	Exports E	Demand for products X + M
Factors		Factor payments F_{dom}							Factor income from ROW F_{in}	Factor income F
Institutions	Households			Labour income H1		Distributed profits H2	Transfers to households H3		Remittances from ROW H4	Household income H
	Enterprises			Income to capital E1			Transfers to enterprises E2		Payments from ROW E3	Enterprise net income E
	Governments	Indirect taxes T1			Direct taxes T2	Direct taxes T3			Transfers from ROW T4	Government receipts T
Savings					Net household savings S1	Net enterprise savings S2	Net government savings S3			Capital account receipts S
	Rest-of-world		Imports M	External factors F_{out}	Remittances to rest-of-world ROW1	Payments to rest-of-world ROW2	Transfers to rest-of-world ROW3	ROW lending or borrowing ROW4		Aggregate outlay to ROW
Total		Cost of producing X	Aggregate supply X + M	Factor income F	Current household expenditure H	Current enterprise expenditures E	Current government expenditures T	Capital outlays S	Aggregate receipts from ROW	

we will treat these as the sums of all activity in each cell. The first row in the table indicates the value of commodities produced by each activity (BX). The second row indicates the value of commodities purchased by activities (UX), households (C), governments (G), and the rest of the world (E), as well as commodities purchased and used for fixed capital formation or changes in inventories (I). The third row indicates how much domestic activities and the rest of the world pay for factors of production (F_{dom} and F_{in}, respectively). The fourth row shows the sources of household income – wages (H1), distribution of profits (H2), transfers from governments (H3), and remittances and payments from the rest of the world (H4). The enterprises and government rows entries are interpreted similarly. Enterprises receive return on investment and profits (E1), transfers and subsidies (E2), and miscellaneous receipts from the rest of the world (E3). Governments collect indirect taxes (T1), direct taxes from households and enterprises (T2 and T3), and transfers from the rest of the world (T4).

The seventh row – combined capital accounts – shows the flows from the current account into the financial capital account.[12] Savings and lending from households (S1), enterprises (S2), governments (S3), and the rest of the world (S4) are all potential sources of financial capital (S). The rest-of-the-world row makes up the balance of transactions.

In general, each row total equals its corresponding column total. Exceptions occur when there are trade, government, or capital account surpluses and deficits.

Extended current account

To link current account economic indicators to comprehensive wealth indicators, the standard current accounts must be adjusted in several ways. The following adjustments are consistent with the extensions proposed for the System of integrated Environmental and Economic Accounts (SEEA) developed by several international agencies (United Nations et al. 2003). Table 3.3 focuses on the interpretation of these adjusted cells. Several columns and rows are redefined, disaggregated, or expanded to accommodate current account flows related to the seven non-financial capitals. The combined capital account is disaggregated into capital formation of each of the non-financial capitals. In addition, the activities section is redefined to include non-market activities that contribute to the production and use of capitals such as environmental remediation, volunteerism, social networking, etc.

The AX cells change when we remove activities previously treated as consumption that should instead be treated as investment, such as education and environmental remediation, or if we add current account activities which affect particular types of capital. The government sector is divided into regional government and non-regional government because the regional government uses some of its funds to build public assets for residents. Government expenditures are limited to consumption activities. Investments in infrastructure (physical capital), education (human capital), or any other capital appear as columns in the capital formation section. Capital formation by non-local governments that affects the wealth of regional residents will also be listed in the disaggregated

Table 3.3 Extended social accounting matrix – current account

		Activities	Commodities	Factors	Households	Enterprises	Regional governments	Non-regional governments
Production	Activities commodities	Intermediate inputs UX	BX		Household consumption C		G_r	G_{nr}
Factors		Factor payments F_{dom}						
Institutions	Households			H1		H2	H3	H4
	Enterprises			E1			E2	E3
	Regional governments	Indirect taxes T_r1			Direct taxes T_r2	T_r3		
	Non-regional governments	Indirect taxes $T_{nr}1$			Direct taxes $T_{nr}2$	$T_{nr}3$		
Savings					S1	S2	S3	S4
	Rest-of-world		M	F_{out}	Remittances to ROW ROW1	ROW2	ROW3	ROW4
Total		Cost of producing X	X + M	F	Household expenditures H	E	T_r	T_{nr}
Changes in capital stocks	Physical capital	$\Delta_{ph}1$			$\Delta_{ph}2$		$\Delta_{ph}3$	$\Delta_{ph}4$
	Human capital	$\Delta_{hu}1$			$\Delta_{hu}2$		$\Delta_{hu}3$	$\Delta_{hu}4$
	Intellectual capital	$\Delta_{in}1$			$\Delta_{in}2$		$\Delta_{in}3$	$\Delta_{in}4$
	Natural capital	$\Delta_{na}1$			$\Delta_{na}2$		$\Delta_{na}3$	$\Delta_{na}4$
	Social capital	$\Delta_{so}1$			$\Delta_{so}2$		$\Delta_{so}3$	$\Delta_{so}4$
	Cultural capital	$\Delta_{cu}1$			$\Delta_{cu}2$		$\Delta_{cu}3$	$\Delta_{cu}4$
	Political capital	$\Delta_{po}1$			$\Delta_{po}2$		$\Delta_{po}3$	$\Delta_{po}4$

(Continued)

Table 3.3 (Continued)

		Physical capital	Human capital	Intellectual capital	Natural capital	Social capital	Cultural capital	Political capital	Rest-of-world	Totals
Production	Activities									X
	Commodities	I_{ph}	I_{hu}	I_{in}	I_{na}	I_{so}	I_{cu}	I_{pa}	E	Demand for products X + M
Factors									F_{in}	F
Institutions	Households								H5	H
	Enterprises								E4	E
	Regional governments								T_r 4	Regional gov receipts T_r
	Non-regional governments								T_{nr} 4	Non-regional gov receipts T_{nr}
Savings		S_{ph}	S_{hu}	S_{in}	S_{na}	S_{so}	S_{cu}	S_{pa}		Capital account receipts S
	Rest-of-world	ROW_{ph}	ROW_{hu}	ROW_{in}	ROW_{na}	ROW_{so}	ROW_{cu}	ROW_{po}		Aggregate outlay to ROW
Total									Aggregate receipts from ROW	
Changes in capital stocks	Physical capital	$\Delta_{ph}5$								Δ_{ph}
	Human capital		$\Delta_{hu}5$							Δ_{hu}
	Intellectual capital			$\Delta_{in}5$						Δ_{in}
	Natural capital				$\Delta_{na}5$					Δ_{na}
	Social capital					$\Delta_{so}5$				Δ_{so}
	Cultural capital						$\Delta_{cu}5$			Δ_{cu}
	Political capital							$\Delta_{po}5$		Δ_{po}

capital formation section.[13] These changes will also effect factor payments (F_{in}), taxes (T1), and imports (M).

Entries in the disaggregated capital formation columns of the commodity row (I_{ph}, I_{hu}, etc.) are purchases of commodities for production of capital stocks. In the case of physical capital and some natural and intangible capital (mineral exploration, and research and development expenditures, for example), the values in the extended framework are simply disaggregation of values already included in the standard definition of combined capital formation entries in a standard SAM. For many others, such as investments in human, cultural, political, and other capital, these values are redefinitions of intermediate inputs, consumption, and government expenditures. For example, purchase of items used to generate social capital may be treated as an intermediate input or as consumption using standard accounting rules. In other cases these may expand our estimates of production if we add previously unaccounted activities such as imputed production of cultural artefacts to the AX section of the account. As Corrado et al. (2009) pointed out, reclassifying these expenditures as investment does not change total production, but increases the measure of saving and capital stocks.

The savings row remains unchanged. The rest-of-the-world row (ROW_{ph}, ROW_{hu}, etc.) is disaggregated to reflect the changes in liabilities for each type of capital. If all new physical capital built during the year is owned by residents, then ROW_{ph} would equal zero. If some or all of the capital was owned by non-residents, then ROW_{ph} would be negative. If residents increased their ownership or local capital, these values would be positive.

One of the most significant changes is that the extended SAM has additional rows to record the accumulation of capital of each type. In general, these entries are recorded in physical units just as employment is recorded as jobs in input-output tables and in standard SAMs. Entries in cells in the activities column ($\Delta_{ph}1$, $\Delta_{hu}1$, etc.) indicate changes in capital of various types as a result of production. For example, activities such as mining and forestry (AX) reduce the stocks of natural resources ($\Delta_{na}1$). Similarly, entries in the household column indicate changes in capital as a result of consumption activities (C). For example, household recycling requires expenditures (part of C) but replenishes stocks of various physical ($\Delta_{ph}2$) and natural resources ($\Delta_{na}2$). Regional and non-regional government activities can also affect the capital stocks ($\Delta_{ph}3$ and $\Delta_{ph}4$, respectively, for example).

At the intersection of capital formation columns and capital stock change rows ($\Delta_{ph}5$, $\Delta_{hu}5$, etc.), increases in capital due to investment are recorded. Environmental remediation (I_{na}) increases stocks of natural resources ($\Delta_{na}5$). Social activities require the purchase of inputs (I_{so}) but increase the stock of social capital ($\Delta_{so}5$).

Extended capital account

Table 3.4 illustrates an example of an annual extended capital account. The first row indicates the quantity of stocks of each capital at the beginning of the year (A_{ph}^{t-1}, A_{hu}^{t-1}, etc.) and the external liabilities associated with these stocks (L_{ph}^{t-1}, L_{hu}^{t-1}, etc.). The last line shows the stocks of assets and the external liabilities at

Table 3.4 Extended social accounting matrix – capital account

	Physical capital		Human capital		Intellectual capital		Natural capital		Social capital		Cultural capital		Political capital	
	Assets	Non-regional liabilities	Assets	Non-regional liabilities	Assets	Non-regional liabilities	Assets	Non-regional liabilities	Assets	Non-regional liabilities	Assets	Non-regional liabilities	Assets	Non-regional liabilities
Initial stocks	A^{t-1}_{ph}	L^{t-1}_{ph}	A^{t-1}_{hu}	L^{t-1}_{hu}	A^{t-1}_{in}	L^{t-1}_{in}	A^{t-1}_{na}	L^{t-1}_{na}	A^{t-1}_{so}	L^{t-1}_{so}	A^{t-1}_{cu}	L^{t-1}_{cu}	A^{t-1}_{po}	L^{t-1}_{po}
Current account changes	Δ_{ph}	ROW_{ph}	Δ_{hu}	ROW_{hu}	Δ_{in}	ROW_{in}	Δ_{na}	ROW_{na}	Δ_{so}	ROW_{so}	Δ_{cu}	ROW_{cu}	Δ_{po}	ROW_{po}
Depreciation	$-D_{ph}$		$-D_{hu}$		$-D_{in}$		$-D_{na}$		$-D_{so}$		$-D_{cu}$		$-D_{po}$	
Proportionate growth	R_{ph}	LR_{ph}	R_{hu}	LR_{hu}	R_{in}	LR_{in}	R_{na}	LR_{na}	R_{so}	LR_{so}	R_{cu}	LR_{cu}	R_{po}	LR_{po}
Exogenous changes	Z_{ph}	LZ_{ph}	Z_{hu}	LZ_{hu}	Z_{in}	LZ_{in}	Z_{na}	LZ_{na}	Z_{so}	LZ_{so}	Z_{cu}	LZ_{cu}	Z_{po}	LZ_{po}
Ending stocks	A^t_{ph}	L^t_{ph}	A^t_{hu}	L^t_{hu}	A^t_{in}	L^t_{in}	A^t_{na}	L^t_{na}	A^t_{so}	L^t_{so}	A^t_{cu}	L^t_{cu}	A^t_{po}	L^t_{po}

the end of the year (A_{ph}^t, A_{hu}^t, etc. and L_{ph}^t, L_{hu}^t, etc.). The remaining rows indicate changes in capital stocks and liabilities during the year. The sources of these changes in stocks correspond to those discussed above – those related directly to the real economy current account levels (Δ_{ph}, Δ_{hu}, etc. from Table 3.3), those related to time (D_{ph}, D_{hu}, etc. and R_{ph}, R_{hu}, etc.), and those changes which are unpredictable or exogenous to the real economy (Z_{ph}, Z_{hu}, etc.). Changes in liabilities come from the current account entries as well (ROW_{ph}^t, ROW_{hu}^t, etc.). These latter values play an important role in calculating the difference between people-based and place-based wealth and change in wealth.

From our earlier discussion we know that at any time t the place-based wealth of the region will be $A_{rr}^t - L_{rr}^t$ which is calculated by adding the changes in capital assets and liabilities of the region to the previous level. On an annual basis, then:

$$A_{rr}^t - L_{rr}^t = A^{t-1} - L_{rr}^{t-1} + \Delta^t - D^t + R^t + Z^t - (ROW^t + LR^t + LZ^t)$$

for each type of capital. The term A_{rr}^t is equivalent to A^t in Table 3.4. The terms L_{rr}^t and L_{rr}^{t-1} are intra-regional liabilities and not explicit elements of the regional accounts.[14] These capital stocks will generally be measured in physical units (such as tons, acres, populations). In some cases, it may be more convenient to measure these stocks in monetary terms (value of physical capital, for example).

Similarly, we know that the people-based wealth of the region is $A_{rr}^t + A_{rw}^t - (L_{rr}^t + L_{rw}^t)$ which is calculated by adding A_{rw}^t and subtracting L_{rw}^t from the place-based wealth. On an annual basis, then:

$$A_{rr}^t + A_{rw}^t - (L_{rr}^t + L_{rw}^t) = A_{rr}^{t-1} - L_{rr}^{t-1} + \Delta^t - D^t + R^t - (ROW^t + LR^t + LZ^t) + A_{rw}^t - L_{rw}^t$$

Here the terms L_{rr}^t, L_{rr}^{t-1}, L_{rw}^t, and L_{rw}^{t-1} are not explicit elements of the regional accounts.[15] Note that all of these variables, except capital stocks and liability stocks, are flow variables and, with the exception of depreciation, may take negative values. A negative value for ROW would indicate a reduction in liabilities, or increase in assets, and thus an increase in wealth gained through repayment of debt or redistribution of ownership, for example. Thus people-based wealth may be higher or lower than place-based wealth, depending on the initial ownership, and the change in ownership of these assets.

Note also that assets and liabilities are not limited to market-based relationships. Externalities may be recorded in any of the liability cells.

Conclusions

Current national economic accounts and their regional counterparts, where available, are the starting place for the comprehensive wealth accounts described herein. Standard national accounting systems such as the US National Income and Product Accounts provide values for current and capital transactions recorded in the market, but with few exceptions do not consider non-market accounts, the distinction between place-based capital and people-based capital, property rights (public or private), and the interrelationships among these components.

The proposed accounting framework is firmly grounded on welfare economics theory but extends the concept of utility and welfare beyond the typical frontiers to include various types of capital that, because they are difficult to measure, are typically ignored when measuring economic performance of nations and regions. These data and measurement issues are as challenging as ever, but advances are being made, as we will see in subsequent chapters.

Notes

1 The views expressed are those of the authors and should not be attributed to the US Department of Agriculture or to the Economic Research Service.
2 Fisherian income is similar to the more common Hicksian income but includes the flow of services generated from intangible capital and the current benefits of future technological change.
3 Schultz (1961) argued that expenditures on education are partially consumption and partially investment. This dual nature of expenditures may be true of other intangibles such as environmental protection and remediation. Even in these cases, the benefits of the expenditures generate a flow of Fisherian income into the future which qualifies these expenditures as investments using the broadest definition of the term.
4 It is important to note that we are using the term "liability" in the accounting sense, not the more colloquial sense of a negative feature. In accounting, a liability is an obligation due to some prior contract or transaction.
5 Pender et al. (2012, p. 37) also discussed the distinction between these concepts.
6 Note that one can sum the wealth of all residents of a region but this is still a measure of people-based wealth much as GNP is an aggregate of people-based income. In this aggregate of regional wealth, many of the liabilities of one resident will be an asset of another.
7 Note that since one person's liabilities are another person's assets, the aggregate net worth of a region's residents includes assets in the balance sheets of both the "owner" and the bond holder. This double-counted asset, equal to intra-regional liabilities, must be subtracted in order to measure a place's assets free of financial arrangements.
8 For a detailed discussion of the accounting identities involved and the structure of SAMs see Round and Pyatt (1985).
9 This is also the basic input-output identity. See Miller and Blair (2009).
10 In many input-output and SAM tables, X is defined as total supply rather than domestic supply, in which case M disappears because it is incorporated in X.
11 Here the term industry or sector which is typical of SAMs is replaced with activity to accommodate non-industrial activities such as environmental remediation, volunteerism, etc.
12 It is important to remember that this is not itself the capital account but rather flows into the capital account.
13 In a traditional SAM for a region, regional governments are explicit rows and columns while non-regional (state and national) governments are included in the rest-of-the-world rows and columns. In the extended SAM described here, non-local government investments in capital should move to the capital formation section. Alternatively, government investments, both regional and non-regional, could be identified as separate columns.
14 While not a typical feature of SAMs the saving row and fixed capital formation column could be disaggregated to record gross savings and intra-regional lending and borrowing. In this way it would be possible to make the intra-regional liabilities explicit.
15 The extra-regional liabilities and assets are embedded in the rest-of-the-world rows and columns. These values could be made explicit by expanding the regional accounts into an inter-regional account.

References

Arrow, K.J., Dasgupta, P., Goulder, L.H., Mumford, K.J., and Oleson, K. (2012) "Sustainability and the measurement of wealth", *Environment and Development Economics*, 17: 317–53.

Baumann, P., and Sinha, S. (2001) "Linking development with democratic processes in India: political capital and sustainable livelihoods analysis", *Natural Resource Perspectives*, 68. London: Overseas Development Institute.

Becker, G.S. (1962) "Investment in human capital: a theoretical analysis", *Journal of Political Economy*, 70(5): 9–49.

Corrado, C., Hulten, C., and Sichel, D. (2009) "Intangible capital and US economic growth", *Review of Income and Wealth*, 55(3): 661–85.

Costanza, R., and Daly, H.E. (2003) "Natural capital and sustainable development", *Conservation Biology*, 6(1): 37–46.

European Commission, Food and Agriculture Organization, International Monetary Fund, Organisation for Economic Co-operation and Development, United Nations, and World Bank (2012) "System of Environmental-Economic Accounting: Central Framework", Paris: OECD.

Fisher, I. (1906) *The Nature of Capital and Income*, London: Macmillan.

Flora, C.B. (1992) *Rural Communities: Legacy & Change*, Boulder, CO: Westview Press.

Gittell, R., and Vidal, A. (1998) *Community Organizing: Building Social Capital as a Development Strategy*, London: Sage.

Hanley, N., Mourato, S., and Wright, R.E. (2001) "Choice modelling approaches: a superior alternative for environmental valuation?", *Journal of Economic Surveys*, 15(3): 27.

Hoffer, D., and Levy, M. (2010) "Measuring community wealth. A report for the Wealth Creation in Rural Communities Project of the Ford Foundation". Online. Available at: <http://www.yellowwood.org/wealthcreation.aspx> (accessed 1 December 2012).

Kennickell, A. (2003) *A Rolling Tide: Changes in the Distribution of Wealth in the US, 1989–2001*, Washington, DC: Federal Reserve Board.

Lev, B., and Schwartz, A. (1971) "On the use of the economic concept of human capital in financial statements", *Accounting Review*, 46(1): 103–12.

Miller, R.E., and Blair, P.D. (2009) *Input-Output Analysis: Foundations and Extensions*, Cambridge: Cambridge University Press.

Nordhaus, W.D. (1995) "How should we measure sustainable income?", Cowles Foundation Discussion Paper.

Nordhaus, W.D. (2000) "New directions in national economic accounting", *American Economic Review*, 90(2): 259–63.

Nordhaus, W.D. (2006) "Principles of national accounting for nonmarket accounts", in D.W. Jorgenson, J. S. Landefeld, and W.D. Nordhaus (eds.), *A New Architecture for the U.S. National Accounts*, Chicago: University of Chicago Press, pp. 143–60.

Pearce, D.W., and Atkinson, G.D. (1993) "Capital theory and the measurement of sustainable development: an indicator of 'weak' sustainability", *Ecological Economics*, 8(2): 103–8.

Pender, J., Marré, A., and Reeder, R. (2012) *Rural Wealth Creation: Concepts, Strategies and Measures*, Economic Research Report No. 131, Washington, DC: US Department of Agriculture, Economic Research Service.

Putnam, R.D. (1993) "The prosperous community", *American Prospect*, 4(13): 35–42.

Romer, P. (1990) "Endogenous technological change", *Journal of Political Economy*, 98(5, pt II): S71–S102.

Round, J.I., and Pyatt, G. (1985) *Social Accounting Matrices: A Basis for Planning*, Washington, DC: World Bank.

Samuelson, P.A. (1954) "The pure theory of public expenditure", *Review of Economics and Statistics*, 36(4): 387–89.

Schultz, T.W. (1961) "Investment in human capital", *American Economic Review*, 51(1): 1–17.

Throsby, D. (1999) "Cultural capital", *Journal of Cultural Economics*, 23(1–2): 3–12.

United Nations, European Commission, International Monetary Fund, Organisation for Economic Co-operation and Development, and World Bank (2003) *Integrated Environmental and Economic Accounting 2003. Handbook of National Accounting, Studies in Methods*, New York: United Nations.

United Nations, Commission of the European Communities, International Monetary Fund, Organisation for Economic Co-operation and Development, and World Bank (2009) *System of National Accounts 2008*, New York: United Nations.

Woolcock, M. (1998) "Social capital and economic development: toward a theoretical synthesis and policy framework", *Theory and Society*, 27(2): 151–208.

Part II
Measuring rural wealth

4 Measuring rural wealth

Valuing human and built capital at the community level

Alexander W. Marré and
John L. Pender[1]

Introduction

Many attempts to measure wealth rely on sets of indicators. Indicators allow people to assess changes in particular types of wealth, especially those that are most important for a particular program or policy. In many cases, indicators may be sufficient for targeting, monitoring, and/or assessing the impacts of a development intervention. However, under certain assumptions and with the right data, wealth and its components can be valued in monetary terms. Such an approach can be useful in making comparisons across geographic areas and between different types of wealth within a given area. Attempts to value multiple kinds of wealth have relied on a concept of comprehensive wealth, which Arrow et al. (2010) define as "the social worth of an economy's entire productive base" that includes all "factors that determine intergenerational well-being".[2] In this chapter we seek to measure and value some of the most important components of comprehensive wealth of rural communities in Oregon.

Several recent studies have sought to measure changes in the value of comprehensive wealth – including both tangible physical and financial capital as well as less tangible or marketable assets such as human and natural capital – at a national level (World Bank 2006, 2011; Arrow et al. 2010; United Nations University International Human Dimensions Programme on Global Environmental Change (UNU-IHDP) and United Nations Environment Programme (UNEP) 2012).[3] As part of the UNU-IHDP/UNEP effort, Mumford (2012) measured comprehensive wealth for each of the lower forty-eight states of the United States. It was the first time comprehensive wealth was measured at a subnational scale in the United States. These studies have helped develop methods of measuring comprehensive wealth and provided valuable insights concerning the sustainability of economic growth across many nations and US states. However, given the scale at which they measured wealth, these studies do not measure wealth or wealth creation specifically in rural areas.

In this chapter we make a first attempt at measuring a few important components of comprehensive wealth at a community level, using data collected by Chen and Weber (Chapter 12) for Oregon municipalities, supplemented by data from the Census of Population and the American Community Survey. We focus on valuing two major components of comprehensive wealth: property values and human capital. We investigate how these forms of wealth changed in Oregon municipalities after implementation of the Northwest Forest Plan (NWFP) in 1994, and how these changes differed between communities in the vicinity of affected forest reserve lands and those more distant.

Studying the effects of the NWFP for municipalities in Oregon provides an interesting case to illustrate the relationships between Federal natural resources policy, human capital and property values in the context of rural communities. The NWFP is a Federal policy aimed at preserving the Northern Spotted Owl – an endangered species – and its habitat by eliminating timber harvesting on 11 million acres of Federal forest land. As discussed in more detail by Chen and Weber (Chapter 12), there are competing hypotheses about how the NWFP has affected development in the Northwest. Some have argued that the NWFP restrictions have undermined economic activity, particularly timber harvesting and milling (Waters et al. 1994). As a result, the wealth of affected communities may have declined as unemployed or underemployed workers and their families were forced to move elsewhere, reducing the human capital base and property values in these communities. Others have argued that by preserving natural amenities, the NWFP may have attracted people to communities near protected forest areas, potentially increasing the human capital base and property values (Eichman et al. 2010; McGranahan 1999). Human capital and property values could have increased not only by attracting more people, but also by attracting people with higher incomes and financial wealth and more education. Chen and Weber test some aspects of these alternative hypotheses econometrically, focusing on changes in property values, population, and income.

Our purpose is not to test hypotheses, but rather to measure these different components of wealth on the same monetary scale, enabling identification of potential tradeoffs or synergies in the impacts of the NWFP on multiple types of wealth, and suggesting hypotheses for further research. Our work adds value to the work of Chen and Weber (Chapter 12) by incorporating changes in the value of human capital into the analysis.

Why focus on property values and human capital?

Human capital and property values likely account for a dominant share of the comprehensive wealth in rural America. According to the estimates of Arrow et al. (2010), human capital accounted for 76 percent of the comprehensive wealth of the United States in 2000, excluding the value of health capital.[4] Human capital is probably also the dominant form of comprehensive wealth in rural America. Property values likely reflect much of all other forms of capital, including not only the value of land and buildings, but also other place-based assets and amenities, such as access to infrastructure, universities, and natural, social, and cultural assets. Indeed, one important method of estimating the value of non-marketed place-based assets and amenities is hedonic price analysis, which measures the implicit value of such assets and amenities based upon their impacts on property values. Although the assumptions necessary for hedonic price analysis to reflect accurately the values of place-based assets and amenities are stringent (Kanemoto 1988), it is still likely true that property values reflect most of the place-based assets of rural communities.

A focus on human capital and property values is highly relevant to any study of the impacts of natural or other amenities in rural areas, such as could be affected by the NWFP. As argued by Roback (1982), places with high amenities are expected to attract workers but not necessarily firms (depending on whether the amenities contribute to firms' productivity), leading to lower wages and possibly higher rents in higher amenity places. Other impacts of preserving natural amenities and discouraging forest exploitation are also possible, as argued by Chen and Weber (Chapter 12). Impacts of policies, such as the NWFP, on wages and rents imply direct impacts on the value of human capital and property values. To date, studies of the wealth impacts of policies, especially human and built capital impacts, are lacking.

Measuring human capital and property values

We measured the value of human capital using the method of Arrow et al. (2010) and Mumford (2012), adapted as indicated below. Their approach requires data on educational attainment, aggregate earnings, population, and size of the labor force to estimate the stock and shadow price of human capital. The stock of human capital per person is assumed to be proportional to $exp(\rho A)$, where A is the average number of years of educational attainment and ρ is the rate of return to an additional year of education, assumed to be 8.5 percent, based on the estimates of Psacharopoulos and Patrinos (2004). This is an estimate of the private and public returns to an additional year of education on wages, averaged across the OECD countries.[5] We estimated the stock of human capital for each municipality in Oregon for those who are likely to have finished their formal education – the population age 25 and older – using municipal-level data for 1990 and 2000 from the Population Census and averages for 2006–2010 from the American Community Survey.[6]

The shadow price of a unit of human capital is the present value of the sum of all wages the unit of human capital is expected to receive over a working lifetime. We assumed a lifetime of work spanning the ages of 25 to 64, or 39 years. The discount rate is assumed to be 8.5 percent, the same as the rate of return to education used in the estimation of the human capital stock. Expected wages are estimated by dividing the aggregate wage and salary income for each municipality by the size of the labor force – resulting in an average wage per worker – which is then divided by the stock of human capital. Data on labor force size and aggregate household wage and salary income were taken from the Population Census and the American Community Survey. For a technical description of the details in deriving these estimates, see the Appendix and UNU-IHDP and UNEP 2012, pp. 281–82.

We used the stock and shadow price estimates to obtain estimates of the levels and change in human capital per capita for the Oregon municipalities in our sample for the periods 1990–2000 and 2000–2010.[7] The approach used by Arrow et al. (2010) and Mumford (2012) to derive these estimates is to hold the shadow price constant in a given base year so that capital gains are removed and only the value of changes in the stock (valued at initial shadow prices) is accounted for. However, in this chapter we do not follow that approach because we seek to compare changes in the value of human capital to changes in property values. The property value data incorporate changes in the market value of property between years; therefore, our estimates of changes in human capital should reflect changes in the shadow price of human capital to be consistent.

For property values, we used the data collected by Chen and Weber (Chapter 12) on community real property values from the Oregon Department of Revenue. These data reflect the value of residential, commercial, and industrial real estate for incorporated places in Oregon in fiscal years 1989–1990, 1999–2000, and 2006–2007. The last year was specifically chosen to avoid mixing in the worst impacts of the 2007 recession on the housing market. A sample of 219 municipalities with more than thirty and fewer than 50,000 people in every year was selected for this analysis. More information about the property value data is available in Chen and Weber's chapter.

Results and discussion

The municipalities in our sample are diverse and cover a wide geographic area. Of the 219 municipalities, 148 are adjacent to forests affected by the NWFP implementation beginning in 1994. Many of the largest municipalities in our sample are adjacent to these NWFP forests and also account for much of the population and changes in property values. For example, the top fifteen cities with the largest growth in property values between 1990 and 2000 accounted for 52 percent of the total growth in property values during that period and had 41 percent of the total population of the sample in 2000. Included in these top cities are two public university towns and towns with close proximity to Portland, the major metropolitan area in Oregon. On the other hand, some municipalities are tourist destinations that are also adjacent to NWFP forests (such as on the coast), with relatively high property values per capita.

Our results are reported in two tables. Table 4.1 gives summary statistics for the levels of community real property value, human capital, and the variables used to estimate human capital in 1990, 2000, 2007 (for property values), or 2006–2010 (for human capital). Statistics are reported in aggregate terms and in per capita terms for the two variables of primary interest: real community property value and human capital. Furthermore, the magnitude and statistical significance of the difference in means between NWFP adjacent and non-adjacent municipalities is reported for both periods. Those municipalities within 10 miles are considered to be adjacent to NWFP forests, following Chen and Weber's (Chapter 12) classification.

The relative magnitude of human capital is consistent with estimates by Arrow et al. (2010), who estimated that the value of human capital in the United States

Table 4.1 Mean property values, human capital, and components by adjacency to Northwest Forest Plan forests

	1990 Mean (S.E.)	2000 Mean (S.E.)	2007 or 2006–2010 Mean (S.E.)
Community real property value, millions			
All sample municipalities	115 (230)	352 (840)	523 (1,002)
NWFP adjacent	154 (268)	474 (993)	707 (1,154)
Non-adjacent	36 (68)	99 (178)	139 (330)
Human capital, millions			
All sample municipalities	713 (1,392)	1,072 (2,100)	1,298 (2,407)
NWFP adjacent	918 (1,621)	1,406 (2,447)	1,705 (2,784)
Non-adjacent	285 (494)	376 (658)	448 (825)
Per capita community real property value			
All sample municipalities	43,552 (39,462)	100,946 (94,961)	135,450 (171,262)
NWFP adjacent	49,900 (46,041)	117,774 (109,133)	164,267 (200,224)
Non-adjacent	30,319 (11,639)	65,869 (35,008)	75,380 (41,717)
Per capita human capital			
All sample municipalities	270,293 (57,418)	309,028 (75,770)	318,708 (96,578)
NWFP adjacent	280,485 (60,150)	325,510 (83,466)	330,224 (90,424)
Non-adjacent	249,048 (44,632)	274,672 (38,444)	294,704 (104,941)
Years of education			
All sample municipalities	12.6 (0.6)	12.9 (0.6)	13.1 (0.6)
NWFP adjacent	12.7 (0.6)	13.0 (0.7)	13.2 (0.7)
Non-adjacent	12.4 (0.4)	12.6 (0.5)	12.8 (0.5)
Population age 25 and older			
All sample municipalities	2,360 (3,751)	3,050 (4,849)	3,605 (5,628)
NWFP adjacent	2,963 (4,257)	3,877 (5,513)	4,589 (6,338)
Non-adjacent	1,103 (1,839)	1,328 (2,224)	1,554 (2,823)
Labor force			
All sample municipalities	1,763 (3,045)	2,362 (3,991)	2,753 (4,576)
NWFP adjacent	2,227 (3,494)	3,023 (4,573)	3,518 (5,191)
Non-adjacent	795 (1,354)	983 (1,688)	1,159 (2,193)
Real aggregate wage and salary income, ($100,000s)			
All sample municipalities	476 (1,005)	740 (1,516)	881 (1,707)
NWFP adjacent	617 (1,178)	977 (1,772)	1,161 (1,981)
Non-adjacent	181 (320)	246 (442)	295 (565)
Per capita real aggregate wage and salary income			
All sample municipalities	16,835 (5,290)	20,116 (6,804)	19,989 (7,566)
NWFP adjacent	17,660 (5,826)	21,614 (7,495)	21,186 (7,864)
Non-adjacent	15,114 (3,382)	16,994 (3,405)	17,495 (6,251)

Notes: All dollar values are in 2005 dollars. Human capital estimates and aggregate wage and salary income are adjusted using the Consumer Price Index. Property values are adjusted using the fixed investment price index from the 2010 Economic Report of the President, Table B-7.

as a whole averaged $230,000 per capita in 2000 (in 2000 dollars). Our estimates of mean property values are less than those of Mumford (2012) for Oregon as a whole. However, Mumford estimated mean per capita housing wealth for Oregon in 2000 of $99,000 (in 2005 dollars). The differences between our property value estimates and Mumford's housing value estimates likely reflect higher values of housing in urban areas excluded from our analysis, among other factors.[8] Many of the municipalities with the highest aggregate property values are suburbs of Portland. Places with the highest per capita property values tend to be coastal cities, which are tourist destinations with many summer homes. Cities with the highest aggregate and per capita human capital are Portland suburbs or university towns. Summary statistics for the components of human capital are presented after the human capital estimates. These statistics show that, on average, non-adjacent municipalities have a lower level of average education, smaller populations and labor forces, and lower wages.

Table 4.2 shows changes in mean community real property values, human capital, and in the variables used to estimate human capital. As in Table 4.1, mean values are reported for all municipalities in the sample, municipalities adjacent to NWFP lands, and municipalities non-adjacent to NWFP lands. For comparability between the variables shown, we calculated annualized changes of the variables, dividing the total change by ten years for data measured in the 1990 to 2000 period, eight years for data measured in the 2000 to 2006/2010 period, and seven years for the 2000 to 2007 period.

Focusing first on results for all municipalities in the sample, Table 4.2 shows that real property values and human capital both grew in the 1990s and 2000s in Oregon communities. The growth in human capital was larger than the growth in property values during both periods. Our estimates of the average growth in the value of human capital during the 1990s are much larger than Mumford's (2012) for Oregon as a whole (and other states); he estimated that the value of human capital grew by $11,210 in Oregon during that period. The main reason for the difference is that Mumford did not account for changes in the shadow price of human capital. In per capita terms, the average changes in real property values and the value of human capital show a different pattern than the aggregate values.

Considering the components of human capital, the population and labor force grew on average in both the 1990s and the 2000s. Both average educational attainment and average real wages and salaries (total and per capita) grew in both periods, but more rapidly during the 1990s. The growth in real per capita wage and salary income per year declined from $328 to –$16, which is a sizeable decline. The sharp decline in the growth rate of human capital per capita during the 2000s is due to the decline in per capita wages and salaries, perhaps reflecting the effects of the recession that began in 2007.

The magnitude and statistical significance of the difference in means between NWFP adjacent and non-adjacent municipalities is reported for both periods, too. The results provide some evidence of important differences between NWFP adjacent and non-adjacent municipalities. In the 1990 to 2000 period, NWFP adjacent municipalities experienced greater average growth in population, the

Table 4.2 Mean annualized changes in property values, human capital, and components by adjacency to Northwest Forest Plan forests

	1990s Mean (S.E.)	Difference in means	2000s Mean (S.E.)	Difference in means
Change in community real property value, millions				
All sample municipalities	24 (63)		21 (48)	
NWFP adjacent	32 (6)	26 (9)***	29 (5)	24 (7)***
Non-adjacent	6 (1)		5 (3)	
Change in human capital, millions				
All sample municipalities	36 (79)		28 (57)	
NWFP adjacent	49 (8)	40***	37 (5)	28***
Non-adjacent	9 (3)		9 (4)	
Change in per capita community real property value				
All sample municipalities	5,739 (6,590)		4,313 (12,772)	
NWFP adjacent	6,787 (607)	3,232***	5,812 (1,241)	4,623**
Non-adjacent	3,555 (435)		1,189 (455)	
Change in per capita human capital				
All sample municipalities	3,874 (5,264)		1,210 (8,974)	
NWFP adjacent	4,503 (443)	1,940*	589 (454)	–1,915
Non-adjacent	2,562 (565)		2,504 (1,611)	
Change in years of education				
All sample municipalities	0.03 (0.03)		0.02 (0.04)	
NWFP adjacent	0.03 (0.00)	0.01**	0.02 (0.00)	0.00
Non-adjacent	0.02 (0.00)		0.02 (0.01)	

(*Continued*)

Table 4.2 (Continued)

	1990s Mean (S.E.)	Difference in means	2000s Mean (S.E.)	Difference in means
Change in population age 25 and older				
All sample municipalities	69 (135)		69 (137)	
NWFP adjacent	91 (13)	67***	89 (12)	61**
Non-adjacent	23 (7)		28 (13)	
Change in labor force				
All sample municipalities	60 (116)		49 (105)	
NWFP adjacent	80 (11)	61***	62 (9)	40**
Non-adjacent	19 (6)		22 (11)	
Change in real aggregate wage and salary income ($100,000s)				
All sample municipalities	26 (58)		18 (38)	
NWFP adjacent	36 (6)	29***	23 (4)	17**
Non-adjacent	7 (2)		6 (3)	
Change in per capita real aggregate wage and salary income				
All sample municipalities	328 (378)		−16 (473)	
NWFP Adjacent	395 (32)	207***	−53 (32)	−116*
Non-adjacent	188 (38)		63 (71)	

Notes: Statistical significance is indicated by ***, **, and * that correspond to 0.001, 0.01, and 0.05 levels, respectively. All dollar values are in 2005 dollars. Human capital estimates and aggregate wage and salary income are adjusted using the Consumer Price Index. Property values are adjusted using the fixed investment price index from the 2010 Economic Report of the President, Table B-7.

size of the labor force, educational attainment, and household wage and salary income, both in aggregate and per capita terms, than non-adjacent municipalities. Unsurprisingly, this resulted in more growth of human capital in NWFP adjacent municipalities in both aggregate and per capita terms, since all the components of human capital increased more in NWFP adjacent municipalities than in non-adjacent ones. Combined with greater growth in average property values for adjacent cities, a picture emerges of NWFP adjacent municipalities achieving more growth in wealth than non-adjacent municipalities immediately after the implementation of the NWFP in the 1990s, which is true in per capita terms too.

The picture changes somewhat after 2000. During the 2000s, NWFP adjacent municipalities still had greater growth than non-adjacent ones with respect to population, size of the labor force, total wages and salaries, and total human capital. These findings are consistent with other research that found that proximity to the NWFP was associated with greater population growth (Eichman et al. 2010). We also found larger increases during the 2000s in per capita property values for NWFP adjacent communities. We found no statistically discernible differences between NWFP adjacent and non-adjacent municipalities in the growth of per capita human capital, educational attainment, or wages and salaries per capita after 2000. The differences between growth in NWFP adjacent and non-adjacent communities appear to be due primarily to differences in population growth during this period. It is unclear how much of the statistically significant differences between NWFP adjacent and non-adjacent communities is due to the higher levels of these variables for NWFP adjacent communities shown in Table 4.1.

Overall, our results show many significant differences between NWFP adjacent and non-adjacent municipalities during the 1990s. However, the differences between these two groups declined substantially after 2000, with mainly differences in population growth evident in this period. However, the population effects seem not to be related to education: we find no evidence of improved average educational attainment given the changes in population.

Conclusions

This chapter has shown how the value of human capital can be estimated for rural places in the United States using publicly available data, and compared with values of other types of wealth. We build on theoretical work by Arrow et al. (2010) and empirical work by Mumford (2012) and are the first study to measure human capital at the sub-state level. The human capital estimates presented in this chapter have a number of limitations and rest on a variety of assumptions that are discussed in more detail by Arrow et al. (2010) and Mumford (2012). For example, we assume that the human capital stock depends only on formal educational attainment, though it is well established that human capital also depends on work experience and conditions of family upbringing. We do not include health capital in our estimates, in part because of concerns raised by Arrow et al. (2010) about the validity of their approach. Furthermore, the estimates of property values that we use do not include all types of wealth, though they should reflect many kinds of place-based assets, including non-marketable assets and amenities that are not directly measurable. For these reasons, our estimates are likely to underestimate the total value of comprehensive wealth in the Oregon municipalities studied. Nevertheless, this chapter provides a starting point to begin measuring the comprehensive wealth of rural communities, and illustrates how such data could be used to assess impacts of a policy such as the NWFP on rural wealth creation.

Assessing the wealth effects of the NWFP (or any other policy) must control for other factors that could affect human capital and property values. We have not sought to do that in this chapter, and do not claim to have shown the wealth impacts of the NWFP. Other studies can build on our work to measure more comprehensive notions of wealth and its components in rural regions and communities to answer important policy and research questions. Future research could seek to identify values of the various components of place-based wealth that are reflected in property values, and study the tradeoffs or synergies between human capital and the various components of place-based wealth.

Appendix[9]

The stock of human capital per worker, h, is a function of educational attainment, A, and the returns to the level of educational attainment, ρ, which is assumed to be fixed at 8.5 percent. The economy is assumed to be in steady state, with the amount of human capital per person increasing exponentially with respect to educational attainment and its return, specifically, $h = e^{(\rho A)}$.

Given h, it is a straightforward step to the total amount of human capital, H. The amount of human capital per person is simply multiplied by the population for which A is measured. Note that since the returns to education are assumed to be fixed, human capital in a given area increases either through an increase in the level of educational attainment, an increase in the working-age population, or both.

The stock of human capital in this framework is valued at the shadow price per unit of human capital, P_k. This value is equal to the present value of the average labor compensation per unit of human capital, r, over an entire working period, T (UNU-IHDP and UNEP 2012).

Therefore, $P_k = \int_{t=0}^{T} re^{-\delta t} dt$. In our case, we assume a work span over the ages of 25 until 64, or 39 years of work. Consistent with the rate of return to human capital, the discount rate is assumed to be 8.5 percent.

Notes

1   The views expressed are those of the authors and should not be attributed to the Economic Research Service or the US Department of Agriculture.
2   The definition of comprehensive wealth used by Arrow et al. (2010) implies that there exists a single measurable metric of social worth. Pender et al. (2012) provide an alternative definition that does not require such a metric, defining comprehensive wealth as the "stock of all assets, net of liabilities that can contribute to the well-being of an individual or group".

3   Various terms have been used in the literature to refer to broad measures of wealth or changes in wealth, including "genuine savings", "genuine investment", "comprehensive wealth", "inclusive wealth", and others. For simplicity, we refer to comprehensive wealth and changes in comprehensive wealth.
4   Arrow et al. (2010) defined health capital as the value of life expectancy, and changes in health capital as the value that people attach to the additional years of life that result from health improvements. This definition of health capital uses life expectancy and the value of a statistical life to calculate the value of an additional "life year". When health capital was included, the value of health capital estimated by Arrow et al. (2010) amounted to more than 95 percent of comprehensive wealth in the United States in 2000. The authors raised concerns about the validity of these estimates and indicated that the estimation of health capital deserves further study, but that this is clearly an important component of comprehensive wealth.
5   There is relatively little variation in the estimated rate of return to education across the OECD countries.
6   Due to sample size limitations, data for communities with a population of fewer than 20,000 are available from the American Community Survey only in five-year moving averages.
7   These estimates are only an approximation of per capita values, since the stock is estimated per person over the age of 25 and the shadow price is estimated over workers in the labor force.
8   Unlike Mumford (2012), our property value data includes other types of property besides housing, which also likely affects the differences.
9   This Appendix is drawn from UNU-IHDP and UNEP (2012, pp. 281–82).

References

Arrow, K.J., Dasgupta, P., Goulder, L.H., Mumford, K.J., and Oleson, K. (2010) "Sustainability and the measurement of wealth", NBER Working Paper No. 16599, Cambridge, MA: National Bureau of Economic Research.

Eichman, H., Hunt, G.L., Kerkvliet, J., and Plantinga, A. (2010) "Local employment growth, migration, and public land policy: evidence from the Northwest Forest Plan", *Journal of Agricultural and Resource Economics*, 35(2): 316–33.

Kanemoto, Y. (1988) "Hedonic prices and the benefits of public projects", *Econometrica*, 56(4): 981–89.

McGranahan, D. (1999) *Natural Amenities Drive Rural Population Change*, Economic Research Report AER 781, Washington, DC: US Department of Agriculture, Economic Research Service.

Mumford, K.J. (2012) "Measuring inclusive wealth at the state level in the United States", in UNU-IHDP and UNEP, *Inclusive Wealth Report 2012: Measuring Progress toward Sustainability*, Cambridge: Cambridge University Press.

Pender, J., Marré, A., and Reeder, R. (2012) *Rural Wealth Creation: Concepts, Strategies and Measures*, Economic Research Report No. 131, Washington, DC: US Department of Agriculture, Economic Research Service.

Psacharopoulos, G., and Patrinos, H.A. (2004) "Returns to investment in education: a further update", *Education Economics*, 12(2): 111–34.

Roback, J. (1982), "Wages, rents, and the quality of life", *Journal of Political Economy*, 90(6): 1257–78.

United Nations University-International Human Dimensions Programme (UNU-IHDP) and United Nations Environment Programme (UNEP) (2012) *Inclusive Wealth Report 2012: Measuring Progress toward Sustainability*, Cambridge: Cambridge University Press.

Waters, E.C., Holland, D.W., and Weber, B.A. (1994) "Interregional effects of reduced timber harvests: the impact of the Northern Spotted Owl listing in rural and urban Oregon", *Journal of Agricultural and Resource Economics*, 19(1): 141–60.

World Bank (2006) *Where is the Wealth of Nations? Measuring Capital for the 21st Century*, Washington, DC: World Bank.

World Bank (2011) *The Changing Wealth of Nations: Measuring Sustainable Development in the New Millennium*, Washington, DC: World Bank.

5 The net worth of households

Is there a rural difference?[1]

Alexander W. Marré

Introduction

As communities, regions and nations draw on wealth to generate flows such as income and employment, so too do individuals and households acquire and deplete asset stocks over their lifetimes to generate income for consumption and saving. Just as researching the wealth that is tied to places is critical to improve our understanding of how places grow and prosper, research on the wealth owned and used by households improves our understanding of their economic resiliency and prosperity, and of the economic vitality and potential of the communities and regions in which they live. This chapter explores the dynamics of household wealth for residents in metropolitan (urban) and nonmetropolitan (rural) areas in the United States and seeks the drivers of differences in rural and urban household wealth and wealth accumulation.[2]

Previous research has shown the important role that living in a rural area plays in conditioning and determining economic outcomes like income, employment, and poverty (Irwin et al. 2010; Weber et al. 2005). However, there is little understanding of the wealth possessed by individuals and households in rural areas or how the patterns and trends in the wealth owned by households in rural areas compare with those in urban areas. Indeed, place- and people-based wealth have received less attention in the academic literature than income, employment, and poverty. While these flows are important, especially from a policy standpoint, so are the assets that generate those flows. And just as the level and distribution of income in an area are important indicators of a region's well-being, so too are the level and distribution of household assets important for a region's economic vitality and prospects.

This chapter focuses on a subset of the wealth available to households, namely net worth. Household net worth is defined as total value of marketable assets owned by the households minus liabilities. Other forms of wealth include human (partially reflected by education, skills, and health), social, and political capital. However, net worth is a particularly convenient entry into measuring the wealth of households since it is comprised of marketable assets, which have accompanying market prices that reflect the value of those assets. Included in this measure are financial assets such as checking and savings accounts, annuities, individual retirement accounts, other investments such as stocks and bonds, the value of life insurance policies, home equity and the value of other real estate, vehicles, and the value of farms and businesses. Therefore, net worth gives an important, yet incomplete, picture of household assets and liabilities.

Conceptual framework

A household's net worth is an indicator of its economic well-being. Traditionally, much of the research on the economic well-being of rural people and places has focused on flows or measures derived from flows such as income, employment, and poverty. The major difference between net worth and income is that net worth is the value of a stock of assets, while income is a flow. Households can draw on their assets during poor economic conditions to support consumption (Fisher and Weber 2004). Under better economic conditions, households can use their wealth to make investment or take risks that allow for increased asset accumulation over time, such as opening a new business, or paying for a college education or training.[3]

Furthermore, household net worth provides additional information about the economic status of a household beyond income. While income is related to wealth, the correlation between the two can be quite low (Keister and Moller 2000; Lerman and Mikesell, 1988).[4] Lastly, household net worth may be related to political capital and prestige in a community and as such can affect future economic opportunities. In the final analysis, if rural households have less net worth than their urban counterparts, then they have fewer opportunities to leverage their assets into new and successful enterprises. In this way, the wealth of rural households is directly linked to the economic prosperity of the places they live in.

On a national scale, the most recent literature on household net worth has unsurprisingly focused on the effects of the recession beginning in the fourth quarter of 2007. The recession has highlighted the importance of net worth to households. Many homeowners saw the value of their homes decline while a decline in the stock market affected retirement savings and other investments. The Federal Reserve estimated that median and mean household net worth declined by 38.8 percent and 14.7 percent, respectively, between 2007 and 2010 (Bricker et al. 2012). The authors used data from the Survey of Consumer Finances and found that median net worth for all families decreased from $126,400 to $77,300 between 2007 and 2010.

A more recent study also looked at how net worth varies by place of residence. Marré and Pender (2013) used the Panel Study of Income Dynamics' (PSID) wealth supplement files to look at trends and the distribution of household net worth between 2001 and 2009 by different regions and metropolitan statuses. The authors found lower overall net worth in nonmetropolitan areas and significant effects of the 2007 recession across most regions and percentiles. The one area of the United States where the authors found increasing net worth was for Corn Belt residents in nonmetropolitan counties not adjacent to metropolitan areas. There, an increase in overall net worth appeared to be driven by an increase in the value of the farm and business assets. The authors conjectured that the increase for these residents was most likely driven by high prices for farmland due to high commodity prices.

Other research has examined the role that wealth plays in helping households cope with a sudden loss of income. Fisher and Weber (2004) used the PSID to examine the asset poverty of metropolitan and nonmetropolitan households. Conventional poverty measures compare a household's income with a predetermined threshold. Asset measures of poverty are aimed at an improved understanding of poverty and poverty dynamics. Since households use assets to help weather adverse economic events, comparing wealth rather than income against a threshold helps indicate whether households have the assets they need to be resilient in the face of poor economic conditions. The authors found that living in nonmetropolitan counties increased the likelihood of asset poverty, even after controlling for demographic characteristics like age, race, and education.

Both Fisher and Weber (2004) and Marré and Pender (2013) showed that differences in net worth and assets are at least in part affected by living in nonmetropolitan areas. This echoes other literature that has shown a "rural effect" on a wide variety of other outcomes (Weber et al. 2005). To date, no literature has examined the potential causes of differences in household net worth between rural and urban households. There are a number of factors that could potentially drive differences in rural and urban net wealth: a demographic effect, a wage effect, and a property value effect.

Previous research has shown that demographic characteristics influence the net worth of households and individuals. The life-cycle hypothesis of wealth accumulation suggests that people accumulate an increasing amount of wealth as they progress through their working lives, and then use those assets for consumption during retirement. As an indicator of human capital, educational attainment is also likely to increase net worth, not only by increasing wages but also by improving financial literacy and increasing access and opportunities for advancement in other ways. There are racial and ethnic differences in net worth accumulation, too (Oliver and Shapiro 1995; Hurst et al. 1998). In particular, African-American households overall have lower net worth than Caucasian households, even when controlling for other characteristics such as educational attainment. Gittleman and Wolff (2004) found that at least some of the difference can be attributed to differences in inheritances.

While the relationship between income and wealth can sometimes be weak, the amount of income earned by a household can clearly affect its ability to make new investments. Across the country, rural areas typically have labor markets that lead to lower wages. New growth theory suggests that the lower wages offered in rural labor markets are due to a lack of knowledge spillovers that are present in urban areas, where people are in closer proximity to each other. Glaeser and Maré (2001) found that when rural residents move to cities, they are able not only to command a higher wage than that received in rural areas, but their wages grow at a faster rate too. This suggests that differences in the overall wage structure between rural and urban areas may lead to lower net worth for rural households.

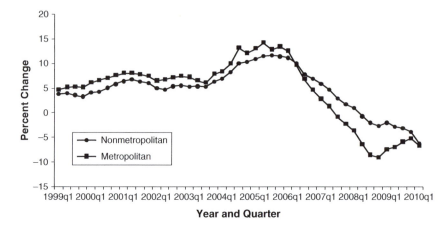

Figure 5.1 Housing prices in metropolitan and nonmetropolitan areas, percent change
from same quarter last year, 1996–2011

Source: ERS calculations using Federal Housing Finance Agency's metropolitan area housing price
indices and state-level nonmetropolitan price indices. These are combined into aggregate metropolitan
and nonmetropolitan averages by weighting each area by its share of total owner-occupied housing
units, taken from the Census Bureau's American Community Survey, using the 2006–2010 five-year
averages by county.

Property values are another potential source of differences in household net
worth between rural and urban areas. Home equity and the net value of any other
form of real estate, farmland, etc. are perhaps the components of net worth that
are most tied to geography, given the wide geographic variation in real estate and
land prices. In addition, for many households, home equity is the largest component of overall net worth. For rural households there are two potentially offsetting effects of property values on net worth. Home prices are generally lower in
rural areas relative to urban areas. During the most recent recession, rural households were spared the worst of the burst of the housing bubble (Figure 5.1). On
the other hand, as Marré and Pender (2013) note, farmland values, especially in
the Corn Belt region, grew substantially in the latter half of the 2000s. For rural
households that own farmland, the high land values may boost net worth relative
to urban households.

Data on household net worth

The Panel Study of Income Dynamics (PSID) began in 1968 as a joint project
between the Office of Economic Opportunity and the University of Michigan
(Brown et al. 1996). A nationally representative sample of roughly 5,000 households was selected for the longitudinal survey with an initial focus on income
dynamics. However, the survey has expanded over the years to include a broad
range of social and economic topics. One of the additional areas explored by
the PSID is household wealth, specifically net worth. The survey offers a set of

variables that give the value, net of liabilities, for the following broad asset categories: checking and savings accounts, annuities, individual retirement accounts (IRAs) and other retirement investments, stocks and bonds, the cash value of other assets such as life insurance policies or rights to an estate, home equity, other types of real estate, vehicles, and the net value of any farms and/or businesses owned. The PSID has followed the original households in the sample frame and their descendants annually (from 1969 to 1999) or every other year (since 1999). Perhaps most importantly for this study, the PSID provides a Beale code for each respondent and survey year, which allows the researcher to identify the metropolitan status of the county where the respondent resides.[5]

The PSID, therefore, gives household net worth and, crucially, provides the geographic identifiers necessary for rural research. There are some caveats to using the PSID data. Overall, the PSID performs well compared with the other two national surveys of household wealth: the Survey of Consumer Finances (SCF) and Survey of Income and Program Participation (SIPP) (Curtin et al. 1989).[6] However, it does a relatively poor job of estimating the net worth of the very wealthy. This is also a common issue for the SCF and the SIPP, although the SCF includes an over-sample of very wealthy households to help offset the problem. A second drawback of the PSID wealth supplement is that it does not include the value of pensions, which may play a significant role in a household's asset portfolio. Lastly, the various subcategories of net worth in the PSID are quite large. For example, a researcher is unable to separate the net value of farmland in the farm and business category from any other farm or business asset. Despite these shortcomings, the PSID provides a promising data set to examine the net worth of rural households.

Obtaining the sample

To begin examining the net worth of households by metropolitan status, a sample of household heads was selected from the PSID. For consistency, these are respondents who are heads of household in the survey years 1999 and 2009. Prior to 1999, wealth questions were only asked intermittently and Beale codes are unavailable in some years. Of the original 4,893 household heads that meet the aforementioned criteria, 302 household heads were removed due to a lack of geographic identifying information. An additional 109 household heads were removed that had missing values for the other variables included in the analysis.

Characteristics of the household heads are given in Table 5.1, both weighted and un-weighted, and compared with data from the 2000 Census.[7] In the PSID sample, the median age of household heads is 42 years of age in 1999. A majority of the household heads are male, married, and white. About 29 percent are black and 6.5 percent are Hispanic. Most have a high school diploma or higher level of educational attainment and are married. The most relevant comparison with the Census data is among householders, although figures for the total population in the United States are also reported.[8] Once weighted, the PSID sample is roughly similar to the Census data in the characteristics examined here, except that the sample has more female and nonmetropolitan household heads than in the general population.

Table 5.1 Sample household head characteristics

	PSID sample (1999)		Census (2000)	
	Un-weighted	Weighted	Householders	Total population
Median age	42	34.4	–	35.3
Female	25.6%	24.4%	12.2%	50.9%
Black	29.4%	11.1%	7.8%	12.9%
Hispanic[1]	6.5%	8.4%	7.0%	12.5%
Education[2]				
Less than a high school diploma	20.0%	18.6%	–	19.6%
High school diploma or equivalent	32.5%	30.5%		28.6%
Some college	23.0%	22.7%		27.4%
Bachelor's degree	14.8%	16.3%		15.5%
Postgraduate	9.6%	11.9%		8.9%
Married[3]	57.6%	56.7%	51.7%	54.4%
Nonmetropolitan residence[4]	26.7%	31.6%	17.8%	17.4%

Source: Author's estimates, using data from the Panel Study of Income Dynamics, University of Michigan, Institute for Social Research and 2000 Census, US Census Bureau. The overall sample size is $N = 4,482$.

Notes:
[1] The Hispanic variable comes from the 2005 PSID wave.
[2] Age and educational attainment data in the 2000 Census are not available for householders. The figures presented here in the total population column are for the population age 25 and older.
[3] Census figures reported here for marital status are for the population age 15 and older.
[4] The Census figures on nonmetropolitan residence were coded by the author with the 2003 metropolitan area definitions from the Office of Management and Budget.

The metropolitan or nonmetropolitan status of each household is determined by the Beale code provided by the PSID. The Beale code is assigned at the time of the interview, usually in the spring of the interview year. This means that it is conceivable that households residing in nonmetropolitan counties could be re-classified as metropolitan residences later in the sample time frame if that county grows in population to meet the metropolitan definition. Overall, however, the sample is fairly stable in terms of the share of households classified as residing in metropolitan or nonmetropolitan areas between 1999 and 2009. Less than one-third of the sample is nonmetropolitan. Between 1999 and 2009, 392 households moved between metropolitan and nonmetropolitan counties or resided in counties that changed classification. The remainder – 1,010 nonmetropolitan house-holds and 3,080 metropolitan households – stayed in their respective county types or resided in counties that were not reclassified as metropolitan or nonmetropolitan over the time period. In the remaining analysis, nonmetropolitan households are defined as those that remain in nonmetropolitan counties in each survey year between 1999 and 2009.

Data from the PSID's wealth supplement consists of a number of wealth categories, typically reflecting the net value of each asset type. To simplify the analysis, the financial capital and other property categories were constructed as the sum of various types of assets and liabilities. The components of net worth are defined as follows:

1   Financial capital: the sum of the value of checking and savings accounts, certificates of deposit, savings bonds, value of private annuities or individual retirement accounts, stocks, mutual funds, investment trusts, rights in estates, less credit card, student loan, or other forms of debt.
2   Home equity: net value of primary home.
3   Farm and business: net value of farm and/or business (including farmland).
4   Other property: net value of any second homes, land, rental real estate plus the net value of vehicles, recreational vehicles, boats, etc.

Financial capital is generally the most liquid of all the asset types, while home equity, farm and business, and other property are generally less liquid, meaning that these components of net worth are the more difficult to convert to cash.

Trends in the size and distribution of household net worth

In Table 5.2, weighted means and medians of the major wealth categories are shown with standard deviations in parentheses. The values are reported only if the household has assets or liabilities in a particular category. For example, mean and median home equity is shown only for home owners. In addition, each weighted mean and median is reported in 2009 dollars to allow for comparability across years. These figures show mean household net worth increasing from $309,993 to $531,844 (in 2009 dollars). For comparison, Wolff (2010, Table 1) uses data from the Survey of Consumer Finances and reports mean net worth increasing from $343,800 to $536,100 between 1998 and 2007 (in 2007 dollars). Results from the PSID show median household net worth increasing from $88,019 to $139,000 between 1999 and 2009, while Wolff found median net worth increasing from $77,200 in 1998 to $102,500 in 2007.

Table 5.2 provides a few noteworthy findings. First, both mean and median financial capital are higher in metropolitan areas than nonmetropolitan areas and grew more between 1999 and 2009. For nonmetropolitan households, home equity and the net value of farm and business assets (for those that own them) are large sources of net worth. Taken together, these findings suggest that the composition of net worth for nonmetropolitan households is more heavily weighted toward less liquid assets, which may adversely affect the ability of nonmetropolitan households to use these assets during periods of economic stress or reduce their ability to move to new economic opportunities. Second, the results show increases in mean and median net worth and their components between 1999 and 2009. The only declines were in the mean value of farm and business for metropolitan households and in the median value of other property for nonmetropolitan households.

Table 5.2 Weighted means and medians of household net worth and components, 2009 dollars

	Mean (std. dev.)		Median		Share of sample households with zero net value (%)	
	1999	2009	1999	2009	1999	2009
Net worth	309,993 (1,116,950)	531,844 (3,248,315)	88,019	139,000	5.0	4.8
Metro	346,196 (1,350,508)	535,620 (2,504,691)	92,975	158,650	3.9	3.9
Nonmetro	243,206 (486,527)	590,327 (5,191,971)	92,717	121,000	1.0	0.9
Financial capital	122,378 (495,426)	166,859 (644,412)	12,877	20,000	13.9	13.0
Metro	140,320 (591,690)	189,836 (727,311)	17,771	24,500	10.3	9.4
Nonmetro	83,186 (213,220)	87,599 (211,611)	10,044	11,000	3.6	3.5
Home equity	111,118 (137,839)	164,931 (246,195)	77,264	100,000	37.6	30.5
Metro	125,784 (161,174)	185,125 (257,526)	83,703	120,000	29.2	23.4
Nonmetro	84,272 (76,737)	111,841 (119,409)	66,962	84,000	8.4	7.1
Farm and business	425,495 (2,140,541)	528,131 (1,581,981)	64,387	75,000	90.0	89.9
Metro	616,745 (2,897,889)	550,110 (1,717,957)	32,193	50,000	67.2	66.6
Nonmetro	203,920 (375,112)	542,722 (1,412,252)	97,868	150,000	22.8	23.2
Other property	60,264 (216,499)	189,714 (3,156,181)	14,809	15,000	13.3	14.1
Metro	58,474 (223,181)	153,066 (2,217,670)	12,877	15,000	10.8	11.2
Nonmetro	61,521 (213,560)	343,640 (5,295,811)	17,384	15,000	2.5	2.9

Source: Author's estimates, using data from the Panel Study of Income Dynamics, Institute for Social Research, University of Michigan.

Table 5.3 Inequality in net worth among households

	Gini coefficients	
	1999	*2009*
All households	0.770	0.805
Metropolitan households	0.787	0.789
Nonmetropolitan households	0.712	0.842

Source: Author's estimates, using data from the Panel Study of Income Dynamics, Institute for Social Research, University of Michigan.

These data may also be used to get a sense of the overall distribution of household net worth among the whole sample and among households by metropolitan residence (Table 5.3). Wolff's (2010) study reported rising inequality in net worth. Between 1998 and 2007, the Gini coefficient of net worth using the SCF data increased from 0.822 to 0.834. The PSID sample used in this analysis shows the weighted Gini coefficient increasing from 0.770 to 0.805 for the entire sample between 1999 and 2009.[9] Inequality was lower among nonmetropolitan households in 1999 than among metropolitan households, but grew among nonmetropolitan households to surpass inequality among metropolitan households in 2009. The rising value of farmland over the period and the difference in the housing market between more remote rural areas and those adjacent to metropolitan areas could be explanations of rising nonmetropolitan inequality in net worth during this period.

Modeling rural/urban differences in household net worth

The first model used to examine the differences in household net worth between rural and urban households is a simple ordinary least squares regression of household net worth and its major subcategories: financial capital, home equity, the value of farms and businesses, and other property. Explanatory variables include an indicator variable for households that resided in nonmetropolitan counties in all sample periods between 1999 and 2009 and a constant. The estimated coefficient associated with nonmetropolitan households may therefore be interpreted as a difference in means test with metropolitan households and those households that moved between nonmetropolitan and metropolitan areas. Results for these regressions are reported in Table 5.4.

These results show no statistically significant difference in rural and urban total household net worth and the farm and business and other property subcategories. The nonmetropolitan household coefficient remains statistically insignificant even if the sample is restricted only to those with farm and business assets or other property assets. In contrast, there is a sizeable difference in the financial capital category of household net worth between nonmetropolitan households and metropolitan households and in home equity. In both cases, the

Table 5.4 Rural/urban differences in net worth and its subcategories, 2009 dollars

	Net worth est. coeff. (S.E.)	Financial capital est. coeff. (S.E.)	Home equity est. coeff. (S.E.)	Farm and business est. coeff. (S.E.)	Other property est. coeff. (S.E.)
Nonmetro household	−12,642 (108,784)	−65,343*** (12,311)	−29,426*** (4,873)	29,121 (21,777)	53,006 (103,713)
Constant	388,795*** (36,624)	130,235*** (10,760)	103,732*** (3,614)	59,141*** (10,211)	95,687*** (30,461)

Source: Author's estimates, using data from the Panel Study of Income Dynamics, Institute for Social Research, University of Michigan.

Notes: Asterisks indicate statistical significance: ***, **, and * correspond to 0.01, 0.05, and 0.1 levels of statistical significance, respectively. Standard errors are Huber-White heteroskedasticity robust.

estimated coefficient is negative, indicating that nonmetropolitan households have less net worth in these categories than metropolitan households.

The next set of models focuses on exploring possible explanations for the difference in financial capital and home equity between households in nonmetropolitan areas. For these two subcategories of household net worth three models are estimated. Model I is the same model discussed above and reported in Table 5.4. Model II adds demographic characteristics and initial financial capital or home equity in 1999 as explanatory variables. Model III adds the wages of the household head and wife/partner (if any) in 2009 as an explanatory variable. Comparing these results shows how the difference in financial capital and home equity for nonmetropolitan households can be partially explained by demographic characteristics and wages, as hypothesized in the conceptual framework of this chapter.

For each model, the dependent variable is financial capital or home equity in 2009. Explanatory variables include age and age squared (measured in 2009) to test for any life-cycle effects of household net worth, and indicator variables for female, black, and Hispanic household heads and for various levels of educational attainment, all measured in 1999. Various types of marital status are controlled for by four indicator variables. The variables *married* and *widowed* are measured in 2009, while *became married* and *became divorced* capture these important household changes between 1999 and 2009. As mentioned above, nonmetropolitan residence, levels of financial capital or home equity in 1999, and household wages in 2009 are also controlled for. Results for these models are reported in Tables 5.5 and 5.6.

There is a sizeable difference in mean financial capital between nonmetropolitan and metropolitan households in 2009 of $65,343 (Table 5.5). This difference is reduced to $21,664 when demographic characteristics and initial levels of financial capital in 1999 are controlled for in Model II. The results have expected signs, pointing to life-cycle effects, large and negative effects on financial capital for black and Hispanic household heads, and positive effects for educational

Table 5.5 Models of household financial capital in 2009, 2009 dollars

	Model I est. coeff. (S.E.)	Model II est. coeff. (S.E.)	Model III est. coeff. (S.E.)
Nonmetro[1] household	−65,343*** (12,311)	−21,664** (10,286)	−9,402 (10,015)
Age		5,043** (2,298)	3,653 (2,257)
Age squared		−46.81** (21.51)	−25.62 (21.51)
Female		−8,786 (16,677)	−9,437 (16,623)
Black		−36,120*** (11,850)	−24,624** (11,704)
Hispanic		−46,630*** (16,863)	−34,275** (16,774)
High school diploma		4,423 (8,554)	−1,685 (8,598)
Some college		15,384 (13,701)	1,161 (13,885)
College degree		64,009** (27,753)	24,434 (27,313)
Postgraduate		93,820** (44,531)	53,968 (43,094)
Married[2]		2,126 (18,426)	−30,298 (18,781)
Widowed[2]		67,061 (78,784)	54,719 (79,481)
Became married[3]		−13,868 (19,093)	−12,405 (18,934)
Became divorced[3]		−62,963** (32,066)	−67,813** (31,978)
Initial financial capital		0.92*** (0.18)	0.92*** (0.19)
Household wages[4]			0.73*** (0.17)
Constant	130,235*** (10,760)	−93,229 (64,164)	−98,870 (63,957)

Source: Author's estimates, using data from the Panel Study of Income Dynamics, Institute for Social Research, University of Michigan.

Notes: Asterisks indicate statistical significance: ***, **, and * correspond to 0.01, 0.05, and 0.1 levels of statistical significance, respectively. Standard errors are Huber-White heteroskedasticity robust. The R^2 for Models II and III is 0.59, and 0.61, respectively.
[1] Household resided in a nonmetropolitan county for all survey years between 1999 and 2009.
[2] Variable measured in 2009.
[3] Variable measured between 1999 and 2009.
[4] Wages are for household head and wife/partner in 2009.

attainment. Notably, the effect of educational attainment is not statistically significant until a college degree and beyond. Each additional dollar of net financial capital in 1999 is associated with an additional $0.92 in financial assets in 2009. However, the estimated coefficient is not statistically different from $1, so there is not sufficient statistical evidence from the results in Models II and III to indicate whether inequality in financial capital declined.

In Model III, the difference in nonmetropolitan and metropolitan household financial capital becomes statistically insignificant with the addition of household wages in 2009. In fact, the addition of wages to the model results in age and educational attainment to become statistically insignificant and a reduction in the magnitude of race and ethnicity, which suggests that the effects of these factors on financial capital are mainly through their effect on wages. The marginal effect of initial financial capital in this model remains the same as in Model III and remains statistically significant.

Table 5.6 Models of household home equity in 2009, 2009 dollars

	Model I est. coeff. (S.E.)	Model II est. coeff. (S.E.)	Model III est. coeff. (S.E.)
Nonmetro[1] household	−29,426*** (4,873)	−14,510*** (3,721)	−10,554*** (4,070)
Age		2,826*** (830)	2,420*** (842)
Age squared		−27.89*** (7.28)	−20.48*** (7.49)
Female		−1,008 (8,431)	−1,135 (8,478)
Black		−15,691*** (5,343)	−12,466** (5,501)
Hispanic		−24,643** (10,082)	−20,659** (9,970)
High school diploma		51 (4,130)	−1,786 (4,217)
Some college		11,847** (5,652)	7,518 (5,920)
College degree		36,692*** (10,369)	23,757** (11,828)
Postgraduate		48,074*** (13,508)	35,588** (14,993)
Married[2]		19,617* (10,205)	9,105 (11,193)
Widowed[2]		−12,820 (16,750)	−16,456 (16,684)
Became married[3]		−1,659 (8,491)	−1,857 (8,296)
Became divorced[3]		−35,745*** (11,188)	−36,846*** (11,078)
Initial home equity		1.09*** (0.16)	1.06*** (0.15)
Household wages[4]			0.26*** (0.10)
Constant	103,732*** (3,614)	−46,436* (26,684)	−51,986** (26,373)

Source: Author's estimates, using data from the Panel Study of Income Dynamics, Institute for Social Research, University of Michigan.

Notes: Asterisks indicate statistical significance: ***, ** and * correspond to 0.01, 0.05 and 0.1 levels of statistical significance, respectively. Standard errors are Huber-White heteroskedasticity robust. The R^2 for Models II and III is 0.48 and 0.50, respectively.
[1] Household resided in a nonmetropolitan county for all survey years between 1999 and 2009.
[2] Variable measured in 2009.
[3] Variable measured between 1999 and 2009.
[4] Wages are for household head and wife/partner in 2009.

In the home equity models reported in Table 5.6, the $29,452 difference in mean home equity between nonmetropolitan and metropolitan households is cut in half by including demographic characteristics and initial home equity in 1999 in the model. As in the financial capital models, the effects of age and educational attainment are large and statistically significant. The variables for age have expected signs. In contrast with financial capital, there was a statistically significant effect for attending college (no degree) on home equity. All else equal, an otherwise similar black household head had $15,691 less home equity and a Hispanic household head had $24,643 less home equity. Model II shows that each additional dollar of home equity in 1999 was associated with $1.09 in additional home equity in 2009, although this coefficient is not statistically different from $1.

With the addition of total household wages in 2009 in Model III, the effect of nonmetropolitan residence on home equity is further reduced, but not eliminated. In contrast with financial capital, adding wages as an explanatory variable did not change the statistical significance of most of the demographic characteristics, although it did reduce their estimated magnitudes. Wages also reduced the estimated effect of initial home equity in 1999, from $1.09 to $1.06. Each additional dollar of household wages in 2009 was associated with $0.26 more in home equity.

Conclusion and discussion

The research presented here used data from the PSID to examine trends and differences in household net worth between rural and urban areas. Although the PSID over-samples more households in nonmetropolitan areas, other demographic characteristics are roughly similar to those from the Census when appropriately weighted. Furthermore, the mean and median values of net worth from the survey are roughly similar in magnitude and change over time to the Survey of Consumer Finances. In terms of the size and distribution of net worth, this study found higher mean and median values of net worth for urban areas in financial capital and home equity, but similar or lower values in the farm and business and other property categories. In addition, this study found increasing inequality in household net worth between 1999 and 2009, with nonmetropolitan households catching up in inequality with metropolitan households during that time period.

Rural and urban differences in household net worth were found in only two of four subcategories of net worth: financial capital and home equity. The difference in home equity is likely due to a variety of factors including the fact that home prices are lower overall in rural areas and that rural areas were less affected by the housing bubble than urban areas. The rural and urban difference in financial capital and home equity between 1999 and 2009 was attributable to a combination of factors including demographic characteristics, initial wealth, and wages. The rural and urban difference in financial capital was entirely explained by the demographic, initial wealth, and wage variables. These same characteristics sizeably reduced but did not eliminate the estimated "rural effect" for home equity. Part of the issue may be that home values are heavily affected by local characteristics, rather than individual or household characteristics. It could also be that housing values affect the selection of a rural residence, i.e., that some people choose to live in rural areas because of lower housing values. This is likely not the case for financial assets, which are more mobile.

From a policy perspective, these results suggest that improving educational attainment in rural areas would not only increase wages but would also reduce the rural and urban gap in financial capital and home equity. As such, they complement the existing literature on rural and urban differences in wages and poverty. Additional research is needed in a few areas. First, the question of rural and urban differences in home equity should be examined more thoroughly with community and regional characteristics included in the model. The question of rising inequality in net worth is of great interest at the national level, and additional research is needed to examine how rising inequality overall has played out among rural households versus urban households and what the causes and consequences of those trends might be.

Notes

1 The collection of data used in this study was partly supported by the National institutes of Health under grant number R01 HD069609 and the National Science Foundation under award number 1157698. The views expressed are those of the author and should not be attributed to the Economic Research Service or the US Department of Agriculture.
2 The terms "metropolitan" and "urban" are used interchangeably in this chapter, as are "nonmetropolitan" and "rural". See Isserman (2005) for a discussion of the strengths and weaknesses of various urban and rural definitions.
3 For example, a study from the Pew Charitable Trusts found that an increase in $10,000 of home equity increased the likelihood that students from families with incomes below $70,000 would enroll in college by six percentage points, and that gains in housing wealth increased college graduation and the quality of schools selected too (Lovenheim 2011).
4 Lerman and Mikesell (1988) estimate the correlation at 0.50 and as low as 0.26 when asset income is removed from total income. Households may therefore have low wealth and high income or high wealth and low income.
5 Beale codes, or rural–urban continuum codes, are a county-level typology on a nine-part scale that classifies counties by population size and adjacency to metropolitan areas. See Economic Research Service (2012) for more information.
6 The SCF is perhaps the most detailed of the three national surveys of household wealth and is used for many government publications, especially from the Federal Reserve, that describe the composition and trends of household net worth in the United States. In contrast, the Survey of Income and Program Participation, maintained by the US Census Bureau, is primarily aimed at better understanding the income of the households surveyed, particularly income from government transfer programs. While both of these data sets provide information on household net worth and its components, neither is well suited for examining the spatial dimensions of household net worth. The SCF does not provide geographic information at the county level in the publicly available data. Some geographic information is available in the SIPP, but county and metropolitan identifiers are suppressed for some states.
7 Individual cross-sectional weights from the PSID are used in this analysis for characteristics of the household head. Otherwise, family cross-sectional weights are used for household-level variables, such as household wealth and nonmetropolitan residence.
8 The terms "householder", used by the Census, and "household head", are not equivalent. Householders are identified as the person in the household in whose name the housing unit is owned or rented. Household heads are the reference person for each household and are usually the adult male head.
9 Care should be taken when interpreting these estimates. Gini coefficients typically fall between zero and one, with the value one indicating perfect equality. However, in this case, a sizeable number of households have negative values of net worth, making it possible for the Gini coefficient to exceed the value of one since the Lorenz curve falls below the horizontal axis (Jenkins and Jäntti 2005).

References

Bricker, J., Kennickell, A.B., Moore, K.B., and Sabelhaus, J. (2012) "Changes in U.S. family finances from 2007 to 2010: evidence from the Survey of Consumer Finances", *Federal Reserve Bulletin*, 98(2): 1–80.
Brown, C., Duncan, G.J., and Stafford, F.P. (1996) "Data watch: the Panel Study of Income Dynamics", *Journal of Economic Perspectives*, 10(2): 155–68.
Curtin, R.T., Juster, F.T., and Morgan, J.N. (1989) "Survey estimates of wealth: an assessment of quality", in R. Lipsey and H. Stone (eds.), *The Measurement of Saving, Investment, and Wealth*, Chicago: University of Chicago Press.

Economic Research Service (2012) "Rural–urban continuum codes". Online. Available at: <http://www.ers.usda.gov/data-products/rural-urban-continuum-codes.aspx> (accessed 1 July 2012).

Fisher, M., and Weber, B.A. (2004) "Does economic vulnerability depend on place of residence? Asset poverty across metropolitan and nonmetropolitan areas", *Review of Regional Studies*, 34(2): 137–55.

Gittleman, M., and Wolff, E.N. (2004) "Racial differences in patterns of wealth accumulation", *Journal of Human Resources*, 39(1): 193–227.

Glaeser, E.L., and Maré, D.C. (2001) "Cities and skills", *Journal of Labor Economics*, 19(2): 316–42.

Hurst, E., Ching Luoh, M., and Stafford, F.P. (1998) "The wealth dynamics of American families, 1984–94", *Brookings Papers on Economic Activity*, 1: 267–337.

Irwin, E.G., Isserman, A.M., Kilkenny, M., and Partridge, M.D. (2010) "A century of research on rural development and regional issues", *American Journal of Agricultural Economics*, 92(2): 522–53.

Isserman, A.M. (2005) "In the national interest: defining rural and urban correctly in research and public policy", *International Regional Science Review*, 28(4): 465–99.

Jenkins, S.P., and Jäntti, M. (2005) "Methods for summarizing and comparing wealth distributions", Institute for Social and Economic Research Working Paper No. 2005–05, University of Essex.

Keister, L.A., and Moller, S. (2000) "Wealth inequality in the United States", *Annual Review of Sociology*, 26: 63–81.

Lerman, D.L., and Mikesell, J.J. (1988) "Rural and urban poverty: an income/net worth approach", *Policy Studies Review*, 7: 765–81.

Lovenheim, M. (2011) "Housing wealth and higher education: building a foundation for economic mobility", The Pew Charitable Trusts, December. Online. Available at: <http://www.pewtrusts.org/uploadedFiles/wwwpewtrustsorg/Reports/Economic_Mobility/Pew_EMPProject_FamilyWealth.pdf> (accessed 5 December 2012).

Marré, A. and Pender, J. (2013) "The distribution of household net worth within and across rural areas: Are there links to the natural resource base?", *American Journal of Agricultural Economics*, 95(2): 457–62.

Oliver, M.L., and Shapiro, T.M. (1995) *Black Wealth/White Wealth*, New York: Routledge.

Panel Study of Income Dynamics, public use dataset (2013) Survey Research Center, Institute for Social Research, University of Michigan, Ann Arbor, MI.

Weber, B., Jensen, L., Miller, K., Mosley, J., and Fisher, M. (2005) "A critical review of rural poverty literature: is there truly a rural effect?", *International Regional Science Review*, 28(4): 381–414.

Wolff, E.N. (2010) "Recent trends in household wealth in the United States: rising debt and the middle-class squeeze – an update to 2007", Working Paper No. 589, Levy Economics Institute of Bard College.

6 The role of wealth measurements in improving practice

Lessons from the field

Shanna Ratner and Melissa Levy

Introduction

The Ford Foundation's Wealth Creation in Rural Communities – Building Sustainable Livelihoods (WCRC-BSL) initiative (now WealthWorks) intends to improve the livelihoods of rural people by creating multiple forms of wealth that are owned, controlled, and reinvested in rural places so that rural places become valued partners in resilient regions.[1] This initiative has focused on three of the poorest rural regions in the United States: Central Appalachia, the South, and Texas' Lower Rio Grande Valley.

WCRC-BSL set an explicit goal of working with grantees to learn how to create multiple forms of wealth without undermining any one to create another. Grantees received assistance in developing and implementing measures of seven forms of wealth to help them more fully understand and improve their impacts.[2] This chapter describes the wealth creation approach to measurement, provides on-the-ground examples of measures of seven forms of wealth, and discusses practitioner insights from this process.

Wealth creation in rural communities: building sustainable livelihoods

In its first year, WCRC-BSL conducted research to determine the extent to which rural economic development practitioners in the United States: (1) intentionally defined desired impacts on the economy, the environment, and social inclusion, and (2) incorporated impact measures in their practice (Stark and Markley 2008). Researchers concluded, "while entrepreneurship can be an intervention that builds all forms of capital, the key challenge is getting practitioners to value and measure changes across all types of capital. Right now, they are not doing so in a systematic and rigorous way" (Stark and Markley 2008, p. 2).

The practice of measurement is not widespread among practitioners, and there are no widely accepted metrics associated with community development (Dorius 2011). The conventional economic development metrics are jobs and income, which are flows derived from stocks of wealth. When stocks are depleted or depreciated, the flows dry up. The concept of measuring underlying stocks of wealth as a basis for creating sustainable livelihoods is relatively new. As far as we know, WCRC-BSL is the first program to attempt measuring multiple forms of wealth at the level of individual wealth creation value chains in the United States.

A wealth creation value chain is the vehicle used to build multiple forms of wealth on the ground using this approach. A wealth creation value chain is a business model based on shared economic, social, and environmental values, in which buyers, processors, producers, and others work together for mutual benefit to create value in response to market demand. Wealth creation value chains:

- respond to consumer demand for goods and services that embody values such as transparency, environmental protection, use of recycled materials, and fair labor practices;
- intentionally include low-wealth individuals and communities in producing products and services that meet market demand while delivering multiple forms of wealth that remain in poor places;
- are demand driven and based on satisfying the self-interests of participants.

These features distinguish wealth creation value chains from conventional supply chains. A supply chain is a process wherein materials are converted into final products, "traditionally characterized by a forward flow of materials and a backward flow of information" (Beamon 1998, p. 28) by several independent firms involved in steps to placing it in the hands of the end user (Mentzer et al. 2001). According to Handfield and Nichols 1999, "By optimizing along the entire sequence of steps that are involved in the production of a product whether it is a good or service, the greatest value can be produced at the lowest possible cost (in Linton et al. 2007, p. 1078)". In many cases, this approach requires organizations to operate sub-optimally from a cost perspective to create the greatest possible value along the entire supply chain (Leenders and Blenkhorn 1988).

A wealth creation value chain intentionally contributes to building seven forms of wealth (in the context of cultural capital), not simply financial profits. The eight forms of wealth are described in Chapter 2.

WCRC-BSL builds on participatory research and evaluation, emphasizes impacts over activities, incorporates eight forms of wealth, and provides a framework for planning and evaluation. Measurement takes place in "real time" as the work is planned and executed, not after the fact. The wealth matrix defines seven forms of wealth for measurement (the eighth form, cultural capital, is measured through measures of the other seven forms), but practitioners determine the specific impacts measured for each form of wealth based on the conditions they seek to create on the ground and the levers of change they move. Rather than posit a set of measures, we allow practitioners to define measures meaningful to them that provide information they can use to improve their decision making and performance.

This measurement approach was designed to overcome barriers to engaging practitioners in measurement in the pursuit of improved outcomes. Typical barriers to measurement include lack of training in measurement techniques, lack of capacity to implement measures, and distrust of measurement as an extractive activity not beneficial to practitioners or beneficiaries.

The act of measuring informs practitioners' understanding of the world they seek to impact and leads to adjustments in approach as needed to improve impacts. Practitioners received training and support in identifying, developing, and sometimes implementing measurement. Practitioners committed to measuring as a core function of their work, not an add-on. Social change is a complex world where external forces are at play, and controlled experimentation is difficult. We do not expect measures of impacts on wealth to establish grounds for attribution; rather, we expect practitioners to use measurement to better understand their own and others' contributions to desired impacts and to define areas for improvement.

Measures can illustrate five impact pathways that the wealth creation approach provides to improve the livelihoods of poor people, households, and communities through:

1   Engagement as producers, for example of agricultural products.
2   Engagement as laborers, for example as firms providing renewable energy services expand.
3   Avoided cost as in lower energy costs through improved efficiency for homeowners or shared certification costs for minority forest landowners.
4   Opportunities for shared ownership, through, for example, owning shares in a community-based destination tourism company.
5   Opportunities to create value chains that provide wealth-enhancing affordable products and services to poor consumers.

The wealth creation approach to economic development

Three fundamental constructs are used in the wealth creation approach to economic development: (1) wealth creation value chains, (2) eight forms of wealth, and (3) structures of ownership and control.

A wealth creation value chain may work with and transform an existing supply chain (in which each participant's relationships are generally limited to those from whom they purchase inputs and those to whom they sell), or a new wealth creation value chain may be developed in response to emerging market demand. Constructing a wealth creation value chain requires an intentional change in the way practitioners approach development, identify partners, and relate to the market. Focus shifts from supply to demand. Rather than asking, "Who wants what we've got?" the question becomes "What can we provide that meets a real need in the marketplace?" A wealth creation value chain begins by understanding the full range of values the marketplace wants the product to incorporate and the benefits of each value to the buyers. The next step is effectively to engage low-wealth people, places, and businesses in meeting demand in a manner that is profitable while creating seven forms of wealth for local benefit.

Value chain coordinators provide leadership for wealth creation work, act as the "glue" for wealth creation value chains by holding the vision of the value chain at scale, build the relationships among and between all the participants, and design strategic interventions to bring the value chain to scale. Current value chain coordinators in WCRC-BSL are nonprofit organizations, though this is not a requirement.

The wealth creation value chain coordinator analyzes existing production activity in their area related to the value chain, identifies gaps, and finds ways to fill those gaps that intentionally benefit low-wealth people, places, and businesses and appeal to the self-interests of all value chain participants. The coordinator works with stakeholders to build and operate the wealth creation value chain in a manner that creates multiple forms of wealth that stick in poor areas.

Structures of ownership and control are those that keep wealth local and give low-wealth people and communities control over how that wealth is maintained and re-invested over time.

The wealth matrix as a measurement framework

The wealth matrix tool helps practitioners plan ways to create strong value chains that simultaneously create multiple forms of wealth without destroying any one form to create another.

The wealth matrix requires value chain coordinators to think through the impact of every intervention on each form of wealth and then identify measures, baselines, and a measurement methodology related to the most significant impact they expect to have on each form of wealth. Coordinators begin to see the system and identify new and interesting ways to strengthen multiple forms of wealth at the same time. For example, instead of bringing a contractor from outside the region to provide needed intellectual capital and leave a report behind, value chain coordinators set up opportunities to enrich the intellectual capital of their place by having outside contractors provide training and/or mentorships as part of their engagement. Instead of acting as outside experts, contractors engage as facilitators with content expertise. Not every intervention will necessarily affect each form of wealth, but the suite of interventions is expected to have positive impacts across the board. Practitioners develop measures of impacts on wealth based on the intervention they expect to have the strongest impact on that form of wealth.

The wealth matrix also helps value chain coordinators track the condition of different stocks of capital over time, identify gaps, and find ways to invest the "income" from healthy stocks into weaker stocks for greater benefit. The wealth matrix is useful not only in assessing assets that do and do not exist, but in recognizing how to use some assets to build others. For example, one coordinator identified a gap in the area of political capital and realized they could build it using (and expanding upon) existing social and intellectual capital, but they needed to change the focus of their relationship building activities and reframe their impacts to appeal across political parties. Grantees find the wealth creation work helps them think about the full spectrum of outcomes they are working toward, and they benefit from stepping back and thinking about all their work through this lens.

Four wealth creation value chains

The measures of wealth illustrated in this chapter were developed and implemented by four WCRC-BSL coordinators, all located in Central Appalachia. Measures from these grantees are highlighted because they have been implementing the framework longer than any other grantees and have created baseline measures and re-measures. The baseline period for all measures was 2009/2010 or earlier with re-measurements in 2011/2012. This was a period of economic stagnation in the United States, which makes the progress of these wealth creation value chain efforts particularly significant. The four coordinators are:

*   The Central Appalachian Network (CAN), a network of six nonprofits that have worked together for almost twenty years to create a more just and sustainable Appalachia. CAN members work together to build wealth creation value chains in and across Kentucky, Ohio, Tennessee, Virginia, and West Virginia in the sustainable agriculture sector.
*   The Federation of Appalachian Housing Enterprises (FAHE), a network of Appalachian organizations committed to sustainable growth and measurable impact through collective voice. FAHE provides access to capital that creates housing and promotes community development. FAHE is constructing a wealth creation value chain in Kentucky, Tennessee, Virginia, and West Virginia in affordable, energy-efficient housing construction and rehabilitation.
*   Mountain Association for Community Economic Development (MACED) works with people in eastern Kentucky to create economic opportunity, strengthen democracy, and support the sustainable use of natural resources. MACED is constructing a wealth creation value chain in energy efficiency retrofits and renewable energy in the Appalachian counties of Kentucky.
*   Rural Action builds model sustainable development projects and encourages a broad civic conversation around Appalachian Ohio's assets in order to create sustainable development paths for the region. Rural Action is building a wealth creation value chain in sustainable forestry and certified wood products.

Each value chain coordinator brought diverse partners together to meet (and, in some cases, create) market demand while creating multiple forms of wealth to be retained by poor households and communities.

Examples of measures of seven forms of wealth

Practitioners define measures after they identify impact pathways and key assumptions. Specifically, before developing measures, practitioners:

*   identify their development goals;
*   research the demand-driven wealth creation value chain they wish to build to meet those goals;

- identify gaps in the chain that must be addressed to enable it to satisfy market demand while producing multiple forms of wealth that are retained by low-wealth people, communities, and businesses;
- determine what they will do to address those gaps.

This process is important because "Outcomes are generally described in global and abstract terms, yet for performance-based measurement to both improve accountability and improve effectiveness of outcomes, such as vital communities or healthy ecosystems, outcomes must be made concrete and linked to inputs, activities and outputs" (Flora et al. 1999, p. 4).

Practitioners are coached in the use of You Get What You Measure® as a tool for identifying and defining measures of impact across each of the forms of wealth in relation to the interventions they undertake to strengthen their value chains (Ratner 2012; Penna 2011). Measures strive to relate interventions to intended impacts. The process of measurement and reflection allows practitioners to identify and consider unintended impacts.

Intellectual capital

Measurements of intellectual capital focus on behavioral changes and outcomes resulting from new knowledge and understanding of new possibilities (Table 6.1). Particularly in poor rural areas, new thinking and exposure to new practices and lessons learned can be hard to come by. Targeted interventions that increased knowledge and understanding and changed ways of thinking led to changes in behavior that strengthened each of the four wealth creation value chains.

The first gap in MACED's wealth creation value chain in energy efficiency retrofits and renewable energy was the lack of effective demand by low-income households. Creating demand meant researching and then engaging rural electric utilities in learning about a new model that would allow low-income households to participate in and benefit from energy retrofits. In 2009, no rural electric utilities in Kentucky were familiar with on-bill financing.[3] By 2012, due to strategic interventions, MACED had introduced them to this unfamiliar concept and initiated a pilot program (How$mart) with four utilities to support energy retrofits for two to three hundred residential units over two years. Over a hundred retrofits have been completed. Currently, the Kentucky Public Service Commission (PSC) is considering the case for a permanent tariff brought to it by participating utilities. If approved by the PSC, MACED's How$martKY pilot would become a permanent program, creating an already approved blueprint for other utilities to adopt the How$mart model without having to worry about clearing the regulatory hurdles. MACED created intellectual capital among the original four utilities, and spread this new way of thinking to the PSC and to additional utilities, approximately ten of which are now looking to adopt How$mart. Here new intellectual capital led to improved built capital. This is the type of institutionalized impact at scale that the WCRC-BSL initiative strives to achieve.

Table 6.1 Selected measures of intellectual capital

Organization	Sector	Baseline	Re-measure
MACED	Residential energy efficiency	# of utilities in KY with on-bill programs for affordable residential energy retrofits: Zero	# of utilities in KY with on-bill programs for affordable residential energy retrofits: 4
Rural action	Certified wood products	# of producers selling through value chain: Zero	# of producers selling through value chain: 8 with 8 more in line

Rural Action identified the need to educate wood product suppliers about market demand before they could enlist their participation in the sustainable forestry and certified wood products wealth creation value chain. Rural Action increased its own intellectual capital first by understanding urban demand for certified wood products, then transferred this knowledge to producers. As a result, there are eight firms now active in the value chain and eight more in the wings.

We identified three aspects of intellectual capital measureable through qualitative research. The first is the introduction of new ideas and ways of thinking. A baseline can be established before new ideas are introduced and the impact of those ideas, assuming they are introduced with specific intention and can be measured over time through documented changes in language and resulting behavior.

The second aspect of intellectual capital often lacking in poor areas relates to information sharing. Reasons for this include the tendency to equate information with power and the lack of modern technology (e.g., broadband access) to support information sharing. The result is often reliance on outdated or limited information and false assumptions that prevent effective economic development. Changes in information sharing are measureable.

The third aspect is establishing a common language among participants in the value chain. Value chain partners must share understanding of market demand, the language of buyers, value chain goals, gaps, strategies, and desired outcomes. Most value chain participants do not begin with knowledge of buyers or each other, and do not have a common language to understand their and others' roles. As this language develops, the entire chain becomes more effective. The development and diffusion of a common language is measured through review of meeting minutes and other methods.

Social capital

Measurements of social capital evaluate the strength and diversity of relationships developed to further the success of the value chain and its wealth creation impacts (Table 6.2). The continuum of networking, coordinating, cooperating, and collaborating defined by Himmelman (2004), with minor modifications by Yellow Wood Associates, is used to measure social capital. Measuring social

Table 6.2 Selected measures of social capital

Organization	Sector	Baseline	Re-measure
CAN	Agriculture and food systems	Number, diversity, and quality of relationships engaged in all value chains: # relationships: 4,093 Diversity: varies among sub-regional value chains Quality: varies among sub-regional value chains	Number, diversity, and quality of partnerships engaged in all value chains: # relationships: 3,977 Diversity: improving Quality: improving
Rural action	Certified wood products	# of market partners for the value chain that buy and invest: Zero	# of market partners for the value chain that buy and invest: 2

capital caused value chain coordinators to intentionally and deliberately foster relationships and networks needed to grow their value chains. Value chain coordinators discovered that social capital is a prerequisite for effective political capital.

At the outset of their work, members of the CAN had no way to visualize their value chains, or to communicate with each other about their core competencies in building relationships with different types of partners. CAN member organizations created maps of their value chains to measure social capital that served both these purposes. Periodic re-mapping helps members see where new relationships are being built and where gaps remain. By sharing maps among themselves, they see who has expertise in establishing particular types of relationships such as relationships with Cooperative Extension, the media, or buyers. Though the total number of connections in CAN's maps decreased somewhat, the quality of the relationships and overall value chain performance improved as CAN deliberately intervened to bring specific buyers, sellers, and supporters together.

CAN's measure of social capital begins with a visualization of each sub-region's value chain (Figure 6.1). The boxes in the center circle represent the transactional partners in the value chain that buy and sell to meet market demand. The boxes in the outer circle represent supporters with the potential to influence the success of the chain.

Every grantee found value in measuring social capital through the strength, diversity, and characteristics of relationships in their value chains. For example, a systems analysis with stakeholders indicated that the single most important thing that would strengthen Rural Action's value chain under current conditions was more relationships with buyers who understood and supported the goals of the value chain. The measure became the number of buyers engaged in creating value chain opportunities as market partners and the variety of ways they engage, not just through purchasing product, but through assistance in marketing and spreading the story, bringing other buyers on board, helping with distribution, and development and testing of product specs and order forms.

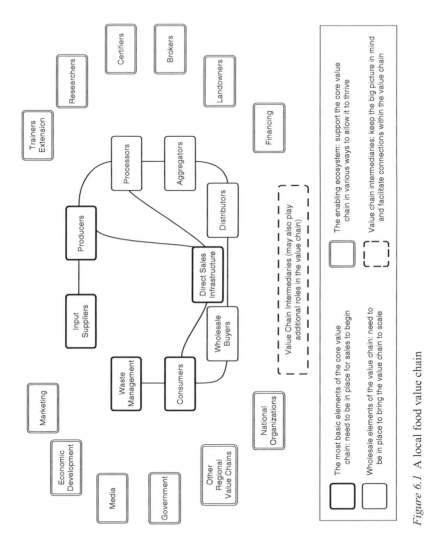

Figure 6.1 A local food value chain

Source: Based on a graphic created by the Central Appalachian Network.

As a result of interventions targeted to impact this measure, two market part-ners joined the value chain in its first year of operation, one with repeat pur-chases, and Rural Action increased the resources targeted to networking events that build buyer relationships. Rural Action focused its interventions more effec-tively by going beyond simple measures of the number of buyers to define the characteristics of buyers that "count". Stronger social capital led to the potential for financial capital (savings and investment) as a result of increased sales.

Individual capital

Measures of individual wealth focus on behavioral changes and outcomes that can only occur when new skills are mastered or human health improves (Table 6.3). Targeted interventions intentionally build the skills of producers or laborers resulting in increased engagement in value chain transactions and opening up new opportunities for future growth.

FAHE focused on developing Building Performance Institute (BPI) certified contractors with Home Energy Rating System (HERS) training to serve rural areas of Central Appalachia. The baseline condition was zero; there were no certified contractors located in or serving rural areas in the region. Today, FAHE has assisted twenty individuals based in rural areas to become BPI certified contractors with HERS training. Their presence is essential to a functioning wealth creation value chain. They provide certification services that will establish a higher value for energy-efficient housing relative to conventional housing, enabling appropriate financing and greater asset value for the homeowner and their community.

CAN focused its individual capital-related interventions on enabling producers to enter and stay in wholesale markets. Rather than measure technical assistance pro-vided, CAN measured the consequences of the assistance in terms of participation and sales. Their baseline measure showed ninety-six producers with value chain derived sales of $3,568,452.61. Targeted, research-driven technical assistance to small producers resulted in an increase in participation to 149 producers and an increase in value chain derived sales over two years to $6,031,527.60. Prior to receiv-ing technical assistance, growers lacked the skills to participate in wholesale markets.

Table 6.3 Selected measures of individual capital

Organization	Sector	Baseline measure 2009	Re-measure 2011
FAHE	Energy efficient affordable housing construction	# of BPI certified contractors: Zero	# BPI certified contractors: 16
CAN	Agriculture and food systems	# of producers with value chain derived sales and value of sales: 96 producers and $3,568,453 in sales	# of producers with value chain derived sales and value of sales: 149 producers and $6,031,528 in sales

Grantees measuring individual capital were encouraged to look beyond the services they provide to identify evidence of changes in skill level or health either through a third party certification (e.g., HERS certificate) or by measuring the difference those services have made (e.g., number participating in wholesale markets and value of wholesale sales). For FAHE and CAN, increases in individual capital contributed to improvements in built capital and natural capital, respectively.

Natural capital

Measures of natural capital are designed to capture the impact of interventions on the quantity and quality of renewable and non-renewable natural resources and on the capacity of those resources to provide ecosystem services (Table 6.4). Each wealth creation value chain affects natural capital differently. This is the first time most practitioners have thought about measuring natural capital impacts.

MACED measures natural capital impacts through reduced carbon emissions from the increased energy efficiency of commercial and residential structures. These reductions continue on an annual basis for all retrofitted structures. As the number of retrofitted structures grows, so will the positive impact on natural capital. The value chain also contributed to renewable solar energy installations that produced increases of from 5,000 to 39,940 kWh over two years, with additional installations in the works. These improvements in built capital led to improvements in natural capital.

CAN's sub-regional agricultural value chains encourage producers to use sustainable growing practices. To construct this measure, CAN first identified the

Table 6.4 Selected measures of natural capital

Organization	Sector	Baseline 2009	Re-measure 2011
MACED	Commercial and residential energy efficiency	# tons of greenhouse gas (GHG) emissions reduced: Residential: Zero Commercial: Zero	# of tons of greenhouse gas (GHG) emissions reduced: Residential only: 315 tons (2012) Commercial: 940 tons
CAN	Agriculture and food systems	# acres moving toward more sustainable production: total acres that contributed to CAN-supported value chain: 2,178.3 certified organic: 130.8 acres chemical-free but uncertified: 689.5 acres unspecified or conventional: 1,358 acres	# acres moving toward more sustainable production: total acres that contributed to CAN-supported value chain: 2,939.55 certified organic: 255.25 acres chemical-free but uncertified: 789.3 acres unspecified, conventional, or certified for different practices: 1,775 acres

practices recognized by producers, creating categories for measurement that reflected reality. They discovered the prevalence of chemical-free but uncertified production and identified other types of certifications with market value, beyond those pertaining to chemical use or organics.

The increase in organic and chemical-free but uncertified acres shows movement in the desired direction. Here, a combination of intellectual and individual capital led to improvements in natural capital.

Rural Action promotes a value chain based on wood products from third-party certified sources to impact positively the way forests are managed. At the outset, Rural Action determined the baseline number of acres certified by the Forest Stewardship Council (FSC) in Central Appalachia. FSC certification currently has the greatest demand in the marketplace. FSC-certified acreage was inadequate to meet growing demand, and the high cost of becoming FSC certified for individual landowners and businesses was a significant barrier to increasing the volume of certified product. Rural Action worked with its partners to create the Center for Forest and Wood Certification that now serves landowners and chain of custody participants throughout Central Appalachia, providing them with affordable certification services.[4]

The impacts of value chain interventions on natural capital are sufficiently diverse that we have not yet attempted to develop shared tools. This quandary is not unique to US practitioners; data for measuring natural capital stocks is universally weak (Heal 2011). However, every intermediary is encouraged to consider how material waste in the chain can be reduced, eliminated, or turned into a resource.

Built capital

Measures of built capital focus on the extent to which the built capital in a given wealth creation value chain exists and is able to add value to the chain without undermining any of the other forms of wealth (Table 6.5). Deficiencies in built

Table 6.5 Selected measures of built capital

Organization	Sector	Baseline	Re-measure
CAN	Agriculture and food systems	Widespread gaps in built infrastructure identified by sample of value chain producers that limit volume and reliability of production: improved access to season extension equipment (high tunnels and greenhouses) and improved irrigation equipment	6 producers reported having constructed new high tunnels, 4 reported having built or made improvements to greenhouses, 5 producers reported improving their irrigation or water collection systems

capital (e.g., absence of warehouse space, broadband, or efficient technologies) are common gaps in wealth creation value chains. Opportunities to fill these gaps through shared ownership can contribute to the goals of WCRC-BSL. When wealth creation value chains function properly, there should be sufficient revenue to support the investments and re-investments in built capital necessary for improving production quality and increasing sales. Instead of measuring income, wealth creation value chains measure the capacity of value chain partners to re-invest financial capital in other forms of capital, including built, that contribute to value chain sustainability and performance.

Focusing on built capital, CAN identified infrastructure gaps they needed to fill to bring their value chains to scale. These included: cooling and storage facilities, irrigation equipment, season extension equipment, greenhouses to supply trans-plants, access to slaughterhouses, and organic compost or other soil. CAN meas-ured the extent to which value chain producers reinvested in improving built capital related to food production. CAN tracks producer investment in greenhouses, high tunnels, irrigation equipment, and water collection systems among others.

Ideally, measures of built capital impacts would include not only the value of investments in built capital, but measures of its performance and value added to the individual producer and/or the value chain as a whole. This is an area for future work.

Political capital

Measures of political capital show the extent to which members of wealth crea-tion value chains and their supporters influence public and private policies affecting their value chains (Table 6.6). Two types of decisions affecting resource

Table 6.6 Selected measures of political capital

Organization	Sector	Baseline	Re-measure
FAHE	Energy efficient affordable housing construction	Degree of consistency in the definition of what qualifies a unit to be labeled as "green" across FAHE membership: Low Among FAHE member states: Low	Degree of consistency in the definition of what qualifies a unit to be labeled as "green" across FAHE membership: High Among member states, and federal programs: Increasing
MACED	Residential energy efficiency	Capacity of value chain to influence decisions of regulators (Public Service Commission) on a permanent basis: None	Capacity of value chain to influence decisions of regulators (Public Service Commission) on a permanent basis: Permanent tariff for on-bill financing under active consideration by PSC with support of utilities

allocation proved to be leverage points in value chain construction. One involves improving regulatory consistency at the local, state, and federal levels. Outdated regulatory practices and regulatory inconsistency are key barriers to scale in many wealth creation value chains. The second involves affecting the policies of buyers in both the public and private sectors.

The tool we developed for measuring political capital helps users identify the specific policies they seek to influence and then research and document the steps required to bring their influence to bear. Table 6.7 describes the steps needed to affect buyer decisions in support of local foods. By breaking this down stepwise, practitioners can track their progress toward the desired changes. This tool helps practitioners focus on influencing specific policies that actually impact the wealth creation value chains they construct.

In exploring the energy efficient affordable housing value chain, FAHE discovered that the market does not reward green, energy-efficient housing production,

Table 6.7 Sample tool for measuring progress toward political capital

Policy priority to be addressed – ACEnet	Purchasing policies of local and regional wholesale buyers support and promote the purchase of locally produced foods, especially produce, meat, and dairy products	Progress towards completing step (incomplete, in progress, or complete)
Step 1	Local and regional consumers are more aware of, and exhibit more demand for, local foods. This is encouraged through campaigns such as 30 Mile Meal and Food We Love, as well as through direct outreach such as town hall meetings	In progress
Step 2	Local and regional wholesale buyers and sellers are made aware of the increased demand for local foods	In progress
Step 3	Potential buyers and sellers are given the information they need to understand the local food sales and procurement process, through programs such as the "Market Ready" curriculum	In progress
Step 4	Information is gathered from wholesale buyers and sellers about policy barriers to local food procurement by local and regional wholesale buyers	Incomplete
Step 5	ACENet works with local, regional, and national partners to draft clear suggestions for policy changes to support local foods procurement	Incomplete
Step 6	Policy suggestions are presented to buyers	Incomplete
Step 7	Technical support is provided for implementing the recommended policies through programs like "Market Ready"	Incomplete

Note: This information supplied to the Central Appalachian Network by ACEnet in 2011.

regardless of the number of units FAHE members produce. This is because energy-efficient units are appraised no differently than inefficient units. In response, FAHE convened a summit of four State Housing Finance Agencies, the US Department of Agriculture (USDA), the Department of Housing and Urban Development (HUD) Atlanta field office, and several key Green Performance Compact participants from the FAHE membership to influence appraisal practices and begin to work toward common definitions of energy efficiency. As a result of the summit, the USDA Tennessee (TN) office committed to pilot test an energy-efficient mortgage product utilizing the methodology from the Summit. In addition, USDA TN is preparing to train appraisers within the pilot service area in the methodology to value the energy savings on the unit. The willingness of USDA TN to sponsor a pilot is spawning conversations to replicate the USDA pilot in Kentucky. From a baseline of zero, FAHE will measure the number of units of energy-efficient housing properly appraised going forward. Convincing USDA to allocate resources toward changing appraisal practices is a successful application of political capital that will significantly strengthen FAHE's value chain and impact the financial capital of low-wealth households.

MACED works toward new energy legislation supporting a renewable energy portfolio at the state level in Kentucky, while CAN members (like ACEnet in the figure below) focus on policy targets at the sub-regional level such as: state-level policymakers making increased amounts of resources available for local food production and support; Farm to School value chains being strengthened across the state; and flexible purchasing policies of local institutions, including hospitals and schools, supporting the use of locally produced foods and food products.

In each instance, coordinators intentionally build social capital across diverse constituencies to achieve political capital. For coordinators working in a wealth creation framework, these relationships are multi-purpose; they contribute to political capital, to other forms of capital, and to the capacity of the value chain overall to deliver goods and services to buyers.

Financial capital

Measures of financial capital are measures of the value of savings and the uses to which those savings are put, in the form of investments in other forms of capital that strengthen the value chain and/or provide meaningful returns to low-income households and communities (Table 6.8). Financial capital can be "internal", representing savings and investments by members participating in value chain transactions, or it can be "external", representing investments in the form of grants, loans, or other types of financing made by those not directly participating in value chain transactions. Fully functional wealth creation value chains should, by definition, be profitable for their participants, providing the means for ongoing re-investment.

MACED measured the annual energy savings for low-income households due to energy retrofits. This number fluctuates with energy prices, which are projected to increase over time. Savings continue to accrue each year after retrofits

Table 6.8 Selected measures of financial capital

Organization	Sector	Baseline	Re-measure
MACED	Residential energy efficiency	Value of annual energy savings for low-income households due to energy retrofits: Zero	Value of annual energy savings for low-income households due to energy retrofits: $4,553.93 (2011); $50,288.26 (2012)
CAN	Agriculture and food systems	# of external and internal investors and value of investment in value chain # of external investors: 37 # of internal investors: N/A value of external investment: $1,475,601.00 value of internal investment: $104,503.00	# of external and internal investors and value of investment in value chain # of external investors: 49 # of internal investors: 12 of 15 surveyed value of external investment: $1,360,532.33 value of internal investment: $265,950.00

are completed. Here, improvements in built capital led to increased financial capital.

CAN compared the value of internal and external investments over time. In 2011, internal investment represented almost 24% of the total investment in the value chains, demonstrating significant strides toward sustainability over a short period of time. Gathering investment data from each sub-regional value chain allows CAN to show progress toward sustainability, contributes to understanding where additional investments are needed, and provides data to think about how different forms of support can be used as leverage to strengthen their wealth creation value chains.

Lessons learned

Our experience to date with this approach, assisting practitioners with the development of measures and providing measurement tools for multiple forms of wealth, suggests:

1 It is possible to use a common framework, like the wealth matrix, to consider impacts on multiple forms of wealth (and ownership) without imposing a set of common measures.
2 Measures developed in context, specific to the work of each value chain, provide information practitioners can and will use to improve their practices. For example, because the discipline of measurement requires careful definition of terms, Rural Action was able to target specific types of buyers that could support their wealth creation value chain in multiple ways.

3   Practitioners are unlikely to adopt comprehensive measurement practices without training and support. However, once demonstrated, practitioners can and do recognize the value of measurement in improving their focus, practice, and ability to engage others in their work and will internalize measurement in ongoing operations. All the value chain coordinators described in this chapter continue to refine and implement outcome measures.

We are still early in the development of wealth measurement practice on the ground; for example, we have not specifically focused on measurements that distinguish between place-based and people-based wealth. However, the wealth creation approach recognizes the imperative to bring these two aspects of wealth into alignment in ways that eliminate historic patterns of exploitation and begin to shift the balance of control over place-based wealth to structures that benefit people in place. The field would benefit from research illustrating how measures that distinguish between people-based and place-based wealth can be used to achieve these goals. Methods, tools, and measures for understanding positive and negative interactions among and between different forms of wealth, including any adverse impacts on some forms of wealth that occur when we focus on building other forms of wealth, are likewise underdeveloped. Since so little data on stocks of wealth is readily available, it is difficult to compare results across regions or initiatives. Additional research would be helpful in these areas. Participatory research involving researchers as co-principals with practitioners would be particularly helpful in identifying valid and reliable approaches that are also practical and useful.

Next steps

As the number of interventions based on the wealth creation framework increases, there will be more opportunities for researchers to partner with practitioners to improve the potential for attribution by collecting measures from comparable communities, and/or supply chains in given sectors. Although not as reliable as a controlled experiment, this could provide additional insights into which aspects of the wealth creation approach are most efficacious and under which circumstances. This would add another dimension of learning to the before and after measures already built into the wealth creation approach.

Notes

1   For an archive of reports from Wealth Creation in Rural Communities – Building Sustainable Livelihoods (now WealthWorks) please go to <http://www.yellowwood.org/wealthcreation.aspx>. Additional materials are available at the National Community of Practice on Wealth Creation site at <http://www.ruralwealth.org> and at <http://www.wealthworks.org>.
2   WCRC-BSL recognizes eight forms of wealth; cultural capital is included in the wealth creation approach but not in the wealth matrix because its influence is measured through measures of the other seven forms of wealth.

3 On-bill financing allows customers of electric utilities to make installment payments on energy efficiency improvements as part of their monthly utility bills. This removes one key obstacle to energy efficiency improvements for low-income homeowners – the ability to capitalize improvements upfront – by spreading payments out over time that can generally be covered by reduced electricity costs associated with efficiency improvements.

4 FSC chain of custody certification is a system for tracking the flow of certified wood through the supply chain and across borders through each successive stage – including processing, transformation, and manufacturing – to the final product.

References

Beamon, B. (1998) "Supply chain design and analysis: models and methods", *International Journal of Production Economics*, 55(3): 281–94.

Dorius, N. (2011) "Measuring community development outcomes: in search of an analytical framework", *Economic Development Quarterly*, 25(3): 267–76.

Flora, C.B., Kinsley, M., Luther, V., Wall, M., Odell, S., et al. (1999) "Measuring community success and sustainability: an interactive workbook, v3.1", North Central Regional Center for Rural Development, Iowa State University, Ames, IA.

Handfield, R.B., and Nichols, E.L. (1999) *Introduction to Supply Chain Management* (Vol. 183), New Jersey: Prentice Hall.

Heal, G. (2011) "Sustainability and its measurement", National Bureau of Economic Research, Working Paper Series #17008. Online. Available at: <http://www.nber.org/papers/w17008> (accessed 10 May 2013).

Himmelman, A.T. (2004) "Collaboration for a change: definitions, decision-making models, roles, and collaboration process guide". Online. Available at: <http://depts.washington.edu/ccph/pdf_files/4achange.pdf> (accessed 10 May 2013).

Leenders, M.R., and Blenkhorn, D.L. (1988) *Reverse Marketing: The New Buyer–Supplier Relationship*, New York: Free Press.

Linton, J.D., Klassen, R., and Jayaraman, V. (2007) "Sustainable supply chains: an introduction", *Journal of Operations Management*, 25(6): 1075–82.

Mentzer, J.T., DeWitt, W., Keebler, J.S., Min, S., Nix, N.W., et al. (2001) "Defining supply chain management", *Journal of Business Logistics*, 22(2): 1–25.

Penna, R.M. (2011) *The Nonprofit Outcomes Toolbox: A Complete Guide to Program Effectiveness, Performance Measurement, and Results* (Vol. 1), Hoboken, NJ: John Wiley & Sons.

Ratner, S. (2012) "You Get What You Measure®: a process to determine and measure progress in community development", *CDPractice*, 18. Online. Available at: <www.commdev.org/index.php/publications/cd-practice> (accessed 10 May 2013).

Stark, N., and Markley, D. (2008) "Rural entrepreneurship development II: measuring impact on the triple bottom line". Online. Available at: <http://www.yellowwood.org/Rural%20Entrepreneurship%20Development%202.pdf> (accessed 10 May 2013).

7 Defining and measuring public sector wealth

How much control does the public have over public wealth in a fiscally stressed world?

J. Matthew Fannin and Beth Walter Honadle

Introduction

In Chapter 3, Johnson et al. presented an overall wealth accounting framework that included a regional public wealth category that contributed to both people- and place-based regional wealth. In this chapter, we focus our lens on the "regional public" category they highlight. We review definitions of public goods, public services, and public wealth, how public wealth can be measured (including indicators of fiscal health), and how public wealth generates a stream of benefits for residents.

Public goods versus public services

The public sector is not to be confused with the term public good. A pure public good is both non-rival and non-excludable (Cowen 1988; Stiglitz 2000) in consumption and may or may not be provided by government (the public sector). A *non-rival* good is consumable by multiple people simultaneously without any one person diminishing other people's ability to consume the good. A *non-excludable* good is one for which it is not feasible to prevent nonpayers from consuming the good once it has been produced. This second characteristic is the root of the classic "free rider" problem in economics in which beneficiaries of non-excludable goods are able to avoid paying for those goods since it is impossible to prevent them from enjoying the benefits. Goods that have both 100 percent non-rival and 100 percent non-excludable properties are considered pure public goods and those goods that are 100 percent rival and 100 percent excludable are considered pure private goods. Public safety is an example of a pure public good in that additional people can consume the good at the same time at a zero increase in marginal cost. A pair of shoes would represent a pure private good in that no two people can wear a pair of shoes at the same time, and the shoes can be withheld from consumption until someone pays for them.

Many goods consumed by people have various degrees of rivalry and excludability. For example, an unfilled movie theater represents a non-rival good that is excludable. Once customers pay to enter the theater, they can enjoy watching a movie without inhibiting others from watching it (until all the seats are filled). By contrast, a fishing spot at a publicly owned lake may be non-excludable but rival in consumption. While there may be no cost to an individual to access a specific spot on the lake, no two individuals (boats) can be positioned in the exact same geographic location.[1]

The properties of public goods often get intertwined in the definitions of the public sector institutions that deliver public goods. Public services represent a stream of benefits that accrue to residents (and in many cases non-residents) of a region typically based on organizing public assets. The public service may generate a public good. For example, public safety is a public service generated from combining physical capital, human capital, and intellectual capital assets among other assets (inputs) to procure (produce) the public service. Hence, the public sector both determines the level of public service to provide and simultaneously makes the decision on *how* to procure the public service (i.e., organize public sector assets into a stream of public service outputs (Johnson and Watson 1991)). We first elaborate on how assets used to generate public services help to define public wealth as a subset of overall regional wealth.

Public wealth as a subset of regional wealth

In Chapter 3, residents' aggregate total wealth was defined as a combination of the private capital assets and the share of public assets owned, or $(A_{rr} + A_{rw} + A_{pr} + A_{pw}) - (L_{rr} + L_{rw} + L_{pr} + L_{pw})$ where A_{rr} is defined as private assets located in the region owned by residents of the region, A_{rw} is the residents' private assets located outside the region, $A_{pr} + A_{pw}$ is the public assets of the region's residents (whether located inside or outside the region), L_{rr} is the private in-region liabilities of residents of the region, L_{rw} is the private liabilities of the region's residents to people outside the region, L_{pr} is the public liabilities of the region held by residents, and L_{pw} is the public liabilities of the region held by non-residents.

One of the challenges surrounding assigning ownership of public assets in a region is that residents are members of multiple public sector institutions. Public sector institutions are typically defined by geographic boundaries, and the geographic boundaries served by a given public sector institution are often nested within other larger geographic boundaries served by other public sector institutions. For example, a town may be nested within a county which is nested within a state or province which is nested within a nation-state (Honadle 2013). Residents living in the town have both a share of ownership of the assets of each public sector jurisdiction in which they reside as well as a share of the liabilities of ownership. Conceptually, a smaller region's proportion of ownership in the assets of a higher level public sector entity could be estimated as the total assets of the higher level public sector entity multiplied by the share of population in the smaller region.

This breakdown is highlighted in Table 7.1. In this table, public sector assets and liabilities of the county's residents are highlighted in the county row.

Table 7.1 People-based public sector wealth of a region

		Public sector					
		County		State		Nation	
		Assets	Liabilities	Assets	Liabilities	Assets	Liabilities
Residents	County	A^r_{cc}	L^r_{cc}	A^r_{cs}	L^r_{cs}	A^r_{cn}	L^r_{cn}
	Rest of state	N/A	N/A	A^r_{ls}	L^r_{ls}	A^r_{ln}	L^r_{ln}
	Rest of nation	N/A	N/A	N/A	N/A	A^r_{mn}	L^r_{mn}

Table 7.2 Place-based public sector wealth of a region

		Public sector		
		County	State	Nation
Place	County	A^p_{cc}	A^p_{cs}	A^r_{cn}
	Rest of state	N/A	A^p_{ls}	A^p_{ln}
	Rest of nation	N/A	N/A	A^p_{mn}

A^r_{cc} represents the county public assets owned by county residents, A^r_{cs} refers to the state public assets owned by county residents, and A^r_{cn} refers to the national public assets owned by county residents. Liabilities are also shown similarly. Given that only the county's residents have ownership rights to the county's public sector assets, then A^r_{cc} represents 100 percent of the county's public sector institution assets in the table. Further, A^r_{cs} would then equal the total value of the state assets times the percentage of the population residing in the county, and A^r_{cn} would equal the total value of national assets times the percentage of the national population residing in the county. The liabilities of the county residents from the county, state, and nation would be calculated similarly.

On the other hand, a region's place-based public sector institution assets are calculated differently. This difference is highlighted in Table 7.2. There are likely specific physical capital assets and other assets of the state or federal government geographically located in a region that provide differential benefits to the region of its location. A^p_{cs} in Table 7.2 refers to the total state-financed public wealth assets geographically located in the county and A^p_{cn} refers to the specific federally financed public wealth assets that are geographically located in the county.

For example, both residents and non-residents of Hardin County, KY, benefit from national defense services provided by Fort Knox, which is geographically located within the county's borders. However, Hardin County residents gain additional benefits from the national assets invested in the county through the incomes earned by Hardin County residents that are employed at the army post, among other county-specific benefits. These benefits accrue to Hardin County because the physical assets of the military installation are located within its borders. Public sector assets for a state or nation are not distributed geographically in the same proportion as the population. Military installations such as Fort Knox will disproportionately provide regions like Hardin County, KY, with a greater value of place-based assets (Table 7.2) than the people-based value they would receive (based on the small proportion of the national population residing in Hardin County), and as a result, the additional returns that come from these place-based investments.

Financial versus real public sector wealth

Much of the public sector wealth assets that are quantifiable are in financial capital form. As discussed in Chapter 3, financial capital represents an intermediate form of capital before its investment into "real (non-financial) capital" that generates benefits to a region. However, we suggest that public financial capital in the form of liquidity accrues benefits to both people and places similar to other forms of "real capital" owned and invested by the public sector.

We use the distinction between potential and kinetic energy from physics as a metaphor to explain what happens when liquidity is used to acquire real capital. When liquidity is transformed into one of the other "real capital" forms, the benefits or returns that accrue to a region from its investment are analogous to the conversion of potential to kinetic energy. At the same time, liquidity that is controlled by a public sector entity can be considered potential "energy" prior to its transformed state into real capital.

For example, liquidity provides a return to its owners through the cost savings of organizing and enforcing transactions. A couple of public sector examples highlight the returns to liquidity. For example, if a local government needs to purchase a physical asset, for example a $100,000 road grader, it may need to save up for a year in order to obtain the funds to pay cash. However, by waiting a year, the cost of this physical asset may increase 10 percent to $110,000. By having a line of credit (liquidity) that costs 5 percent per year if exercised, the returns to that liquidity would be 5 percent, or $5,000 in this example ($110,000 – $105,000).

Liquidity also provides returns when less frequent negative events occur such as natural disasters. For example, residents receive reduced benefits from local public sector investments in roads when flooding makes roads impassable. Debris on roads from flooding may be driven by events such as tropical storms with a known probability of occurrence and cost of cleanup. With sufficient planning, a local government may have time to organize the financing of cleanup from a future tropical storm through a line of credit with a lending institution or longer payment terms through an advanced contract with a debris removal contractor. However, if the public sector underestimates the level of debris created from a future storm, the line of credit may not be sufficiently large, and/or the existing contractor may be unable to clean up the additional debris in a timely fashion. Liquidity in the form of cash on hand saves on the transaction costs of organizing another contractor to clean up the additional debris or renegotiating the line of credit.

The optimal level of liquidity that should be held by a public sector is based on the relative return that liquidity extracts in each transaction. For those transactions where cost savings exceed the cost of obtaining liquidity externally (e.g., interest payment on a line of credit), then a line of credit sufficiently large to execute those transactions should be considered. For transactions that generate savings below the cost of obtaining liquidity externally, the level of cash necessary to execute those transactions should be held. Attributes that impact the ratio of internal to external liquidity may include the frequency and uncertainty of the transactions.

Measuring public wealth

In this section, we present a simple approach to empirically measure people-based versus place-based public wealth assets in a region. In particular, we create a simplified version of Tables 7.1 and 7.2 focusing on people- and place-based public wealth considering county and state wealth for the case parish (county) of Lincoln Parish, LA. We then discuss the strengths and limitations to this approach.

Lincoln Parish, LA

Lincoln Parish, LA, is located in the north central portion of Louisiana. It is a nonmetropolitan parish with a 2010 Census population of 46,735. Some of its major private sector industries include the forest products industry as well as the poultry production and processing industries.

In addition to the private sector, the public sector is a major contributor to the parish's economy. Louisiana Tech University and Grambling State University, two public universities within the University of Louisiana System, are both located in the parish.

People-based wealth

First, we attempt to highlight the role that these local (parish) and state wealth assets have on the people-based local and state public wealth of Lincoln Parish, LA. To accomplish this, we obtained the audited financial statements (AFS) from the Louisiana Legislative Auditor for both Lincoln Parish Government and the State of Louisiana.[2] Assets and liabilities for both the parish and state governments were obtained from their respective Government-wide Statement of Net Assets table. For the State of Louisiana, both their governmental activities and component units' (state-controlled organizations such as state-funded universities that are audited separately) assets and liabilities were included in the state's totals.

We filled in each of the cells of Table 7.3 using both the parish and state AFS data. For the parish column, 100 percent of the assets and liabilities of the parish government are located in the cells of the county row and county assets and county liabilities columns. In particular, Lincoln Parish government lists just over $62 million in total assets. These include many types of assets including financial assets such as cash, as well as physical capital assets such as roads, bridges, and other infrastructure. Against these assets, the parish owes approximately $8 million in liabilities.

In the parish residents' row and state assets and liabilities columns, we estimated the proportions of state assets and liabilities owned and owed by residents of Lincoln Parish. We estimated these values by simply multiplying the percentage of total state residents residing in Lincoln Parish (1.03 percent from 2010 US Census data) by the total state assets and liabilities. Given the state assets totaling $45.5 billion in 2010, the people of Lincoln Parish own approximately $470 million dollars in assets ($10,050 per resident) and $233 million in liabilities ($4,981 per resident). The rest of the state row and state assets and liabilities column show the ownership of state assets and liabilities by residents of the other sixty-three parishes in Louisiana.

When summing across the assets of the parish row, we obtain total assets of $532 million and liabilities of $241 million. The total public sector net worth owned by residents of Lincoln Parish (assets minus liabilities) slightly exceeds $291 million. Of total local and state public assets owned by people of Lincoln Parish, 11 percent of these assets are controlled by the parish public sector and 89 percent controlled by the state public sector. In contrast, only 3 percent of the public sector liabilities of Lincoln Parish residents are controlled by the parish government as compared to 97 percent controlled by state government.

Place-based wealth

The challenge with estimating place-based public wealth is properly identifying all wealth assets a particular public sector entity has located in a given geographic region. To address this challenge, we assume that 100 percent of the place-based assets of the parish government are geographically located in the parish. Second, we assume that 100 percent of the assets of two state chartered and financed public sector entities (two universities) are located in the same geographic location as their campuses. Further, we include only non-financial capital assets of these local governments in our place-based wealth calculations.[3] Finally, because many other state-owned assets (state-owned roads, state parks or museums, etc.) located in Lincoln Parish are difficult to quantify separately or data are unavailable, we focus on only the university place-based state capital asset subset for the example.

As was the case in Table 7.2, we focus only on assets in the place-based regional wealth of Lincoln Parish in Table 7.4. The combination of capital assets of parish government and capital assets of the two state-financed universities in the parish exceeds $355 million. This amount exceeds the $291 million in net

Table 7.3 People-based local and state public wealth accounting example, Lincoln Parish, LA

($)	Lincoln Parish government		State of Louisiana		Total (Lincoln Parish + State)	
	Assets	Liabilities	Assets	Liabilities	Assets	Liabilities
Lincoln Parish residents	62,479,766	8,306,285	469,687,929	232,771,088	532,167,695	241,077,373
Rest of Louisiana residents			45,090,815,071	22,346,407,912	45,090,815,071	22,346,407,912
Total	62,479,766	8,306,285	45,560,503,000	22,579,179,100	45,622,982,766	

Table 7.4 Place-based local and state public wealth accounting example, Lincoln Parish, LA

($)	Lincoln Parish government	State of Louisiana	Total
Lincoln Parish	27,040,029	328,779,730	355,819,759
Rest of Louisiana		22,607,916,270	22,607,916,270
Total	27,040,029	22,936,696,000	

worth of Lincoln Parish resident-owned parish and state government. In this case, the place-based public wealth of the parish exceeds the people-based wealth.

What are the implications for this high concentration of state-based public wealth assets? It is important to understand the type of assets invested in these places. Much of the place-based assets of the state in these universities are in-built capital, such as buildings and equipment. The returns to these investments come in a number of forms.

First, the built capital investment combined with the rental of human capital (wages and salaries paid to faculty and staff) allow for creation of additional human capital in students to occur. Some of this human capital migrates outside the parish, while some remains in the parish. The additional human capital then generates a stream of benefits directly to its owners. It also benefits other residents of the parish when those college graduates choose to start their own businesses in the parish and generate incomes earned by other residents employed. Second, since the human capital production process requires the hiring of professors, instructors, administrative staff, and facility maintenance staff, it generates a stream of benefits in income to those individuals who hold those jobs. The parish then gets to claim much of the people-based benefits when these employed individuals reside in Lincoln Parish. Lincoln Parish had the lowest average annual unemployment rate of any parish in Louisiana for fifteen out of sixteen years between 1985 and 2000 and maintained an unemployment rate between 2.4 and 6.4 percent over that period (Area Resource File 2011–2012). The parish maintained an unemployment rate below the statewide average unemployment rate until 2006, when post Hurricane Katrina and Rita recovery employment opportunities resulted in many south Louisiana parishes seeing measurable reductions in the unemployment rate relative to their North Louisiana counterparts.

Wealth measurement limitations

There are a number of limitations in the use of audited financial statement data for distinguishing place-based and people-based public sector wealth. First, an audited financial statement in most cases does not identify specifically the geographic location of assets. While certain assumptions about locations of assets may be reasonable (e.g., county-owned roads are located within the county's geopolitical boundaries), audited financial statement data typically needs to be supplemented with additional detailed place-based data to distribute adequately assets of particularly larger public sector jurisdictions such as states inside individual county boundaries.

Second, audited financial statement data does not typically provide information about the geographic origin of those who own the liabilities (debts) taken on by the public sector. In Table 7.3, the liabilities column for Lincoln Parish government totaled just over $8.3 million. Unfortunately, we do not know who is owed these liabilities. When calculating the net worth of Lincoln Parish residents' ownership of public assets ($291 million), we implicitly assumed that zero dollars of these public sector liabilities were held as assets by Lincoln Parish residents. If parish residents own any of these public sector liabilities (e.g., parish or state municipal bonds), then the public sector net worth of residents estimated· in Table 7.3 is underestimated by the value of local ownership of these public sector liabilities.

A third and more fundamental limitation is the use of data from audited financial statements as a proxy for public sector wealth. In most cases, public sector roads and bridges are valued on audited financial statements at cost. Since these public sector assets are not typically traded in the private sector, there is not a market to determine their value to consumers. Johnson et al. in Chapter 3 argue that an asset's value should be identified as the net present value of the lifetime consumption of the asset by all consumers. In this way, the value of the public sector assets would fluctuate based on the changing value consumers place on public assets over time.

The measurement of public wealth including its breakdown into financial and capital asset forms has important implications for the fiscal health of the public sector and its ability to deliver public services. We investigate the financial condition of public sector institutions in the next section.

Measuring fiscal health

The ability of the public sector to be sustainable over the long term in delivering benefits from investments in financial and non-financial public sector capital is dependent on a fiscally healthy public sector. This section of the chapter focuses on the measurement of the fiscal health of local governments and explores its relevance for public sector wealth.

The measurement of fiscal health of local governments has been a subject of longstanding interest to practitioners and academicians. Forty years ago the now defunct Advisory Commission on Intergovernmental Relations published *City Financial Emergencies: The Intergovernmental Dimension* (US ACIR 1973). By its very title one can see that a local government is not an island when it comes to understanding the state of its financial affairs. The International City and County Management Association (ICMA) has created tools to measure the fiscal health and condition of local governments starting with the *Financial Trend Monitoring System* workbook (1980) and currently in the form of *Evaluating Financial Condition: A Handbook for Local Government*, which is now in its fourth edition. In 1993, Ken Brown published his very influential ten-point test of financial condition, which uses a simple set of ratios of revenues, expenditures, operating condition, and debt structure and has local governments compare their results with a Government Finance Officers Association database (Brown 1993). Experts on county government research have called for the creation of databases that will enable the analysis of "fiscal condition (revenue capacity, utilization of such revenue capacity, bonded indebtedness, elasticity of tax base, degree of fiscal stress), intergovernmental fiscal assistance from the federal and state government" and other features.

In short, there is a variety of measurement tools available to measure a local government's current financial situation and project its viability into the future based on an evaluation of recent trends and an assessment of factors having the potential to impact its finances (Honadle and Lloyd-Jones 1998).

A key point to understand about local governments' fiscal health is that there is relatively little that these governments *control* about their environment (Honadle 2003, 2013; Honadle et al. 2004; LaPlante and Honadle 2011). States through their constitutions and legislation literally define the terms of the existence of local governments, but, in addition, can decide what forms of revenues local governments may use, or mandate expensive services that the local governments have to fund. In addition, a state can unilaterally choose to cut or eliminate state aid to local governments, a form of revenue on which local governments are highly dependent for providing essential services. In addition, state governments also enact tax expenditure limitations that can result in short-run under-investment of critical public sector capital assets and that can impact long-run reduction in local public service delivery (Deller and Stallman 2007). These external conditions placed on local governments by larger units of government (state and federal) represent a loss of autonomous control over the provision, financing, and procurement of public services highlighted in the conceptualized framework of the previous section. At the extreme, states can place local governments in a form of receivership by appointing financial control boards or overseers who report to the state and usurp local elected officials' legal authority to manage their finances.

In addition, local governments – because of their proximity to the people – are necessarily the first responders to natural disasters and unanticipated events requiring public safety personnel and other resources. Local governments in "snowbelt" cities consider the likelihood of heavy snowfall and the need to pay for snow removal personnel, equipment, and supplies. But catastrophic events are, by their nature, unplanned for and can cripple a local government's ability to maintain other essential services because the budget is diverted to paying for the disaster.

Local governments are vulnerable to economic conditions over which they have no control. If a recession causes local retail sales to drop or a terrorist attack causes tourists to stay away, a local government loses revenues at the same time as it may have more demand for human services. Likewise, to the extent that a local government depends on wage taxes, it could reap a benefit when the economy is booming, but experience sudden loss when businesses close, move, or reduce production. Property tax valuations are relatively stable (compared with changes in the sales or income tax bases), but changes in the value of the local property tax base are also important considerations in understanding the fiscal health in the short and long term. This relative elasticity of taxes is reason for local governments to attempt to diversify revenue sources as a hedge against sudden economic changes causing abrupt changes in revenue.

Furthermore, there are political reasons why local officials delay the day of financial reckoning using "shell game" tactics that obscure the underlying health of their finances and that create additional obligations in the future. Simply put, it is not popular with voters to raise taxes or add user fees to pay for services when such necessities can be avoided in the short run. It is not uncommon for local officials to announce plans to pay for large capital expenditures with revenues from sources that have yet to generate any money. This may create the illusion of budget balancing, but is often just a way of gaining support for projects by asserting that there is a way to pay for them.

The point of this section has been to discuss some of the issues related to measuring local fiscal health. There are good tools available for conducting analyses. However, there are limitations to the tools, because there are important variables that cannot be captured in simple ratios or trend lines that are needed to present a fuller picture. In other words, it takes more than simple accounting techniques to determine the fiscal health and condition of a local government. This is one reason why ratings agencies look at the overall economy, quality of local government management, history of tax collections, and other subjective indicators in assessing the creditworthiness of local governments in addition to more technical measures.

Conclusion

In this chapter, we extended the wealth accounting framework as presented by Johnson et al. in Chapter 3. In particular, we reviewed the foundational concepts of public goods and how they related to definitions of the public sector and public services generated. We broke down people- and place-based distinctions of public wealth and how these distinctions can result in differential returns to residents based on their relative location to place-based public capital investments. We presented an example of how to measure empirically both people- and place-based public wealth, and discussed how these differences impact the stream of benefits residents receive.

In addition, we highlighted the role of fiscal health and its relationship to public wealth. While many measurements of fiscal health exist, no one tool is comprehensive in measuring fiscal health, and contextual judgments are necessary to develop an accurate picture of a locality's fiscal health or condition.

This chapter also highlighted how much control local residents have in leveraging a local government's wealth collectively to generate community-wide benefits. It was noted states ultimately define the rules by which residents can organize an autonomous government. They have much control over the institutional environment by creating rules that may limit both revenue and expenditure options which have impacts on the ability of a local public sector to add to its public wealth stocks and accrue returns from those investments. Local public sector stakeholders interested in maximizing the returns to public sector investments would be wise to understand the scope of the institutional environment in their region before proposing strategic public sector wealth capital investments to know if the rules impact the rate of accumulation of public sector capital or how it might be leveraged to generate returns to residents.

The local public sector should consider how the procurement of public services impacts their financial wealth and associated fiscal health. When a local government procures a higher percentage of public services, they invest a higher percentage of their total assets in capital assets that depreciate requiring regular re-investments of public sector financial capital. Higher levels of public capital assets may or may not be desirable given the local public sector's ability to re-invest in them over time.

Further, local governments should consider how vulnerable their public wealth capital is to changes in compensation from other public sector governments. Abrupt changes in inter-governmental transfers to schools or roads can impact long-term infrastructure investments and the returns these investments make to local residents. In addition, changes to how these larger governments financially support local governments to negative events such as economic or natural disasters have implications for fiscal health. Local governments need to identify their financial vulnerabilities and develop strategies to bring fiscal health back to pre-event levels in order to maintain public sector wealth so that local residents maintain the returns they historically receive from these investments.

Notes

1 It should also be noted that not all seats in a movie theater have the same desirability, and since most theaters do not have reserved seating, some level of rivalry exists for these desired seats just like the fishing location at the lake. These attributes highlight the reality that few goods have absolute non-rival or non-excludable properties.
2 Lincoln Parish Government data are located in the audited financial statements of the Lincoln Parish Police Jury, and State of Louisiana data are in the state's Comprehensive Audited Financial Statements. Due to differences in fiscal years, comparison is made based on Lincoln Parish government's fiscal year ending December 31, 2010 and the State of Louisiana's fiscal year ending June 30, 2010. Capital assets for Grambling State University and Louisiana Tech University were calculated based on the fiscal year ending June 30, 2010.
3 Due to the nature of many financial statements, cash on hand is often not distinguished from cash equivalents or other current assets that are highly liquid, but represent ownership of assets not located in the region. For simplification, we chose to remove these assets for consideration in our place-based analysis.

References

Area Resource File (ARF) (2011–2012) US Department of Health and Human Services, Health Resources and Services Administration, Bureau of Health Professions, Rockville, MD.

Brown, K.W. (1993) "The 10-point test of financial condition: toward an easy-to-use assessment tool for smaller cities", *Government Finance Review*, 21–26 December. Online. Available at: <http://gfoa.org/services/dfl/bulletin/BUDGET-Ten-point-test.pdf> (accessed 21 February 2013).

Cowen, T. (1988) "Introduction", in T. Cowen (ed.), *The Theory of Market Failure*, Fairfax, VA: George Mason University Press, pp. 1–26.

Deller, S.C., and Stallmann, J. (2007) "Tax and expenditure limitations and economic growth", *Marquette Law Review*, 90(3): 497–54.

Honadle, B.W. (2003) "The states' role in U.S. local government fiscal crises: a theoretical model and results of a national survey", *International Journal of Public Administration*, 26(13): 1431–72.

Honadle, B.W. (2013) "Local government fiscal health: an intergovernmental perspective", in H.L Levine, J.B. Justice, and E.A. Scorsone (eds.), *Handbook of Local Government Fiscal Health*, Burlington, MA: Jones & Bartlett Learning.

Honadle, B.W., and Lloyd-Jones, M. (1998) "Analyzing rural local governments' financial condition: an exploratory application of three tools", *Public Budgeting & Finance*, 18(2): 69–86.

Honadle, B.W., Costa, J.M., and Cigler, B.A. (2004) *Fiscal Health for Local Governments: An Introduction to Concepts, Practical Analysis, and Strategies*, Boston: Academic Press/Elsevier.

Johnson, G.W., and Watson, D.J. (1991) "Privatization: provision or production of public services", *State & Local Government Review*, 23(2): 82–9.

LaPlante, J.M., and Honadle, B.W. (2011) "Beyond the storm: surmounting challenges of the new public finance", in J.M. LaPlante and B.W. Honadle (eds.), "Symposium, 'Beyond the Storm: Surmounting the Challenges of the New Public Finance'", *Journal of Public Budgeting, Accounting and Financial Management*, 23(2&3): 189–214.

Stiglitz, J.E. (2000) *Economics of the Public Sector*, 3rd edn, New York: W.W. Norton.

8 Measuring the wealth of regions

Geospatial approaches to empirical capital estimation

Hodjat Ghadimi, Trevor M. Harris,
and Timothy A. Warner

Introduction

As national and regional economies strive for sustainable development, the need for empirical metrics with which to measure wealth at scales below that of the nation are highly desirable, if not essential. As this volume demonstrates, wealth estimation is challenging in its own right and is only compounded when seeking to measure wealth at sub-national or even sub-regional scales necessary for calculating rural wealth. Geographic Information Systems (GIS) and remote sensing technologies have made dramatic advances in recent years (Bossler et al. 2010; Warner et al. 2009; Wilson and Fotheringham 2007), and a vast quantity of well-attributed geospatial data is now available in Spatial Data Infrastructures (SDI) for many nations at a variety of scales and spatial resolutions (van Loenen and Kok 2004; Masser 2010). Conceived as a framework of authenticated spatial data with embedded metadata and established standards, SDI have been the backbone of the GIS community for some time, with nodes managed by government agencies and key database stakeholders. More recently, the Geospatial Web (Scharl and Tochtermann 2007) and crowd-sourced spatial data in the form of Volunteered Geographic Information (VGI) (Sui et al. 2013) provide additional sources of geospatial data to augment official authenticated databases. These latter data options provide an ever-expanding capacity for capturing geospatial data for both data-rich regions and especially for traditionally data-sparse regions.

In this chapter we contend that the use of scaled spatial data layers, coupled with GIS and remote sensing, represent valuable proxies for place-based capital estimation to complement national aggregate estimates of wealth. To that end we explore new and innovative approaches to regional wealth assessment based on geospatial technologies and associated SDI as a basis for generating metrics for place-based multi-scalar wealth estimation. An assessment of these empirically based geospatial approaches to capital estimation is made and we illustrate how such an approach might be operationalized using the rural and natural resource and energy rich state of West Virginia as a limited case study. An empirical geospatial data approach to capital estimation in West Virginia reinforces both the need for sub-regional approaches to capital estimation for rural areas and the differentiation made by Johnson et al. (Chapter 3) between people-based and place-based wealth whereby capital ownership is distinguished from the geographic location of wealth. West Virginia makes an ideal case study as it clearly reveals the irony of 'a rich place with poor people' typical of many rural energy rich regions.

Wealth estimation and regional geospatial data

As Pender and Ratner (Chapter 2) suggest, regional wealth is broadly embodied in the multifarious forms of physical, financial, natural, human, intellectual, social, political, and cultural capital. All regional economies are endowed with varying levels of these capital assets which in totality amount to the wealth of a region and provide the essential pillars for regional development. However, while the wealth of regions has long been recognized as central to societal well-being and to regional and national development, the measurement and assessment of regional wealth is fraught with difficulties, dominated as it is by aggregate estimates of wealth derived at national scales. At the international level, the first unified and standard system of national accounting for measuring the capital and wealth of nation-states dates back to the 1950s and yet despite the availability of ever more statistical data in recent years, measuring the components of capital is still no easy task.

A central issue in capital estimation is to assess the status of regional capital stocks and to monitor changes that result from resource depletion, government policies, or public-private investment. Kendrick's (1976, 1979) seminal contributions to broadening concepts of capital, production, and productivity as part of national wealth measures through expanded economic accounts are well known. Yet despite the availability of estimates of national economic wealth there are few assessments of capital wealth at the regional level. The World Bank study of the wealth of nations (2006), and the OECD manual *Measuring Capital* (OECD 2009) are additional valuable contributions to the practice of measuring national capital, but they are again characteristically scaled to the national level and represent a heavy emphasis on the use of estimation in the assessment of capital assets. The World Bank, for example, measures intangible wealth, the "dark matter" referred to by Pender et al. (Chapter 1), as the residual difference between total wealth and the sum of produced and natural capital. Given that intangible wealth can amount to as much as 60 percent of the total wealth of all countries and 80 percent of capital stock in developed countries, this degree of estimation represents a significant challenge. These deficiencies are well acknowledged by the World Bank and OECD but there is clearly a need for mechanisms and metrics that can generate better estimators of capital wealth and can do so for regions below the national level.

The deconstruction of wealth into the eight constituent parts laid out by Pender and Ratner (Chapter 2) provides a valuable framework for exploring how geospatial data might provide critical metrics for capital estimation. Authenticated SDI have expanded considerably in recent years and contain unprecedented volumes of highly accurate and near-real-time spatial data that span the spectrum of human, ecological, and physical systems. National and regional SDI such as for West Virginia (<http://wvgis.wvu.edu/data>), the US national SDI portal at

Geospatial One Stop (<http://www.data.gov>), or Global SDI such as the European Commission's INSPIRE geoportal (<http://inspire-geoportal.ec.europa.eu>) promise considerable advantages in leveraging the attribute-rich spatial information and providing the critical data required to generate accurate regional capital estimates. Harnessing this information and geospatial technologies to realize effective wealth metrics at multiple scales is, however, at an embryonic stage.

In this chapter we provide an introduction to how geospatial data might generate capital estimates through vignettes of specific geospatial data examples and how data may be utilized and processed to create metrics of capital estimation for the rural state of West Virginia. These examples focus on quantifying capital estimates of (1) residential properties through the linking of E911 databases developed for routing responders to emergency telephone calls and social media-generated residential housing sales; (2) coal reserves for the state and by depositional horizon; (3) educational attainment based on decennial census data; and (4) the estimation and valuation of ecosystem services. These vignettes are clearly not intended to be exhaustive of all the capital wealth indicators possible but do provide example snapshots of the overall value of an empirical geospatial approach. Second, using West Virginia again as a case study, the currently available SDI for the region is examined in terms of how the various spatial data sets might contribute to identifying place-based wealth estimates for the state. A matrix of spatial data and wealth metrics is constructed that identifies the available components of SDI that could contribute singly or in combination to wealth estimation. A gap analysis is also performed to identify sectors that are currently not well covered by these data sets. Third, because SDI are generally representative of advanced economies, we identify alternative sources of geospatial data and technologies that are increasingly gaining ground in geospatial data processing and assuming an ever-growing place in geospatial data generation. The growing availability of geotagged information created through location intelligent devices such as smart-phones and cameras and social media technologies such as Twitter are generating vast quantities of crowd-sourced VGI. In combination with the capabilities of remote sensing to capture massive quantities of data for large swaths of the earth's surface, crowd-sourced information may play an increasingly important role in providing spatial metrics of regional wealth for areas traditionally considered data sparse.

Vignette 1: testing indicators of physical capital

Three geospatial indicators of produced wealth are examined to generate assessments of capital wealth based on a geospatial approach. Residential housing, non-residential structures, and road infrastructure are core indicators contributing to capital estimates of produced wealth.

Residential housing stock

West Virginia is fortunate to have available a database of residential housing units generated for the entire state that is accurate to within meters of the exact position of the housing unit. This database was generated from high-spatial-resolution aerial imagery and was designed to support E911 and the creation of a city-style addressing system. Each residential unit was identified from the database at 1:4,800 scale. Using individual housing units at such high resolution is likely unnecessary in this instance, thus using GIS to aggregate housing units into more useful spatial scales for linking to other spatial units is probably appropriate (Figure 8.1). Thus acquiring geospatial data at the very highest resolution available may not, perhaps counter to expectation, be required in all instances of capital estimation.

Valuing these housing units is somewhat more problematic since house prices vary markedly not only across the state but within local areas. Here again is an opportunity to blend spatial data sets and valuation metrics by linking the housing stock to valuation procedures contained in nationwide house valuation data sets. Such information may be obtainable from Multiple Listing Service or local and state property transfer records, but websites such as Trulia (<http://www.trulia.com>) and Zillow (<http://www.zillow.com>) provide particularly convenient access, and regularly updated information. While individual house valuations might be possible (in which case hedonic valuation in conjunction with GIS to model local spatial variation could be useful), Trulia average listing prices of houses for counties or for postal zip codes can be used in combination with the housing count also aggregated to the zip code (Figure 8.2). The value of the housing stock can thus be calculated in near real time for combinations of areas across the state. Figure 8.2 shows that the housing stock of individual counties in West Virginia varies from just over half a billion dollars to almost twenty billion

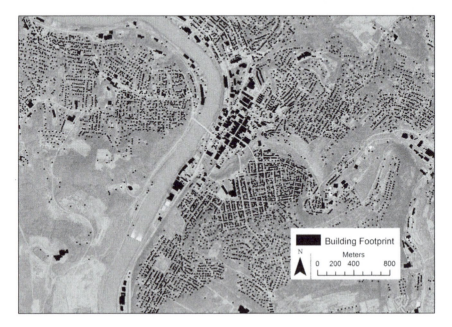

Figure 8.1 Residential structures near Morgantown, West Virginia

dollars. The lowest values tend to be clustered in the southern coalfields and the northwest of the state. Though the state is predominantly rural, the highest values are associated with the larger urban areas.

Non-residential structures

Non-housing structures can likewise be identified from the above database or from alternative geospatial sources such as the Geographic Names Index database maintained by the United States Geological Survey (USGS). These structures appear on the USGS 1:24,000 topographic map sheets. Not all structures can be easily attributed through this database, though some structures, such as schools and colleges, churches, bridges, correctional institutions, and state government buildings, are specified (Figure 8.3). Many other structures, however, are not attributed and thus it is difficult to estimate possible value. In this instance, an average value per square foot based on construction prices or previous sales can be assigned to these structures and then aggregated to an acceptable spatial unit such as census tract, county, or even state. Location variation in property within these aggregated regions could potentially be modeled using GIS, as described above.

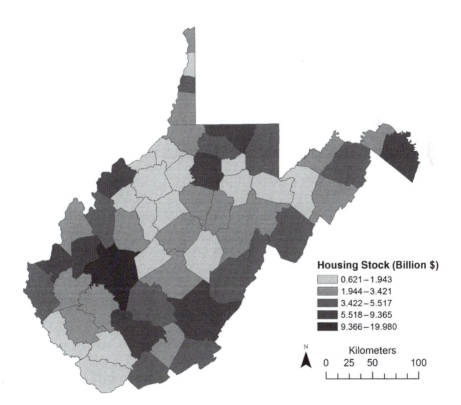

Figure 8.2 Housing stock of West Virginia, calculated by county

Road stock

The United States is well endowed with geospatial information on the spatial configuration of the road network and its attribution that identifies the categories of roads from interstate multi-lane highways to unpaved tracks. The USGS, for example, through its Digital Line Graph maps, and the state Department of Highways maintain extensive databases of such road networks. A variety of scales exist for these road data sets ranging anywhere from 1:2,000,000 to

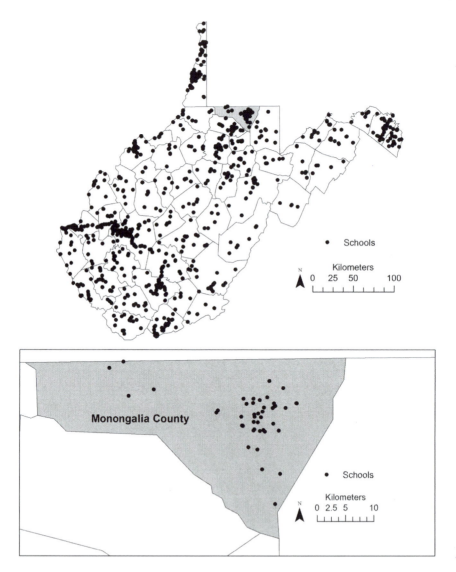

Figure 8.3 West Virginia school locations. Top: West Virginia. Bottom: Monongalia
County. Each circle represents one school

1:4,800, and for West Virginia these resources allow the calculation of road infrastructure at a scale of 1:4,800. For the United States, common data layers such as this are available for the entire country and form part of what are called *framework layers* – essential geospatial coverages that are important and available for all regions. While the geometry of these road networks may be discerned from satellite and aerial imagery the quality of the available digital spatial data makes this recourse unnecessary. However, in instances where such digital databases were not available, remote sensing would in most cases be important in generating such a digital layer.

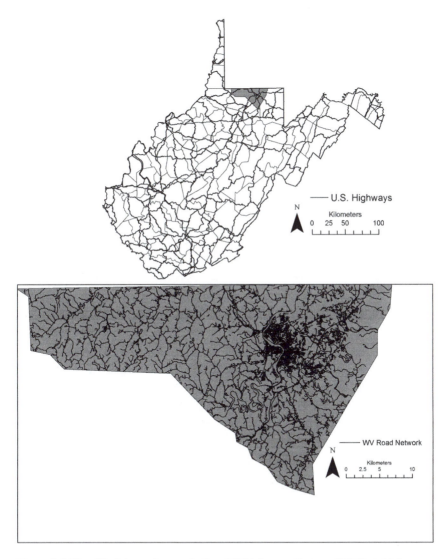

Figure 8.4 West Virginia road network. Top: US highways. Bottom: WV State highways for Monongalia County

For West Virginia, a road network was constructed from established data-bases, and the lengths and type of road structures can relatively easily be determined (Figure 8.4). Valuation procedures can then be applied to determine capital estimation. The basic spatial unit could include any configuration from census tract, to zip code, to the state, and above. What constitutes an optimal scale for data representation, in this case for wealth determination at the regional level, is a significant research question, since in GIS parlance one is confronting the issue of line generalization or densification – just how dense do the coordinates describing the road need to be to produce an "accurate" estimate of road length? The denser the coordinate geometry, the more detailed becomes the road configuration, and the "longer" the road becomes because it now represents twists and turns that are not present when the digital road is generalized at a coarser scale. These scale issues permeate many of the geospatial data coverages discussed in this chapter.

Vignette 2: testing indicators of natural wealth

To illustrate the geospatial assessment of natural capital, we draw upon two specific forms of natural capital: coal and ecosystem services.

Coal stocks

Coal is a traditional industrial energy resource and, like other fossil fuels, is a standard component of inventories of natural capital. In West Virginia, the distribution of surface and sub-surface coal resources is well documented, and the level of spatial and attribute detail extends well beyond the state scale. Indeed, digital spatial data rasterized on a 30-meter grid exist for the entire state and provides details of the sixty individual coal beds located in the state (Figure 8.5) (<http://www.wvgs.wvnet.edu/www/coal/cbmp/coalimsframe.html>). This mapping has grown out of over a hundred years of geological surveys and production mining of the region, and a recent effort to produce a digital coal database for taxation purposes (Hansen et al. 2009). Mined areas, as well as areas where the coal has been eroded in the geologic past, have been removed, so that only remaining coal is shown. For each bed, net coal thickness (exclusive of any non-coal partings in the bed) and depth below surface are available as attributes. Together, these attributes can be used to estimate the total tonnage of coal reserves for any location.

Estimating a value for the coal reserves is controversial (Hansen et al. 2009) since the value of coal in the ground is determined both by the market price of delivered coal and the extraction costs; indeed, not all the coal can be mined economically. The West Virginia State Tax Department values individual coal reserve properties using the West Virginia Geological and Economic Survey (WVGES) coal database to estimate the amount of coal present, as well as the sulfur content, and an estimate of when the coal is likely to be mined. Because the process heavily discounts future earnings, the value of coal reserves state-wide average $0.06 per ton, although once mined, coal can sell for as much as

$100 or more per ton. Unfortunately, the parcel-level data the Tax Department uses is not in the public domain – another issue for consideration in the use of geospatial data in capital estimation. However, the annual tax paid on property is public information, and where the coal ownership has been split from the surface property, separating people-based and place-based wealth, it is taxed separately and thus could be used to develop spatially varying estimates of coal value. Alternatively, current county-based prices paid per ton of coal can be obtained

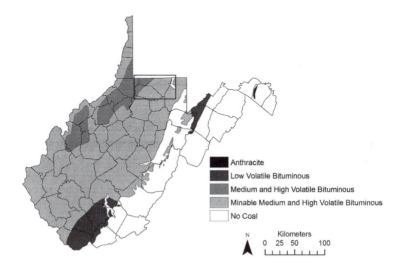

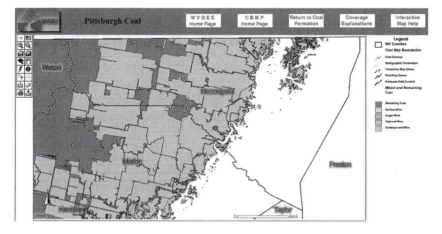

Figure 8.5 West Virginia coal. Top: Coal reserves by type for the state of West Virginia. Bottom: Location of remaining and previously mined coal reserves by geological horizon for Monongalia County

Source: West Virginia Geological and Economic Survey, 2012.

from the US Energy Information Administration, although this would still require subtracting an estimate of the cost of mining, and the data are incomplete due to "data withheld to avoid disclosure". West Virginia also has good county-level historical data on coal production. These data potentially can be used to characterize the depletion rate and the potential lifespan of the remaining resource.

Ecosystem services

Ecosystem services is a relatively new concept in wealth estimation and although it is an important component it is invariably an unrecorded component of capital accounting. Sustainable economic growth is undermined if environmental conditions are degraded, resulting in increased economic costs and reduced quality of life. This concern has led to the call for quantification of ecosystem services, defined as "the goods (such as food) and the services (such as waste assimilation) [that comprise] ... the benefits human populations derive, directly and indirectly, from ecosystem functions" (Costanza et al. 1997, p. 253). Ecosystem functions include "the habitat, biological or system properties or processes of ecosystems" (ibid.). Boyd and Banzhaf (2007) argue that the term "ecosystem services" is too loose for practical use, and instead advocate a focus on "final ecosystem services", defined as "components of nature, directly enjoyed, consumed or used to yield human well-being". Some have philosophically objected to the commodification of nature (Robertson 2004, 2006), while others have called into question the valuation of such services in the absence of a market (Sagoff 2011). The methods of quantifying ecosystem services tend to be simplistic, and generally do not include questions of spatial continuity of the habitat types. Despite these challenges, it is clear that not accounting for the externalities associated with environmental degradation may result in skewed evaluations of the sustainability of economic policies (Costanza et al. 1997).

The primary data used for mapping ecosystem services in this study was the USGS National Land Cover Data (NLCD) (Fry et al. 2011), produced by classification of Landsat Thematic Mapper (TM) and Enhanced Thematic Mapper Plus (ETM+) data, with a pixel size of 30 m. NLCD products are available for 2001, 2006, and 2010. The NLCD maps land cover in twenty-nine classes, though only fifteen have been mapped within West Virginia. These fifteen classes were converted to the equivalent Costanza et al. (1997) biome categories, and the valuations of the ecosystem services from the biomes used to estimate the annual value of ecosystem services for each pixel (Table 8.1). The annual service flows were converted to net present value (NPV) using a discount rate of 4 percent and a hundred-year period. A sensitivity analysis indicated that periods longer than a hundred years resulted in little change in the estimated valuation, therefore a hundred years was assumed to be a reasonable approximation of the potentially infinite time represented by sustainable ecosystems.

The resulting map (Figure 8.6) shows eastern West Virginia, a mountainous region home to the Monongahela National Forest, with the highest ecosystem

Table 8.1 Ecosystem services values from Costanza et al. (1997) applied to NLCD land cover categories

Code	NLCD Category	Costanza et al. Category	Value ($ ha^{-1} yr^{-1})
11	Open water	Lakes, rivers	8,498
21	Developed, open space	Urban	0
22	Developed, low intensity	Urban	0
23	Developed, medium intensity	Urban	0
24	Developed, high intensity	Urban	0
31	Barren land	Ice/rock	0
41	Deciduous forest	Temperate/boreal forest	302
42	Evergreen forest	Temperate/boreal forest	302
43	Mixed forest	Temperate/boreal forest	302
52	Shrub/scrub	Grassland/rangelands	232
71	Grassland/herbaceous	Grassland/rangelands	232
81	Pasture/hay	Grassland/rangelands	232
82	Cultivated crops	Cropland	92
90	Woody wetlands	Wetlands	14,785
95	Emergent herbaceous wetlands	Wetlands	14,785

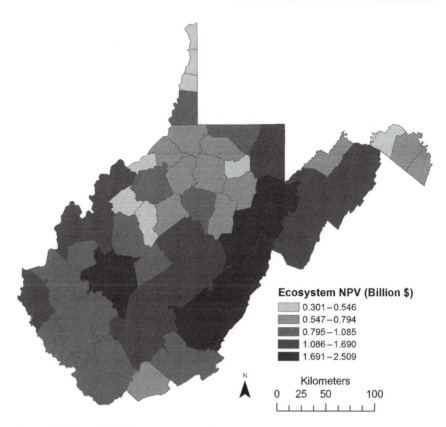

Figure 8.6 West Virginia ecosystem services by county

services, up to $2.5 billion. The lowest values are generally found in the north-west and northern panhandle. It is notable that the ecosystem services are of similar magnitude to the calculated values of the housing stock (Figure 8.2). A comparison of the ecosystems services map with poverty in the state (Figure 8.7) indicates that the region of high values of ecosystem services in the eastern part of the state is also associated with low rates of poverty.

The ecosystem services map poses some immediate questions regarding using ecosystem services in developing a regional capital accounting. First, the conversion of annual flows to capital estimates has notable uncertainty associated with the lack of agreement regarding the appropriate discount rate for valuing future flows (Newell and Pizer 2003; Weitzman 2010). Second, the map is based on a limited number of land use categories. Additional remote sensing analysis could be used to produce additional finer land cover categories, but consistent valuation of the categories is not currently available, reinforcing one of the major criticisms of ecosystem services economics (Sagoff 2011). Indeed, examination of Table 8.1 shows that even the current NLCD categories are finer than the Costanza et al. (1997) valuations. Third, the valuations shown are based on Costanza et al.'s (1997) compilation of 1990s and earlier estimates. Thus, the

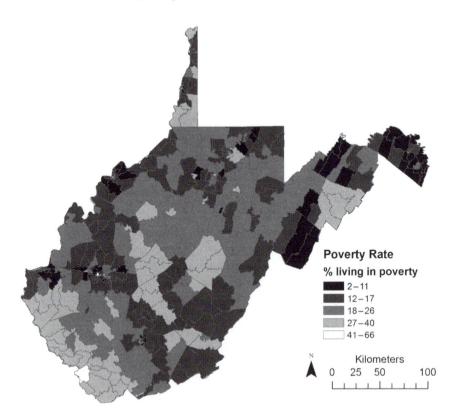

Figure 8.7 West Virginia poverty

values are on average close to twenty years old, and an updated compilation of values would appear warranted. On the other hand, the strength of the map is that it is generated at a fine scale, using consistent and objective methods, and the accuracy is quantified. Aggregation to coarser scales is straightforward.

Vignette 3: testing indicators of human capital

Human and social capital have been the subject of considerable debate and research. The World Bank (2006) used intangible capital as a broad concept to include human capital and the quality of formal and informal institutions. Assessing the sustainability of development in an economy requires monetary estimates for all the types of capital assets that contribute to people's well-being. The measurement of capital forms raises many challenges, in particular for those assets that are not easily observed or are not traded in markets. Human capital is one such case that is not even a common component of any standard wealth and capital stock accounting framework. However, a few studies that have computed monetary estimates of human capital stocks found that they account for more than 80 percent of all wealth in the United States (World Bank 2006; Arrow et al. 2010). Approaches to the measurement of human capital in the economic literature are based on frameworks that recognize investments in education and training as the creators of human capital (Jorgenson and Fraumeni 1989, 1992).

Human capital indicators consist of demographic structure (population and labor force), educational attainment skills and training levels, and talent (occupations in the creative economy). These indicators suggest the extent to which a region's population and labor force are effectively engaged in productive economic activities. In many respects, human capital is perhaps one of the easiest components of capital to be estimated through geospatial data because of the quantity and quality of census data and labor statistics available for a variety of geographical units: spatial units such as counties with concentrations of available and active human capital and/or higher levels of knowledge as measured by educational attainment, and the size of talent measured by high-technology and innovation-related occupations and jobs. The share of younger population (those below 30 years old) and active labor force (ages 18–65) in the total population is relatively easily generated from available databases. The labor force participation rate for areas is also available and provides a gauge to the level of population likely available to expand wealth.

Educational attainment is the most common measure of the skills and knowledge that shape a population's capacity to engage in productive activities, sometimes measured by the proportion of individuals in the labor force that graduated from high school or possess a higher degree (Arrow et al. 2010). Marré and Pender (Chapter 4) estimate human capital of small towns in Oregon using data from the Population Census and American Community Survey. Certainly, as already demonstrated, the number and accessibility of educational facilities – elementary schools, community colleges and vocational schools, and universities – can be captured by GIS technology and be used as an indicator contributing to the quality of labor force. Similarly, talent and the availability of technology-based knowledge occupations are hypothesized to have larger contributions to wealth generation and can be identified by location to indicate regional talent in wealth-creating activities.

Geospatial indicators and wealth estimation

The vignettes demonstrate how exemplar geospatial data can be processed through GIS to provide wealth estimates. Table 8.2 provides a series of selected spatial data taken from about 350 spatial data coverages served by the West Virginia SDI (<http://wvgis.wvu.edu>). The list is not intended to be comprehensive or exhaustive but it does provide an insight beyond these vignettes as to what geospatial data are generally available in the United States and how these coverages can be processed to calculate capital estimates. Table 8.2 broadly structures the geospatial layers according to the eight categories of wealth specified earlier in this chapter. Importantly, the scale of the data set is also recorded in specific ratio terms or in terms of the approximate geographical unit used to aggregate the data. Thus, physical capital and human capital can be seen to be well served by currently available geospatial data stored in the WV SDI. In contrast, some types of wealth appear to have few indicators in this data set, including financial, intellectual, and social capital. This is not to suggest that such data sets do not exist or could not be created, but rather that for West Virginia such data sets are not currently widely available.

Discussion and conclusion

This chapter proposes that geospatial databases allied to geospatial technologies could play a significant role in developing an empirically driven regional approach to rural wealth estimation. Calculating regional wealth estimates for rural areas invariably requires sub-national capital estimations because national approximations of regional wealth and capital are spatially coarse and heavily reliant on estimation. Using a geospatial data approach as outlined above to assess rural capital implies a multi-scalar approach that, at some level, current SDI can support. In this chapter we draw attention to the rapidly growing and highly relevant multi-scalar spatial databases that provide a wealth of information capable of supporting empirical regional capital estimation.

While GIS are important tools for processing and modeling these data sets, it is the availability of authenticated SDI that enables these sub-national empirical approaches to be pursued. It is recognized that the digital divide will contribute to a differentiation in the availability and analysis of appropriate spatial data between advanced and less advanced economies but it is here that the extensive capability of remotely sensed satellite imagery, with ever more precise spatial and spectral resolution imagery, can assist in meeting the need not only in the natural but in the human and produced fields (Warner et al. 2009). The addition of GIS data sets, such as vegetation, crop and other land and water, where available,

Table 8.2 Examples of geospatial measures of wealth and evaluation of availability of associated data sources

Type of capital	Category	Dataset	Source[1]	Scale	Wealth estimator
Physical, produced or built	Electrical	Electricity distribution infra structure	WVDNR	1:4800	Power lines
	Water distribution	Not currently available			Water pipe lines
		Not currently available			Water reservoirs
		Not currently available			Sewage pipelines
		Sewage treatment plants	WVDEP	1:24000	Sewage treatment system
	Oil distribution	WV pipelines	WVGES	1:24000	Pipelines (oil)[3]
	Gas distribution	WV pipelines	WVGES	1:24000	Pipelines (gas)[3]
	Tele-communications	Telephone	Fryer's TowerSource	1:24000	Cell towers
		Internet	WVPSC	County	Broadband availability
	Transportation	SAMB Planimetrics	WVSAMB	1:4800	Roads (divided highways, multilane, paved, unpaved)
		SAMB Planimetrics	WVSAMB	1:4800	Railways
		SAMB Planimetrics	WVSAMB	1:4800	Bridges
		SAMB Planimetrics	WVSAMB	1:4800	Tunnels
		SAMB Planimetrics	WVSAMB	1:4800	Navigable waterways
		SAMB Planimetrics	WVSAMB	1:4800	Airports
	Buildings	SAMB Planimetrics	WVSAMB	1:4800	Single and multi-unit residential buildings
		SAMB Planimetrics	WVSAMB	1:4800	Commercial buildings
		SAMB Planimetrics	WVSAMB	1:4800	Industrial buildings
		SAMB Planimetrics	WVSAMB	1:4800	Institutional/public buildings
	Machinery	Not currently available			Fixed, movable
	Urban land	Built land	USCB	CB[2]	Built and non-built land, public open space
	Other	Industrial sites	WVDO	1:24000	Industrial sites

(Continued)

Table 8.2 (Continued)

Type of capital	Category	Dataset	Source[1]	Scale	Wealth estimator
Financial	Financial institutions	GNIS	USGS	Place	Financial institutions
Natural	Coal	Coal fields of the US	NA	National	Coal strata
		Recoverable coal reserves	USEIA	State	Coal reserves, production
		National coal resource data system	USGS	County	Coal reserves
		WV coal production	WVGES	County	Coal production
		WV coal GIS	WVGES	30 m	Coal reserves
	Oil and gas	Crude oil proved reserves and production	USEIA	State	Oil reserves and production
		Oil and gas permits	WVDEP	Point	Permitted wells
		Oil and gas production	WVGES	Point	Production by well
	Minerals	Mineral resources data system	USGS	County	Mineral reserves, e.g., bauxite, copper, gold, iron, lead, etc.
	Timber	WV timber market report	AHC	Region	Timber sales
	Non-timber forest resources	Not currently available			Ginseng, ramps, deer, fishing, etc.
	Land cover	National land cover data set	USGS	30 m	Ecosystem services
	Renewable resources	Renewable electric power sector net generation	USEIA	State	Renewable energy production
		Wind potential	USDOE	2.5 km	Potential wind energy production
	Agricultural land	The census of agriculture	USDA	County	Crop land and production

Table 8.2 (Continued)

Type of capital	Category	Dataset	Source[1]	Scale	Wealth estimator
Human or individual	Population	American FactFinder	USCB	CB	Population size, density
	Education	American FactFinder	USCB	CB	Formal and informal education
	Health	Health data interactive	CDC	State	Life expectancy
		National vital statistics system	CDC	County	Child mortality
		Overweight and obesity trends	CDC	County	Obesity
	Income	American FactFinder	USCB	CB	Median income
		American FactFinder	USCB	CB	% below poverty line
Intellectual	Innovation	Not currently available			
Social	Networks	Not currently available			
Political	Governance	Voter participation	GMU, US Elections Project	State	Voter participation
Cultural	Cultural features	GNIS	USGS	Place	Cultural features

Notes:
[1] Data sources: AHC – Appalachian Hardwood Center; CDC – Centers for Disease Control; GMU – George Mason University: GNIS – Geographic Names Information System; NA – National Atlas; USCB – US Census Bureau; USDA – US Department of Agriculture; USDOE – US Department of Energy; USEIA – US Energy Information Administration; USGS – US Geological Survey; WVDEP – West Virginia Department of Environmental Protection; WVDNR – West Virginia Division of Natural Resources; WVDO – West Virginia Development Office; WVGES – West Virginia Geological and Economic Survey; WVPSC – West Virginia Public Service Commission; WVSAMB – West Virginia Street Addressing and Mapping Board.

[2] CB – Census block.

[3] Data not generally available due to security concerns.

can be used to considerably refine the remote sensed image classification categories (Mehaffey et al. 2011).

In addition, the recent advent of Neogeography, premised as it is on the WWW 2.0, social media, location-intelligent mobile devices, open-source map data and mapping software, poses significant opportunities to augment these official data sets. Breathtaking technological advances, open source Internet applications and web data services, along with published open-source application programming interfaces provide major opportunities for agencies and communities to participate, contribute, and draw upon spatial data and processing services traditionally confined to an expert GIS community. In closing the gap between data providers and data consumers, this emerging community of citizen sensors is capable of providing vast quantities of real-time, geo-tagged data that can enhance and infill much of the authenticated geography that created the "no data-no geography" conundrum faced by the GIS community. However, in so doing, citizen sensors and VGI challenge the traditional vision of SDI in the core areas of standards, metadata, data management, authenticity, and verification, which are the hallmarks of established SDI and which have yet to be fully played out. What should be apparent, however, is that these geospatial approaches provide a very real opportunity not only to generate realistic assessments of regional capital that are so critical in assessing regional development policy outcomes, but also to provide additional insight into the conundrum of resource-rich regions and rural areas juxtaposed with economic and cultural poverty (Figure 8.7).

Acknowledgments

The West Virginia Regional Research Institute provided financial support for this study. The authors would like to thank Randy Jackson, Frank Lafone, and Amanda Krugh for help with the research, and the WVGES for the WV coal data. The authors also gratefully acknowledge John Pender and two anonymous reviewers whose suggestions on an earlier draft of the manuscript greatly improved this chapter.

References

Arrow, K.J., Dasgupta, P., Goulder, L.H., Mumford, K.J., and Oleson, K. (2010) "Sustainability and the measurement of wealth", NBER Working Paper 16599, Cambridge, MA: National Bureau of Economic Research.

Bossler, J., Campbell, J.B., McMaster, R.B., and Rizos, C. (eds.) (2010) *Manual of Geospatial Science and Technology*, Boca Raton, FL: Taylor & Francis.

Boyd, J., and Banzhaf, S. (2007) "What are ecosystem services? The need for standardized environmental accounting units", *Ecological Economics*, 63: 616–26.

Costanza, R., Arge, R.D., Groot, R.D., Farber, S., Grasso, M., et al. (1997) "The value of the world's ecosystem services and natural capital", *Nature*, 387: 253–60.

Fry, J.A., Xian, G., Jin, S., Dewitz, J.A., Homer, C.G., et al. (2011) "Completion of the 2006 National Land Cover Database for the coterminous United States", *Photogrammetric Engineering & Remote Sensing*, 77: 858–64.

Hansen, E., Boettner, F., White, T., Boettner, T., and Miller, P. (2009) *Taxing West Virginia's Coal Reserves: A Primer*, Charleston, WV: West Virginia Center on Budget & Policy.

Jorgenson, D.W., and Fraumeni, B.M. (1989) "The accumulation of human and non-human capital, 1948–1984", in R.E. Lipsey and H. Tice (eds.), *The Measurement of Saving, Investment, and Wealth*, Chicago: University of Chicago Press, pp. 227–82.

Jorgenson, D.W., and Fraumeni, B.M. (1992) "The output of the education sector", in *Output Measurement in the Service Sectors*, Chicago: University of Chicago Press, pp. 303–41.

Kendrick, J.W. (1976) *The Formation and Stocks of Total Capital*, NBER General Series no. 100, New York: Columbia University Press for NBER.

Kendrick, J.W. (1979) "Expanding imputed values in the National Income and Product Accounts", *Review of Income and Wealth*, 25(4): 349–63.

van Loenen, B., and Kok, B.C. (eds.) (2004) *Spatial Data Infrastructure and Policy Development in Europe and the United States*, Delft: IOS Press.

Masser, I. (2010) *Building European Spatial Data Infrastructures*, Redlands: ESRI Press.

Mehaffey, M., Van Remortel, R., Smith, E., and Bruins, R. (2011) "Developing a dataset to assess ecosystem services in the Midwest United States", *International Journal of Geographical Information Science*, 25: 681–95.

Newell, R.G., and Pizer, W.A. (2003) "Discounting the distant future: how much do uncertain rates increase valuations?", *Journal of Environmental Economics and Management*, 46(1): 52–71.

Organisation for Economic Co-operation and Development (2009) *Measuring Capital, OECD Manual 2009*, Paris: OECD.

Robertson, M.M. (2004) "The neoliberalization of ecosystem services: wetland mitigation banking and problems in environmental governance", *Geoforum*, 35: 361–73.

Robertson, M.M. (2006) "The nature that capital can see: science, state, and market in the commodification of ecosystem services", *Environment and Planning D: Society & Space*, 24: 367–87.

Sagoff, M. (2011) "The quantification and valuation of ecosystem services", *Ecological Economics*, 70: 497–502.

Scharl, A., and Tochtermann, K. (eds.) (2007) *The Geospatial Web: How Geobrowsers, Social Software and Web 2.0 are Shaping the Network Society*, London: Springer.

Sui, D., Elwood, S., and Goodchild, M. (eds.) (2013) *Crowdsourcing Geographic Knowledge: Volunteered Geographic Information (VGI) in Theory and Practice*, New York: Springer.

Warner, T.A., Nellis, M.D., and Foody, G.M. (eds.) (2009) *The SAGE Handbook of Remote Sensing*, London: SAGE.

Weitzman, M.L. (2010) "Risk-adjusted gamma discounting", *Journal of Environmental Economics and Management*, 60(1): 1–13.

Wilson, J., and Fotheringham, A.S. (eds.) (2007) *The Handbook of Geographic Information Science*, Malden: Blackwell.

World Bank (2006) *Where is the Wealth of Nations?: Measuring Capital for the 21st Century*, Washington, DC: World Bank.

9 Absentee forest and farm land ownership in Alabama

Capturing benefits from natural capital controlled by non-residents

Conner Bailey and Mahua Majumdar

Introduction

The social and economic well-being of all communities, and perhaps especially rural communities, is significantly affected by the land, how it is used, and who controls the flow of benefits from the land (Jacobs 1998; Geisler 1995; Zabawa 1991; Gaventa 1998). Ownership of natural capital in the form of land is a fundamental source of wealth. Whether land is owned by people who live on or near the land, or whether they live somewhere else has important consequences for where the flow of income from land is directed. As will be detailed below, our research shows that over half of all land in Alabama is absentee owned. This simple fact has profound implications for how place-based wealth in the form of land affects accumulation of human, built, and financial capital as well as the economic prospects of people who live in communities where absentee owned land is located.

In terms used in this volume, land is considered a stock resource from which revenues flow. Land is inherently a place-based form of wealth (Johnson et al., Chapter 3) that can serve as the foundation for rural economies based on agriculture, forestry, mining, or other activities. Where ownership and control are located elsewhere, however, wealth in land may contribute little to people-based rural wealth creation. We know there are whole regions of the United States where extensive external ownership or control over land has undermined the ability of rural people to accumulate wealth. In central Appalachia, for example, persistent poverty has been linked to absentee ownership of the region's wealth in land and minerals (e.g., Appalachia Land Ownership Task Force 1983; Gaventa 1980; Williams 2002). Similarly, many rural communities in the Pacific Northwest which had depended on harvesting timber from public lands have fallen into economic distress because federal policies resulted in a drastic reduction in timber sales (Sherman 2009). For the communities and regions affected, it did not matter greatly that in one case ownership was in the hands of distant corporations while in the other the resource was controlled by the federal government. In both regions, the fact that outsiders owned or controlled land and associated natural capital undermined local wealth creation. We argue here that absentee forest and farm land ownership undermines the ability of people in rural Alabama to accumulate wealth because revenues from the land flow elsewhere. Specifically, we hypothesize that absentee ownership is negatively correlated with the accumulation of human and financial capital, two important forms of people-based wealth.

Why does it matter who owns the land?

There is a strong consensus within the academic literature that land is not only a productive resource but also provides economic and political power at individual and community levels (Gaventa 1998; Geisler 1995). Ownership of this fundamental asset determines the flow of material benefits, is a store of wealth that can be used to generate additional income and wealth, and provides an important measure of personal independence and satisfaction (Nelson 1978; Zabawa 1991). Ownership and management of land affect employment and income at the individual level and can promote or impede economic and community development (Deininger and Michael 2003; Dudenhefer 1993; Nelson 1978). Gaventa (1998) points out that control over land translates into political power, and landlessness often translates into powerlessness, particularly in rural and resource dependent regions. Molotch's (1976) classic work on urban development demonstrates that the fundamental importance of land ownership to local power is not limited to rural areas.

Several authors have examined the relationship between ownership patterns and quality of life (Bain 1984; Goodstein 1989; Heasley and Guries 1998; Shaffer and Meade 1997), but few studies have focused specific attention on absentee ownership. Results of a national survey of private forestland owners showed that 82 percent of all owners lived in the same county where their land was located (Birch et al. 1978). A study by Shaffer and Meade (1997) found that 25 percent of non-industrial private forestland owners in Virginia were absentee, defined as living in a county other than where their land was located. More widely known and far-reaching studies on absentee ownership are those of Walter Goldschmidt (1978) and the Appalachian Land Ownership Task Force (1983). Goldschmidt's work has become a classic in understanding the social impact of absentee ownership of industrial farming operations (Green 1985; Lobao et al. 1993). The Appalachian Land Ownership Task Force's landmark study, *Who Owns Appalachia?*, has been the subject of continued discussion and has inspired other researchers to make similar studies in the same region (Gaventa and Horton 1984; Goodstein 1989; Horton 1993; Scott 2012). The Appalachian study documented the extent of corporate and absentee ownership of land in the Appalachian region and the impact such ownership had in limiting local ability to pursue economic and social development. Appalachia has been portrayed as an internal colony where natural wealth – primarily in the form of coal – was controlled and extracted by external owners with little benefit accruing to the people of the region (Williams 2002). The result has been persistent rural poverty throughout much of the Appalachian region. Fifteen northern Alabama counties were included in that regional study.

Prior to the study being reported upon here, no systematic research had been conducted on absentee ownership of land in Alabama and the impacts of absentee ownership on the quality of life. Two reporters for the *Birmingham News*, the state's largest newspaper, did analyze tax records for ten counties of Alabama's Black Belt region and found that almost two-thirds of all land was owned by people or corporations located outside the county (Archibald and Hansen 2003). These Black Belt counties, defined demographically in terms of counties where African Americans make up over 40 percent of the population, are among the poorest of Alabama counties and are also located in the heart of the forest products industry of the state. Unfortunately, Archibald and Hansen provided no documentation on how the data were collected or analyzed.

In Alabama, research has shown strong negative correlations between timber dependency (the relative importance of the forest products industry in county-level employment and income) and standard measures of well-being, including income, unemployment, educational attainment, and local investment in public schools (Bailey et al. 1996; Bliss et al. 1998b; Bliss and Bailey 2005; Howze et al. 2003). The work by Sisock (1998) and Bliss et al. (1998a) documented a trend towards concentrated ownership of forestland in Alabama and provided statistical analysis showing that there was a significant negative correlation between this concentration and quality of life. An unpublished paper by Kennealy et al. (2007) confirmed this finding both for Alabama and for eight other states in the Southeastern United States. None of these studies addressed absentee ownership.

The relationship between land ownership patterns and local community well-being is a complex issue. Land represents an important stock of local wealth, but if that land is controlled by absentee owners the flow of income generated by that land may be lost to the community. One mechanism through which revenue from land could be retained in the local economy is through property taxes levied by local (county) governments. However, property taxes in Alabama are the lowest in the nation and special tax consideration is given to owners of forest and farm land (Joshi et al. 2000; PARCA 2009). Hamill (2002) reports that property taxes paid by timberland owners (accounting for 71 percent of the state's total area) account for less than 2 percent of total property tax receipts and average less than $1 per acre. This is possible because owners of both forest and farm lands can either base their property taxes on market value or on the productive capacity of the land to grow crops or timber, a so-called "current use" process that became state law in 1982 (Flick et al. 1989). Once value of the land has been established, the assessed value is set at 10 percent. That assessed value is then applied to the millage rates in place for each county. Millage rates vary from a low of 17.5 to a high of 44.5 ($0.00175 to $0.00445 per dollar valuation), and of course property values vary greatly depending on a wide variety of factors, most notably proximity to urban centers. Alabama's per capita property tax collections are the lowest in the nation ($453) and are considerably lower than those of three neighboring states of Georgia ($1,000), Tennessee ($728), and Mississippi ($755).

The rationale behind current use taxation is that it protects forest and farm land owners from increased property tax assessments if urban sprawl increases the market value of their land. The merits of staunching the spread of urban sprawl notwithstanding, the implications for generating wealth in a rural economy are made clear in statutory language: "provided, that no consideration shall be taken of the prospective value such property might have if it were put to some other possible use" (Alabama Code Sec. 40-7-25.1). Near urban areas this has provided land owners options to keep their land in production (or hold speculatively for further value increases) rather than develop, but in much of rural Alabama this provision has had a dampening effect on the ability of county governments to collect revenues sufficient to support public schools or maintain roads and other infrastructure (Flick et al. 1989; Joshi et al. 2000; PARCA 2009). Low property taxes also have enabled owners simply to hold onto land without the need to generate significant revenue or create employment on the land. Relatively passive uses which generate limited if any employment, such as hunting leases, generate more than enough revenue to cover taxes.

Not surprisingly, land owners are generally reluctant to support property tax increases. This reluctance may be greater in the case of absentee owners who would have limited direct benefit from improvements in public schools or other public expenditures. Research on large corporate absentee owners in the forest products industry made it clear that these owners were opposed to increasing taxes to support local schools or social services (Joshi et al. 2000). Moreover, most of these corporate owners received property tax abatements on their pulp and paper mills, with average land and equipment values well in excess of $1 billion, dramatically reducing funds available to support local schools and county governments (Joshi et al. 2000). These corporations have since divested themselves of most of their timberland. The Real Estate Investment Trusts (REITs) and Timber Management Organizations (TIMOs) which purchased most of this land are corporate absentee owners with a short time horizon for profits on their investments and are unlikely to be any more receptive to tax increases than the previous owners (Bliss et al. 2010).

In Alabama the 1901 Constitution requires that a constitutional amendment be passed any time a county wants to raise its property taxes. To initiate this process, county officials need to hold a public hearing, gain consent of the local legislative delegation, and have a bill introduced and passed in the state legislature. If even a single "no" vote is recorded, the constitutional amendment needs to be approved by a state-wide election; otherwise the election is limited to voters in the affected county (Flynt 2004). Once in the political process, there are powerful organized interests representing forestry and agriculture (e.g., the Alabama Farmers Federation and the Alabama Forestry Association) in place to oppose any property tax increase anywhere in the state. Most recently these organizations opposed an effort in the state legislature to increase the state-wide property tax by 0.5 mill ($0.0005) (White 2012). A recent court test of Alabama's property tax system found in favor of the status quo (Lynch vs. Alabama 2011).

Alabama remains one of the poorest states in the nation (RUPRI 2007; US Census Bureau n.d.a). We hypothesize that the impact of absentee ownership exerts a depressing effect on wealth generation in the state. There are two primary mechanisms by which this happens. First, economic returns from land flow to the owners, and since (as we will show) the majority of land in Alabama is absentee owned, much of this wealth leaves the local economy. Second, the state's tax policies are structured so that land owners, including absentee owners, pay very low property taxes in support of schools, roads, or social services in the counties where the land is located, thus contributing little to the accumulation of local wealth in the form to improve human, financial, or built capital.

Method

The reason few studies on absentee ownership have been conducted in Alabama or elsewhere in the United States is that the data necessary to conduct such a study are extremely difficult to obtain. Land ownership data are managed by individual counties, of which there are sixty-seven in Alabama. For our study, we needed access to county property tax records, which are public documents. Most but not all counties have the data available in electronic format. Some counties use a private firm to manage their data, and we purchased data for $300 per county. Others have their data available on the web, which we were able simply to download. Yet other counties were either reluctant to provide access to public tax records or did not have staff available to provide electronic access to the data, which generally involved tens of thousands of individual property records. In some cases upwards of twenty phone calls were made to individual counties without resulting in success in obtaining the requested data. In the end, we were able to generate ownership data for forest and farm land for fifty of sixty-seven Alabama counties (Figure 9.1).

County tax records report the address to which tax bills are sent, and this is what we have used to determine resident or absentee ownership. We defined absentee owners as those owners with a tax address located in a county other than the county where the land was located, whether the tax address was located within Alabama or a different state or nation. We further distinguished between absentee owners who lived in Alabama and those who did not. In some cases, the addresses used may be the office of a financial advisor or a lawyer representing the owner, and may not reflect the owner's actual residence. There is no way of knowing whether this possible discrepancy increases or decreases the percentage of land reported as absentee. Given the large number of tax records in our database (608,071 separate privately owned parcels), we believe the impact to be negligible.

We used Pearson's correlation to examine relationships between absentee ownership (total, in-state, and out-of-state) and four quality-of-life variables. Data for per capita income is an estimate of how much income is earned in a county divided by the number of people living in that county. School children receiving free or reduced price school meals are reported as percentages which provide a measure of households with low incomes (Park et al. 2002). Children are eligible for free or reduced price meals if they live in households with incomes less than 130 percent and 185 percent, respectively, of the federal poverty line.

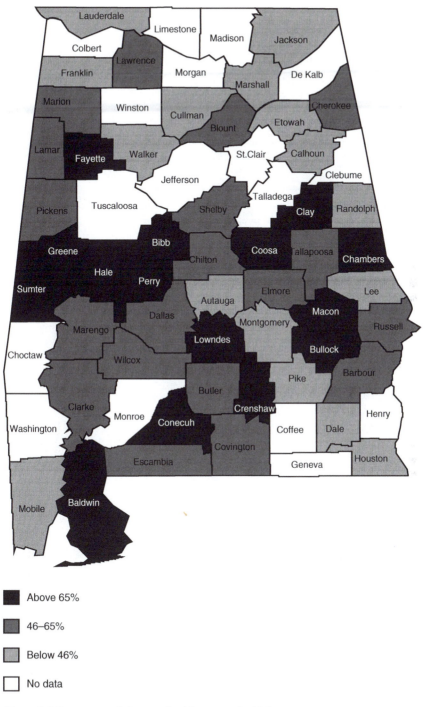

Above 65%

46–65%

Below 46%

No data

Figure 9.1 Percentage of absentee land by county in Alabama

We also examined two measures of human capital, educational attainment, and local funding for public education (Flora and Flora 2013). Educational attainment is defined as the percentage of residents 25 years and older with a high school or higher degree. Local funding for public education is defined as the total amount of local funding available per student in each county. In Alabama, the majority of funding per student in most counties comes from the state, but local tax revenues provide important supplemental funding and often make the difference between a school system which is underfunded or adequately funded. Differences in funding available per student between counties in the state are directly related to differences in local tax revenues dedicated to public schools.

Our unit of analysis was the county. Data on per capita income and educational attainment came from the US Census Bureau (n.d.b). Data on local funding of public schools and percentage of school-aged children receiving free or reduced price meals came from the Alabama State Department of Education (n.d.).

We hypothesize that absentee ownership will be negatively correlated with per capita income, educational attainment, and local funding for public schools, and positively correlated with the percentage of school-age children receiving free or reduced price meals.

Results

Forest and farm land account for 97 percent of all land in Alabama, with forestry accounting for over 71 percent of total land (22.99 million acres); agriculture (row crop and pasture land) represents 26 percent (8.6 million acres) of the state's total area (Hartsell and Brown 2002; USDA n.d.). Virtually all of the state's farm land is privately owned, as is 94.4 percent of all forest land (Hartsell and Brown 2002, p. 20). Compared with other regions, the South has the lowest percentage of publicly owned timber land in the nation (9.4 percent) and Alabama's publicly owned timber land is the lowest in the South at 5.3 percent (Smith et al. 2004, p. 59).

Absentee ownership

Data from county tax records in Alabama show that over 60 percent of all forest land and over 40 percent of all farm land are owned by people who live in a different county from where the land they own is located (Table 9.1). Over one-third of this land is owned by people who live outside the state of Alabama. Until recently, 16 percent of all forest land in Alabama was owned by corporations in the forest products industry (Hartsell and Brown 2002), but in the last decade most of this land has been sold to REITs and TIMOs which manage timber assets for investors who may live anywhere in the world (Bliss et al. 2010; Gunnoe and Gellert 2011).

Some Alabama counties have an extraordinarily high percentage of absentee ownership (Coosa, Lowndes, Macon, and Sumter) while in others absentee

Absentee land ownership in Alabama 141

Table 9.1 Percentage of absentee forest and agricultural land (including land owned by
in- and out-of-state owners) in fifty study counties

Absentee forestland			Absentee agricultural land		
As percent of total forest land in Alabama	Percent out-of-state owners	Percent in-state owners	As percent of total agricultural land in Alabama	Percent out-of-state owners	Percent in-state owners
60.5	35.5	64.5	40.9	29.2	70.8

Source: County tax records for fifty Alabama counties.

ownership is relatively low (Cullman, Lauderdale, Marshall, and Montgomery). The range of absentee ownership runs from a high of 85.5 percent (Coosa County) to a low of 21.2 percent (Cullman County). Figure 9.1 shows graphically the distribution of counties with relatively more and relatively less absentee ownership of forest and agricultural land.

Of total absentee acres, 34.6 percent (3,439,456 acres) is held by owners who live outside Alabama. Of the land owned by out-of-state absentee owners, 90.1 percent land is forested and 9.9 percent is agricultural. Few cases are found where the land was owned by owners who live out of the country (mostly in Canada), and these owners are simply included in the out-of-state records.

Financing, income, and human capital

We included per capita income and percentage of students eligible for reduced price or free meals at public schools in our analysis. In 2009, the average per capita income in the fifty study counties was $19,203. The maximum and minimum range of per capita income varied from $12,258 (Wilcox County) to $33,607 (Shelby County). An average of 68 percent of students in public schools in the fifty counties were eligible for reduced price or free meals which indicates that nearly two-thirds of all households had relatively low incomes. There was considerable variation between counties, with the highest percentages in Alabama's Black Belt counties.

We also included a proxy for human capital stock and human capital investment. On the individual level, we found an average of 76 percent of the population 25 years or over in our fifty-county study area had a high school diploma. There was considerable variation between counties (69 to 92 percent), however. At the county level, we used local funding per student in the fifty study counties, the average of which was $1,257. The local funding varied dramatically from one county to another. Some counties (e.g., Baldwin and Shelby) used local taxes to provide more than $2,000 per student to fund local schools, while other counties (Sumter, Coosa, and Lamar) provided less than $900 per student. Descriptive statistics on these four variables are provided in Table 9.2.

Table 9.2 Descriptive statistics for quality-of-life variables

Variable	N	Mean	Standard deviation	Minimum	Maximum
Income (dollars)	50	19,203	3,526	12,258	33,607
Eligibility for reduced price of free student meals (percent)	50	67.6	16.7	29.2	100.0
Adults with a high school diploma (percent)	50	75.9	5.3	68.5	91.5
Local funding per student	50	1,257	382	695	2,368

Source: US Census Bureau (n.d.b) and Alabama State Department of Education (n.d.).

Table 9.3 Correlation analysis results for total absentee land

	Absentee	Income	Student meal	Education	Local fund
Absentee	1.00				
Income	−0.42 (0.00)***	1.00			
Student meal	0.43 (0.00)***	−0.79 (0.00)***	1.00		
Education	−0.42 (0.00)***	0.73 (0.00)***	−0.51 (0.00)***	1.00	
Local fund	−0.15 (0.31)	0.50 (0.00)***	−0.25 (0.07)*	0.38 (0.01)**	1.00

Notes: *p*-values are given in parentheses; *** – statistically significant at the 0.01 level, ** – statistically significant at the 0.05 level, * – statistically significant at the 0.1 level; *Absentee*: percentage of absentee land; *Income*: per capita income; *Student meal*: percentage of students eligible for reduced or free meals; *Education*: percentage of people (25 years or above) with high school degree or above; *Local fund*: local funding per student in public school.

Results of correlation analysis

We used Pearson's correlation coefficients to examine whether an association exists between our four variables and total absentee land ownership in Alabama. In Table 9.3 and Figures 9.2 and 9.3, we see that strong and statistically significant negative correlations exist between total absentee land ownership and per capita income and educational attainment. We also see a strong and statistically significant positive relationship between total absentee land ownership and the percentage of students receiving free and reduced price meals (Figure 9.4). Understanding that correlations suggest the presence of a relationship but cannot

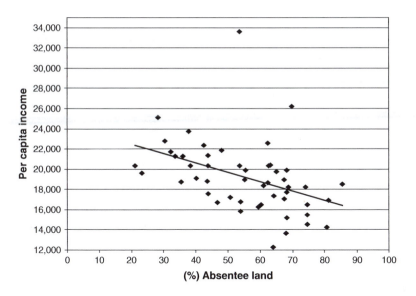

Figure 9.2 Correlation between percentage of absentee land and per capita income in Alabama

Source: US Census Bureau (n.d.b).

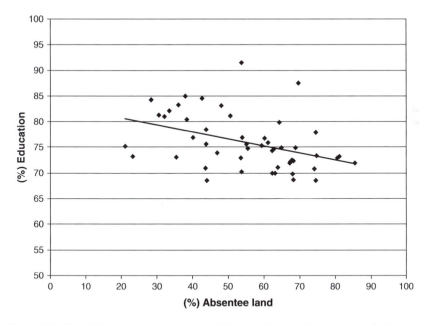

Figure 9.3 Correlation between percentage of absentee land and percentage of Alabama residents 25 years and above with at least a high school education

Source: US Census Bureau (n.d.b).

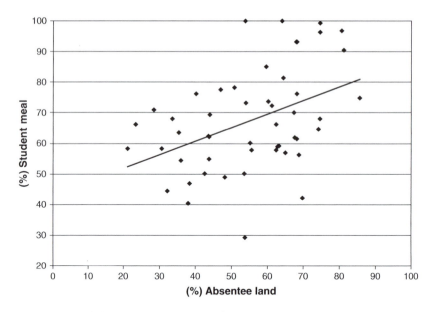

Figure 9.4 Correlation between percentage of absentee land and percentage of public
school students on free or subsidized meals in Alabama

Source: Alabama State Department of Education (n.d.).

provide statistical evidence of causal factors, these findings tend to give support
to hypothesized relationships. A weaker correlation was found between total
absentee land ownership and funding for public schools and the results were not
statistically significant (Figure 9.5). In the case of this variable, there were several outlying cases where counties with significant absentee owned land invested
heavily in their public schools. There were ten counties where per student funding was over $1,600, five of which were metropolitan counties, four were
micropolitan counties, and only one was a non-metro county. At $2,368 per
student, metropolitan Shelby County had the highest level of support of any
county public school system. Metropolitan and micropolitan counties all have
farm and forest land, but the degree of dependence in the local economy on agriculture and forestry is lower because the economies of these counties are more
diversified. Correlations were not statistically significant when we conducted
separate analyses of absentee owners who lived in Alabama and those who lived
elsewhere.

Overall, we found that more than half of all forest and agricultural land in the
fifty counties that we studied is owned by absentee land owners, including owners who live outside Alabama. We found a negative correlation between absentee
ownership and per capita income and educational attainment, and a positive correlation with the percentage of public school children receiving free or reduced
price meals.

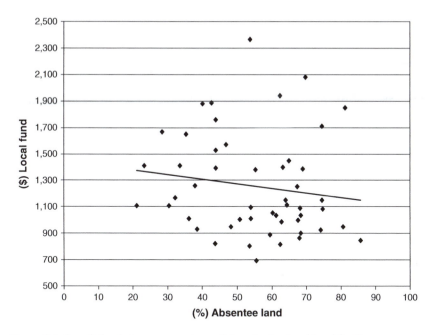

Figure 9.5 Correlation between percentage of absentee land and local funding per student in public schools

Source: Alabama State Department of Education (n.d.).

Discussion

Absentee ownership is not unusual or wrong. People move, perhaps intending to return, and hold onto a family home or piece of property. Others invest in a retirement property. Absentee ownership may become a problem, however, when it becomes a dominant presence in the local economy. Large numbers of absentee land owners may adversely affect the socio-economic well-being of a region because much of the flow of income from the land is likely to be drained away from the local economy. Money spent on labor and money paid in property taxes would be the primary flow of revenue into the local economy from absentee owners. In the case of forestry, there is little local labor involved in most years while the trees are growing, and most of the labor associated with planting trees comes from migrant workers (McDaniel and Casanova 2003). Harvesting is highly mechanized and employs a crew of maybe five individuals for a few days. Depending on the type of crop, agriculture generates more employment on an annual basis, but this sector also is highly mechanized.

The second stream of income into the local economy from absentee owned land comes in the form of property taxes, which are a mainstay of county and municipal governments and school systems. Where a high proportion of the land is absentee owned, one of the few tools left to local governments to ensure some benefit from the land remains available to the local economy is the property tax system. Property taxes contribute to local wealth generation through supporting human capital formation by funding public schools. They also contribute towards improving built capital in the form of roads, bridges, sewer and water systems, and towards social capital by supporting social services as well as police and fire protection.

Second, the ties which link absentee owners to the county where their land is located may be less strong than those of local residents whose lives are intimately affected by the quality of local school systems or other social services. As a result, we hypothesize that they may be little interested in increased property taxes to serve these and other local needs. Available literature suggests that corporate owners are unlikely to support property tax increases. The interests of corporate and other large land owners are well represented in the state capital by the Alabama Farmers Federation and the Alabama Forestry Association, and these organizations are effective advocates of low property taxes. Future research on whether different categories of absentee owners would be supportive, opposed, or neutral to increasing property tax to support local education and other services would help confirm or deny the hypothesis that narrow self-interest of absentee owners would lead them not to support increased property taxes.

Alabama is one of the least heavily taxed states in the nation, and property taxes are the lowest in the nation. Low property taxes benefit not only local land owners but also absentee owners, and since absentee owners own more than half of all farm and forest land in the state, much of the benefits of the tax structure are enjoyed by absentee owners, many of whom live outside the state. Based on the foregoing, two important points can be identified: one, income from forest and farm land is drained away from the local and often from the state economy because most of the land is owned by absentee owners; and two, Alabama's property tax structure obstructs the ability of local governments to raise revenues needed to support public schools and other necessary services.

Conclusions

Absentee ownership of forest and farm land in Alabama is negatively correlated with per capita income and educational attainment, and is positively correlated with the percentage of children receiving free or reduced cost meals in public schools. On the basis of these findings, we believe absentee ownership of land represents an obstacle to local wealth generation in rural Alabama. The academic literature on land ownership supports the view that land is an important prerequisite for people-based wealth creation. Ownership of land also provides personal independence and satisfaction for the present, and security for the future, including for the next generation. Ownership of land determines the right to decide how a piece of land will be used which in turn determines employment and income opportunities associated with land use.

This study revealed the considerable difficulties involved in gaining access to data necessary to understand who owns forest and farm land in Alabama. The question is an important one for understanding wealth generation not only in Alabama but in rural America as a whole. The Alabama case is unusual in that the state's property taxes are the lowest in the nation, limiting the revenue available to local governments to support creation of human capital or physical infrastructure supportive of local wealth generation. We do not know if Alabama is unique in the South or the nation when it comes to absentee ownership of forest or farm land. The reason we do not know is that the data are not easily available. In a digital age, there is no reason why county-level public tax records are not freely available in standardized format through state agencies, allowing for cross-state comparisons of ownership patterns and examination of how ownership of land affects wealth creation.

Who owns the land is a matter of fundamental importance to questions of wealth creation and retention, particularly in rural areas where agriculture and forestry represent the economic basis for personal and community stability. Understanding the nature of land ownership provides local and state governments with information important to designing appropriate tax policies that support improvements in public education and infrastructural improvements. The difficulty we found in collecting data on land ownership illustrates a serious obstacle that researchers have in addressing this need. We believe the USDA should take the lead in developing and maintaining a database on land ownership that would be publicly available to researchers and other government agencies.

References

Alabama Code Sec. 40-7-25.1. Online. Available at: <http://codes.lp.findlaw.com/alcode/40/7/1/40-7-25.1> (accessed 23 December 2012).

Alabama State Department of Education (n.d.) *Annual Report 2009–2010*. Online. Available at: <https://www.alsde.edu/home/Reports/SDEAnnualReports.aspx> (accessed 2 April 2011).

Appalachia Land Ownership Task Force (1983) *Who Owns Appalachia? Landownership and Its Impact*, Lexington, KY: University Press of Kentucky.

Archibald, J. and J. Hansen. (2003) "Land is power, and most who wield it are outsiders", *Birmingham News*, 12 October, 2003.

Bailey, C., P. Sinclair, J. Bliss, and K. Perez (1996) "Segmented labor markets in Alabama's pulp and paper industry", *Rural Sociology*, 61(3): 474–95.

Bain, N.R. (1984) "Nonresident land ownership: a potential factor in rural change", *Land Use Policy*, 1(1): 64–71.

Birch, T.W., D.G. Lewis, and H.F. Kaiser (1978) *The Private Forest Landowners of the United States*, Resource Bulletin WO–1, Washington, DC: USDA Forest Service.

Bliss, J. and C. Bailey (2005) "Pulp, paper, and poverty: forest-based rural development in Alabama, 1950–2000", in R. Lee and D. Field (eds.), *Communities and Forests: Where People Meet the Land*, Corvallis: Oregon State University Press.

Bliss, J.C., M.L. Sisock, and T.W. Birch (1998a) "Ownership matters: forestland concentration in rural Alabama", *Society and Natural Resources*, 11: 401–10.

Bliss, J.C., T.L. Walkingstick, and C. Bailey (1998b) "Development or dependency? Sustaining Alabama's forest communities", *Journal of Forestry*, 96(3): 24–30.

Bliss, J.C., E. Kelly, J. Abrams, C. Bailey, and J. Dyer (2010) "Disintegration of the U.S. industrial forest estate: dynamics, trajectories, and questions", *Small-scale Forestry*, 9: 53–66.

Deininger, K. and K. Michael (2003) "Land policy, poverty alleviation and sustainable rural development", *Agriculture and Rural Development*, 10(2): 44–7.

Dudenhefer, P. (1993) "Poverty in the rural United States", *Focus*, 15(1): 37–45.

Flick, W.A., S.W. Krietemeyer, and C.A. Hickman (1989) *Current-Use Assessment in Alabama*, Bulletin 600, August 2009, Auburn, AL: Alabama Agricultural Experiment Station.

Flora, C. and J. Flora, with S. Fey (2013) *Rural Communities; Legacy & Change*, 4th edn, Boulder, CO: Westview Press.

Flynt, W. (2004) *Alabama in the Twentieth Century*, Tuscaloosa: University of Alabama Press.

Gaventa, J. (1980) *Power and Powerlessness; Quiescence and Rebellion in an Appalachian Valley*, Urbana: University of Illinois Press.

Gaventa, J. (1998) "The political economy of land tenure: Appalachia and the Southeast", in H.M. Jacobs (ed.), *Who Owns America? Social Conflict over Property Rights*, Madison: University of Wisconsin Press.

Gaventa, J. and B. Horton (1984) "Land ownership and land reform in Appalachia", in C.C. Geisler and F.J. Popper (eds.), *Land Reform, American Style*, Totowa, NJ: Rowman & Allenhead.

Geisler, C. (1995) "Land and poverty in the United States: insights and oversights", *Land Economics*, 71(1): 16–34.

Goldschmidt, W. (1978) *As You Sow*, Montclair, NJ: Allanheld, Osmun and Co.

Goodstein, E. (1989) "Landownership, development and poverty in southern Appalachia", *Journal of Developing Areas*, 23(4): 519–34.

Green, G.P. (1985) "Large-scale farming and the quality of life in rural communities: further specification of the Goldschmidt Hypothesis", *Rural Sociology*, 50(2): 262–74.

Gunnoe, A. and P. Gellert (2011) "Financialization, shareholder value, and the transformation of timberland ownership in the US", *Critical Sociology*, 37(3): 265–84.

Hamill, S.P. (2002) "An argument for tax reform based on Judeo-Christian ethics", *Alabama Law Review*, 54(1): 1–112.

Hartsell, A.J. and M.J. Brown (2002) *Forest Statistics for Alabama, 2000*. Research Bulletin SRS–67, Ashville, NC: Southern Research Station, USDA Forest Service.

Heasley, L. and R.P. Guries (1998) "Forest tenure and cultural landscapes: environmental histories in the Kickapoo Valley", in H.M. Jacobs (ed.), *Who Owns America? Social Conflict over Property Rights*, Madison: University of Wisconsin Press.

Horton, B.D. (1993) "The Appalachia land ownership study: research and citizen action in Appalachia", in P. Park, M.B. Miller, B. Hall, and T. Jackson (eds.), *Voice of Change: Participatory Research in the United States and Canada*, Toronto: Ontario Institute for Studies in Education.

Howze, G., L. Robinson, and J.F. Norton (2003) "Historical analysis of timber dependency in Alabama", *Southern Rural Sociology*, 19(2): 1–39.

Jacobs, M. (1998) "Who owns America", in H.M. Jacobs (ed.), *Who Owns America? Social Conflict over Property Rights*, Madison: University of Wisconsin Press.

Joshi, M.L., J.C. Bliss, C. Bailey, L.J. Teeter, and K.J. Ward (2000) "Investing in industry, under-investing in human capital: forest-based rural development in Alabama", *Society & Natural Resources*, 13(4): 291–319.

Kennealy, P., V. Hartarska, C. Bailey, and M. Dubois (2007) "Timberland ownership and social well-being in the South", paper presented at the 2007 meetings of the Rural Sociological Society, San Jose, California, August.

Lobao, L.M., M.D. Schulman, and L.E. Swanson (1993) "Still going strong: recent debates on the Goldschmidt Hypothesis", *Rural Sociology*, 58(2): 277–88.

Lynch et al. vs. The State of Alabama, Civil Action No. 08-S–450-NE (2011) U.S. District Court, Northern District of Alabama.

McDaniel, J. and V. Casanova (2003) "Pines in lines: tree planting, H2B guest workers, and rural poverty in Alabama", *Southern Rural Sociology*, 19(1): 73–96.

Molotch, H. (1976) "The city as a growth machine: towards a political economy of place", *American Journal of Sociology*, 82(2): 309–32.

Nelson, W.E. (1978) "Black political power and the decline of black land ownership", *Review of Black Political Economy*, 8(3): 253–65.

PARCA (The Public Affairs Research Council of Alabama) (2009) *A Progress Report on Research Aimed at Improving State and Local Governments*, Birmingham, AL: PARCA. Online. Available at: <http://parca.samford.edu/PARCA2/newsletters/fall2009.pdf> (accessed 20 June 2011).

Park, J.T., A.P. Turnbull, and H.R. Turnbull (2002) "Impacts of poverty on quality of life in families of children with disabilities", *Exceptional Children*, 68(2): 151–70.

RUPRI (Rural Policy Research Institute) (2007) *Demographic and Economic Profile, Alabama*, updated January 2007, Columbia, MO: Rural Policy Research Institute. Online. Available at: <http://www.rupri.org/Forms/Alabama.pdf> (accessed 3 February 2012).

Scott. S.L. (2012) "What difference did it make? The Appalachian land ownership study after twenty-five years", in S. McSpirit, L. Faltraco, and C. Bailey (eds.), *Confronting Ecological Crisis in Appalachia and the South*, Lexington, KY: University Press of Kentucky.

Shaffer, R.M. and G.S. Meade (1997) "Absentee forest landowners in Virginia", *Virginia Journal of Science*, 48(3): 219–24.

Sherman, J. (2009) *Those Who Work, Those Who Don't; Poverty, Morality, and Family in Rural America*, Minneapolis, MN: University of Minnesota Press.

Sisock, M.L. (1998) "Unequal shares: forest land concentration and well-being in rural Alabama", unpublished MS thesis, Auburn University.

Smith, W.B., P.D. Miles, J.S. Vissage, and S.A. Pugh (2004) *Forest Resources of the United States, 2002*, GTR-NC–241, St. Paul, MN: North Central Research Station, USDA Forest Service.

US Census Bureau (n.d.a) *American Community Survey, 2006–2010*, 5-year estimates, poverty status for the past 12 months, Table S1701. Online. Available at: <http://factfinder2.census.gov/faces/tableservices/jsf/pages/productview.xhtml?pid=ACS_10_5YR_S1701&prodType=table> (accessed 14 September 2012).

US Census Bureau (n.d.b) American Community Survey, 2005–2009. Online. Available at: <http://censtats.census.gov/usa/usa.shtml> (accessed 12 April 2011).

USDA (n.d.) *Alabama Agricultural Statistics, 2008*, Bulletin 50, Montgomery, AL: National Agricultural Statistics Service, U.S. Department of Agriculture.

White, D. (2012) "Support in Alabama House for tax increase proposal wilts under lobbying effort", *Birmingham News*, 1. Online. Available at: <http://blog.al.com/spotnews/2012/03/support_for_tax_increase_propo.html> (accessed 23 December 2012).

Williams, J.A. (2002) *Appalachia: A History*, Chapel Hill, NC: University of North Carolina Press.

Zabawa, R. (1991) "The black farmer and land in south-central Alabama: strategies to preserve a scarce resource", *Human Ecology*, 19(1): 61–81.

Part III

Strategies for rural wealth creation

10 Strategies for rural wealth creation

A progression of thinking through ideas and concepts

Steven C. Deller

Introduction

Wealth creation at the community level is a complex undertaking on multiple levels. To better understand different strategic approaches to wealth creation, it is imperative to understand the progression of our thinking surrounding the enhancement of local well-being from economic growth, economic development, and community development to community economic development and now to rural wealth creation. I accomplish this by reviewing how we came to where we are related to community economic development, then move on to how the wealth creation framework outlined by Pender and Ratner in Chapter 2 and Johnson et al. in Chapter 3 is one approach to place structure on the issues and potential strategies that can be implemented at the community level.

Unfortunately, there is no commonly accepted definition of community economic development upon which practitioners and academics agree. The lack of a common definition hinders the ability to form a foundation upon which to build policies and strategies. The rural wealth creation framework outlined in this volume could be viewed as building that foundation. Second, rural communities are extremely heterogeneous and any given strategy that may work in one community may not work in another. Third, the outcome objectives vary not only across rural communities but also over time. During periods of economic decline or stagnation, rural communities are often narrowly focused on job creation. During periods of economic expansion and growth, job creation becomes secondary to other community objectives such as environmental protection or preservation of community characteristics. Fourth, the planning horizon for community economic development efforts can also vary across rural communities and over time. Many rural communities tend to be more reactive to community crisis, whether it is an economic or another type of crisis. As such, many rural communities tend to have very short reactive planning horizons, seeking immediate solutions to an immediate crisis, with few taking a longer-term proactive view. Such heterogeneity across communities, over time and planning horizons, can make understanding rural wealth creation a moving target for the community, practitioners, and academics.

As Bhattacharyya (2004) notes, many practitioners, as well as academics, can call themselves community developers because the field is "unfenced" and encompasses so many potential efforts. Phillips and Pittman (2009, p. 3) concur, noting that "[u]nlike mathematics or physics where terms are scientifically derived and rigorously defined, community development has evolved with many different connotations". In essence, community development, as well as community economic development, has become all things to all people, thus making it difficult as both a field of practice and an area of study.

Despite this vagueness, there are several recurring themes that can help practitioners, policy makers, and academics think through policies and strategies. First, community development is a forward-looking process, as opposed to "putting out fires" or reacting to a community crisis. Second, citizen involvement at the grassroots level is necessary to ensure citizen solutions. As argued by Daley and Marsiglia (2001), Gaunt (1998), Sharp and Flora (1999), and Sullivan (2004), citizen involvement is essential for local democracy. Local knowledge embodied in the citizenry can help inform issue identification and strategies to affect change. Citizen involvement also helps to promote community "buy-in" and the sustainability of community development efforts. Third, processes are educational, drawing on both internal (i.e., local knowledge) and external resources. Fourth, the outcomes tend to take a holistic view and aim to enhance community vitality, well-being, and quality of life. Fifth, community development embraces change within the community and these changes can range from what appears to be subtle to substantial.[1]

Definitions of economic development tend to be equally diverse. Some focus on increasing flows of economic activity, such as employment, income, or tax collections; others focus on improved indicators of well-being, such as increased consumption of material goods or improvements in health. Still others focus on increases in wealth, broadly defined. As an example of a definition focused on economic activity, Haider (1986, p. 452) argued that "[t]he moral imperative of economic development is to create jobs". In a similar vein, the American Economic Development Council suggested that economic development involves creating wealth, but emphasized expanding job opportunities and the tax base as the objectives:

> [Economic development is] the process of *creating wealth* through the mobilization of human, financial, capital, physical and natural resources to generate marketable goods and services. The economic developer's role is to influence the process for the benefit of the community through *expanding job opportunities and the tax base.*
>
> (AEDC 1984, p. 18, italics added)

The historical perception of wealth creation requires innovation, the discovery of more productive uses of resources, and creating more of the things that people value (Vaughan et al. 1984, pp. 1, 23). More recently, Malizia and Feser (1999, p. 15) suggested that "[a] more logical definition of economic development ... would consider wealth creation more important than job creation, or alternatively job creation as a means to create wealth". Similarly, Blakely and Leigh (2010, p. 73) argued that the "traditional and most widely referenced definition of economic development has long been that of wealth creation". By contrast, Phillips and Pittman (2009) suggested that more current thinking defines economic development as an outcome and/or process but with a focus on growing businesses, creating jobs, increasing income and standards of living, combining considerations of increasing flows of economic activity and improvements in well-being. Sustainably improving well-being generally requires increasing wealth, broadly defined (Arrow et al. 2010), so these definitions do not necessarily conflict.

Shaffer et al. (2004, 2006) and Phillips and Pittman (2009) suggested that the notions of community development and economic development be merged into a broader notion of community economic development.

> Economic development theory and policy have tended to focus narrowly on the traditional factors of production and how they are best allocated in a spatial world. We argue that community economic development must be broader than simply worrying about land, labor and capital. This broader dimension includes public capital, technology and innovation, society and culture, institutions, and the decision-making capacity of the community.
>
> (Shaffer et al. 2006, p. 64)

Shaffer et al. (2006, p. 72) emphasized that community economic development "is about increasing community wealth, both monetary and nonmonetary". Hence, broad-based wealth creation is not a new concept but one that has already been incorporated into community economic development thinking.

Historically, community development has focused on community capitals such as social and political capitals whereas economic development has focused on physical, financial, and human capitals. By blending the two, a more holistic approach to building wealth in the community is possible. As argued by Pender and Ratner in Chapter 2 the different forms of community capitals are inherently interconnected and interdependent to the whole of the community system. To focus on one type of capital without accounting for all types of capital results in a piecemeal and incomplete set of strategies. Effective wealth creation strategies aimed at improving the well-being of the community require a systems-thinking approach.

The rural wealth creation framework outlined in this book provides such a systems-thinking approach, drawing and building upon the notions of community economic development as articulated by Shaffer and his colleagues and Phillips and Pittman (2009). In this framework, particular focus is placed upon understanding and measuring the multiple kinds of wealth that determine the prospects for community economic development, the interactions among different types of wealth, the process of creating different types of wealth, and how wealth creation depends upon the local context. This framework offers an elaboration of and emphasis on particular features of community economic development analysis related to multiple types of wealth and wealth creation.

When using the systems-thinking approach embodied in the rural wealth creation framework, the practitioner can more readily address a fundamental issue that is often overlooked: is this community ready to undertake meaningful economic development efforts? Effective economic development requires that certain local institutions and capacities (or different types of community capitals) are in place and functional. The systems-thinking approach to rural wealth creation helps communities think about their assets and how to invest in those assets (i.e., create rural wealth) to improve the well-being of the community. Within this framework the array of potential strategies becomes much more diverse and robust.

Rural wealth creation, as outlined in this book, attempts more explicitly to quantify capitals in all forms and understand their relationships with economic output (growth), distribution (household income types, spatial), and utility to or well-being of residents. Perhaps more importantly, rural wealth creation outlines a systems-thinking approach that helps us understand the production process of each of the forms of capital, how capital can be transformed from one form to another (Johnson et al.'s notion of stock to flow to stock outlined in Chapter 3), including notions of depreciations of capitals, and how capitals are combined at the community or regional level to generate a desired outcome. The rural wealth creation systems approach helps us understand how there are "interactive" and "multiplicative" effects on how capitals can be jointly invested. This allows us to think about the tradeoffs, both benefits and costs, to various forms of capital for a desired outcome. Wealth creation also makes explicit the notions of privately (people-based) and publicly (place-based) owned capitals and the nature of the policies required to make intelligent investments to achieve the desired outcomes.

A historical backdrop to thinking about strategies[2]

To better appreciate the range of strategies that rural communities can undertake in wealth creation it is imperative to understand notions of community economic development within the US historical context. In a detailed review of subnational US economic development, Eisinger (1988) suggests that most policies have been "supply-sided". In other words, most policies or strategies have been aimed at promoting business investment (physical capital) in the name of job creation. Other than perhaps human capital, all other forms of capital were ignored and/or assumed to be given. Using traditional neoclassical firm location approaches, communities aimed to improve their "business climates" by narrowly focusing on lowering costs to prospective firms. This would include low taxes, limited regulations, and an economical labor force. Through the Mississippi Balance Agriculture with Industry (BAWI) Act, the first "modern" attempt to spur economic growth at the height of the Great Depression, Mississippi promoted itself as a low-cost alternative location to manufacturing firms located in the Northeastern states. Advancing the idea of cheap labor, land, and taxes, Mississippi was successful in recruiting many Northeastern manufacturing firms. The relative success of the BAWI Act at the time set the stage for state and local governments to promote economic growth through a positive business climate (i.e., low costs) with a focus on manufacturing. This type of thinking behind state and local economic policies is still prevalent today.

As noted by Malizia and Feser (1999), economic development as a field of study did not come into being until after World War II. Phillips and Pittman (2009) also trace the origins of modern community development to post World War II reconstruction efforts to help war-torn countries and less developed counties. Several factors came together during the twenty years from about 1930 to about 1950. The Great Depression raised serious questions about the robustness, resilience, and stability of unfettered capitalism. The apparent success of Soviet central planning as well as the success of the US Marshall Plan in Germany and the rapid rebuilding of Japan also challenged faith in a pure market-based economy. In addition, the newly independent India developed a comprehensive plan for economic growth and development that motivated many other former colonies to become more proactive in economic growth and development.

From a federal perspective, community economic development efforts since World War II have focused heavily on urban renewal and have emphasized housing. Title I of the 1949 Housing Act and the 1959 Housing Act increased fiscal resources and explicitly opened a loophole to allow resources to be used for broader urban redevelopment efforts. Many of the programs made available in the Housing Acts along with other miscellaneous programs were combined into community block grants through the 1974 Housing and Community Development Act. In 1953, the federal government established the Small Business Administration (SBA) with the central mission of helping to promote small business development through counseling, loans and loan guarantees, and grants. Unlike most other federal programs of the time, the SBA was not intended to provide support to state and local economic development efforts but rather to provide services directly to small businesses.

The Economic Development Administration (EDA) was established by the Public Works and Commerce Development Act of 1965 with the stated mission "to lead the federal economic development agenda by promoting innovation and competitiveness, preparing American regions for growth and success in the worldwide economy". This is accomplished primarily through the use of federal dollars to support infrastructure investments (Title I); grants, loans, and loan guarantees for industry (Title II); aid in planning at the regional and local level (Title III); and special grants to local communities for economic readjustment in response to economic emergencies such as the closure of a major employer (Title IV).

The US Department of Agriculture (USDA) has been designated as the lead federal agency responsible for advocating and administering programs in rural areas (Honadle 2001, 2011). Historically, much of this policy has been focused on promoting and stabilizing the agricultural sector, because agriculture was considered the economic base of rural areas. While this was perhaps true before World War II, most rural areas outside the Central Plains have now diversified into manufacturing, tourism and recreation, and service-based industries. Federal rural development policy has evolved over time to include nonagricultural programs, covering housing, community development, nonagricultural businesses, and public utilities (Roth et al. 2002).

Honadle (2001, 2011) and Shaffer (2001) observe that, outside of farm support programs, rural development policy has also been fragmented and piecemeal. Part of this is due to the vaguely worded Rural Development Act of 1972, which required the President to form a national rural development policy, and charged the USDA with implementing any subsequent policies. Each administration has either ignored the mandate, such as the Reagan Administration, or embraced the challenge with initiatives, such as the first Bush Administration, with its National Rural Development Partnerships. Many observers believe that the enormous diversity of rural America continues to pose profound challenges to formulating a coherent national rural policy. The many interests in rural areas are simply too diverse to be able to rally stakeholders around a single and effective policy.

Eisinger (1995) eloquently argued that the political structure of the US creates strong incentives to take a very short-term view of economic development policies. There is a strong disincentive to embrace policies of political rivals, such as the former president or governor. There are also strong incentives to embrace policies that have short-term immediate political payoffs, such as the recruitment of a major employer. This view is also supported by the growth machine theory offered by Molotch (1976) and Logan and Molotch (2005), which argues that economic development policies are driven by those who are most likely to gain from short-term economic growth, such as real estate developers. The environment that Eisenger paints suggests that effective and sustainable community economic development must take place at the local or community level. However, local policies that do not garner media headlines but may have economic success in the long term, such as entrepreneurship or the expansion of smaller firms, are not always supported politically.

Waves of development policy

First wave thinking, which today is widely referred to as industry recruitment or "smokestack chasing", is dominated by four central concepts: (1) most job creation is from large firms, thus large firms receive most of the attention; (2) these large firms seek out low-cost alternatives to locate new facilities; (3) export base theory provides the foundation for economic growth, thus growth hinges on promoting industries that produce exportable goods and/or services; and (4) political pressures promote policies that garner short-term economic growth for political gains. But our thinking has evolved over time, and coupled with fundamental changes in the nature of the economy, has resulted in significant challenges to these four central concepts.

Within the traditional context of community economic development, much of this refocusing of our thinking can be traced to the work of Birch (1979, 1987). Birch asked a very simple question: does economic growth flow from large or small firms? His conclusion pointed to small firms. This result, coupled with new thinking about the role of innovation in economic growth, returned the work of Schumpeter (1942, 1961) and the role of the entrepreneur in creative destruction to the forefront. More recently, Beck et al. (2003), Aquilina et al. (2006), Shaffer (2002, 2006), and Deller (2010) laid out the rationale for the promotion of small businesses as an economic strategy. Advocates argue that small businesses stimulate competition and entrepreneurship which, in turn, enhances efficiency, innovation, and aggregate productivity growth. Acs and Audretsch (1990, 1993) maintain that in manufacturing, the development of small-scale, flexible production technologies has enabled small firms to flourish. Because of the small scale of operation, smaller businesses are more flexible and able to adapt to rapidly changing environments. Indeed, much of the recent resurgence in US manufacturing has been with smaller or medium scale firms and has forced economic development practitioners to rethink the role of manufacturing. Further, as sources of experimentation and innovation, small firms play an integral role in the renewal processes (Robbins et al. 2000). This "churning" is at the theoretical heart of the rationale as to why small businesses are vital to the economic welfare of the community and larger economy (Headd 1998).

This fundamental shift in thinking caused many economic development policy makers and practitioners to question not only the effectiveness of industrial recruitment efforts but also the role of small businesses in their own portfolio of policies. Many development agencies re-evaluated their efforts and found that they could be more efficient and effective if they focused on the small- to medium-sized businesses that were already in their communities. As a result of this rethinking, the second wave of economic development strategies came into vogue, emphasizing homegrown economic activity (expansion and retention). Activities associated with these types of strategies were increasing investment capital for local firms, development of incubators, technical assistance for local firms, revolving loan funds, and tax increment financing. But, as noted by Eisinger (1995), the political pressures embodied in growth machine theory create barriers to pursuit of small business development strategies.

Third-wave economic development strategies emphasize public-private partnerships in an attempt to broaden the "responsibility" of economic development beyond a small handful of people. In third-wave strategies, government agencies and economic development organizations worry about creating networks to leverage capital, investing in human resources, and high-skilled and well-paying jobs. Reasons for emphasizing third-wave development strategies are that the delivery of economic development services was fragmented, disjointed, and at times held hostage by politicians and bureaucrats. Third-wave strategies attempt to integrate different programs into a coherent set of policies and strategies. Another key feature of third-wave strategies is to allow for differentiation instead of assuming that *one-size-fits-all* strategies were sufficient. Still other reasons for third-wave strategies include issues of scale, in particular the concept of agglomeration economies. The notion of agglomeration economies within a spatial world is at the core of Porter's (1990, 1996, 2000) approach to economic cluster development, and suggests that communities should form regional cooperative agreements as opposed to engaging in direct competition, as emphasized by first-wave thinking.

The concept of rural wealth creation is a natural extension of the second and third wave of economic development thinking and policies. Here a longer-term, more holistic approach is taken to thinking about the community, the local economy, and policies or strategies that can affect change. This approach is embodied in third-wave thinking, particularly if a Porter-type cluster framework is employed. Here all parts of the puzzle are on the table. While community economic development strategies may be narrowly defined and focused on certain elements of the puzzle, the strategies are implemented in light of the whole system or puzzle. If, for example, the community focuses its energies on small business consulting and education as a strategy, this is done with the understanding that all forms of community capitals are in play and affected.

Also embodied in the third wave of community economic development is the realization that a truly interdisciplinary approach to thinking about the problem and potential strategies is required. Economists, for example, bring certain insights to the table and can help shed light on certain aspects of the puzzle, but cannot provide all the answers or policy insights. Community cultural dynamics (a form of capital) matter (i.e., sociology), as does the institutional decision-making structure (i.e., sociology and political science) and the flexibility afforded local communities through state and federal laws (i.e., political science). As noted in the introductory comments, the study and practice of community economic development is truly interdisciplinary, and the rural wealth creation framework helps place that interdisciplinary approach into perspective and into a policy construct.

The difficulty with this systems approach is that it can become overwhelming and confusing. In the 1960s, there was a movement within community development to adopt a systems approach. This was driven primarily by the renewed interest in environmental protection. By the 1970s, the holistic approach had been abandoned as being too complex and cumbersome. Elected officials and concerned citizens were generally overwhelmed and, in essence, threw their hands up in frustration. The current systems-thinking approach recognizes that one cannot tackle the whole of the system at once, but must compartmentalize components within the context of the whole. Tackling a jigsaw puzzle as a whole does not work; one must work in sections moving towards the complete puzzle. The key is to understand and appreciate that each individual part is related to all other parts of the community system. The rural wealth creation framework allows us to look at individual parts within the context of the whole system.

Lessons for rural wealth creation strategies

A community consciously attempting to alter its socio-economic situation can pursue a comprehensive strategy, or it can simply implement a collection of programs that may or may not be cumulative or even effective in achieving stated objectives (Shaffer et al. 2004). A collection of programs does not make a policy or strategy. Vaughan and Bearse suggest:

> strategic choices bear a positive integral and consistent relationship to the attainment of some objective. The set of actions must possess synergy: that is, have positive, cumulative, and mutually reinforcing effects on the attainment of objectives. Thus, if two actions are both chosen as part of a strategic set, each will reinforce, or at least not diminish, the effects of the other. Timing and phasing of actions are also important. Strategy is not merely the choice of actions but the ordering of each action to best achieve one's aim.
> (Vaughan and Bearse 1981, p. 308)

Bryson (1990) defines a strategy as a pattern of purposes, policies, programs, actions, decisions, or resource allocations that define what an organization (or community) is, what it does, and why it does it. A pattern means that there is some consistency, that this is not just a one-shot event, and that it has an action component. Rural wealth creation requires a continuous process where a community learns from its mistakes and builds on it successes. Defining the "who and what" of rural wealth creation essentially says that strategies define the organization or community. Why a community "does what it does" is really a statement about the values the community or organization possesses.

This latter point is key because it re-emphasizes two fundamental issues: (1) no two rural communities are exactly alike; and (2) no two rural communities have the same vision for their future. Each community varies with the levels of wealth at its disposal. One community may find it necessary to invest in one type of wealth before it can move to the next level, while another may find it has deficiencies in other types of wealth. In an edited volume on community visioning programs by Walzer (1996), the notion of community "success" was at the center of a vigorous discussion. The question was simple: how does one know if the community is successful in its efforts and is there a set of indicators that can quantify that success? Because no two communities are exactly alike, what might be considered a success in one might be a failure in another. For example, getting multiple "warring factions" within the community together in the same room without having to call the sheriff could be a huge success. The type of wealth required of such a community and the corresponding strategies to build that wealth are different from the situation in another community that has well-functioning public and civic engagement. As argued by Ratner and Levy (Chapter 6), the rural wealth creation framework gives us the structure required to move forward in terms of measuring and assessing changes over time.

A necessary condition for creating and implementing a set of rural wealth creation strategies is a clear and widely agreed upon vision of the community. More formally, a strategy statement must include: (1) the community's goals and objectives; (2) the role of local and nonlocal actors/agencies; (3) explicit recognition of the tradeoffs among community goals; and (4) sources and uses of political and technical/professional input. The process of establishing a vision for the community helps delineate priorities, such as identifying key issues and target groups. Adopting a rural wealth creation framework can assist in the allocation of resources by eliminating conflicts and linking apparently unrelated efforts. Within the systems approach embodied in rural wealth creation, strategies aimed at building one type of wealth will influence other types of wealth. A wealth creation strategy can yield an organizational structure and response system that ensures knowledge of who is doing what and when, and that links the community with nonlocal public and private resources. Another reason is that a strategy provides a mechanism to guide the small, incremental events that accumulate into a major event or effort. Thus, a strategy links separate efforts within the context of a conceptual understanding of rural wealth creation, and permits the community to organize actions and resources to achieve objectives more efficiently. Finally, developing strategies can help a community separate symptoms from the true underlying problems.

Often people are more interested in short-term projects than in long-term strategies. Both are important. The long-term strategies provide the overarching direction for the community. The short-term projects provide tangible feedback that local people need to stick with the long-term strategy. Without a long-term strategy within which short-term projects fit, the projects might conflict with each other or not add up to an effective development program. One could think of the long-term strategy as the envelope that collects the short-term projects. For example, a long-term goal or outcome of the community might be downtown revitalization. This goal is achieved through a collection of short-term projects that all fall within a longer-term strategy. One strategy might be to enhance downtown business profitability, and short-term projects might include forming a business association (social capital) and a business improvement district (political capital), using Tax Increment Financing districts for building and infrastructure improvements (physical capital), and focused business counseling and training opportunities (human capital). A simple streetscaping program that improves the visual appeal of the downtown by planting trees (e.g., a form of investing in natural capital) could be a short-term project that is part of a larger long-term strategy.

A critical step in formulating strategy is drawing the distinction between goals and objectives (which define the vision), inputs, outputs, and outcomes. Inputs are the time and efforts of local citizens in undertaking specific projects. Specific projects, such as the creation of a downtown improvement authority, are linked to goals and objectives. If projects are the inputs, the output is enhanced business profitability and the outcome is a revitalized downtown, or, in the extreme, the downtown becomes the heart of the community. Here, through the envelope of a series of short-term projects that make up the long-term strategy, the long-term outcome is a revitalized downtown; inputs are used to complete activities that yield outputs that are aimed at achieving outcomes. Too often attention is focused singly on inputs and outputs, and long-term outcomes are overlooked; or people lose sight of the forest (desired outcomes) for all the trees (specific projects).

The specific strategies that can be put in place to enhance rural wealth creation are as varied as rural communities. Again, no two communities are exactly alike, nor are the long-term visions or desired outcomes identical across communities. But with the wealth creation framework one thinks in terms of the capitals that are at the disposal of the community. This leads to two broad ways of approaching strategies: (1) increase the amount of capitals and (2) use existing capitals differently. Consider specific examples of each in turn.

Increasing the amount of resources available simply means that the community has increased the amount of community capitals available for producing output or facilitating the production of output. This could be local financial institutions making more loans available locally, or an outside business making a local investment, forming a credit union, or establishing a local branch of a community college. It could be building on natural capital to promote recreational activities or retirement migration. It could be expanding cultural capital by organizing community arts fairs, volunteer organizations, sports, recreational, or youth organizations. It could be the creation of social and human capital via a local business association like a chamber of commerce or the creation of a leadership development program. Developing a small business mentoring and/or counseling programs through the chamber of commerce is a form of investing in a focused type of human capital. Creating a welcoming environment for new residents and making schools attractive to young families is another simple approach to investing in community capitals.

Using existing resources differently in traditional economic growth and development generally means that businesses are applying new knowledge and technologies (intellectual capital, in the terminology of Pender and Ratner in Chapter 2). Businesses have found new ways to combine existing capitals to produce greater output per worker. It could also mean that businesses have used existing capitals to produce a new good or service that previously had not been produced locally. In a broader wealth creation framework, it could mean moving from extractive to non-extractive uses of natural resources. For example, it could mean a shift from harvesting forest resources to promoting recreational uses or harvesting in a way that is compatible with recreational uses, including housing development. It could be shifting public resources to promote small business or to help finance young families or retiree in-migration. It could also be how local governments make investments in public services. Communities that are willing to tax themselves to build a new library, expand recreational services, or invest in a simple streetscaping program are not only redirecting resources but also investing in the political capital required to move a community forward. Using resources differently could be as simple as making sure that state and federal elected officials are aware of what the community is doing and are invited to participate in community activities.

This is just a sampling of possible strategies and many of these strategies overlap; one strategy can work toward multiple objectives or outcomes. Because rural communities are heterogeneous, some of these strategies may be inappropriate in particular contexts. For example, if the community already has a high functioning and effective chamber of commerce, energies spent on forming a new business organization may be misdirected. In addition, many of these strategies may not be conducive to the vision or intended outcomes of the community. For example, rural communities that want to become a high-amenity residential area (commuting or retirement) may not want to focus limited resources on the development of an industrial park. Few if any of these strategies are aimed at "hitting a grand slam", as with the short-term thinking of some politicians and key actors in growth machine theory. The community must take the long-term view and look at these strategies as a set of small steps toward a desired long-term outcome. Communities seeking "short-cuts" often face failure or unintended consequences.

Conclusions

Rural wealth creation takes a holistic or systems-thinking approach to improving the lives and well-being of rural residents. Within the context of community economic development, the focus emphasizes a broad concept of development rather than simple growth. A proactive long-term approach is adopted as opposed to short-term reactive policies aimed at addressing some immediate crisis. In the view of Eisinger (1988), communities take on more entrepreneurial characteristics, looking for new opportunities and ways (strategies) to pursue those opportunities, and employing a willingness to try new ideas and learn from mistakes. This may involve communities working independently or making effective partnerships (within and across communities) to achieve those desired outcomes. The rural wealth creation approach emphasizes the need to consider multiple types of wealth, their interactions, and the local context in order to be successful in pursuing community economic development strategies.

Notes

1   Phillips and Pittman (2009) make an interesting distinction between practitioners and academics about what community development is. Practitioners tend to think of community development as outcome-based while academics tend to think in terms of process and the ability of the community to act collectively.
2   This section draws on Deller and Goetz (2009).

References

Acs, Z.J., and Audretsch, D.B. (1990) *The Economics of Small Firms: A European Challenge*, Boston, MA: Kluwer Academic Publishers.
Acs, Z.J., and Audretsch, D.B. (1993) *Small Firms and Entrepreneurship*, Boston, MA: Kluwer Academic Publishers.
American Economic Development Council (AEDC) (1984) *Economic Development Today: A Report to the Profession*, Schiller Park, IL: AEDC.
Aquilina, M., Klump, R., and Pietrobelli, C. (2006) "Factor substitution, average firm size and economic growth", *Small Business Economics*, 26: 203–14.
Arrow, K.J., Dasgupta, P., Goulder, L.H., Mumford, K.J., and Oleson, K. (2010) "Sustainability and the measurement of wealth", NBER Working Paper 16599, Cambridge, MA: National Bureau of Economic Research.

Beck, T., Demirgüç-Kunt, A., and Levine, R. (2003) "Small and medium enterprises, growth and poverty: cross-country evidence", World Bank Policy Research Working Paper 3178, Washington, DC: World Bank.

Bhattacharyya, J. (2004) "Theorizing community development", *Journal of the Community Development Society*, 34(2): 5–34.

Birch, D.L. (1979) *The Job Generation Process: Final Report to Economic Development Administration*, Cambridge, MA: MIT Program on Neighborhood and Regional Change.

Birch, D.L. (1987) *Job Creation in America: How Our Smallest Companies put the Most People to Work*, New York: Free Press.

Blakely, E.J., and Leigh, N.G. (2010) *Planning Local Economic Development: Theory and Practice*, 4th edn, Thousand Oaks, CA: Sage Publications.

Bryson, J.M. (1990) *Strategic Planning for Public and Nonprofit Organizations: A Guide to Strengthening and Sustaining Organizational Achievement*, San Francisco: Josey-Bass.

Daley, J.M., and Marsiglia, F.F. (2001) "Social diversity within nonprofit boards", *Journal of the Community Development Society*, 32(2): 290–309.

Deller, S.C. (2010) "Spatial heterogeneity in the role of microenterprises in economic growth", *Review of Regional Studies*, 40(1): 70–96.

Deller, S.C. and Goetz, S. (2009) "Historical description of economic development policy", in S. Goetz, S. Deller, and T. Harris (eds.), *Targeting Regional Economic Development*, London: Routledge, pp. 17–34.

Eisinger, P. (1988) *The Role of the Entrepreneurial State*, Madison: University of Wisconsin Press.

Eisinger, P. (1995) "State economic development in the 1990s: politics and policy learning", *Economic Development Quarterly*, 9(2): 146–58.

Gaunt, T.P. (1998) "Communication, social networks, and influence in citizen participation", *Journal of the Community Development Society*, 29(2): 276–97.

Haider, D. (1986) "Economic development: changing practices in a changing U.S. economy", *Environment and Planning C: Government and Policy*, 4: 451–69.

Headd, B. (1998) *Small Business Growth by Major Industry, 1988–1995*, Washington, DC: U.S. Small Business Administration, Office of Advocacy.

Honadle, B.W. (2001) "Rural development policy in the United States: beyond the cargo cult mentality", *Journal of Regional Analysis and Policy*, 31(2): 93–108.

Honadle, B.W. (2011) "Rural development policy in the United States: a critical analysis and lessons from the 'still birth' of the Rural Collaborative Investment Program", *Community Development: Journal of the Community Development Society*, 42(1): 56–69.

Logan, J., and Molotch, H. (2005) "The city as a growth machine", in J. Lin and C. Mele (eds.), *Urban Sociology Reader*, London: Routledge, pp. 97–105.

Malizia, E.E., and Feser, E.J. (1999) *Understanding Local Economic Development*, New Brunswick, NJ: Rutgers University.

Molotch, H.L. (1976) "The city as a growth machine: towards a political economy of place", *American Journal of Sociology*, 82(2): 309–32.

Phillips, R., and Pittman, R.H. (2009) "A framework for community and economic development", in R. Phillips and R.H. Pittman (eds.), *An Introduction to Community Development*, New York: Routledge, pp. 3–19.

Porter, M.E. (1990) *The Competitive Advantage of Nations*, New York: Free Press.

Porter, M.E. (1996) "Competitive advantage, agglomeration economies, and regional policy", *International Regional Science Review*, 19(1–2): 85–90.

Porter, M.E. (2000) "Location, competition, and economic development: local clusters in a global economy", *Economic Development Quarterly*, 14(1): 15–34.

Robbins, D.K., Pantuosco, L.J., Parker, D.F., and Fuller, B.K. (2000) "An empirical assessment of the contribution of small business employment to U.S. state economic performance", *Small Business Economics*, 15(4): 293–302.

Roth, D., Effland, A.B.W., and Bowers, D.E. (2002) *Federal Rural Development Policy in the Twentieth Century*, Washington, DC: US Department of Agriculture, Economic Research Service. Online. Available at: <http://www.nal.usda.gov/ric/ricpubs/rural_development_policy.html> (accessed 14 March 2013).

Schumpeter, J.A. (1942) *Capitalism, Socialism & Democracy*, New York: Harper & Row.

Schumpeter, J.A. (1961) *The Theory of Economic Development*, Cambridge, MA: Harvard University Press.

Shaffer, R.E. (2001) "Building a national rural policy and the National Rural Development Partnership", *Journal of Regional Analysis and Policy*, 31(2): 77–91.

Shaffer, R.E., Deller, S.C., and Marcouiller, D.W. (2004) *Community Economics: Linking Theory and Practice*, Oxford: Blackwell.

Shaffer, R.E., Deller, S.C., and Marcouiller, D.W. (2006) "Rethinking community economic development", *Economic Development Quarterly*, 20(1): 59–74.

Shaffer, S. (2002) "Firm size and economic growth", *Economics Letters*, 76: 195–203.

Shaffer, S. (2006) "Establishment size and local employment growth", *Small Business Economics*, 26: 439–54.

Sharp, J.S., and Flora, J.L. (1999) "Entrepreneurial social infrastructure and growth machine characteristics associated with industrial-recruitment and self-development strategies in nonmetropolitan communities", *Journal of the Community Development Society*, 30: 131–53.

Sullivan, D.M. (2004) "Citizen participation in nonprofit economic development organizations", *Journal of the Community Development Society*, 34(2): 58–72.

Vaughan, R.J., and Bearse, P. (1981) "Federal economic development programs: a framework for design and evaluation", in R. Friedman and W. Schweke (eds.), *Expanding the Opportunity to Produce: Revitalizing the American Economy Through New Enterprise Development*, Washington, DC: The Corporation for Enterprise Development, p. 309.

Vaughan R., Pollard, R., and Dyer, B. (1984) *The Wealth of States*, Washington, DC: Council of State Planning Agencies.

Walzer, N. (ed.) (1996) *Community Visioning Programs: Practices and Experiences*, Westport, CT: Praeger.

11 Rural wealth creation and emerging energy industries

Lease and royalty payments to farm households and businesses

Jeremy G. Weber, Jason P. Brown, and John L. Pender[1]

Introduction

In the past decade, energy production has offered new opportunities for wealth creation in many rural areas. Energy from nontraditional sources – especially natural gas from shale and sandstone formations, biomass, and wind energy – account for a growing share of US energy supply. Between 2005 and 2011, more than half of the growth in US primary energy production came from increased natural gas production, and more than one-fourth came from biomass (primarily ethanol) and wind energy production combined.[2] Domestic oil production has also seen an increase as the industry has responded to higher crude oil prices by applying drilling innovations to shale oil formations.

We begin the chapter by discussing the recent development of natural gas and wind energy in rural areas of the United States in light of the conceptual framework for rural wealth creation presented in Chapter 2. We focus on natural gas and wind because they generate payments to households that own land where gas is extracted or wind turbines are placed. The second part of the chapter focuses on the implications of lease and royalty payments from energy companies to farm households and businesses using recent nationally representative data on US farms. We explore several issues that are particularly salient for rural wealth and energy development but that are also concrete examples of broader wealth-related ideas discussed throughout the book.

Emerging energy industries – growth and its causes

Shale gas production has grown rapidly from 2 percent of US natural gas production in 2000 to an estimated 37 percent in 2012 (Mufson 2012). The increase has caused production to reach new historic highs each year since 2007 (EIA 2012). Favorable energy prices in the 2000s and improvements in extractive technology have contributed to the production boom. The refinement of horizontal drilling and hydraulic fracturing ("fracking"), which consists of injecting a mix of water, chemicals, and sand into wells to create fissures in rock formations, has improved the profitability of extraction. Consequently, drilling has expanded across the United States.

State governments have encouraged development to varying degrees, with substantial variation in taxation and regulation of drilling across states (Resources for the Future 2012). Environmental concerns have led the state of New York to place a moratorium on fracking. By contrast, the Pennsylvania legislature has encouraged drilling by not taxing extraction, though it has recently assessed an impact fee on wells. A potentially more important deterrent is the fall in natural gas prices from growth in supply; greater production has already dramatically lowered natural gas prices in the United States (MIT 2011).

From 2007 to 2010, wind energy contributed 36 percent of all new electric generation capacity added to the US power system (Wiser and Bollinger 2011). By 2010, installed wind power capacity could provide more than 5 percent of total electricity supply in thirteen states, with four states above 10 percent (Iowa, Minnesota, North Dakota, and South Dakota).

Supportive policies have spurred growth in wind energy, including the federal production tax credit, the Rural Energy for America Program, state renewable energy portfolio standards, and financial incentives by state and local governments (Bird et al. 2005; Lu et al. 2011). The American Recovery and Reinvestment Act of 2009 also included investment tax credits and grants for community wind investors. Other causes of growth include higher energy prices and public support for renewable energy (ELPC 2009).

Implications for different types of wealth

In a broad sense, extracting natural gas or harnessing wind for electricity involves converting a stock of natural capital into a flow of marketable goods. In addition to wind or gas endowments, the conversion draws upon stocks of multiple types of capital. Focusing on natural gas, extraction draws on human, physical, natural, and even social capital.

Initially, most natural gas workers and supporting firms come from outside the drilling area, especially in areas that have historically produced little gas and therefore have few workers with industry experience. Over time, however, local firms and residents tend to supply more labor and services. In the initial stages of exploration of the Marcellus Shale, roughly 70 percent of gas company employees came from out of state; by 2010 the situation had reversed, with in-state employees accounting for 70 percent (Kelsey et al. 2011).

Large-scale extraction also requires public infrastructure to access drilling sites (public physical capital, water for fracking (natural capital), and treatment and storage options for waste (potentially a mix of physical and natural capital)). Drilling one gas well in shale can involve up to a thousand truckloads of equipment and materials (National Park Service 2009). It also requires between two and ten million gallons of water (Kargbo et al. 2010). Extraction also depends in part on social capital as represented by trust or the lack thereof between residents and the industry. In states such as Texas and Louisiana, which have a long history of energy development, fracking has met little local opposition compared with New York, which does not have such a history.

Converting gas endowments into marketable gas generates payments for labor employed in the industry, for landowners with mineral rights, and for governments through tax revenues. Payments to labor can be substantial. One study found that counties experiencing a boom in gas production in Colorado, Texas, and Wyoming saw wage and salary income increase by $69 million over the growth period (Weber 2012). Extraction also generates billions of dollars in payments to landowners and in tax revenues for state and local governments.

The long-term implications of gas development on local wealth depend on the industry's direct effect on local capital (e.g., roads or air quality) and on how workers, landowners, and government use income from development. The two effects are tightly connected. If saved, income from development will form part of the stock of financial capital that residents or local institutions can channel into other types of capital. The incentive to invest locally, however, depends on how gas development affects the area's physical and natural capital. A decline in property values near drilling areas, which has been observed in some areas, reflects perceived health risks or deterioration of infrastructure, landscape aesthetics, or groundwater quality from drilling (Boxall et al. 2005; Muehlenbachs et al. 2012; Hill 2012). This in turn reduces the incentive for residents to invest locally, for example in residential property development. On the other hand, public revenue generated by production and invested in schools, roads, and public recreational infrastructure can complement and stimulate local private investment. And where gas development has not changed the returns to investment, payment streams may finance greater investment.

Similar to natural gas development, local endowments of several types of wealth are likely to affect and be affected by wind power development. Wind development has principally drawn upon a region's wind resource, land (natural capital), and access to electrical transmission lines (physical capital). Compared with natural gas, wind energy has little effect on natural capital like air and water quality. The interruption of the landscape by wind turbines is probably the most salient disamenity associated with wind energy.

Little is known about the impacts of wind power development on local wealth. A recent econometric study of local economic impacts of wind power development estimated that wind power was associated with about $11,000 of additional annual personal income and 0.5 of additional jobs per megawatt of wind power capacity installed (Brown et al. 2012). Some communities have invested wind dollars in education. One school district in West Texas reported that by the 2018–2019 school year, it will have received about $35 million from a wind farm company (Smith 2011).

In the long term, the eyesore of wind turbines may reduce people's desire to live, visit, or work in the community, in turn affecting migration, commuting flows, and income from tourism, with subsequent potential impacts on property values and tax revenues (Hoen et al. 2009; Heintzelman and Tuttle 2011). Opposition to wind turbines in some areas suggests that some people strongly prefer not to have wind turbines interrupting the horizon. Examples include opposition to proposed off-shore wind turbines in Cape Cod, Massachusetts (Levitz 2012) and to the first community-based wind project in Utah (Hartman et al. 2011).

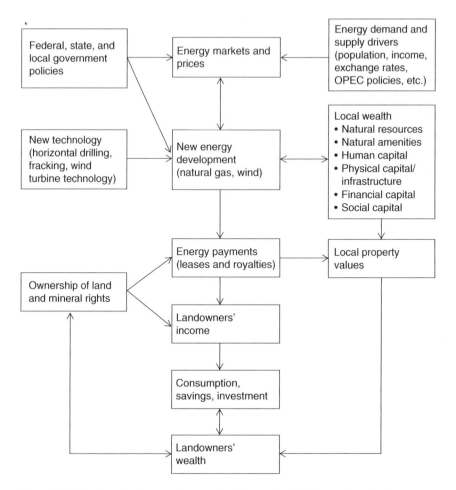

Figure 11.1 Factors affecting rural energy development and its impacts on landowners

The long-term local effects from energy development are unknown and complex. To better understand the complexity, a flow diagram (Figure 11.1) shows the various potential factors and local actors involved with energy development. Market forces, government policies (federal, state, and local), and stocks of local wealth influence energy development. Owners of land and mineral rights receive energy payments, which in turn affect property values. Thus, payments have a direct effect on income and wealth, both of which influence consumption, savings, and investment.

Energy payments to farm households and businesses

As mentioned earlier, natural gas and wind development generate lease and royalty payments to many farm households and businesses. We use "energy payments" to refer to the payments from private energy companies or brokers to owners of surface or mineral rights. For oil and natural gas, the payments represent the conversion of a *stock* of a non-renewable natural resource into cash. For wind the payments represent the conversion of a *flow* of a renewable resource into cash. The differences suggest that wind has a greater potential to support long-term wealth accumulation. Despite their potentially different effect on wealth, we study the two types of payments together, largely because only 49 of the 426 (unweighted) respondent farms with payments were associated with wind. However, in the empirics on land values we estimate the model with and without farms with wind payments.

Typical leases for natural gas are for five years with royalty payments of 12.5 percent of the value of gas removed. Often one-time bonus payments are made to landowners upon signing a lease. Companies drilling in the Marcellus shale in Pennsylvania paid landowners $2 billion in 2008 (Considine et al. 2009). Those drilling in the Haynesville shale in Louisiana reported paying $1.2 billion in 2009 (L.C. Scott and Associates 2009).

Wind leases are more long term at twenty to twenty-five years with different combinations of annual payments ranging between $4,000 and $8,000 per turbine and royalty payments of 3 to 6 percent of gross revenues (Aakre and Haugen 2010). Of course, typical payments can vary over time with market conditions and from landowner to landowner based on bargaining power and parcel attributes.

What households do with the payments will influence the long-term effects of energy development on producing regions. There is no nationwide source of information on energy payments and the households who receive them. However, in 2011 the Agricultural Resource Management Survey (ARMS) – a nationally representative survey of farm businesses and the households who operate them – included for the first time a question on lease and royalty payments from energy activities.[3] Specifically, the question asked for "income from royalties or leases associated with energy production (*e.g. natural gas, oil, and wind turbines*)".

Much of the existing information on rural wealth focuses on farms (Pender et al. 2012). Farm households generally differ from nonfarm rural households, especially in terms of wealth. However, the majority of rural households own little land and are therefore not in a position to receive energy payments. Payments to farms merit attention because they shed some light on payments to landowning households in general. Payments to the two groups likely differ only to the extent that they lease different quantities of land to energy developers and therefore receive different total payments.

Another advantage of looking at farm households is that many of them run a business – a farm. (Admittedly, only 42 percent of farms are labeled a farm business by the USDA in that they have at least $250,000 in sales or the principal operator defines farming as his or her primary occupation.) This allows us to study one dynamic channel through which energy development affects rural wealth – the conversion of natural capital into financial capital (payments), which the farm household may then turn into physical capital (equipment) to improve the profitability of their farm business and their accumulation of wealth. The ARMS is well suited for such an endeavor. Its detailed information on the household of the farm's principal operator, including consumption expenditures and nonfarm assets, liabilities, and income, permit researching household responses to payments. Furthermore, the ARMS is nationally representative, allowing us to draw conclusions about the frequency and magnitude of energy payments to farms in the entire lower 48 states.

In 2011 an estimated 3.4 percent of all farms, roughly 74,000 farms, received lease or royalty payments from energy activities. In line with the magnitude of payments suggested by the previously mentioned studies, payments to farms were economically significant – totaling $2.3 billion. By comparison, 35 percent of farms received some type of farm program payments from the Federal government. However, payments from the single largest farm program, direct payments, only totaled around $5 billion per year under the 2008 Farm Act. From 2008 to 2011, all government payments, including crop insurance and conservation payments, averaged $11.8 billion a year (USDA-ERS 2012a). Thus, energy payments are about half of direct payments and 19 percent of the total Federal government support to farms. Furthermore, the median government payment was $3,642 while the median energy payment was $7,000, with a quarter of farms receiving $25,000 or more (Table 11.1).

The geography of energy payments is also distinct from that of Federal farm program payments. Energy payments are concentrated in the Plains region, as shown in Table 11.2. Farm program payments are highest in the Midwest and

Table 11.1 Payments to farm businesses

Payment level	Percentage of farm businesses
$1–1,000	21.0
$1,001–5,000	26.8
$5,001–25,000	27.7
$25,001–5,0000	9.5
$50,001 or more	15.0
Median payment	7,000
Average payment	30,613

Source: 2011 Agricultural Resource Management Survey, Version 1.

Table 11.2 Energy and government payments by region

Region	Median energy payment	Percentage of farms receiving payments	Percentage of total energy payments	Percentage of total government payments
Atlantic	$4,400	2.4	21.0	11.8
South	$5,000	1.1	2.5	13.9
Midwest	$1,079	2.0	3.8	30.8
Plains	$7,859	8.0	61.5	29.2
West	$13,000	2.5	11.2	14.3

Source: 2011 Agricultural Resource Management Survey, Version 1.

Plains but are more uniformly distributed across regions. Because of the concentration of energy payments in the Plains, many of them go to livestock producers, with roughly half of farms that receive energy payments specializing in raising beef cattle. In contrast, crop farms are more likely to receive farm program payments (White and Hoppe 2012).

The wealth effect of energy payments

There are two main channels through which energy payments and the activities that generate them can affect the wealth of recipient households. First, payments may be saved, in which case they form part of the household's wealth. Second, the capitalization of payments or any amenities or disamenities created by energy development will affect the value of the household's landholdings and therefore their wealth.

The implications of payments and energy activities on rural wealth extend beyond their direct effects on the wealth of recipient households. Consumption of payments or their capitalized value in land will increase the sales of local businesses, to the extent that households consume local goods and services. Households may also expand their farm business if payments allow them to overcome financing constraints. Greater farm business investment would increase the sales of businesses operating locally, thereby increasing employment and income. Prior research has suggested that 50 to 60 percent of farm business expenditures are spent locally (Foltz and Zeuli 2005; Lambert et al. 2009).

We use the 2011 Agricultural Resource Management Survey (ARMS) to explore three empirical questions:

1   How much of each energy payment dollar is consumed?
2   Are payments associated with greater farm investment?
3   Are payments associated with higher land values?

In all the empirical models we take energy payments to be exogenous. The option to lease land for energy developers is likely determined by long-established geological characteristics. It's also unlikely that the farmer would have chosen where to farm based on the potential for energy payments. Leasing land, however, is clearly a choice of the farm operator and may be related to unobserved farm characteristics. This is most likely an issue with payments and land values, since the quality of the land may influence the decision to allow energy development – a possibility whose implications we discuss below.

How much of each energy payment dollar is consumed?

Here we estimate how much of each energy payment dollar received by farm households is consumed in the year received. We assume that households consume out of their current income and wealth, and that they may have different propensities to consume out of different types of income and wealth. Whitaker

(2009) estimated the propensity for US farm households to consume out of different types of income. We estimate a similar model:

$$C_{i,t} = \alpha + \sum_j \beta_j Y_{i,t}^j + \delta_f W_{i,t}^f + \delta_{nf} W_{i,t}^{nf} + \gamma_1 Age_{i,t} + \gamma_2 Age_{i,t}^2 + \varepsilon_{i,t} \qquad (1)$$

where $C_{i,t}$ represents household i's consumption expenditures in period t, $Y_{i,t}^j$ denotes income for household i from source j, $W_{i,t}^f$ and $W_{i,t}^{nf}$ are the household's farm and nonfarm net worth, and $Age_{i,t}$ is the age of the farm's principal operator. Separating income by its source allows for the possibility that income streams are not perfect substitutes for each other (Carriker et al. 1993). We include four types of income: energy payment income, net farm income (including government payments), and earned and unearned off-farm income. We also separate total net worth (household assets minus debt) into farm and nonfarm wealth. We account for life-cycle effects by including the age and age squared of the principal operator of the farm.

An implication of the permanent income hypothesis is that the more transitory the income, the less inclined households are to consume it (Friedman 1957). Whitaker (2009) found that farm households consumed 10 cents of every dollar of off-farm income but only 1 cent of every dollar of net farm income. Whitaker's relatively low propensities to consume out-of-farm income are not an anomaly. Carriker et al. (1993) estimated a similarly small marginal propensity to consume farm income for a panel of Kansas farm households: each dollar in adjusted net farm income increased consumption by just 2.6 cents. In comparison, recent estimates on all households' marginal propensity to consume in the US range between 0.10 and 0.40 (Gross and Souleles 2002; Shapiro and Slemrod 2003, 2009; Johnson et al. 2006; Agarwal et al. 2007).

It is unsurprising that the marginal propensity to consume income is lower for farm households than for US households in general. Johnson et al. (2006) found that households with more liquid assets consumed less of their tax rebates. This is important because 96 percent of farm households have more wealth than the median US household (USDA-ERS 2012b). (See Table 11.A1 for sample mean and median wealth.)

We estimate the consumption model for all farm households and then for a sample trimmed in two ways. Because of uncertainty regarding how energy payments to the farm business are allocated when multiple households share in net farm income, we drop observations where more than one household shares in the income. We also trim households who rent their dwelling to avoid inappropriate comparisons. In many cases, the farm business owns the house of the farm household. Expenses associated with the house are therefore paid for in the form of lower net farm income to the household. We do not attempt to value housing consumed by the households. But for the few households who rent their dwelling, their rental expense is included in consumption expenditures, which is why we drop them.

When we look at all farm households we find a statistically insignificant effect of energy payments on household consumption (Table 11.3). Excluding cases where multiple households share in income from the farm and where the household rents its dwelling reduces the point estimate, but it reduces the standard

Table 11.3 Responses to energy payments: consumption and farm investment

	Consumption		Farm investment	
	All farms Coeff./S.E.	Farms owned by one household Coeff./S.E.	All farms Coeff./S.E.	Farms owned by one household Coeff./S.E.
Energy payments	0.073	0.042**	0.096	0.103
	(0.046)	(0.018)	(0.137)	(0.126)
Farm income	0.009***	0.007***	0.124***	0.107***
	(0.003)	(0.002)	(0.032)	(0.030)
Off-farm income – earned	0.055***	0.059***	0.012	0.013
	(0.014)	(0.014)	(0.021)	(0.019)
Off-farm income – unearned	0.019	0.028*	−0.003	−0.012
	(0.013)	(0.017)	(0.022)	(0.013)
Farm net worth	0.001***	0.001***	0.019***	0.016***
	(0.000)	(0.000)	(−0.003)	(−0.002)
Nonfarm net worth	0.019***	0.019***	−0.005	0.001
	(0.002)	(0.002)	(0.013)	(0.005)
Age of primary operator	378	667***	−1492*	−1,194***
	(363)	(193)	(771)	(455)
Age squared	−5.690**	−7.838***	8.100	6.412*
	(2.748)	(1.598)	(6.198)	(3.713)
Intercept	27,736**	17,560***	61,622***	49,052***
	(11,717)	(5,816)	(23,701)	(13,766)
Observations	9,096	7,837	9,096	7,954
R-squared	0.077	0.103	0.133	0.168

Notes: *** – $p < 0.01$, ** – $p < 0.05$, * – $p < 0.1$. Standard errors are calculated using the jackknife estimator produced with thirty replicate weights.

error even more, leading to a statistically significant relationship at the 5 percent level. The estimates of the coefficients on the other variables change little.

Each dollar in energy payments is associated with 4.2 cents of additional consumption expenditures, below the estimate for off-farm income (5.9 cents) but much larger than that of net farm income (0.70 cents). Earned off-farm income is largely from wages and salaries and is arguably the most stable income for many farm households. The finding that energy payments are more likely to be consumed than farm income but less likely to be consumed than earned income suggests that farm households perceive energy payments as moderately stable income. The stability of payments of course rests largely on the details of the leases with energy companies and the energy source. One interpretation of our findings is that on average the leases are specified so as to provide households with relatively consistent payments.

The estimates for farm income and earned income are in line with Carriker et al. (1993) and Whitaker (2009), but are lower than estimates for US households in general. Estimates for the propensity to consume out of nonfarm net worth are similar to prior estimates for US households. For each dollar in nonfarm wealth, farm household consumption increases by 0.019. Estimates for US households have been around 0.02 (Levin 1988; Bostic et al. 2009).

Are payments associated with greater farm investment?

We assume that household consumption and investment decisions depend on each other and are therefore influenced by the same factors. Consumption and investment decisions may affect each other if farm households are forced to self-finance investment because of imperfect credit markets. The equation we esti-mate has the same specification as in (1) but with farm investment as the dependent variable. We define farm investment as the sum of capital expenses made in the survey year, including purchases of or improvements to land (e.g., drainage tile, manure lagoons), construction of buildings, and the purchase of vehicles, tractors, or equipment.

On average, a dollar in energy payments was associated with 10 cents in farm investment, but the estimate was statistically insignificant (Table 11.3). Unlike with consumption, excluding farm businesses with multiple households has little effect on the point estimate or its precision. The imprecision partly reflects the small number of households in the ARMS Version 1 sample with energy pay-ments (fewer than 400). In the future a larger sample from pooling multiple years could give a more precise estimate.

Are payments associated with higher land values?

Prior research has showed that farm program payments are capitalized in land values (Weersink et al. 1999; Shaik et al. 2005; Goodwin et al. 2011). There may be a similar capitalization of energy payments, particularly if most farms own the rights to the minerals below their land. On average energy payment farms received $40 per acre in 2011. The ARMS asks farmers how much land they own and its estimated value, excluding the value of any buildings or perennial crops. To explore whether the payments are associated with higher land values we estimate

$$V_i = \alpha + \gamma_1 E_i + \gamma_2 A_i + \gamma_3 G_i + X_{i,k}\beta_k + State_i + \varepsilon_i, \qquad (2)$$

where V is the total value of land owned by the farm business, E is the energy payment received, A is the number of acres owned, G is the value of direct pay-ments received, X is a vector of factors influencing farm land values, and *State* is a dummy variable for the state. The vector includes variables related to land qual-ity and urban influence (Plantinga et al. 2002). To control for land quality, we include dummy variables for the farm's land resource region (there are twenty such regions in the United States) and the percentage of the county's total area in each land capability class as defined by the National Resource Conservation Service. Also somewhat related to land quality is the farm's production specialty as defined by the commodities that make up the majority of its sales, for which we also control. To capture the effect of local demand and urban influence, we include the median household income of the county and a linear and quadratic term for the driving time to the nearest city with a population of 250,000 or more.

We note that unlike the first two sets of results, which used the household as the unit of analysis, the land value model is based on farm businesses. The practical difference is that farm businesses includes nonfamily farms, where 50 percent or more of the farm is owned by people who are not related.

Because the specificiation in (2) holds total acres constant, the coefficient on energy payments has the same interpretation as if all the variables were in per acre terms.[4] Consequently, γ_1 is the per acre increase in land values associated with an additional dollar per acre in energy payments.

We find that each dollar per acre in energy payments is associated with $2.6 in additional value of an acre of land (Table 11.4). Unlike natural gas or oil leases, where the norm is for the entire property to be leased, wind payments are often for the use of only a few acres of the farm. We therefore also estimated the model excluding farms receiving wind payments. Doing so gives a similar coefficient estimate but a smaller standard error. Because energy development may affect land values for farms not receiving payments, we also estimate the model excluding farms that did not receive a payment but were in a county where at least half

Table 11.4 Energy payments and land values

	With wind Coeff./S.E.	Excluding wind Coeff./S.E.
Energy payments	2.605*	2.492**
	(1.478)	(1.209)
Median county household income	8.558***	8.637***
	(2.837)	(2.913)
Driving distance to city with a population of 250K or more	1,362***	1,384***
	(483)	(463)
Driving distance squared	−2.373***	−2.435***
	(0.618)	(0.634)
Acres owned	521	525
	(327)	(356)
Direct government payments	35.2***	33.7***
	(7.5)	(7.3)
Intercept	217,765	166,371
	(357,805)	(345,123)
Controls for land resource region	yes	yes
Controls for land capability classes in county	yes	yes
Controls for farm production specialty	yes	yes
Controls for state	yes	yes
Number of observations	9,938	9,866
R squared	0.30	0.29

Notes: *** – $p < 0.01$, ** – $p < 0.05$, * – $p < 0.1$. Standard errors are calculated using the jackknife estimator produced with thirty replicate weights.

of the county covered an unconventional oil or gas formation. Again, doing so gives very similar estimates (not shown).

By comparison, our results indicate that each dollar in direct government payments is associated with about $35 in land value. Prior estimates of capitalization of farm program payments in land values using ARMS have ranged from almost nothing to roughly $30 an acre (Goodwin et al. 2003a, 2003b, 2011). Care is needed when interpreting the estimates due to unobserved land quality characteristics. Direct payments are based on historic yields, meaning that more productive land receives higher payments. Because more productive land is also worth more, the true effect of direct payments on land values is likely smaller than we have estimated. For energy payments, the bias likely works in the other direction. Farmers with marginal land are perhaps more likely to lease land for energy development, meaning that the true effect of energy payments on land values may be higher.

Taking the point estimate of 2.6 as a lower bound, it suggests that farmers expect payments to dissipate quickly over the ensuing years. (At a 5 percent discount rate, the discounted value of a dollar paid in each of the next three years is about $2.70.) This is roughly consistent with evidence that production from natural gas declines exponentially as the well ages (MIT 2011). An alternative interpretation is that energy development makes the land less desirable for other uses. A well pad may make the parcel less attractive for residential development since people probably prefer to see a pristine landscape instead of one dotted with tanks, tubes, and concrete slabs. They may also be concerned about effects on well water. Thus, the expected flow of energy payments may be large but is partially offset by disamenities associated with wells or turbines.

Total effects on consumption and wealth

In our consumption model we estimated the effect of current payments on consumption. Taking the total derivate of (1) with respect to energy payments (and assuming that payments have no effect on farm and nonfarm income) gives:

$$\frac{dC}{dE} = \frac{\partial C}{\partial E}\frac{\partial E}{\partial E} + \frac{\partial C}{\partial W_{nf}}\frac{\partial W_{nf}}{\partial E} + \frac{\partial C}{\partial W_f}\frac{\partial W_f}{\partial E} \tag{3}$$

where W denotes wealth and f and nf denote farm and nonfarm. We directly estimated

$$\frac{\partial C}{\partial E} = \beta_E, \quad \frac{\partial C}{\partial W_{nf}} = \delta_{nf}, \text{ and } \frac{\partial C}{\partial W_f} = \delta_f$$

in equation 1. Although we do not directly estimate the effect of energy payments on nonfarm wealth, we approximate it by assuming that all energy payments not consumed or paid in taxes form part of nonfarm wealth. We suppose a tax rate of

20 percent. On average, farm proprietors paid an effective income tax rate of 15 percent in 2010 (Williamson et al. 2013). We add another 5 percent to account for any state and local taxes. Using τ to refer to taxes paid on energy payments, each dollar in energy payments adds $1 - \tau - \beta_E$ to nonfarm wealth. This assumes that energy payments are not saved as farm wealth, which although unrealistic, may be a good approximation given the statistically insignificant effect of energy payments on farm investment. Energy payments, however, do affect farm wealth by affecting land values. We assume that $\dfrac{\partial W_f}{\partial E} = \gamma_1$, with γ_1 coming from estimating equation 2. The total consumption effect of the 2.3 billion in energy payments is then:

$$\Delta C = \frac{dC}{dE} E = \beta_E E + \delta_{nf}(1 - \tau - \beta_E)E + \delta_f \gamma_1 E \tag{4}$$

where the last two terms reflect the effect of payments on consumption via wealth, and the $\beta_E E$ term captures the direct effect of payments on consumption.

We estimate that the \$2.3 billion in energy payments to farm businesses and households would stimulate \$140 million in consumption in the year paid, most of which corresponds to consumption of current payments as opposed to consuming the wealth created by the capitalization of expected payments into land values (Table 11.5).

The components of equation (4) allow us to calculate a total wealth effect, from saving energy payments and from payments affecting land values.

$$\Delta W = (1 - \tau - \beta_E)E + \gamma_1 E \tag{5}$$

The first term on the right-hand side equals \$1.74 billion; the second term, \$5.98 billion. With roughly 74,000 farms receiving payments, the total effect implies an average wealth effect of about \$104,000 per recipient farm, or about 5 (10) percent of the average (median) recipient farm wealth. This is the current wealth effect from saving current energy payments and the effect of future payments (and the activity that generates them) on land values. It is not an annual flow: presumably payments in the following year would be associated with a small decline in land values since the resource stock has declined, at least in the case of natural gas and oil.

Table 11.5 Energy payments and consumption and wealth

	Calculation	*Total effect ($, billions)*
Consumption	$(0.043 \times 2.3) + (1 - .20 - .043) \times (0.019 \times 2.3) + (0.001 \times 2.6 \times 2.3)$	0.14
Wealth	$((1 - .20 - .042) \times 2.3) + (2.6 \times 2.3)$	7.72

Conclusion

New technologies for accessing energy resources, changes in global energy markets, and government policies at all levels influenced energy development in the 2000s. Local wealth endowments – particularly of natural resources, but also of human, physical, and other types of capital – have affected where development has occurred. Energy development in turn has affected local wealth endowments by generating income and government revenue that can be invested locally, or by affecting natural amenities or social capital.

We highlight several observations from our look at energy payments. First, there is potential for the distribution of costs and benefits of energy development and energy payments to undermine social capital in a community. Energy payments are substantial – 15 percent of farms receiving payments received more than $50,000 – but are concentrated among few farms. The same is likely true for landowning households in general. Moreover, only a minority of rural households own much land. Rural residents without land or mineral rights may benefit from development in other ways (employment, for example), but many will have to bear greater congestion on the roads or the unwanted view of wind turbines on the horizon without receiving much benefit. The uneven distribution of costs and benefits could cause tension between neighbors as some work ardently to limit energy development while others welcome it.

Second, the effects of energy development on public and private wealth may be quite different. We estimate that energy payments added about $104,000 on average to the net worth of farm households receiving payments. But energy development, especially for natural gas, uses public infrastructure and potentially degrades natural assets. With natural gas, it's unclear if public revenues generated by the industry offset the depreciation of public physical and natural assets. The same concern may apply to wind: although it has fewer public costs, many local and state governments have given the industry favorable tax treatment.

Third, because real estate accounts for a large share of the asset portfolios of many rural households (as with US households in general), the largest effect of energy development on private wealth will likely come through property values. In our study, higher land values accounted for roughly three-quarters of the total estimated private wealth effect. The estimated effect may mask two competing effects – the positive effect of payments on land values and the negative effect from any deterioration of local amenities such as water quality, scenic beauty, and infrastructure. If so, properties adjacent to areas with energy development but without payments could decline in value. In time, even properties that receive payments may depreciate as payments decline and any disamenities created from development persist or worsen (e.g., failure of cement casing in older wells causing gas to enter well water). Clearly, there are important spatial and temporal questions regarding property values on which empirical research is needed. Thus, this chapter is only a small step towards further understanding the consequences of energy development on rural wealth and economic well-being.

Appendix

Table 11.A1 Descriptive statistics

Variable	Mean	S.E.	Median
Consumption expenditures	38,022	454	32,750
Energy payments	952	230	0
Farm income	20,751	1,128	−1,823
Earned nonfarm income	50,871	1,701	32,500
Unearned nonfarm income	21,316	819	12,500
Farm net worth	751,832	9,323	382,436
Nonfarm net worth	253,883	6,751	166,250
Operator age	59	0.32	59

Note: Standard errors are calculated using the jackknife produced with thirty replicate weights.

Notes

1 The views expressed are those of the authors and should not be attributed to the US Department of Agriculture or to the Economic Research Service.
2 Total US primary energy production grew from 69.44 quadrillion Btu (qBtu) in 2005 to 78.15 qBtu in 2011, while natural gas production grew from 18.56 qBtu to 23.51 qBtu (accounting for 57 percent of the growth in total production), biomass energy production grew from 3.10 qBtu to 4.51 qBtu (16 percent of growth in total production), and wind energy production grew from 0.18 qBtu to 1.17 qBtu (11 percent of growth in total production) (US Energy Information Administration, October 2012).
3 More information on the ARMS is available at: <http://www.ers.usda.gov/data-products/arms-farm-financial-and-crop-production-practices.aspx>.
4 If the intercept in (2) were omitted, the interpretation of the coefficients could be shown to be the same as if all continuous variables were put on per acre terms. Suppose an initial per acre specification: $\frac{V}{Acres} = \alpha + \beta\left(\frac{E}{Acres}\right) + \eta$. Multiplying by *Acres* would would give $V = \alpha Acres + \beta E + \eta Acres$. If the covariance between *Acres* and the error term is zero, we can rewrite the equation as $V = \alpha Acres + \beta E + \varepsilon$. Relative to a per-acre specification, controlling for acres owned as an independent variable and having the total value of land as the dependent variable reduces statistical noise from measurement error in acres, thereby improving precision in estimates. However, error in measuring acres will bias its coefficient towards zero. With extreme measurement error the coefficient will be zero and is similar to simply omitting *Acres* from the model. Thus, as measurement error increases, so does the potential for omitted variable bias.

References

Aakre, D., and Haugen, R. (2010) "Wind turbine lease considerations for landowners". Online. Available at: <https://www.wind-watch.org/documents/wind-turbine-lease-considerations-for-landowners/> (accessed 5 March 2012).
Agarwal, S., Liu, C., and Souleles, N.S. (2007) "The reaction of consumer spending and debt to tax rebates – evidence from consumer credit data", *Journal of Political Economy*, 115: 986–1019.
Bird, L., Bolinger, M., Gagliano, T., Wiser, R., Brown, M., et al. (2005) "Policies and market factors driving wind power development in the United States", *Energy Policy*, 33(11): 1397–407.

Bostic, R., Gabriel, S., and Painter, G. (2009) "Housing wealth, financial wealth, and consumption: new evidence from micro data", *Regional Science and Urban Economics*, 39(1): 79–89.

Boxall, P.C., Chan, W.H., and McMillan, M.L. (2005) "The impact of oil and natural gas facilities on rural residential property values: a spatial hedonic analysis", *Resource and Energy Economics*, 27: 248–69.

Brown, J.P., Pender, J., Wiser, R., Lantz, E., and Hoen, B. (2012) "Ex post analysis of economic impacts from wind power development in U.S. counties", *Energy Economics*, 34(6): 1743–54.

Carriker, G.L., Langemeier, M.R., Schroeder, T.C., and Featherstone, A.M. (1993) "Propensity to consume farm family disposable income from separate sources", *American Journal of Agricultural Economics*, 75(3): 739–44.

Considine, T.J., Watson, R., Entler, R., and Sparks, J. (2009) "An emerging giant: prospects and economic impacts of developing the Marcellus Shale natural gas play", University Park, PA: Pennsylvania State University, Dept. of Energy and Mineral Engineering.

Energy Information Administration (EIA) (2012) "Natural gas gross withdrawals and production". Online. Available at: <http://www.eia.gov/dnav/ng/ng_prod_sum_dcu_NUS_m.htm> (accessed 1 November 2012).

Environmental Law & Policy Center (ELPC) (2009) *Community Wind Financing*. Online. Available at: <http://elpc.org/wpcontent/uploads/2009/11/ELPC-Community-Wind-Book–09.pdf> (accessed 6 October 2011).

Foltz, J.D., and Zeuli, K. (2005) "The role of community and farm characteristics in farm input purchasing patterns", *Review of Agricultural Economics*, 27(4): 508–25.

Friedman, M. (1957) *A Theory of the Consumption Function*, Princeton: Princeton University Press.

Goodwin, B.K., Mishra, A.K., and Ortalo-Magné, F.N. (2003a) "Explaining regional differences in the capitalization of policy benefits into agricultural land values", in C.B. Moss, and A. Schmitz (eds.), *Government Policy and Farmland Markets*, New York: Wiley Online Library, pp. 97–114.

Goodwin, B.K., Mishra, A.K., and Ortalo-Magné, F.N. (2003b) "What's wrong with our models of agricultural land values?", *American Journal of Agricultural Economics*, 85: 744–52.

Goodwin, B.K., Mishra, A.K., and Ortalo-Magné, F. (2011) "The buck stops where? The distribution of agricultural subsidies", NBER Report No. w16693, Cambridge, MA: National Bureau of Economic Research.

Gross, D.B., and Souleles, N.S. (2002) "Do liquidity constraints and interest rates matter for consumer behavior? Evidence from credit card data", *Quarterly Journal of Economics*, 117(1): 149–85.

Hartman, C., Stafford, E., and Reategui, S. (2011) "Harvesting Utah's urban winds", *Solutions* 2(3). Online. Available at: <http://www.thesolutionsjournal.com/node/930> (accessed 20 March 2012).

Heintzelman, M.D., and Tuttle, C.M. (2011) "Values in the wind: a hedonic analysis of wind power facilities". Online. Available at: <http://ssrn.com/abstract=1803601> (accessed 8 March 2012).

Hill, E.L. (2012) "Unconventional natural gas development and infant health: evidence from Pennsylvania", Cornell University Applied Economics and Management Working Paper No. 128815. Online. Available at: <http://dyson.cornell.edu/research/researchpdf/wp/2012/Cornell-Dyson-wp1212.pdf> (accessed 12 August 2012).

Hoen, B., Wiser, R., Cappers, P., Thayer, M., and Sethi, G. (2009) "The impact of wind power projects on residential property values in the United States: a multi-site hedonic analysis", Lawrence Berkeley National Laboratory, LBNL–2829E. Online. Available at: <http://eetd.lbl.gov/ea/ems/reports/lbnl–2829e.pdf> (accessed 13 March 2012).

Johnson, D.S., Parker, J.A., and Souleles, N.S. (2006) "Household expenditure and the income tax rebates of 2001", *American Economic Review*, 96(5): 1589–610.

Kargbo, D.M., Wilhelm, R.G., and Campbell, D.J. (2010) "Natural gas plays in the Marcellus Shale: challenges and potential opportunities", *Environmental Science and Technology*, 44: 5679–84.

Kelsey, T.W., Shields, M., Ladlee, J.R., and Ward, M. (2011) "Economic impacts of Marcellus Shale in Pennsylvania: employment and income in 2009", Williamsport, PA: Marcellus Shale Education and Training Center.

Lambert, D., Wojan, T., and Sullivan, P. (2009) "Farm business and household expenditure patterns and local communities: evidence from a national farm survey", *Review of Agricultural Economics*, 31(3): 604–26.

Levin, L. (1988) "Are assets fungible? Testing the behavioral theory of life-cycle savings", *Journal of Economic Behavior & Organization*, 36(1): 59–83.

Levitz, J. (2012) "Cape Cod wind farm tiptoes ahead", *Wall Street Journal*, 10 August. Online. Available at: <http://online.wsj.com/article/SB10000872396390444900304577581460741815638.html> (accessed 13 November 2012).

Lu, X., Tchou, J., McElroy, M., and Nielsen, C. (2011) "The impact of Production Tax Credits on the profitable production of electricity from wind in the U.S.", *Energy Policy*, 39(7): 4207–14.

Massachusetts Institute of Technology (MIT) (2011) "The future of natural gas". Online. Available at: <http://mitei.mit.edu/publications/reports-studies/future-natural-gas> (accessed 16 March 2012).

Muehlenbachs, L., Spiller, E., and Timmins, C. (2012) "Shale gas development and property values: differences across drinking water sources", No. w18390. Cambridge, MA: National Bureau of Economic Research.

Mufson, S. (2012) "The new boom: shale gas fueling an American industrial revival", *Washington Post*, 14 November.

National Park Service (2009) "Development of the natural gas resources in the Marcellus Shale". Online. Available at: <http://www.nps.gov/frhi/parkmgmt/upload/GRD-M-Shale_12–11–2008_high_res.pdf> (accessed 11 November 2010).

Pender, J., Marré, A., and Reeder, R. (2012) *Rural Wealth Creation: Concepts, Strategies, and Measures*, Economic Research Report No. 131, Washington, DC: US Department of Agriculture, Economic Research Service.

Plantinga, A.J., Lubowski, R.N., and Stavins, R.N. (2002) "The effects of potential land development on agricultural land prices", *Journal of Urban Economics*, 52: 561–81.

Resources for the Future (2012) "A review of shale gas regulations by state". Online. Available at: <http://www.rff.org/centers/energy_economics_and_policy/Pages/Shale_Maps.aspx> (accessed 12 March 2012).

Scott, L.C. and Associates (2009) "The economic impact of the Haynesville Shale on the Lousiana economy in 2008". Online. Available at: <http://dnr.louisiana.gov/assets/docs/mineral/haynesvilleshale/loren-scott-impact2008.pdf> (accessed 12 November 2010).

Shaik, S., Helmers, G.A., and Atwood, J.A. (2005) "The evolution of farm programs and their contribution to agricultural land values", *American Journal of Agricultural Economics*, 87: 1190–97.

Shapiro, M.D., and Slemrod, J. (2003) "Consumer response to tax rebates", *American Economic Review*, 93(1): 381–96.

Shapiro, M.D., and Slemrod, J. (2009) "Did the 2008 tax rebates stimulate spending?", *American Economic Review*, 99(2): 374–79.

Smith, M. (2011) "Wind money fuels spending and benefits in small schools", *New York Times*, 10 November. Online. Available at: <http://www.nytimes.com/2011/11/11/us/wind-money-fuels-spending-and-benefits-in-small-schools.html?_=1&ref=windpower> (accessed 3 March 2012).

US Department of Agriculture – Economic Research Service (USDA-ERS) (2012a) "U.S. and state farm income and wealth statistics". Online. Available at: <http://www.ers.usda.gov/data-products/farm-income-and-wealth-statistics.aspx#27428> (accessed 21 May 2013).

USDA-ERS (2012b) "Farm household well-being: wealth, farm programs, and health insurance". Online. Available at: <http://www.ers.usda.gov/topics/farm-economy/farm-household-well-being/wealth,-farm-programs,-and-health-insurance.aspx#.Ua9W49LtXol> (accessed 21 May 2013).

Weber, J. (2012) "The effects of a natural gas boom on employment and income in Colorado, Texas, and Wyoming", *Energy Economics*, 34: 1580–88.

Weersink, A., Clark, S., Turvey, C.G., and Sarker, R. (1999) "The effect of agricultural policy on farmland values", *Land Economics*, 75: 425–39.

Whitaker, J.B. (2009) "The varying impacts of agricultural support programs on U.S. farm household consumption", *American Journal of Agricultural Economics*, 91(3): 569–80.

White, T.K., and Hoppe, R.A. (2012) *Changing Farm Structure and the Distribution of Farm Payments and Federal Crop Insurance*, Economic Information Bulletin No. 91, Washington, DC: US Department of Agriculture, Economic Research Service.

Williamson, J.M., Durst, R., and Farrigan, T. (2013) *The Potential Impact of Tax Reform on Farm Businesses and Rural Households*, Economic Information Bulletin No. 107, Washington, DC: US Department of Agriculture, Economic Research Service.

Wiser, R., and Bolinger, M. (2011) "2010 Wind technologies market report", DOE/GO–102011 3322. Washington, DC: US Department of Energy Office of Energy Efficiency and Renewable Energy.

12 Natural capital and rural wealth creation

A case study of Federal forest policy and community vitality in the Pacific Northwest[1]

Yong Chen and Bruce A. Weber

Introduction

Natural resources in the Pacific Northwest have long been recognized as a source of wealth. Settlers of European descent started migrating to the region in significant numbers to harvest these resources in the mid-1800s. Beaver pelts, salmon and trees have all at various times provided important economic bases for the region.

In this chapter, we apply the wealth creation framework outlined in Chapter 2 in a case study of how a Federal decision about forest management changed the distribution of benefits of local forest wealth among Oregon rural communities, improving the economic trajectories of some local communities while damaging – at least initially – the prosperity of others. We look first at the economic, institutional and policy context, and then examine what happened to population and income flows and real property wealth in Oregon's rural communities as Federal policies toward forest management changed after the 1980s. These changes in local population, income and physical property wealth were outcomes of the work, migration and investment decisions of households and firms during the 1990s and early 2000s, partly in response to the Federal decisions about the use of federally owned natural capital in forests.

Natural capital and Federal policy in the Pacific Northwest: the economic, institutional and policy context

In order to understand rural community wealth in Oregon and the Pacific Northwest, one needs to know two important things about the economic and institutional context. The first is that natural capital has historically supported – and still undergirds – a significant share of Oregon's jobs. In the early 1990s, the extractive natural resource sectors (agriculture and agricultural products, forestry and forest products, fishing and seafood, and mining) provided the economic base that supported over 20 percent of the state's jobs (Waters et al. 1999). And logging, wood and paper products were the most important natural resource industries: 12.9 percent total employment in Oregon in 1993 was supported by these forest-related sectors.

The second thing to understand is that a very large share of the natural wealth is in Federal ownership. More than half (51 percent) of Oregon's land – and almost

60 percent of the state's forestland – is federally owned. Thus, Federal forest policy decisions are very important for the rural communities in this region.

In 1994, the Federal government put into place the Northwest Forest Plan (NWFP), which established a new forest management framework for the 24 million acres of Federal forestland in Washington, Oregon and California within the range of the Northern Spotted Owl. The NWFP reduced harvests on public lands in order to protect old-growth trees and provide habitat for the Spotted Owl and other threatened species. This highly contentious policy change shifted 11 million acres of Federal forestland from timber production to old-growth forest protection. In so doing, the policy shifted management of the natural capital in forests for its extractive value to managing it for its non-extractive values.

Implementation of the NWFP speeded up a decline in timber harvests that had begun in Oregon in 1990 (Figure 12.1). Almost 5 billion board feet of timber were harvested in 1989 in Oregon on Federal land managed by the US Forest Service and the Bureau of Land Management. Harvests on Federal land steadily declined to less than 200 million board feet in 2001, and averaged less than 330 million board feet per year during the 2000s. Oregon harvests on private timberland during the 1980s, 1990s and early 2000s, in contrast, continued to

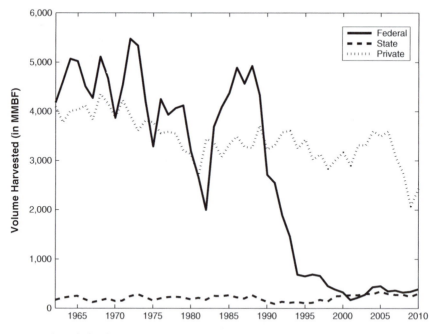

Figure 12.1 Timber harvest by ownership, 1962–2010

Source: Oregon Department of Forestry, State Timber Harvest by Ownership Graph, <http://www.oregon.gov/ODF/STATE_FORESTS/FRP/Charts.shtml> (accessed 20 March 2011).

average over 3 billion board feet a year, suggesting that the change in public land harvesting was not driven by changes in the demand for lumber.

The NWFP hastened a massive structural transition in the Pacific Northwest woods products industry that had been in process since at least the 1980s (Figure 12.2). In 1980, 405 lumber mills were operating in about half (113) of Oregon's communities. Two-thirds of these mills (282) closed during the following three decades, and by 2007 there were mills in only one-quarter (58) of Oregon's communities. For Oregon's small communities, mill closures usually deal a serious blow to community employment. The average direct job loss per mill closure was about a hundred jobs. With the median population of Oregon's communities being fewer than two thousand, a mill closure can be expected to have a significant impact.

Federal forest policy and wealth creation: what previous studies show about possible impact pathways

Economic returns to forests can be realized through harvest of logs (which provide earnings from the harvest, processing and sale of wood products) or through

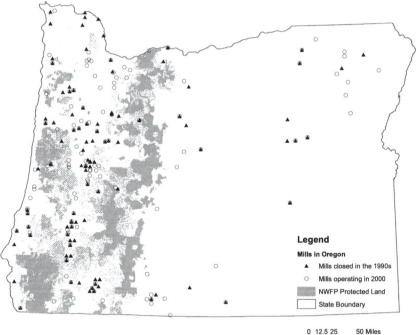

Figure 12.2 Oregon lumber mills, mill closures and Federal forest land protected under the Northwest Forest Plan

Source: Data supplied to the Oregon Department of Forestry by Paul F. Ehinger and Associates.

conservation of forests (which can generate recreation-oriented business income and jobs and/or create amenity values that affect local wages and real property values). Changes in forest management policy that restrict logging can therefore be expected to affect employment and wealth in both the wood products sectors and sectors related to amenity-seeking migrants and tourists.

Some studies of forest management impacts have analyzed income and employment impacts of harvest restrictions through the path of firm decisions about operation of mills that are based on extraction of natural wealth in trees. These studies find large job losses and other economic damages resulting from policies such as the NWFP. Beuter (1990), Anderson and Olson (1991), Waters et al. (1994) and Charnley (2006) used input-output models to estimate that employment reduction from such policies would range from 13,000 to 147,000 jobs. Charnley (2006) conducted case studies and found a negative impact of the NWFP on county employment.

There is a set of studies that has considered the impact that the amenities might have on household and firm decisions, without specifically linking these amenities to forest management policies. These studies consider alternative pathways to economic impacts: one pathway is through decisions of households about residential location and work that consider the natural-wealth-related amenities. Many studies have found that amenities affect migration decisions. Chi and Marcouiller (2012) found that the presence of public lands was a significant determinant of in-migration to "frontier" areas of low population density. Clark and Hunter (1992) and Clark et al. (1996) found that migration patterns follow a "life cycle" structure, with different factors affecting migration at different points in the lifespan. Clark and Hunter (1992) report that migration of working-age males is strongly influenced by labor market opportunities and not by amenities. Migration of middle-aged and older males, on the other hand, is influenced by amenities. Ferguson et al. (2007), in a study of migration in rural and urban Canadian communities, found that different factors affect the migration in rural and urban areas and of different age cohorts. Economic factors were uniformly important for rural people, while in urban areas economic and amenity variables had about equal importance in explaining migration.

Using Geographically Weighted Regression (GWR), Partridge et al. (2008, p. 261) found significant spatial variation in the effect of natural amenities on migration: "For some amenity variables, global regression estimates suggested there was no 'average' effect on growth, while the GWR estimates indicated positive effects in some regions and negative effects in other regions." Jensen and Deller (2007) also found significant spatial variation in the impacts of both built and natural amenities on elderly migration, and that these effects varied as elderly migrants aged. Older people are attracted to areas with warmer climates though not necessarily to areas with lakes and agriculture. They found that built amenities that complemented and supported natural amenities (such as camping facilities, hiking trails, marinas and golf courses) strongly predicted the migration of those over 55 years of age.

Following Rosen (1979) and Roback (1982), some studies expect that income levels in amenity-rich communities will be lower because people are willing to accept lower wages and higher unemployment rates in places with higher natural amenities. Blomquist et al. (1988), Gyourko and Tracy (1991) and Schmidt and Courant (2006) investigated individual location decisions and found that amenities in and outside metropolitan areas do indeed generate compensating wage and land differentials, with workers willing to accept lower wages and pay higher rent. By contrast, Deller (2009), in a study of nonmetropolitan US counties, found that natural and built amenities positively affect wages, rent and unemployment levels – a result that is not completely consistent with expectation.

Other studies come to different (though not necessarily contradictory) conclusions about the impact of household decisions to migrate to these high-amenity locations. A review article by Waltert and Schläpfer (2010) found conflicting results about the impact of amenities on income: among the eleven articles included in their analysis that reported amenity impact on income (seven on income per capita and four on wages and transfers), four reported significant positive impact. Shumway and Otterstrom (2001) found that in the 1990s counties characterized by environmental amenities, recreation-based economies and retirement communities experienced higher population growth. They also gained income because in-migrant income is on average about $10,000 higher than out-migrant income (Shumway and Otterstrom 2001, p. 498). Reeder and Brown (2005), in their study of the impact of amenity-related growth on rural communities, found that recreation and tourism development attracts population growth, increases county income and pushes up housing costs. Deller et al. (2001) and English et al. (2000) also found that amenity-based development had a positive impact on income. Nzaku and Bukenya (2005), on the contrary, found that natural amenities are negatively associated with per capita income in the Southeastern US.

Another pathway to increased jobs related to amenities is through the decisions of firms to locate in high-amenity communities to serve amenity-related development. Some studies of this pathway find that amenity-related development, though it creates jobs, is less desirable than resource extraction because it increases the service employment with low-paying jobs (McKean et al. 2005) and results in less equitable income distribution (Gibson 1993; Marcouiller and Green 2000).

There is a small group of studies that looks specifically at the impact of resource protection on rural economies, and implicitly at the pathway from forest protection policy to natural capital amenities to household and firm decisions to locate in high-amenity places. Lorah and Southwick (2003) find that population and income growth rates in nonmetropolitan counties with protected lands are much higher than in those without protected lands. Rasker (2006) found similar results in the Western United States. Looking at the Northern Forest region, Lewis et al. (2002) found that net migration rates were higher in counties with more conservation lands but that employment growth was not higher. In a later study in the same region, Lewis et al. (2003) found that the public conservation lands had no significant impact on wage growth. Eichman et al. (2010) looked specifically at the impact of the NWFP. In a simultaneous equations estimation of determinants of employment change and net migration using county-level data from Oregon, Washington and Northern California, their study provides evidence that the NWFP did in fact reduce employment in the region, and that this negative effect was not offset by the small positive net migration associated with the NWFP.

Most previous studies have used county-level data that may not capture the spatially differentiated effects that occur at a smaller geographic scale. This is particularly important for analysis in the Western United States, where counties are quite large geographically. In the only study we encountered that used community-level data in analyzing the impact of the NWFP on amenity migration and community well-being, Charnley et al. (2008, pp. 751–2) found that the links between the NWFP, amenities and amenity migration were more complex and varied than implied by county-level studies. They found that the NWFP "contributed to an increase in some recreation-related natural amenity values, but caused a decrease in others." And among the 1,314 nonmetropolitan communities in the NWFP region, they found (in a comparison that did not control for other factors) mixed evidence about amenity migration: population, for example, grew more slowly in forest communities (those within 5 miles of the Federal forests and thus with better access to forest amenities) between 1990 and 2000 than in communities more distant from the forests, and forest communities were more likely to have lost population during the decade.

The impact of the NWFP on rural community population, income and property wealth: an examination of alternative impact pathways

In our analysis of the effects of this change in Federal forest policy, we also use community-level data. We examine the effects of the implementation of the Northwest Forest Plan on population growth, changes in property wealth (real property value) and changes in median household income in Oregon's 234 rural communities – incorporated cities with fewer than 50,000 people. Our model, like many models of regional growth, views community growth as the outcome of interactions between firm and household location decisions. Like Carlino and Mills (1987) and Deller et al. (2001), we assume that households and firms are free to migrate. Households migrate to seek higher levels of utility from both market goods and services and nonmarket amenities. Firms migrate to seek lower production costs and be closer to market demand.

Modeling two pathways of NWFP impact

We hypothesize that the NWFP affects our three outcome variables through two pathways: the decreased forest harvest pathway that causes firms to close mills and lay off loggers and mill workers, and the increased forest amenities pathway that induces households and firms to move to the enhanced amenity locations and build new physical wealth and create jobs. Our modeling strategy assumes that these two pathways operate at different spatial scales, and that we will be able to distinguish empirically the relative strength of these two pathways for NWFP impact by examining three NWFP impact pathway indicator variables that have different spatial distributions.

Our *decreased harvest pathway* hypothesizes that the impact of NWFP-induced reductions in forest harvest on local economies is manifested in two ways: through mill closures anywhere in the state and through reduced logging employment in communities near NWFP-protected land. Mills and mill towns are located all over the state and are often at some distance from forests that provide their raw logs, so mills all over the state are at risk when harvests anywhere in the state decrease. And we hypothesize that communities with mill closures will experience more negative NWFP impacts than those without mill shutdowns. Loggers are more ubiquitous than mills and we expect that loggers living in communities close to the protected land are more at risk than those in more distant communities. Thus we hypothesize that NWFP-induced reductions in forest harvest will have a greater negative impact on NWFP-adjacent communities in which greater shares of residents work in logging. Our *enhanced amenity pathway*, by contrast, hypothesizes that the impact of NWFP on amenity-related migration and tourism development is strongest among the communities closest to the protected forest under the NWFP, and is manifested most clearly in NWFP-adjacent communities.

We expect that the decreased harvest pathway and the enhanced amenity pathway may have different time paths. So we analyze the impact of the NWFP through these two pathways in both the decade in which the NWFP was implemented and in the following decade. We expect that the reduced harvest pathway impact on the local economy will be an immediate impact. For instance, as a mill closes, the real property value of a community's industrial property will go down. The associated job losses are expected to decrease the community income. Whether these negative impacts are long-lasting may depend on other local contextual variables, so that in the longer term, the expected direction of the impact is undetermined. The impact under the enhanced amenity pathway, however, may exhibit a different pattern over time. If the implementation of the NWFP did attract amenity migration, we should first observe an increase in community population, which may push up the local demand and increase the real property value for commercial and industrial use. At the same time, as more and more people move into the community, the real property value for residential houses should also go up. This will reduce the incentive for in-migration and may increase the incentive for out-migration of low-income people.

Our empirical model has three dependent variables: (1) average annual changes (over each decade) in community population; (2) average annual changes in community real property value; and (3) average annual changes in community median household income. Community real property is mainly composed of industrial/commercial and residential real property.[2] The same model was estimated for two time periods: 1990–2000 and 2000–2010. We employed generalized method of moments (GMM) to estimate our simultaneous equations model. The three dependent variables were modeled as functions of NWFP impact pathway indicator variables (mill closures, NWFP-adjacency, and the interaction of NWFP-adjacency and logging dependence), plus a series of exogenous contextual variables drawn from the rural economic development literature that capture community characteristics in the base year that could affect changes in population, property wealth and income. The details of the model specification can be found in Chen and Weber (2013).

NWFP impact pathway indicators

We expect that the effect of the NWFP through the *enhanced amenity pathway* will be most pronounced in communities close to the protected land. We attempt to capture the enhanced amenity effects of the NWFP by creating a dummy variable that indicates whether a community is within a 10-mile buffer of the "reserved land" designated in the NWFP for species protection. From now on, we will refer to the communities within the 10-mile distance as "NWFP-adjacent communities."

We hypothesize that the *reduced harvest pathway* effect of the NWFP on a given community can be captured in two ways. The first is through a variable measuring the number of mill closures during the 1990s, the decade in which the NWFP was implemented. Mills can close for many reasons, including downturns in demand because of business cycles or competition from other regions, and obsolete or damaged equipment. Indeed mills had been closing for decades prior to the NWFP. But shortages of regional supply of timber have also affected the profitability of many mills, and have been cited by mill owners as one of the reasons for mill closures. And the NWFP dramatically reduced the supply of logs available to Oregon mills. The effect of reducing Federal timber harvests is not confined to communities adjacent to the harvested timberland because harvested logs often travel long distances to mills; the effect is spread to mill towns across a broader region.[3]

We also expect that loggers living in communities close to the protected land are more at risk from the NWFP than those in more distant communities and create a second variable to capture this reduced harvest pathway. We hypothesize that NWFP-induced reductions in forest harvest will have a greater negative impact on NWFP-adjacent communities in which greater shares of residents work in logging. Our data allow us to identify the share of each community's workers employed in farming, fishing and forestry occupations. Since about 2000, over one-quarter of those in farming, fishing and forestry occupations in Oregon have been working in logging jobs.[4] We explore the hypothesis that the effect of the NWFP in adjacent communities may depend on how important logging is in each community by creating a variable that identifies communities that both are adjacent to NWFP-protected land and have 10 percent or more of workers in farming, fishing and forestry occupations. Since we expect that the farm, fishing and forestry workers living in NWFP-adjacent communities were more likely to be employed in logging than those living in more non-NWFP-adjacent communities, we call the NWFP-adjacent communities with 10 percent or more

Table 12.1 Impact of Northwest Forest Plan on Oregon rural communities

	Community had mill closures in 1990s	*Community within 10 miles of NWFP-protected forestland*	*Logging-dependent community within 10 miles of NWFP-protected forestland*
1990s			
Population change	Negative impact*	Positive impact*	0
Wealth change	Negative impact**	Positive impact**	0
Income change	0	0	Negative impact**
2000s			
Population change	0	0	0
Wealth change	0	Positive impact***	0
Income change	0	0	0

Source: Chen and Weber (2013).

Notes: Estimated total effects are shown for variables in which there were significant partial effect coefficients in a. simultaneous equations model estimated in Chen and Weber (2013). The Delta Method is used to generate the test for the statistical significance of the total effect: *** – significant at 0.01, ** – significant at 0.05, * – significant at 0.1.

of workers in farming, fishing and forestry "NWFP-adjacent logging-dependent communities." The third NWFP indicator variable, then, equals 1 for NWFP-adjacent communities with 10 percent or more of their workers in farming, fishing and forestry occupations, and equals 0 for other communities.

To account explicitly for the interactions among population growth, real property value change and change in household income in our impact estimates, we estimated the total effects of each of the three NWFP impact pathway indicators. The results are summarized in Table 12.1. Econometric results for the full model are presented in Chen and Weber (2013).

Findings: how did the NWFP affect rural community population, income and property wealth?

There is evidence that the NWFP has affected community population, property wealth and income in Oregon through both the reduced harvest and the enhanced amenity impact pathways, and that these impacts were different in the 1990s than in the 2000s.[5]

Mill towns and logging towns experienced some adverse effects from reduced harvests under the NWFP. Communities with mill closures experienced slower population growth and less growth in community property values in the 1990s than communities without mill closures. And NWFP-adjacent logging-dependent communities experienced slower growth in median household income during the decade in which the NWFP was implemented.

More generally, however, the enhanced amenity pathway appears to have been dominant during the 1990s. Communities close to NWFP-protected forests (whether they were logging-dependent or not) grew faster in population and community real property value than the more distant communities during this decade. And the positive impact on population growth and community property wealth of being adjacent to NWFP-protected land was larger than the negative impact of a mill closing.

In the 2000s, the main NWFP effect appears to have been through the enhanced amenity pathway: real property values grew faster in the NWFP-adjacent communities than in those farther away from NWFP-protected forests, even though their populations were not growing significantly faster. This is consistent with the perception of approaching spatial equilibrium. That is, in the amenity-rich communities, increased demand for property (e.g., by businesses to serve tourists, by those seeking second homes or by in-migrants driving out current residents) will push up real property values even if the population is not growing rapidly. This increases the cost of living and dampens the incentive for further in-migration.

Mill closures in the 1990s do not appear to have had the same negative impacts on population growth or real property values in the 2000s as they had in the 1990s. Indeed, during the 2000s, changes in population, property wealth and median income were not significantly different in communities with mill closures during the 1990s compared with communities without mill closures. This conclusion also holds for logging towns adjacent to NWFP-protected lands. The differences in median household income growth between the logging and non-logging communities that had been observed in NWFP-adjacent communities in the 1990s had disappeared by the following decade. Whereas the NWFP effects were detrimental to nearby logging and mill towns in the 1990s, this no longer appeared to be the case after 2000.

It is likely that, as has been found in other studies of amenity-related development, there are important intra-community distributional shifts in well-being between new residents and original residents. Property value increases associated with new residents, for example, may price original residents out of local housing. The impacts of the NWFP on inequality and the distribution of costs and benefits needs further study.

It is worth noting that our conclusions about the population impacts of the NWFP support those of county-level analyses for the 1990s that found positive effects of protected lands on population growth (Lorah and Southwick 2003) and net migration (Lewis et al. 2002). Our results suggest, however, that these early effects are short-lived and may be choked off by rising property values.

This is not inconsistent with the recent slowdown in amenity-related migration (Partridge et al. 2012) and the converging population growth of the top tier of high-amenity places in America (Rickman and Rickman 2011). In retrospect, while the implementation of the NWFP imposes direct employment pressures on timber-dependent communities, it also opens new opportunities for a change in these timber-related communities and other communities close to NWFP.

Through adjustments in economic structure and investment, communities can redirect their local economy onto a more environmentally sustainable path by attracting migrants with higher incomes. Through entrepreneurship and technology, they can add additional impetus to the local economy. This amenity-driven growth can lead to local concentration rather than the dispersion of population, as found by Chen et al. (2013). This implies that staying environmentally sustainable does not necessarily mean that the local economy has to stay small in size.

Rural wealth creation framework in retrospect

The rural wealth creation framework provides a very useful lens for examining how Federal decisions about the management of the natural capital in forests affect the rural people and communities in this region (Figure 12.3). Natural capital clearly plays a key role in rural wealth creation and rural well-being in the Western United States. And because a very significant share of natural capital is owned by the Federal government, Federal decisions about the use of natural

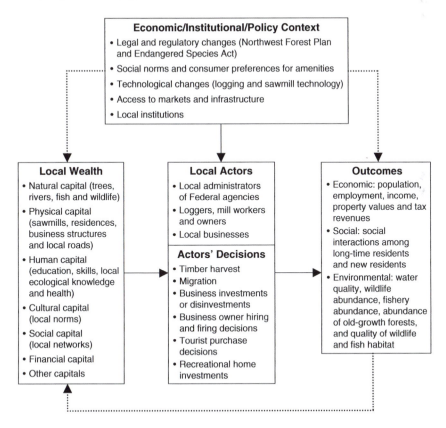

Figure 12.3 Impact of Northwest Forest Plan on rural community outcomes

capital are critical to rural wealth creation in this region and to the distribution of income and wealth in rural places.

Our findings highlight some of the key themes of the rural wealth creation framework outlined in Chapters 1 and 2: (1) the importance of many forms of capital and their interactions in creating and sustaining human well-being; (2) the roles of stocks of capital (in our case natural capital) in stimulating other forms of capital (built capital) and flows (income and population); (3) the significance of nonlocal ownership of a local asset (a major stock of natural capital in rural Oregon owned and managed by "nonlocals", in this case, the Federal government); and (4) how public capital (national forestland) affects private capital (real property embodied in homes and lumber mills).

Implications for Federal policy and rural wealth creation

There are two important sets of implications of our research. The first relates to the role of Federal policy in wealth creation. The Federal government, by preserving natural capital instead of harvesting it, has redistributed the returns to this publicly owned forest wealth across the communities in the region.

> Historically, the major benefits came from the timber production, which went mainly to the timber-dependent communities. The implementation of the NWFP, signaling that the Federal government wanted to protect old-growth forestland, appears to have promoted community property wealth in communities close to the protected land, and to have redistributed the economic benefits from the timber-dependent communities to a broader set of NWFP-adjacent communities.
>
> (Weber and Chen 2012, p. 5)

Discussion of the Federal roles in capital investment for economic development often focuses on Federal built infrastructure investments (highways, airports) and subsidies for private built capital (loans and grants for housing and businesses), or human capital (health care and support for education), or intellectual capital (Federal support for research and innovation). These are indeed important roles for the Federal government. Our analysis suggests that the management of natural capital by the Federal government has important effects on the value of privately owned built capital and particularly the distribution of wealth among people and places across the landscape. The enormous stock of natural capital owned and managed by the Federal government, particularly in the Western United States, is a complement to the privately owned built, human, natural and other forms of capital distributed over geographic space. The use and management of the Federal assets greatly affect the opportunities and fortunes of those who live nearby. Many decisions about Federal land use and management involve formal processes for citizen input and an opportunity for local interests to shape the management decisions. Our results suggest that the impacts on local economic well-being of Federal land management are not trivial and thus deserve to be given at least some weight in the Federal decision-making process.

The other main set of implications of our research is for the development of wealth creation strategies. A key implication of our study is that government has a central role to play in rural wealth creation. In part this is because the Federal (and to a much lesser extent, state) government owns and manages a significant part of the natural capital of rural America, and there is an interaction between stocks of public natural capital and private built capital and between these stocks and flows of private income.

Another implication for rural wealth creation is that, just as there are various national interests in forest management, local interests in local public capital are multiple and complex. Because capital (in our case, natural capital) has multiple attributes that value different uses differently, decisions about the uses of natural capital can lead to very different outcomes and different sets of winners and losers. Thus public involvement in decisions about public (and private) investments and management can be messy, and determining what is in the "public interest" is not straightforward. (This is also true for decision making about local private capital investments, as in zoning and land development decisions or decisions about subsidies to specific firms.)

A final implication for rural wealth creation is that, because the interactions among the various capitals are dynamic and change over time and space, it is not evident who should be included in any decisions about the use of public capital. In our study, it appears that the policy change on the use of public capital disadvantaged mill towns and communities near the protected areas that had a historical dependence on logging, and it advantaged those nearby communities that were not logging towns. And, while the added growth in property wealth in the nearby non-logging towns appears to be enduring and extended over two decades, the lower growth rates in income and property wealth in the nearby logging towns appear to have subsided by the second decade. Many of the winners and losers from the change in forest management policy did not live in nearby communities and, even if they had been identifiable prior to the decision about the forest policy change, would have been difficult to involve in the public input process.

Notes

1 Funding for this chapter was provided by the Economic Research Service under cooperative agreement No. 58-6000-0-0053 and by the Oregon Agricultural Experiment Station. Earlier versions of this chapter were presented at the 2011 annual meetings of the North American Regional Science Council, Miami, FL, and the 2012 annual meetings of the Agricultural and Applied Economics Association, Seattle, WA. The authors are grateful for the helpful suggestions of John Pender, Economic Research Service, USDA and Steve Deller of the University of Wisconsin.

2 There is no state-wide database that separates residential real property value from industrial/commercial real property at the city level. The values of centrally assessed property (such as large power plants and railroad property) are reported separately, however. These property values are not dependent on local economic forces and thus not expected to be affected by policy affecting local timber harvests. We excluded centrally assessed properties from our local real property value dataset.

3 The wood products industry has been in transition for many decades, with mill closures occurring before and after the implementation of the NWFP. The spike in mill closures

during the 1990s could have been due to other causes besides the NWFP. Even if one believes that mill closures were not directly caused by the NWFP and thus should not be considered an NWFP-induced phenomenon, a mill closure variable would need to be included in the analysis as a predictor of population, income and property wealth change. Reconceptualizing the mill closure variable as a control variable rather than a pathway indicator would not affect the results or interpretation of variables representing other pathways.

4 In 2012, the Bureau of Labor Statistics reported 13,050 workers in farming, fishing and forestry occupations in Oregon. Over one-quarter (29 percent) of these (3,750) were employed as loggers (fallers, logging equipment operators, log graders and scalers, and other logging occupations) (source: <http://www.bls.gov/oes/current/oes_or.htm#45-0000>). In 2000, the BLS reported 11,990 workers in this occupational group, 27 per-cent of whom (3,190) were loggers (source: <http://www.bls.gov/oes/2000/oes_or.htm#b45-0000>). In 1993, Oregon's wood products industry (logging and wood product manufacturing) employed 47,300 people: 9,400 in logging and 37,900 in wood product manufacturing (Rooney 2012).

5 Population and income growth in rural communities were also different during these two decades in Oregon. Whereas Oregon saw income growth and significant in-migration during the 1990s, the decade of the 2000s was a time of reduced economic growth and slower in-migration in rural areas of Oregon and the nation.

References

Anderson, H.M., and Olson, J.T. (1991) *Federal Forests and the Economic Base of the Pacific Northwest: A Study of Regional Transitions*, Washington, DC: Wilderness Society.

Beuter, J.H. (1990) *Social and Economic Impacts in Washington, Oregon, and California Associated with Implementing the Conservation Strategy for the Northern Spotted Owl: An Overview*, Report for the American Forest Resource Council, Portland, OR: Mason, Bruce, & Girard.

Blomquist, G.C., Berger, M.C., and Hoehn, J.P. (1988) "New estimates of quality of life in urban areas", *American Economic Review*, 78: 89–107.

Carlino, G.A., and Mills, E.S. (1987) "The determinants of county growth", *Journal of Regional Science*, 27: 39–54.

Charnley, S. (2006) *Northwest Forest Plan – The First Ten Years (1994–2003): Socioeconomic Monitoring Results*, 6 Vols. General Technical Report PNW-GTR–649. Portland, OR: US Department of Agriculture Forest Service, Pacific Northwest Research Station.

Charnley, S., McLain, R.J., and Donoghue, E.M. (2008) "Forest management policy, amen-ity migration and community well-being in the American West: reflections from the Northwest Forest Plan", *Human Ecology*, 36: 743–61.

Chen, Y., and Weber, B. (2013) "Federal forest policy and community vitality in the Pacific Northwest: how did the Northwest Forest Plan affect population, wealth and income in rural communities?", Working Paper 13-01, Corvallis, OR: Oregon State University Rural Studies Program.

Chen, Y., Irwin, E., and Jayaprakash, C. (2013) "Population dispersion vs. concentration in a two-region migration model with endogenous natural amenities", *Journal of Regional Science*, 53(2): 256–73.

Chi, G., and Marcouiller, D.W. (2012) "Recreational homes and migration to remote amenity-rich areas", *Journal of Regional Analysis and Policy*, 42(1): 47–60.

Clark, D.E., and Hunter, W.J. (1992) "The impact of economic opportunities, amenities and fiscal factors on age-specific migration rates", *Journal of Regional Science*, 32(3): 349–65.

Clark, D.E., Knapp, T.A., and White, N.E. (1996) "Personal and location-specific characteristics and elderly interstate migration", *Growth and Change*, 27: 327–51.

Deller, S.C. (2009) "Wages, rent, unemployment and amenities", *Journal of Regional Analysis and Policy*, 39(2): 141–54.

Deller, S.C., Tsai, T., Marcouiller, D.W., and English, D.B.K. (2001) "The role of amenities and quality of life in rural economic growth", *American Journal of Agricultural Economics*, 83(2): 352–65.

Eichman, H., Hunt, G.L., Kerkvliet, J., and Plantinga, A.J. (2010) "Local employment growth, migration, and public land policy: evidence from the Northwest Forest Plan", *Journal of Agricultural and Resource Economics*, 35(2): 316–33.

English, D.B.K., Marcouiller, D.W., and Cordell, H.K. (2000) "Tourism dependence in rural America: estimates and effects", *Society and Natural Resources*, 13: 185–202.

Ferguson, M., Ali, K., Olfert, M., and Partridge, M. (2007) "Voting with their feet: jobs versus amenities", *Growth and Change*, 38(1): 77–110.

Gibson, L.J. (1993) "The potential for tourism development in nonmetropolitan areas", in D.L. Barkley (ed.), *Economic Adaptation: Alternatives for Nonmetropolitan Areas*, Boulder, CO: Westview Press, pp. 145–64.

Gyourko, J., and Tracy, J. (1991) "The structure of local public finance and the quality of life", *Journal of Political Economy*, 99(4): 774–806.

Jensen, T., and Deller, S. (2007) "Spatial modeling of the migration of older people with a focus on amenities", *Review of Regional Studies*, 37(3): 303–43.

Lewis, D.J., Hunt, G.L., and Plantinga, A.J. (2002) "Public land conservation and employment growth in the northern forest region", *Land Economics*, 78(2): 245–59.

Lewis, D.J., Hunt, G.L., and Plantinga, A.J. (2003) "Does public lands policy affect local wage growth?", *Growth and Change*, 34(1): 64–86.

Lorah, P., and Southwick, R. (2003) "Environmental protection, population change, and economic development in the rural western United States", *Population and Environment*, 24(3): 255–72.

McKean J.R., Johnson, D.M., Johnson, R.L., and Garth, T.R. (2005) "Can superior natural amenities create high-quality employment opportunities? The case of non-consumptive river recreation in central Idaho", *Society and Natural Resources*, 18: 749–58.

Marcouiller, D.W., and Green, G.P. (2000) "Outdoor recreation and rural development", in G.E. Machlis and D.R. Field (eds.), *National Parks and Rural Development: Practice and Policy in the United States*, Washington, DC: Island Press, pp. 33–49.

Nzaku, K., and Bukenya, J.O. (2005) "Examining the relationship between quality of life amenities and economic development in the southeast USA", *Review of Urban & Regional Development Studies*, 17(2): 89–103.

Oregon Department of Forestry (various years) *Annual Timber Harvest Reports*. Online. Available at: <http://www.oregon.gov/ODF/STATE_FORESTS/FRP/Charts.shtml> (accessed 20 March 2011).

Partridge, M.D., Rickman, D.S., Ali, K., and Olfert, M.R. (2008) "The geographic diversity of U.S. nonmetropolitan growth dynamics: a geographically weighted regression approach", *Land Economics*, 84(2): 241–66.

Partridge, M.D., Rickman, D.S., Olfert, M.R., and Ali, K. (2012) "Dwindling U.S. internal migration: evidence of a spatial equilibrium or structural shifts in local labor markets?", *Regional Science and Urban Economics*, 42: 375–88.

Rasker, R. (2006) "An exploration into the economic impact of industrial development versus conservation on western public lands", *Society & Natural Resources*, 19(3): 191–207.

Reeder, R.J., and Brown, D.M. (2005) *Recreation, Tourism, and Rural Well-being*, Economic Research Report ERR 7, Washington, DC: US Department of Agriculture, Economic Research Service.

Rickman, D.S., and Rickman, S.D. (2011) "Population growth in high-amenity nonmetropolitan areas: what's the progress?", *Journal of Regional Science*, 51(5): 863–79.

Roback, J. (1982) "Wages, rents, and the quality of life", *Journal of Political Economy*, 90(4): 1257–78.

Rooney, B. (2012) The Oregon wood products industry since the Northwest Forest Plan was implemented. Oregon Employment Department website. Online. Available at: <http://www.qualityinfo.org/olmisj/ArticleReader?itemid=000083517> (accessed 26 March 2014).

Rosen, S. (1979) "Wage-based indexes of urban quality of life", in P. Mieszkowski and M. Straszheim (eds.), *Current Issues in Urban Economics*, Baltimore, MD: Johns Hopkins University Press, pp. 74–104.

Schmidt, L., and Courant, P.N. (2006) "Sometimes close is good enough: the value of nearby environmental amenities", *Journal of Regional Science*, 46(5): 931–51.

Shumway, J.M., and Otterstrom, S.M. (2001). "Spatial patterns of migration and income change in the mountain west: the dominance of service-based, amenity-rich counties", *Professional Geographer*, 53(4): 492–502.

Waltert, F., and Schläpfer, F. (2010) "Landscape amenities and local development: a review of migration, regional economic and hedonic pricing studies", *Ecological Economics*, 70(2): 141–52.

Waters, E.C., Holland, D.W., and Weber, B.A. (1994) "Interregional effects of reduced timber harvests: the impact of the Northern Spotted Owl listing in rural and urban Oregon", *Journal of Agricultural and Resource Economics*, 19(1): 141–60.

Waters, E.C., Weber, B.A., and Holland, D.W. (1999) "The role of agriculture in Oregon's economic base: findings from a social accounting matrix", *Journal of Agricultural and Resource Economics*, 24(1): 266–80.

Weber, B., and Chen, Y. (2012) "Federal forest policy and community prosperity in the Pacific Northwest", *Choices*, 27(1). Online. Available at: <http://www.farmdoc.illinois.edu/policy/choices/20121/2012109/2012109.html> (accessed 26 March 2014).

13 Entrepreneurship and rural wealth creation

Sarah A. Low[1]

Introduction

Previous chapters have introduced eight types of wealth. Undoubtedly, each type of wealth can support entrepreneurship in various ways, and entrepreneurship can support wealth creation. Of course, entrepreneurs deplete some types of wealth, but entrepreneurial activities may yield sufficient returns in wealth or other outcomes, such as economic growth, to offset this depletion.

It is widely held that entrepreneurship and long-term employment growth are positively correlated (Acs and Armington 2006; Glaeser et al. 2012). Recent research has even found evidence of rural entrepreneurship creating economic growth and reducing poverty rates (Stephens and Partridge 2011; Rupasingha and Goetz 2013). The relationship between entrepreneurship and economic outcomes has important policy implications as entrepreneurship is often considered a more sustainable economic development strategy than alternatives, such as business recruitment incentives.

This chapter focuses on the relationship between the wealth a community has, or could invest in, and entrepreneurship as a livelihood strategy. Drawing on the conceptual framework for rural wealth creation (see Chapter 2, Figure 2.1), this chapter focuses on the arrow connecting the "Local Wealth" box to the "Actors' Decisions" box, specifically the hypothesized relationship between local wealth and livelihood strategies related to entrepreneurship. The principal contribution of this chapter is to assess empirically how five types of local wealth (physical capital, financial capital, natural capital, human capital, and intellectual capital) affect various types of local entrepreneurship.

I begin by discussing various motivations for entrepreneurship and presenting several proxies for measuring entrepreneurship that work for US regions, across time, and for the purpose at hand. I then review literature on the link between entrepreneurship as a livelihood strategy and economic outcomes (or the arrow connecting the "Actors" box to the "Outcomes" box in Chapter 2, Figure 2.1), indicating why entrepreneurship is important to economic outcomes in rural America. Available literature does not address the relationships indicated by the arrow from the "Outcome" box back to the "Local Wealth" box, that is, the effects of entrepreneurship on changes in wealth over time. This chapter concludes with a discussion about the relationship between local wealth and entrepreneurship as a livelihood strategy in nonmetropolitan America, using insights from the literature and original empirical analysis.

Who are entrepreneurs and how do we measure them?

In the context of regional and rural development, there are many ways to think about, define, and measure entrepreneurship. Entrepreneurs can be defined by their motivation or goals and the same entrepreneur can be viewed through multiple lenses. Appropriate entrepreneurship measures will vary across US regions, across time, and for the purpose at hand. Let us begin the discussion by thinking about the motivation for being an entrepreneur.

Necessity-based entrepreneurship reflects an individual's perception that entrepreneurship is the best employment option available, but not necessarily the preferred one; while *opportunity-based entrepreneurship* represents voluntary participation (Acs and Varga 2005). Parker (1996) hypothesized that a lack of wage and salary job opportunities can "push" individuals into entrepreneurship, i.e., from a period of high unemployment come more necessity-based entrepreneurs. Conversely, a buoyant economy may pull an individual into entrepreneurship when he or she sees a market opportunity. Based upon an opportunity, a new product or new market, *innovative entrepreneurship* is the type of entrepreneurship that most people think of when they hear the word "entrepreneurship", and is also most likely to create jobs and increase income and financial wealth (Low 2009). *Mundane entrepreneurship* describes a non-innovative response to demographic growth, for example opening a coffee shop near a new residential development (Julien 2007). *Lifestyle entrepreneurs* may be mundane and/or necessity-based; they open a business to support a certain lifestyle, for example striking out as an independent consultant to have more control over their work–life balance. Necessity and lifestyle entrepreneurs are unlikely to be innovative, and mundane entrepreneurs are not innovative by definition.

Rural residents have a long tradition of innovation by necessity. Rural residents are driven to solve problems with available resources, creating an entrepreneurial culture in rural America (Markley and Low 2012). For example, a farmer covered his wooden mouldboard plough with steel to cut thick sod; with that innovation, the era of modern farm implements and an entrepreneurial venture were born. Perhaps as a result of some combination of necessity and entrepreneurial culture, the highest non-farm proprietorship rates in the country are in rural America (Low et al. 2005).

It can be difficult to assess the outcomes associated with different types of entrepreneurship, in part because definitions are subjective and entrepreneurs can have multiple motivations. For example, what are the economic impacts of one additional innovative entrepreneur versus one additional lifestyle entrepreneur? Surveys may be able to distinguish between different types of entrepreneurs based on their motivation and level of innovation, but administrative data cannot. Figueroa-Armijos et al. (2012) used survey data from the Global Entrepreneurship

Monitor and found that before the most recent recession individuals in rural America were more likely to become opportunity-based entrepreneurs than individuals living in urban America. During the recession, however, there was a decline in opportunity-based entrepreneurship and an increase in necessity-based entrepreneurship among rural residents.

Necessity-based entrepreneurship may increase local quality of life by providing local residents with better access to services and goods they would otherwise have to drive to a metropolitan area to obtain. Although the opportunity-based self-employed supported more growth in Appalachia than necessity-based self-employed, more self-employed (of either type) were correlated with increased growth (Stephens and Partridge 2011). Individuals with incomes below $50,000 and those employed part-time were more likely to become necessity entrepreneurs (Figueroa-Armijos et al. 2012). This suggests that increased access to resources, such as human capital, financial capital, and intellectual capital, might spur more opportunity-based entrepreneurship. We do know that self-employment in innovative industries creates higher rates of employment growth than self-employment, overall (Gallardo and Scammahorn 2012; Low 2009).

Entrepreneurship is a dynamic and complex phenomenon and this complexity makes a single empirical definition of entrepreneurship impossible. Assessing empirically whether an individual or firm has engaged in innovation or new market opportunities is difficult. Consequently, measures of entrepreneurship utilized in economic development research and policy making are based, not on ideal definitions of entrepreneurship, but on what data are available – a class of "second best" measures (Green et al. 2007). Additionally, it is difficult for one measure to capture individuals and firms, stocks and flows, or risk-bearing and innovation (Gartner and Shane 1995). Indices of entrepreneurship are fraught with weighting and measurement problems of their own. As a result, widely used entrepreneurship measures are nothing more than proxies for entrepreneurship: self-employment, establishment births, and average firm size (establishment rates).

Self-employment rates

The self-employment rate and its variants are the most widely used proxies of entrepreneurship in economic development applications and regional research (Iversen et al. 2008). The US self-employment rate can be measured with publicly available county-level data that are based on administrative records and calculated using filings of federal tax Form 1040 (Schedule C) for sole proprietorships, and Form 1065 for partnerships. Self-employment is a stock measure, taken at one point in time. Stock measures are more stable year to year than flow measures, thus making them more suitable for cross-sectional studies (Gartner and Shane 1995). Unfortunately, self-employment is broad and captures all types of small business activity, not necessarily new or innovative activity, and not necessarily full-time activity. For example, a professor with a full-time university job will be counted as self-employed when he submits a Schedule C for a textbook review.

Despite farm self-employment being integral to rural America, it is routinely excluded from the self-employment rate because farming is influenced heavily by subsidies and there is a relatively high proportion of unpaid family labor in farming operations (Blanchflower 2000; Meager 1992). Additionally, there is wide disparity in regional levels of farm self-employment – as high as 79.1 percent and as low as zero in US counties, with a mean of 20.0 percent (Bureau of Economic Analysis 2006). A nascent literature on farm entrepreneurs is developing, however, and has only recently been addressed with US data (Vogel 2012).

Empirical analysis in this chapter utilizes three measures of *self-employment* that have been used in the relevant literature – the non-farm proprietorship rate, the nonemployer rate, and the innovative nonemployer rate – each with its own benefits and caveats. The non-farm proprietorship rate (proprietorship rate, here-after) can be calculated from annual estimates prepared by and available from the Bureau of Economic Analysis' Regional Economic Information System; it is the ratio of non-farm proprietors to total employment (Low 2004). The proprie-torship rate is the most widely utilized measure of self-employment in US regional literature and includes proprietors with employees. The nonemployer establishment rate (nonemployer rate, hereafter), the ratio of nonemployer estab-lishments to total employment, is a way to assess the self-employed without employees, and is calculated from the US Census Bureau's Nonemployer Statistics. The nonemployer rate includes only proprietors with no paid employ-ees in most private-sector industries (again, production agriculture constitutes a majority of the excluded nonemployers). Finally, the innovative nonemployer rate is the number of nonemployers in innovative industries, normalized by total employment.[2] For details on how innovative industries are defined in the calculation of this proxy, see Low (2009), and see Gallardo and Scammahorn (2012) for a practical application of this measure in three, relatively rural, Southern states.

Establishment rates

The establishment rate, defined in a variety of ways, is widely used in regional entrepreneurship studies because it indicates entrepreneurial environment. I assume a higher density of smaller firms, or smaller average firm size, creates a more entrepreneurial environment. I define the establishment rate as the number of establishments divided by employment and calculate it using data from the 2003 Census Bureau's County Business Patterns, which excludes production agriculture. The establishment rate is suited for longitudinal entrepreneurship research due to its availability and stability over time (Saxenian 1994). Establishment measures are readily available, easy to compute across time and space, and are relatively stable across time (Gartner and Shane 1995). The estab-lishment rate is spatially dependent; it is high in sparsely populated areas due to market structure, and so care must be taken when using the establishment rate for regions, particularly nonmetropolitan regions.

Establishment birth rates

The flow of establishments, births and deaths, represents an alternative to stock measures of entrepreneurship. Such dynamic data, however, are more difficult to obtain and they ignore existing businesses. Dynamic data are increasingly being used in the entrepreneurship literature because establishment births and deaths are considered a better indicator of innovation than other widely used entrepreneurship proxies (Acs and Armington 2003; Acs and Mueller 2008; Lee et al. 2004; Luger and Koo 2005; Mueller 2007). Micro datasets, such as the Census' Longitudinal Business Database, are available, and public-use dynamic establishment databases are in development: for example, Statistics of US Businesses from the Census Bureau and Business Employment Dynamics from the Bureau of Labor Statistics. In this analysis, I use single-unit employer establishment births over population, calculated with county-level data from the Census Bureau, 2003. Single-unit births are chosen because they are not part of a distant multi-unit firm. I also employ the single-unit employer establishment birth rate in innovative industries, as described in Low (2009) and akin to the innovative nonemployer rate described above.

Why are entrepreneurs important to the rural economy?

Until recently, little research on entrepreneurship as an economic growth strategy in *rural* areas existed; most research was national or metropolitan in scope. New research discussed in this section suggests that entrepreneurship *can* improve rural well-being by creating job growth and income growth, and reducing poverty. Economic well-being improvement is most notable when certain types of wealth exist in a community, for example connectivity with urban areas (Henderson and Weiler 2010) or natural capital and an entrepreneurial local context (McGranahan et al. 2011). The studies I reviewed examined the flow of income and jobs and did not examine the *stock of wealth* created by entrepreneurs in rural America. No research on entrepreneurship's impact on rural wealth creation exists, to the best of my knowledge, and this is an area for future research. Growth in the flow of income and jobs *may* increase wealth; for example, income growth *may* increase financial capital if part of the increased income is saved.

Henderson and Weiler (2010) found that self-employment-driven wage and salary employment growth is higher in metropolitan and metro-adjacent counties than nonmetro non-adjacent counties. Results suggest that, while self-employment rates are higher in rural America, higher self-employment rates do not translate into economic growth in these counties. Henderson and Weiler's finding that less employment growth is created by *rural* self-employment may explain why studies have shied away from focusing on entrepreneurship in *rural* areas alone. Henderson and Weiler posited that their result is due to higher levels of lifestyle-based or necessity-driven self-employment in the most rural areas. That is, it is not self-employment driven by innovation or motivated by growth ambitions, but rather self-employment to maintain a certain lifestyle or because suitable employment was not available. Yu et al. (2011) suggested that it may be riskier for rural entrepreneurs to innovate or be growth-oriented. Yu et al. concluded that rural entrepreneurs require a higher probability of success than those in urban markets, likely because rural entrepreneurs do not have access to the thick markets, higher salvage values, and spillover benefits afforded to comparable firms in urban areas. Henderson and Weiler also suggested that the spillover benefits of self-employment are larger in urban labor markets than rural.

Rupasingha and Goetz (2013) found that self-employment rates are positively correlated with future per capita income growth, employment growth, and reduction in poverty rates in nonmetropolitan counties. In metropolitan counties, self-employment rates were associated with income and employment growth, but not poverty rates. Rupasingha and Goetz's results suggest there may be differences in rural and urban self-employment or entrepreneurship policies; their findings also suggest that promoting small and local businesses in rural America may accelerate local economic growth and reduce poverty. These findings suggest that investment in self-employment may be good policy and that future research should examine the importance of human capital and training programs for small nascent entrepreneurs in rural America.

For Appalachia, Stephens and Partridge (2011) concluded that a 1 percent increase in self-employment was associated with a 4 percent increase in employment growth over the following sixteen years; they also find a 1 percent increase in self-employment is associated with a 0.65 percent increase in per capita income growth. That is, in Appalachia, a remote and economically lagging rural region, self-employment does contribute to positive economic outcomes, even if it is less growth than would be created in an urban area. Stephens and Partridge's result suggests self-employment is a viable growth strategy in Appalachia, and their conclusion could hold in other lagging regions of the United States, but is yet to be tested.

In rural America, entrepreneurship may be a more viable growth creation strategy in regions with certain types of local wealth. McGranahan et al. (2011) found that the interaction of entrepreneurial context with creative class (the share of people employed in creative occupations) was strongly associated with job growth and growth in the establishment birth rate, particularly in areas high in natural capital. This finding suggests that entrepreneurship may be a better job growth creation strategy in areas with higher levels of natural capital.

How do investments in local wealth impact entrepreneurship?

Rupasingha and Goetz (2013) found that entrepreneurship, measured as the proprietorship rate, is important to rural economic outcomes and suggested that more research into policy-relevant drivers of entrepreneurship is important. I discuss in this section the relationship between five different types of local wealth (financial, physical, human, intellectual, and natural capitals) and six proxies for entrepreneurship (the proprietorship rate, the nonemployer rate, the innovative nonemployer rate, the establishment rate, the establishment birth rate, and the innovative establishment birth rate). I draw from recent literature and ordinary least squares (OLS) regressions of local wealth on next period entrepreneurship rates. I limit my analysis to counties defined as nonmetropolitan by the 2000 decennial census.

Counties are chosen as the unit of analysis because they are a widely understood regional unit and many county-level data are available annually. Goetz and Rupasingha (2009) argue that county averages of individuals' characteristics can serve as an alternative to individual-level data, which is arguably the best. I conduct analysis for nonmetropolitan counties because this has not been done in the literature; rather, most multivariate econometric analyses of entrepreneurship rates include a binary variable indicating a county's metropolitan status (e.g., Goetz and Rupasingha 2009; Henderson et al. 2007). I control for the percentage of rural residents in a county, as this varies substantially, even within nonmetropolitan counties. Per Renski (2012), I control for industry mix with the percentage of employment in higher-level industries; race/ethnicity; and the percentage of youth and retirement-age adults.[3] These data are from the 1990 decennial census. I use lagged values to reduce endogeneity concerns, as have Stephens and Partridge (2011), Henderson and Weiler (2010), and others.

Financial capital

Regional research suggests that financial capital, or the stock of money available for productive use within a community, affects entrepreneurship in rural America (Goetz and Rupasingha 2009; Henderson et al. 2007). Most financial capital is privately held and, while it may be utilized to create a public good, it can be taken away by its owner, putting it outside a community's locus of control. Community banks, foundations, and revolving loan funds are examples of financial capital within the locus of control but are difficult to measure across times and regions, and may be best studied using a case study methodology. Despite its relative rarity in rural America, venture or equity capital deals in rural America can be just as successful as urban ones (Scruggs 2010); however, most entrepreneurs are funded through credit cards or personal loans backed by collateral. Collateral facilitates borrowing for entrepreneurial ventures and some empirical research has found home values and home ownership rates are positively related to self-employment (Goetz and Freshwater 2001), likely because home equity can be converted into financial capital by a nascent entrepreneur.

Local bank deposits give insight into the region's availability of financial capital and have been used widely as a proxy for the regional availability of financial capital. I use bank deposits per capita, from the Federal Deposit Insurance Corporation, 1990 – a period of time when relationship banking was more common than centralized decision making, or score-carding, at rural banks. Several studies have found that local bank deposits per capita have a statistically significant relationship with regional entrepreneurship, including Garofolli (1994), Goetz and Rupasingha (2009), and Henderson et al. (2007).[4]

Deposits per capita are positively correlated with the establishment birth rate and the innovative industry establishment birth rate (Table 13.1).[5] A one standard deviation increase in deposits per capita ($4,500) was associated with a 0.24 standard deviation increase in the establishment birth rate. Interestingly, the coefficient on deposits per capita is not positive when regressed on the establishment rate, the nonemployer rate, and the proprietorship rate. A small (0.05) negative coefficient resulted in the innovative nonemployer rate and the nonemployer rate regressions.

Results suggest that deposits per capita may not be an essential ingredient for the self-employed (nonemployers and proprietors) in rural America, but that it is more important for establishment births.[6] This result suggests new establishments are more likely to require financial capital (as indicated by the establishment birth regressions). Consequently, investing in a mechanism to distribute financial capital may aid the entrepreneurs; for example, a community microloan program may most benefit the self-employed entrepreneur who needs a small amount of capital unavailable from a bank.

Physical capital

Highways and broadband Internet are examples of physical capital found to be related to regional entrepreneurship rates (Henderson et al. 2007; Gallardo and Scammahorn 2012), but are generally outside a region's locus of control. Buildings, say a community center or school, are within a local locus of control but are conceptually less likely to be drivers of entrepreneurship. Anecdotal tales of communities banding together to increase their wireless Internet access exist, but proximity to an urban area is correlated with the presence of these types of physical capital.

As a proxy for measuring physical capital empirically, I use the Federal Reserve Bank of Kansas City's infrastructure index, which is un-weighted and includes standardized highway expenditure, commercial air traffic, and broadband Internet prevalence in 2002 and 2003 (and is not available for prior time periods). The index controls for connectivity infrastructure in each US county (available at: <http://www.kansascityfed.org/publications/research/mse/regional-asset-indicators.cfm>).[7]

The results suggest a positive correlation between the infrastructure index and both establishment birth rates (Table 13.1). These results are consistent with the notion that self-employment will occur regardless of the level of available infrastructure, but higher establishment birth rates and births in innovative industries are correlated with better access to transportation infrastructure (highway spending and flight connectivity) and the Internet. It is not surprising that communities with higher stocks of physical capital would foster higher establishment birth rates because the physical capital increases connectivity to thick markets, enhances the flow of knowledge, inputs, inexpensive financing, and more. My physical capital proxy may be uncorrelated with self-employment because many self-employed are necessity entrepreneurs and if they were located in a community with more

Table 13.1 Standardized OLS regressions for nonmetropolitan counties

	Nonfarm proprietorship rate, 2003	Nonemployer rate, 2003	Innovative industry nonemployer rate, 2003	Establishment rate, 2003	Establishment birth rate, 2003	Innovative industry establishment birth rate, 2003
Coefficients and standard errors on capitals						
Financial	-0.038 (0.024)	-0.055** (0.023)	-0.052** (0.021)	-0.018 (0.026)	0.239*** (0.027)	0.093*** (0.025)
Physical	-0.024 (0.028)	-0.030 (0.028)	-0.011 (0.024)	0.047 (0.03)	0.132*** (0.033)	0.118*** (0.03)
Human	0.095*** (0.029)	0.008 (0.028)	0.072* (0.025)	0.314*** (0.031)	0.569*** (0.033)	0.376*** (0.031)
Intellectual	-0.149 (0.113)	0.184* (0.109)	0.393*** (0.098)	-0.317*** (0.12)	0.042 (0.131)	0.055 (0.121)
Natural	0.204*** (0.022)	0.210*** (0.021)	0.108*** (0.019)	0.191*** (0.023)	0.291*** (0.025)	0.123*** (0.023)
N	1956	1949	1956	1940	1955	1953
Adjusted R^2	0.418	0.420	0.209	0.431	0.402	0.217

Notes: Control variables (race/ethnicity, age, rurality, industry employment) omitted due to space constraints; *** – $p < 0.01$, ** – $p < 0.05$, * – $p < 0.1$.

physical capital and greater connectivity the necessity-based self-employed might instead work in the wage and salary labor market. This finding suggests investment in physical capital may be important for promoting entrepreneurship. At a minimum, communities may try to ensure they have adequate Internet access, as that is increasingly in the local locus of control, versus transportation infrastructure investment, which is largely made at federal and state levels.

Human capital

Research has found a positive relationship between growth in a region's economic outcomes (per capita income, employment, establishment births) and the level of human capital when measured as the percentage of adults age 25 and over with a four-year college degree (Rupasingha and Goetz 2013). A relationship between college education and self-employment growth has not been observed, however (Goetz and Rupasingha 2009; Low and Weiler 2012; Stephens and Partridge 2011). Human capital requires a huge public investment which tends to pay dividends to both the individual and the community in which they live. Research has found that the effect of human capital varies not only with the type of entrepreneurship, but also temporally; during times of recession human capital has less effect on entrepreneurship than during times of growth (Acs et al. 2007). Another type of human capital is creativity; Stephens et al. (forthcoming) found that in lagging rural regions, creativity was more important for growth than education-based human capital, while Gallardo and Scammahorn (2012) found both to be drivers of self-employment. Creativity and education are correlated; for this reason we do not include both in our multivariate analysis, using only education as a proxy for human capital.

All but one of the entrepreneurship proxies I use has a positive relationship with the human capital metric, defined as the percentage of adults age 25 and over with a four-year college degree (Table 13.1). The magnitude of the coefficient on human capital was relatively large in the birth, innovative birth, and establishment rate regressions, indicating that a one standard deviation increase in the percentage of college-educated adults would increase the birth rate by over one-half standard deviation (0.57). While the proprietorship rate had a positive correlation with human capital, the nonemployer rate did not; this may be driven by necessity, i.e., due to job loss, a person is engaging in self-employment and has no employees, but survey research would be needed to test this suggestion.

Intellectual capital

Intellectual capital is the stock of knowledge, innovation, and ideas in intellectual products in a community. Examples include new products, new methods, research and development, inventors, patents, and copyrights – all things that seemingly spur innovative entrepreneurship. Research facilities, universities, and high-tech firms, which are most likely to generate patents, tend to exist in populated areas, thereby creating an endogeneity problem for researchers interested in teasing out the causality between innovation, place, and entrepreneurship (Carlino et al. 2007; Ó hUallacháin 1999). Rural areas lend themselves to incremental patenting, i.e., building on prior inventions (Orlando and Verba 2005). Although larger cities tend to generate most ground-breaking innovations, the cumulative effect of incremental patents can be just as big (Henderson and Weiler 2010). Measuring intellectual capital, like other capitals, is challenging. Patents have been used as a proxy for innovative entrepreneurship but they are not always assigned to a firm and it is unknown if the invention ever makes it to market; nevertheless, I use county-level patents per capita, 1990–1999, as a proxy for intellectual capital and acknowledge it consists of much more.

Results from the patents per capita coefficient were interesting, partly because patenting principally occurs in urban areas. I found a relatively large, positive, and statistically significant coefficient on patents per capita when regressed on innovative nonemployers (0.39) and all nonemployers (0.18). Are inventors in rural America likely to be lone-eagle types, doing invention independently of a firm, i.e., are they unaffiliated nonemployers? Interestingly, neither birth rate had a significant relationship with patents per capita in nonmetropolitan counties, suggesting that patenting activity is not correlated with single-unit employer establishment births (a positive relationship was found for metropolitan counties). A negative coefficient on patents per capita in the establishment rate regression suggests patenting may be associated with larger firm size in nonmetropolitan areas. Perhaps patenting in nonmetropolitan America is too sporadic to be a useful indicator of intellectual capital? A deeper understanding of patenting and intellectual capital in rural America is needed to answer these questions and I leave this to future work.

Natural capital

Natural capital, the natural assets of a community, particularly non-market amenities, is regional wealth in its truest form. Public goods that can be considered natural capital include weather and topography, while privately held goods, including mineral rights and real estate not accessible to the public, have less value to the public. Natural capital is difficult to create, and is easier to destroy, for example mountain-top removal for resource extraction. Managing natural resources and increasing access for recreation purposes can increase the usefulness of natural capital. Many regional studies of entrepreneurship utilize a county-level natural amenity index developed by the USDA Economic Research Service (McGranahan 1999); this scale is consistently positively linked with various entrepreneurship proxies and their growth (Goetz and Rupasingha 2009; Low and Weiler 2012) and I use it as a proxy for natural capital. I find a strong, positive relationship between the natural capital proxy and all the entrepreneurship proxies used, with the standardized coefficient on natural capital ranging from 0.11 (innovative nonemployer rate regression) to 0.29 (establishment birth rate regression). This positive relationship suggests investment in natural capital may promote entrepreneurship as a rural livelihood. Future research could investigate how investment in natural capital, for example improving access to the outdoors or preserving natural areas, may increase other types of local wealth.

Social, cultural, and political capital

Social, cultural, and political capital are likely important to entrepreneurship, but we do not include them in our empirical work because measuring these capitals is difficult with secondary data and for each county in the US. These forms of capital are perhaps best understood using case study methods and regional surveys. Entrepreneurship culture, a subset of a region's cultural capital, does appear in the entrepreneurship literature and deserves a brief discussion.

Cultural capital reflects the values rooted in a place; for example, entrepreneurial culture and its intergenerational transfer can positively affect communities' entrepreneurship rates over the long run. Research has demonstrated that regional entrepreneurial culture persists over time, even in the face of adversity, as demonstrated in Germany 1925–2005 by Fritsch and Wyrwich (2012). Cultural capital is both a people- and place-based wealth; while people maintain the culture, it is intrinsic to place, no individual owns culture, and it is hard to take away from a region. It has been suggested that rural America has particularly high levels of entrepreneurial culture, as demonstrated by high self-employment rates. Others have stated that fostering a culture, or context, in which entrepreneurship thrives can benefit a region's economy (Lee et al. 2004; Tamasy 2006). Of course, a region's entrepreneurial culture or cultural capital is difficult to measure. Research using individual-level survey data suggests entrepreneurial attitudes (goal-setting, confidence in abilities) drive self-employment and firm birth rates (Acs and Armington 2006; Evans and Leighton 1989; Lee et al. 2004).

Local wealth portfolio

As the literature suggests and empirical results have illustrated, a portfolio of local wealth may be utilized to spur and maintain entrepreneurship as a livelihood strategy in rural regions. It is also important to acknowledge that entrepreneurship consumes some wealth but likely creates other types of wealth, the types and extent of which are yet unknown and should be pursued in future research. Just as a community reliant on employment from one dominant industry may be at risk should that industry slow down or exit, investing in only one type of asset may not be optimal. Low and Weiler (2012) found that risk in a county or labor market area's wage and salary jobs spurs both establishment birth and proprietorship rates in the next period. A community with a variety of capitals provides more fodder for entrepreneurship and may even reduce its employment risk (volatility). Chinitz (1961) wrote about the US Steel culture in Pittsburgh during the mid twentieth century – Pittsburgh was reliant on US Steel and is still in the process of re-inventing itself. Having an entrepreneurial core might have increased the region's resilience to changes in the steel industry. For example, New York was able to re-invent itself after the demise of the garment industry – part of this success was because of the entrepreneurial culture already persistent in the city at the time.

Given the need for a portfolio of capital, how can a rural region know which type of capital should receive the most investment? That is, what interactions among capitals are most crucial when using entrepreneurship as an economic development strategy? Very little regional research on this question exists. Stephens et al. (forthcoming) find that in lagging rural regions, creativity is more important for growth than human capital, patents, or high-tech industry employment. Kravchenko et al. (2011) find that rural counties with high levels of human capital have higher levels of lending to small firms. Are human and financial capital interrelated? Must investment in one precede the other?

Recent research suggests entrepreneurship is a vehicle for incorporating human capital and intellectual capital into the economy (Glaeser 2007; Lee et al. 2004). Building upon this idea, McGranahan et al. (2011) examined how the nexus between entrepreneurship and creative occupations (creative class) affects economic growth in nonmetropolitan counties. They developed a model of county growth incorporating natural amenity levels and tested to what extent entrepreneurship (defined as both self-employment and establishments per employee) and human capital drives nonmetropolitan growth in the presence of different amenity levels. McGranahan et al. found that counties with a higher proportion of creative class and entrepreneurship experienced more growth during the 1990s than other counties. Their results suggest that the entrepreneurship/creative class nexus is particularly strong in high natural amenity areas, for example mountainous and coastal areas, but that the relationship is less relevant in low-amenity areas, for example the Great Plains. McGranahan et al. represent one of the few studies on the interrelatedness of rural wealth. Clearly, more research on interactions and sequencing is necessary.

Conclusion

Literature reviewed and the empirical work presented in this chapter suggest that the determinants of regional entrepreneurship rates are complex, with many determinants and interactions between them playing an important role in the entrepreneurial process (Tamasy 2006). Unfortunately, little, if any, research examines these interactions or the sequence in which they are needed, explicitly. Such research may be best conducted using case studies and survey data as it is difficult to tease out interactions and sequencing between types of capital using multivariate analysis and secondary data. Empirical work using secondary data might be useful in helping county leaders ask the right type of questions, however. For example, given a set of assets, what wealth investments would best promote entrepreneurship as a rural livelihood strategy?

Much research is limited by data availability, thus many drivers of entrepreneurship are immeasurable with publicly available or administrative data. Place-based and region-specific case studies must be done and must supplement more generalizable research, such as econometric analysis. Using both quantitative and qualitative methods may provide a better understanding of the connection between wealth and entrepreneurship, and provide greater insight to local leaders.

A county with relatively high self-employment may want to assess its financial capital stock and invest in the creation of non-bank financial institutions, for example micro-lending or a community loan fund, because results from this chapter suggest formal bank lending (a type of financial capital) is more closely linked with establishment births than self-employed. A county with high levels of intellectual capital may want to ask if it has the financial capital, human capital, and entrepreneurs needed to commercialize innovations locally.

I hope this chapter can serve as a foundation for future research on the relationship between entrepreneurship and rural wealth. I reviewed literature examining entrepreneurship's role in economic growth in rural counties. I discussed how entrepreneurship differs, both by the entrepreneur's motivation and intention, but also by mentioning many of the proxies for measuring entrepreneurship that are available to the regional researcher. I have shown the connection between several forms of wealth and entrepreneurship. Gaps in the literature include research on the interactions between types of wealth and sequencing of investment in wealth necessary to support entrepreneurship, and research on how entrepreneurship may affect rural wealth, not just economic outcomes. Research points towards much of the influence of wealth on entrepreneurship being place-based and varying spatially. Again, this points to the necessity of case studies or region-specific analysis in conjunction with more generalizable research before policy and investment decisions are made.

Notes

1 The views expressed are those of the author and should not be attributed to the Economic Research Service or the US Department of Agriculture.
2 See Low and Isserman (forthcoming) for a detailed discussion on the difference between the proprietor rate, the nonemployer rate, and the innovative nonemployer rate, and the theoretical reason to use total employment as the denominator in all three rates. All three types of self-employment rates used in this analysis are calculated for 2003 because one explanatory variable was not available prior to 2003.
3 Due to space constraints, I do not discuss the regression results for the control variables; the full set of results are available from the author.
4 As an anonymous reviewer helpfully noted, bank deposits are not money on hand. Rather, bank deposits are a proxy for the flow of money on hand, loans made, and interest income from those loans. Cited studies have found deposits to be a practical and useful proxy for the availability of financial capital in US counties.
5 As noted by an anonymous reviewer, this correlation may be due to other factors. I do not intend for this association to be taken as causal.
6 In metropolitan counties, a positive relationship between financial capital and the innovative nonemployer rate was observed (results available from the author upon request).
7 The infrastructure index contains data on the use or maintenance of capital stocks and is not a measure of capital stock itself. In the absence of timely, accurate data on capital stocks in rural counties, proxies are necessary, however.

References

Acs, Z., and Armington, C. (2003) "Endogenous growth and entrepreneurial activity in cities", Discussion Papers, Washington, DC: Center for Economic Studies, Bureau of the Census.

Acs, Z., and Armington, C. (2006) *Entrepreneurship, Geography, and American Economic Growth*, New York: Cambridge University Press.

Acs, Z., and Mueller, P. (2008) "Employment effects of business dynamics: mice, gazelles and elephants", *Small Business Economics*, 30: 85–100.

Acs, Z.J., and Varga, A. (2005) "Entrepreneurship, agglomeration and technological change", *Small Business Economics*, 24: 323–34.

Acs, Z., Armington, C., and Zhang, T. (2007) "The determinants of new-firm survival across regional economies", *Papers in Regional Science*, 86: 367–91.

Blanchflower, D.G. (2000) "Self-employment in OECD countries", *Labor Economics*, 7: 471–505.

Bureau of Economic Analysis (2006) *Regional Economic Information System*. Online. Available at: <http://www.bea.gov/regional/> (accessed 1 December 2012).

Carlino, G., Chatterjee, S., and Hunt, R. (2007) "Urban density and the rate of innovation", *Journal of Urban Economics*, 61: 389–419.

Chinitz, B. (1961) "Contrasts in agglomeration: New York and Pittsburgh", *American Economic Review*, 51: 279–89.

Evans, D., and Leighton, L. (1989) "The determinants of changes in U.S. self-employment, 1968–1987", *Small Business Economics*, 1: 111–19.

Figueroa-Armijos, M., Dabson, B., and Johnson, T.G. (2012) "Rural entrepreneurship in a time of recession", *Entrepreneurshp Research Journal*, 2, Article 3.

Fritsch, M., and Wyrwich, M. (2012) "The long persistence of regional entrepreneurship culture: Germany 1925–2005", DIW Berlin Working Paper 1224, DIW Berlin.

Gallardo, R., and Scammahorn, R. (2012) "Determinants of innovative versus non-innovative entrepreneurs in three southern states", *Review of Regional Studies*, 41(2/3): 103–17.

Garofolli, G. (1994) "New firm formation and regional development: the Italian case", *Regional Studies*, 28: 381–93.

Gartner, W.B., and Shane, S.A. (1995) "Measuring entrepreneurship over time", *Journal of Business Venturing*, 10: 283–301.

Glaeser, E. (2007) "Entrepreneurship in the city", NBER Working Paper Series #13551, Cambridge, MA: National Bureau of Economic Research.

Glaeser, E.L., Kerr, S.P., and Kerr, W.R. (2012) "Entrepreneurship and urban growth: an empirical assessment with historical mines", NBER Working Paper Series #18333, Cambridge, MA: National Bureau of Economic Research.

Goetz, S., and Freshwater, D. (2001) "State-level determinants of entrepreneurship and a preliminary measure of entrepreneurial climate", *Economic Development Quarterly*, 15: 58–70.

Goetz, S., and Rupasingha, A. (2009) "Determinants of growth in non-farm proprietor densities in the US, 1990–2000", *Small Business Economics*, 32: 425–38.

Green, G., Wise, G., and Armstrong, E. (2007) "Inventor and entrepreneur clubs: investment in an innovative approach to entrepreneurship", conference paper presented at: Frameworks for Entrepreneurship Research in Food, Agriculture, Natural Resources and Rural Development: A National Conference on Entrepreneurship Research, Kauffman Foundation, Kansas City, MO.

Henderson, J., and Weiler, S. (2010) "Entrepreneurs and job growth: probing the boundaries of time and space", *Economic Development Quarterly*, 24: 23–32.

Henderson, J., Low, S.A., and Weiler, S. (2007) "The drivers of regional entrepreneurship in rural and metro areas", in N. Walzer (ed.), *Entrepreneurship and Local Economic Development*, Lanham, MD: Lexington Books, pp. 81–102.

Iversen, J., Jorgensen, R., and Malchow-Moeller, M. (2008) "Defining and measuring entrepreneurship", *Foundations and Trends in Entrepreneurship*, 4: 1–63.

Julien, P.A. (2007) *A Theory of Local Entrepreneurship in the Knowledge Economy*, Cheltenham: Edward Elgar.

Kravchenko, N., Weiler, S., and Phillips, R. (2011) "Geographic informational asymmetries and small bank lending", Economics Department Working Paper Series, Colorado State University.

Lee, S., Florida, R., and Acs, Z. (2004) "Creativity and entrepreneurship: a regional analysis of new firm formation", *Regional Studies*, 38: 879–91.

Low, S. (2004) "Regional asset indicators: entrepreneurship breadth and depth", *Main Street Economist (Federal Reserve Bank of Kansas City)*, September.

Low, S.A. (2009) *Defining and Measuring Entrepreneurship for Regional Research: A New Approach*, Doctorate of Philosophy dissertation, University of Illinois at Urbana-Champaign.

Low, S.A., and Isserman, A.M. (forthcoming) "Where are the innovative entrepreneurs? Identifying innovative industries and measuring innovative entrepreneurship", *International Regional Science Review*, DOI: 10.1177/0160017613484926.

Low, S.A., and Weiler, S. (2012) "Employment risk, returns, and entrepreneurship", *Economic Development Quarterly*, 26: 238–51.

Low, S.A., Henderson, J., and Weiler, S. (2005) "Gauging a region's entrepreneurship", *Economic Review (Federal Reserve Bank of Kansas City)*, 90: 61–89.

Luger, M.I., and Koo, J. (2005) "Defining and tracking business start-ups", *Small Business Economics*, 24: 17–28.

McGranahan, D.A. (1999) *Natural Amenities Drive Rural Population Change*, Economic Research Report, AER 781, Washington, DC: US Department of Agriculture, Economic Research Service.

McGranahan, D.A., Wojan, T.R., and Lambert, D.M. (2011) "The rural growth trifecta: outdoor amenities, creative class and entrepreneurial context", *Journal of Economic Geography*, 11: 529–57.

Markley, D.M., and Low, S.A. (2012) "Wealth, entrepreneurship, and rural livelihoods", *Choices*, 27(1): 27.

Meager, N. (1992) "Does unemployment lead to self-employment?", *Small Business Economics*, 4: 87–103.

Mueller, P. (2007) "Exploiting entrepreneurial opportunities: the impact of entrepreneurship on growth", *Small Business Economics*, 28: 355–62.

Ó hUallacháin, B. (1999) "Patent places: size matters", *Journal of Regional Science*, 39: 613–16.

Orlando, M., and Verba, M. (2005) "Do only big cities innovate? Technological maturity and the location of innovation", *Economic Review (Federal Reserve Bank of Kansas City)*, 90: 31–57.

Parker, S. (1996) "A time series model of self employment under uncertainty", *Economica*, 63: 469–75.

Renski, H. (2012) "The influence of industry mix on regional new firm formation in the United States", *Regional Studies* (ahead of print): 1–18.

Rupasingha, A., and Goetz, S.J. (2013) "Self-employment and local economic performance: evidence from US counties", *Papers in Regional Science*, 92: 141–61.

Saxenian, A. (1994) *Regional Advantage: Culture and Competition in Silicon Valley and Route 128*, Cambridge, MA: Harvard University Press.

Scruggs, P. (2010) "The role of equity capital in rural communities", Report to the Ford Foundation. Online. Available at: <http://www.yellowwood.org/The%20Role%20of%20 Equity%20Capital%20in%20Rural%20Communities.pdf> (accessed 15 January 2013).

Stephens, H.M., and Partridge, M.D. (2011) "Do entrepreneurs enhance economic growth in lagging regions?", *Growth and Change*, 42: 431–65.

Stephens, H.M., Partridge, M.D., and Faggian, A. (forthcoming) "Innovation, entrepreneurship, and economic growth in lagging regions", *Journal of Regional Science*. DOI: 10.1111/jors.12019.

Tamasy, C. (2006) "Determinants of regional entrepreneurship dynamics in contemporary Germany: a conceptual and empirical analysis", *Regional Studies*, 40: 365–84.

Vogel, S. (2012) *Multi-Enterprising Farm Households: The Importance of their Alternative Business Ventures in the Rural Economy*, Economic Information Bulletin 101, Washington, DC: US Department of Agriculture, Economic Research Service.

Yu, L., Orazem, P.F., and Jolly, R.W. (2011) "Why do rural firms live longer?", *American Journal of Agricultural Economics*, 93: 673–92.

14 Evaluating the impact of farmers' markets using a rural wealth creation approach

Becca B.R. Jablonski[1]

Introduction

Ask most Americans where they go to purchase "locally grown" food and they will answer: farmers' markets. Located in parking lots, public parks, and community centers, farmers' markets require little infrastructure, and thus represent a relatively easy-to-implement "sustainable development" strategy to many planners, policy makers, and economic developers. As consumer demand for locally grown food has increased, and communities seek opportunities to support agricultural producers, farmers' markets have proliferated. Between 1994 and 2012, the number of farmers' markets nationally increased from 1,755 to 7,864 (USDA AMS 2012b).

Aggregate growth in farmers' markets obscures the fact that some markets fail (Stephenson et al. 2008). The mainstream media overwhelmingly report positive impacts derived from farmers' markets to agricultural producers – particularly small- and mid-scale farmers, consumers, local surrounding businesses, and communities (Malone and Whitacre 2012). As a result, farmers' markets have sprouted in all types of communities as a one-size-fits-all agricultural development strategy without adequate examination of where markets should locate, how they contribute to sustainable development, what support they need to be successful given their specific context, and what opportunity costs are associated with that support.

Using the rural wealth creation framework (defined in Chapter 2), this chapter critically evaluates farmers' markets' impacts on four of the eight forms of capital.[2] By beginning to measure how, in what ways, and under what circumstances farmers' markets contribute or might contribute to sustainable rural development, my goal is to provide insight into how planners, policy makers, and economic developers can more critically evaluate local and regional food system initiatives.

Farmers' markets as rural wealth creation

One of the major challenges in assessing the impact of farmers' markets is the lack of requisite data. Official tracking of direct-to-consumer sales has not kept pace with the sector's growing importance, and where data do exist, they are not delineated by market channel (Tropp 2008). The US Department of Agriculture's Agricultural Marketing Service (USDA AMS) collects annual information on the number and location of markets nationally and conducts a farmers' market manager survey every several years to assess operations, management, sales, and organizational structures (USDA AMS 2012a). However, obtaining farmers' market data from managers is problematic and unreliable for a number of reasons. Most significantly, many markets do not have managers, or to the extent that they do, they are volunteers and do not collect sales information from farmers. Additionally, the USDA AMS survey is voluntary, and information is only collected from existing markets. Thus, information about markets that close or fail may not be adequately captured (Stephenson et al. 2008). The USDA National Agricultural Statistics Service collects information from farms about "direct sales" as part of the Agricultural Resource Management Survey. Low and Vogel (2011) provide some of the most useful analysis of these data, but point to many of the data's challenges, including small sample size, internal and external inconsistencies, inability to separate the value of sales of food and nonfood products, and inability to link the value of sales to the use of a particular marketing channel (such as a farmers' market).

In the absence of readily available data, many researchers have conducted case studies to assess the contribution of farmers' markets to various aspects of sustainable community and economic development. Most farmers' market research involves a case study approach due to the level of detail and effort required to obtain the data as well as the fact that producers who sell through direct-to-consumer channels are a heterogeneous group (Hardesty and Leff 2010; LeRoux et al. 2010). These studies tend to focus on specific aspects of farmers' markets relating to economic, social, health, and environmental outcomes (in other words, financial, social, human, and natural capitals). Though not standardized in their data collection methods, survey questions or sample size, in aggregate, these studies shed light on the potential for farmers' markets to enhance asset building and capital creation in rural communities.

A contribution of this chapter is to use the existing literature to consider the interrelationships of the capitals and the influence they exert on each other, which are perhaps of greater importance than their individual impacts. The accumulation or depletion of one capital has a strong bearing on the others. Additionally, where one capital is lacking or absent, a development initiative may not have the desired effect. The rest of this chapter is devoted to examining the ways in which farmers' markets may affect financial, social, human, and natural capitals, and the interrelationships and transactions of these impacts.

Financial capital

As described in Chapter 2, financial capital is instrumental in facilitating transactions in other forms of capital. If farmers' markets do not meet threshold levels of financial capital generation, there is strong evidence that the other potential capital accumulation benefits will not ensue.[3] Though farmers have economic and noneconomic reasons for attending farmers' markets, the financial motivation appears to be the most important reason for their participation. Studies show that where farmers are not deriving net income from a market, there is high vendor turnover (e.g., Alkon 2008; Stephenson et al. 2008).[4] Stephenson et al. (2008) provide the only systematic exploration of markets that failed and report five intertwined factors, two of which are insufficient numbers of participating farms and farm products. If a market is not profitable for participating vendors, it may be in jeopardy. Financial capital accumulation is therefore a necessary but not sufficient condition of farmers' markets as a rural wealth creation strategy.

The literature shows wide variability in the ability of farmers' markets to enhance farm household income. On the whole, farmers' markets appear to increase farms' gross sales. For example, in his study of farmers selling at Maine markets, Hunt (2007) found participating farmers reporting gross incomes higher than those of other farmers in Maine, and at least as high, if not higher incomes than other farmers nationally. However, farmers' markets often have higher associated marketing and labor costs than other market channels. Higher gross sales do not necessarily translate into increased profitability or financial capital creation. Hardesty and Leff (2010) found that the labor to revenue ratio was the highest in the farmers' market channel (compared with the other market channels they explored). Similarly, LeRoux et al.'s (2010) study looking at producer marketing strategies found that farmers' markets had the lowest overall desirability ranking due in part to the higher associated labor demands.

Much of this variation in farm household income derived from farmers' market sales appears to be based on the population density of the market location. Urban, or more densely populated market locations provided better farm returns in every study I examined (Brown et al. 2007; Gale 1997; Otto and Varner 2005; Varner and Otto 2008; Timmons and Wang 2010). Studies of rural farmers' markets corroborate this conclusion. Malone and Whitacre (2012) found that the most rural counties were under-represented in direct-to-consumer sales generally. Schmit and Gómez (2011) and Jablonski et al. (2011) reported limited overall vendor sales in their studies of rural markets across northern and central New York, respectively. Even in studies of rural communities demonstrating consumer willingness to pay a premium for "locally grown" produce, evidence shows that there are often not enough customers to overcome the production and harvesting expenses (Biermacher et al. 2007).

Community financial capital

Communities may accumulate financial capital from farmers' markets even when farmers are not increasing their household income or profitability.[5] For example, several studies show increased sales at businesses adjacent to farmers' markets on market days. Not only do these additional sales support the businesses themselves, they generate extra tax revenue for the communities in which the markets are located (e.g., Lev et al. 2003). There is also some evidence that farmers' markets increase property values in the market district (Brown 2002).

Perhaps the greatest financial benefit of a farmers' market is its ability to increase the amount of money circulated in a local economy. A farmers' market can increase the amount of money circulated locally in two ways. First, a market can supplant non-local expenditure with local expenditure, thereby reducing leakage (money that leaves a local economy) and increasing total local sales. This direct impact results in important indirect and induced impacts. As farms increase sales, they must purchase more inputs (seeds, fertilizers, packaging, etc.) to produce the additional output. If these indirect purchases are made in the local economy, they have a multiplier impact. As the demand for these input purchases grow, businesses must increase their purchases of inputs and number of employees to make these products. Employees earn wages, and the additional revenue generated from wages is also spent (at least to some extent) in the local economy, resulting in induced impacts. Thus farmers' markets may serve to strengthen local inter-industry linkages, resulting in important community economic impacts.

Second, if farm vendors have greater local linkages (multiplier impacts) than the other local stores from which customers are currently purchasing foodstuffs, even in the absence of additional total local sales there may be a community economic impact. In other words, if farm-vendors spend a greater share of their input expenditure per unit of output locally, compared with the other local outlets where consumers shop, then the multiplier impact associated with market sales is higher than that of other outlets. Thus supplanting local grocery stores' sales, for example, with increased market sales may result in financial wealth creation within a local community.

Surprisingly, despite the widely purported claim that farmers' markets generate positive economic impacts on communities, only a few studies calculate the multiplier impacts of farmers' markets (Henneberry et al. 2009; Hughes et al. 2008; Otto and Varner 2005). A significant problem with all but one of these economic impact assessments is that they calculate the gross impact of farmers' markets without considering the opportunity costs. In order to get at the true impact, researchers must know the extent to which farmers' markets increase total local expenditure or have greater multiplier impacts than other local sales outlets. Otto and Varner (2005), for example, assume that all sales at Iowa farmers' markets represent new or increased local sales. In practice, this is very unlikely to be true as a stable population is more likely to divert purchases of foodstuffs from another source (i.e., reducing grocery store purchases in favor of farmers' market purchases).

Hughes et al. (2008) provide the only study that calculates the net impact of farmers' markets by estimating the loss in grocery store sales due to expenditures at farmers' markets. They find that the economic impact of farmers' markets is still significant, but substantially reduced when accounting for the opportunity cost of such spending.

Social capital

By definition, the intent of a "local" food system is to establish meaningful connections between consumers and producers in a specific place (Hinrichs 2000;

Smithers et al. 2008). Successful farmers' markets, as the quintessence of local food systems, are inherently social and may serve to enhance social capital. Studies consistently show that consumers learn about markets through word of mouth, visit markets with friends and family, interact with vendors, meet community members they know at the market, and feel more tightly linked to the community after visiting (Alkon 2008; Brown 2002; Brown and Miller 2008; Feenstra et al. 2003; Henneberry et al. 2009; Hinrichs 2000; Hunt 2007; Smithers et al. 2008; Stephenson and Lev 2004).

Lyson and Green (1999) assert that these recurring social interactions have the potential to bring the community together and build its capacity for creative problem solving and conflict resolution. However, I could only find limited evidence to support this claim. For example, Sharp and Smith (2003) examined the relationship between farmers and non-farmers at the rural–urban periphery and found that tolerance for agriculture is stronger when non-farmers report the existence of social capital with farmers.

Interrelationship between social and economic capitals

Some literature argues that the social and economic outcomes of farmers' markets are linked. Farmers' markets are social institutions mediating economic activity; they facilitate an environment where market and nonmarket transactions can take place (Gillespie et al. 2007; Hinrichs et al. 2004). Hunt (2007), for example, concludes that consumer spending at farmers' markets is affected by both economic and social considerations, and that consumer–vendor interaction plays an important role. However, it is unclear if this is a spurious correlation. It may be the case that customers who intend to spend more money need to talk to vendors more than customers who are just browsing. Regardless, this phenomenon appears to be self-reinforcing as studies show that consumers choose to shop at farmers' markets, at least in part, because they think it is socially beneficial (Brown 2002; Brown and Miller 2008; Henneberry et al. 2009; Stephenson and Lev 2004).

The social interaction facilitated through farmers' markets also appears to play an important role in instilling trust relationships between producers and consumers, which can result in improved vendor sales (DuPuis 2006). Farmers' markets provide a venue for interaction and meaningful connections in a large economy characterized increasingly by indirect and impersonal connections (Feenstra et al. 2003). Trust serves as a way to mitigate risk for farmers, as they can feel more confident about continued sales to repeat customers (Hunt 2007). Additionally, trust relationships can support expanded marketing channels for producers. For example, a farmer may meet future Community Supported Agriculture members or restaurant customers by virtue of coming to the market (Hardesty and Leff 2010). Thus markets serve to increase the density of local food networks and relations, which is a key component of increasing inter-industry linkages (community economic impact) (Gillespie et al. 2007).

Many researchers have noted the inherent tension that exists between social and financial capital generation at markets; individual farms want to maximize their financial gains, while at the same time, collective efforts may ultimately benefit everyone involved. For example, farm vendors may not publicize their participation in a market via their customer email lists or social media channels, preferring that customers purchase directly from the farm where there is no risk of lost sales to competing vendors. However, if all farmers promoted the market, it might result in net gains for all vendors. The implication of social capital as a collective resource is that farm vendors who develop relationships with customers may not realize its full benefit. There is evidence that customers often view vendors as a unit and thus relationships developed with one vendor can benefit all vendors, while at the same time vendors who act in a manner that diminishes non-farmers' trust and confidence may hurt all market vendors (Sharp and Smith 2003). I could not find research on incentives to overcome these problems of collective action in the literature. Most of the existing literature presenting evidence of vendor cooperation utilizes very limited examples from case studies (e.g., Alkon 2008; Griffin and Frongillo 2003). Griffin and Frongillo (2003), for example, found that farmers cooperate at the market by covering each other's stalls during breaks.

Enhanced social capital developed through farmers' markets may play a key role in supporting the long-term economic viability of small- and mid-scale farmers. As many farmers are not supported financially through farmers' market sales alone, recommendations for improved profitability often center on diversification of sales outlets. Particularly for small- and mid-scale farms, successful market diversification may require additional grower collaboration and coordination to expand product availability and streamline delivery and ordering processes (Hardesty 2008; Tropp 2008). This type of coordination may be facilitated through social capital, which can be generated through grower participation in farmers' markets. Successful coordination strategies may result in asset accumulation for farmers, as well as for the community at large.

Human capital

Chapter 2 of this volume draws its definition of wealth creation in part from Arrow et al. (2010), who define human capital as encompassing health, education, and skills. There is growing evidence that health is both human capital and an input to producing other forms of human capital. Bleakley (2010), for example, demonstrates empirically that being unhealthy inhibits productivity and investment in human capital. With this broader definition of human capital in mind, farmers' market studies typically focus on two types of human capital outcomes: improved nutrition through access to healthy ("local") foods; and farmers' business skill development and entrepreneurship.

Health

Many rural communities are experiencing limited food access. Food retailers have become more consolidated and shifted business models to include larger retail storefronts that require greater numbers of shoppers. Concomitantly, rural populations have declined. Thus, it has become more difficult for supermarkets to thrive in rural places. Many studies demonstrate the link between limited food access and increases in food insecurity and obesity. As planners and policy makers seek ways to reverse this trend, farmers' markets are more commonly being thought of as an affordable, easy-to-implement method to improve rural food access (Schmit and Gómez 2011).

Though the rigor of some of the studies appears to be in question (many of the studies, for example, do not include control groups), there is consensus among researchers that the presence of a farmers' market in a community is positively correlated with health outcomes (e.g., Dollahite et al. 2005; McCormack et al. 2010; Ruelas et al. 2012). McCormack et al. (2010) reviewed twelve studies published between 1980 and 2009 focused on the nutrition outcomes of farmers' market initiatives. Seven studies investigated the impact of farmers' market nutrition programs for women, infants, and children participants and five focused on the influence of farmers' market programs for seniors. All of the studies involved some type of subsidy to support the increased consumption of fruits and vegetables, and the majority of the results validated the improved health outcomes.

One major deficit of these studies is that they fail to examine the opportunity costs associated with farmers' markets as a food access strategy. In order to make their product attractive to low-income consumers, do farmers and communities deplete their financial capital by reducing the costs of products, or require government subsidies? What is the impact on wealth creation – all community assets, net of liabilities? Alkon (2008) writes that there are often contradictions between financial and ethical goals – environmentally sustainable products often cost more, and are unaffordable to many low-income households. He cites a vendor at the North Berkeley, CA farmers' market who reported interest in supporting positive environmental and health outcomes for Latina/o community members. When asked why he did not sell his product at a nearby, predominantly Latina/o market, he answered that he could not make enough money. Farmers at markets often donate produce for cooperative extension agents or other nonprofit agencies to use in demonstrations about healthy eating. Though this may serve to attract additional customers to markets, most evidence points to the philanthropic nature of this act (Griffin and Frongillo 2003). The long-term implications of these tradeoffs and implications for rural wealth creation require further investigation.

Intersection of social and human capitals

Another vein of research examines the impact of social capital on health outcomes, and thus human capital. There is evidence that increased participation in civic society can decrease the risks of food insecurity and increase the capacity of at-risk households to obtain healthy, affordable foods. As farmers' markets can play a role in increasing interpersonal connections and civic structures, they may serve to support enhanced health outcomes (e.g., Dollahite et al. 2005; Morton et al. 2005; Walker et al. 2007). Walker et al. (2007), for example, conducted the first study of the Farmers' Market Nutrition Program (a federal–state partnership initiative to support increased consumption of locally grown fruits and vegetable by low-income consumers) on food security and social capital and found them to be positively correlated. However, much more research is needed in this area before a conclusion can be reached.

Intersection of economic and human capitals: skill development and entrepreneurship

Increasing consolidation and coordination across supply chains has decreased access of small- and mid-scale farms to conventional markets, such as supermarkets (e.g., Gillespie et al. 2007; Griffin and Frongillo 2003). To some extent, farmers' markets (and other "alternative" local food markets) have emerged in response. There is a significant amount of research demonstrating that farmers' markets can play a key role in supporting the development of beginning and small farms by providing an easy, low barrier to entry market, with an existing customer base for locally grown products (Alkon 2008; Brown 2002; Brown and Miller 2008; Brown et al. 2007; Feenstra et al. 2003; Hardesty and Leff 2010; Hunt 2007; Schmit and Gómez 2011; Thilmany and Watson 2004).

Many researchers argue that successful farmers' markets function as business incubators, and help to support entrepreneurship. They can provide key infrastructure to build skills and provide business experience for new and expanding farm businesses (Feenstra et al. 2003; Gillespie et al. 2007). The same direct farm-to-consumer interaction that serves to strengthen social capital assets also builds human capital assets. Repeated interactions can "generate and circulate knowledge that vendors might use to develop new products and creative ways of marketing them" (Hinrichs et al. 2004, pp. 32–33). Feenstra et al. (2003), for example, explored New York, Iowa, and California farmers' market contributions to the development of vendors' capacity as entrepreneurs, and found that 66 percent of vendors expanded an existing product line, 50 percent added a new product category, and 40 percent made new business contacts. Hinrichs et al.'s (2004) study of innovation at farmers' markets found that social learning between vendors and customers most strongly influenced vendors' intensity of innovative practices.

The ability of farmers' markets to build vendors' skills and enhance entrepreneurship opportunities raises an important question as to the significance of direct vendor sales at the market, and how to evaluate financial capital accumulation. Even the small amount of sales derived by vendors from farmers' markets may provide an important source of (often supplementary) income for small and beginning farm households. Gross sales may be less important than the skills and business experience provided by farmers' markets (Brown et al. 2007). In other words, looking solely at the direct financial capital generated through farmers' markets may be shortsighted; farmers' markets may play a more critical role in developing human capital assets required for long-term financial viability.

However, without threshold levels of human capital assets, farmer vendors are unlikely to benefit from opportunities to build skills and entrepreneurship through market participation. Hinrichs et al. (2004), for example, found that social learning is moderated by human capital and structural factors. In their study having higher levels of educational attainment significantly increased the intensity of innovative practices resulting from market participation.

Natural capital

The rural wealth creation framework behooves one to consider how development initiatives impact a community's natural assets. The framework explicitly acknowledges that without maintained (or improved) farmland, other capital creation benefits cannot result, as there will not be farmers to grow product(s) to sell at farmers' markets.

There are several studies that examine the ability of farmers' markets to build natural capital assets. Many of these studies begin with the assumption that certain agricultural production practices (e.g., non-GMO, organic, heirloom) are ecologically superior to other farming practices (Bjorklund et al. 2009; Hunt 2007; Lyson and Green 1999). Thus they conclude that increasing agricultural outputs with these attributes builds a community's natural capital assets.

Perhaps more to the point, several studies demonstrate growing demand for products marketed with certain production attributes, and consumer willingness to pay a premium price for these products (e.g., Alkon 2008; Hunt 2007; La Trobe 2001; Lyson and Green 1999). To the extent that many farmers (particularly small- and mid-scale) gain market access via farmers' markets, which improves farm profitability, natural capital assets may be benefitted (maintained or perhaps enhanced) as farmland continues in production. Though natural capital assets may increase more if the land is not kept in farming (i.e., farmland might be put into the Conservation Reserve or other more ecologically valuable use), given the current conversion rate of rural land to developed use of 1,498,200 acres annually, it is perhaps most likely that non-economically viable farmland will be developed (American Farmland Trust 2007). Thus, maintaining land in agriculture is perhaps a realistic way to preserve a rural community's natural capital assets.

It is also worth noting that these natural capital benefits may result by virtue of rural farmers increasing their access to markets, regardless of the market location or type. In fact, there may be an argument that natural capital would be most significantly enhanced through rural farmers' participation in markets most successful in increasing farms' financial assets, which may mean participation in urban markets. This is an area of research that requires further investigation.

Conclusion

This chapter demonstrates that using wealth creation to measure the impacts of local food initiatives paints a far different picture than evaluating the same strategy by its economic impact alone. The charge of the wealth creation framework, to capture the impact on all community assets and their interrelationships, has key implications to long-term sustainable development.

A careful reading of the farmers' market literature demonstrates that farmers' markets must meet farm-vendors' financial requirements or vendors will not participate and the markets may fail. But most other impacts resulting from farmers' markets require additional research. In terms of economic impact: Do farms purchase more of their inputs, per unit of output, locally than other outlets for foodstuffs? To what extent do farmers' markets divert purchases from another "local" outlet versus increase overall purchases (i.e., how do we measure the opportunity costs of farmers' markets)? If farmers' markets in rural areas require public subsidy so that threshold levels of remuneration are met to ensure farmer participation (i.e., salaries for market managers or advertising) what are the opportunity costs? What other local food or agricultural development strategies might be implemented that do not require public subsidy or elicit higher returns on investment? The rural wealth creation framework requires investigation of the *net* impact of an initiative on community wealth. Unsuccessful farmers' markets, particularly those implemented where threshold financial wealth creation asset requirements are absent, may actually serve to deplete wealth.

Likewise, this literature review points to a number of areas for future research in social and human capital. Do farmers' markets facilitate a community's capacity for problem solving and conflict resolution? Is there evidence that efforts focused on vendor collaboration elicit wealth creation (i.e., net gains in social or financial capital)? Are there examples of governance structures or interventions that facilitate vendor collaboration? Does social capital facilitated through interactions at farmers' markets lead to improved nutrition outcomes?

The use of a broader capitals framework also raises the question as to whether or not all of the capitals are of uniform importance, and contribute equally to rural wealth creation. Communities must be very clear about the goals and intended beneficiaries of an initiative. Some communities will have to choose between strategies that elicit the greatest amount of capital accumulation versus specific distributional effects (i.e., increasing food access in underserved communities or supporting enhanced farm profitability).

Finally, more research is needed on where a market needs to be located in order to enhance rural wealth creation most effectively. Unlike the discussion of ownership (and people-based versus place-based wealth) in other parts of this book, local food system assets are inherently owned and managed locally. These local businesses have little ability to relocate, and are thus committed to the long-term future of the community. Many of the financial, social, human, and natural wealth creation benefits described throughout this chapter can occur as long as the farm is physically located in the rural community; the resulting benefits are not dependent on the market's location. Though there are a few impacts that require markets to be physically located in rural communities (i.e., increasing sales for adjacent businesses on market days), many of the rural wealth creation outcomes may result from enhanced marketing opportunities for producers generally. Thus, does it make more sense for rural communities to develop farmers' markets in more urban centers where farmers' markets may yield more financial asset creation that can be spent in rural communities (and may serve to enhance their long-term sustainability)?

The question of market location raises another about the impact of market ownership. Farmers' market ownership, or more specifically the way in which it governs, has significant consequences on capital creation. The governance structure of a market is politically charged, as it determines who wins and who loses based on its rules and regulations (DuPuis 2006). For example, a farmers' market located in New York City (on the border of New Jersey), may establish rules that only New York State farmers are considered "local" and thus eligible to participate. The market may therefore result in capital accumulation and rural wealth creation in New York at the expense of New Jersey. If rural communities become dependent on urban markets, will they lose the ability to make decisions about market governance?

There is a significant need for further research on the best ways to utilize the growing demand for "locally grown" food to support rural communities, as well as ways to evaluate initiatives. There are many facets to consider, but exploring all of a community's assets, and the interaction of these assets, through the wealth creation approach is in the best interest of a community concerned with long-term sustainability and enhanced well-being.

Notes

1 This project was supported by the Agriculture and Food Research Initiative Competitive Grant No. 2012-67011-19957 from the USDA National Institute of Food and Agriculture. The sponsor played no role in the study design, collection, analysis, interpretation of data, writing of the report, or decision to submit the chapter for publication.
2 See Pender and Ratner (Chapter 2) for a more detailed definition of "wealth" and the "community capitals" paradigm. Pender and Ratner define "wealth" in terms of eight types of capital, including: physical, financial, natural, human, intellectual, social, political, and cultural.
3 Threshold levels of financial capital vary given specific contexts, and thus there is no dollar amount attributed to the definition of "threshold".
4 In this chapter, I use increased income as a proxy for creation of financial wealth. As pointed out by Pender and Ratner in Chapter 2, creating financial wealth requires net financial savings, which is not the same as increasing income, although it is easier to generate net savings if income is increased. I found no studies that investigated impacts of farmers' markets on financial wealth per se.
5 Though community financial capital accumulation may not depend directly on enhanced farm profitability through farmers' market sales, farmers generally require a financial incentive in order to participate in markets, and thus community financial capital accumulation may depend indirectly upon net farm sales at a market.

References

Alkon, A. (2008) "From value to values: sustainable consumption at farmers markets", *Agriculture and Human Values*, 25(4): 487–98.

American Farmland Trust (2007) "National Statistics Sheet", *Farmland Information Center*. Online. Available at: <http://www.farmlandinfo.org/agricultural_statistics/> (accessed 23 April 2013).

Arrow, K.J., Dasgupta, P., Goulder, L.H., Mulford, K.J., and Oleson, K. (2010) "Sustainability and the measurement of wealth", NBER Working Paper 16599, Cambridge, MA: National Bureau of Economic Research.

Biermacher, J., Upson, S., Miller, D., and Pittman, D. (2007) "Economic challenges of small-scale vegetable production and retailing in rural communities: an example from rural Oklahoma", *Journal of Food Distribution Research*, 38(3): 1–13.

Bjorklund, J., Milestad, R., Ahnstrom, J., Westberg, L., and Geber, U. (2009) "Local selling as a driving force for increased on-farm biodiversity", *Journal of Sustainable Agriculture*, 33(8): 885–902.

Bleakley, H. (2010) "Health, human capital, and development", *Annual Review of Economics*, 2(1): 283–310.

Brown, A. (2002) "Farmers' market research 1940–2000: an inventory and review", *American Journal of Alternative Agriculture*, 17(4): 167–76.

Brown, C., and Miller, S. (2008) "The impacts of local markets: a review of research on farmers' markets and community supported agriculture (CSA)", *American Journal of Agricultural Economics*, 90(5): 1298–302.

Brown, C., Miller, S., Boone, D., Boone, H., Gartin, S., et al. (2007) "The importance of farmers' markets for West Virginia direct marketers", *Renewable Agriculture and Food Systems*, 22(1): 20–29.

Dollahite, J., Nelson, J., Frongillo, E., and Griffin, M. (2005) "Building community capacity through enhanced collaboration in the farmers' market nutrition program", *Agriculture and Human Values*, 22(3): 339–54.

DuPuis, E.M. (2006) "Civic markets: alternative value chain governance as civic engagement", *Crop Management*. Online. Available at: <http://www.plantmanagementnetwork. org/pub/cm/symposium/organics/DuPuis/> (accessed 11 September 2012).

Feenstra, G.W., Lewis, C.C., Hinrichs, C.C., Gillespie, G.W., and Hilchey, D. (2003) "Entrepreneurial outcomes and enterprise size in US retail farmers' markets", *American Journal of Alternative Agriculture*, 18(1): 46–55.

Gale, F. (1997) "Direct farm marketing as a rural development tool', *Rural Development Perspectives*, 12(2): 19–25.

Gillespie, G.W., Hilchey, D., Hinrichs, C.C., and Feenstra, G.W. (2007) "Farmers' markets as keystones in rebuilding local and regional food systems", in C.C. Hinrichs and T.A. Lyson (eds.), *Remaking the North American Food System: Strategies for Sustainability*, Lincoln, NE: University of Nebraska Press.

Griffin, M.R., and Frongillo, E.A. (2003) "Experiences and perspectives of farmers from Upstate New York farmers' markets", *Agriculture and Human Values*, 20(2): 189–203.

Hardesty, S.D. (2008) "The growing role of local food markets", *American Journal of Agricultural Economics*, 90(5): 1289–95.

Hardesty, S.D., and Leff, P. (2010) "Determining marketing costs and returns in alternative marketing channels", *Renewable Agriculture and Food Systems*, 25(1): 24–34.

Henneberry, S.R., Whitacre, B., and Agustini, H.N. (2009) "An evaluation of the economic impacts of Oklahoma farmers' markets", *Journal of Food Distribution Research*, 40(3): 64–78.

Hinrichs, C.C. (2000) "Embeddedness and local food systems: notes on two types of direct agricultural market", *Journal of Rural Studies*, 16(3): 295–303.

Hinrichs, C.C., Gillespie, G.W., and Feenstra, G.W. (2004) "Social learning and innovation at retail farmers' markets", *Rural Sociology*, 69(1): 31–58.

Hughes, D.W., Brown C., Miller, S., and McConnell T. (2008) "Evaluating the economic impact of farmers' markets using an opportunity cost framework", *Journal of Agricultural and Applied Economics*, 40(1): 253–65.

Hunt, A.R. (2007) "Consumer interactions and influences on farmers' market vendors", *Renewable Agriculture and Food Systems*, 22(1): 54–66.

Jablonski, B.B.R., Perez-Burgos, J., and Gómez, M.I. (2011) "Food value chain development in Central New York: CNY Bounty", *Journal of Agriculture, Food Systems, and Community Development*, 1(4): 129–41.

La Trobe, H. (2001) "Farmers' markets: consuming local rural produce", *International Journal of Consumer Studies*, 25(3): 181–92.

LeRoux, M.N., Schmit, T.M., Roth, M., and Streeter, D.H. (2010) "Evaluating marketing channel options for small-scale fruit and vegetable producers", *Renewable Agriculture and Food Systems*, 25(1): 16–23.

Lev, L., Brewer, L., and Stephenson, G. (2003) *How Do Farmers Markets Affect Neighboring Businesses?*, Corvallis, OR: Oregon State University Extension Service.

Low, S.A., and Vogel, S. (2011) *Direct and Intermediated Marketing of Local Foods in the United States*, Economic Research Report ERR 128, Washington, DC: US Department of Agriculture, Economic Research Service. Online. Available at: <http://www.ers.usda.gov/publications/err-economic-research-report/err128> (accessed 13 March 2013).

Lyson, T.A., and Green, J. (1999) "The agricultural marketscape: a framework for sustaining agriculture and communities in the Northeast", *Journal of Sustainable Agriculture*, 15(2–3): 133–50.

McCormack, L.A., Laska, M.N., Larson, N.I., and Story, M. (2010) "Review of the nutritional implications of farmers' markets and community gardens: a call for evaluation and research efforts", *Journal of the American Dietetic Association*, 110(3): 399–408.

Malone, T., and Whitacre, B. (2012) "How rural is our local food policy?", *Daily Yonder*. Online. Available at: <http://www.dailyyonder.com/local-food-policy-it-it-truly-focussed-rural/2012/08/24/4364> (accessed 23 October 2012).

Morton, L.W., Bitto, E.A., Oakland, M.J., and Sand, M. (2005) "Solving the problems of Iowa food deserts: food insecurity and civic structure", *Rural Sociology*, 70(1): 94–112.

Otto, D., and Varner, T. (2005) *Consumers, Vendors, and the Economic Importance of Iowa Farmers' Markets: An Economic Impact Survey Analysis*, Ames, IA: Iowa State University.

Ruelas, V., Iverson, E., Kiekel, P., and Peters, A. (2012) "The role of farmers' markets in two low income, urban communities", *Journal of Community Health*, 37(3): 554–62.

Schmit, T.M., and Gómez, M.I. (2011) "Developing viable farmers' markets in rural communities: an investigation of vendor performance using objective and subjective valuations", *Food Policy*, 36(2): 119–27.

Sharp, J., and Smith, M. (2003) "Social capital and farming at the rural–urban interface: the importance of nonfarmer and farmer relations", *Agricultural Systems*, 76(3): 913–27.

Smithers, J., Lamarche, J., and Joseph, A.E. (2008) "Unpacking the terms of engagement with local food at the farmers' market: insights from Ontario", *Journal of Rural Studies*, 24(3): 337–50.

Stephenson, G., and Lev, L. (2004) "Common support for local agriculture in two contrasting Oregon communities", *Renewable Agriculture and Food Systems*, 19(4): 210–17.

Stephenson, G., Lev, L., and Brewer, L. (2008) "I'm getting desperate: what we know about farmers' markets that fail", *Renewable Agriculture and Food Systems*, 23(3): 188–99.

Thilmany, D., and Watson, P. (2004) "The increasing role of direct marketing and farmers' markets for Western US producers", *Western Economics Forum*, 3(2): 19–25.

Timmons, D., and Wang, Q. (2010) "Direct food sales in the United States: evidence from state and county-level data", *Journal of Sustainable Agriculture*, 34(2): 229–40.

Tropp, D. (2008) "The growing role of local food markets: discussion", *American Journal of Agricultural Economics*, 90(5): 1310–11.

US Department of Agriculture, Agricultural Marketing Service (USDA AMS) (2012a) *Farmers Market Fact Sheet*, Washington, DC: US Department of Agriculture, Agricultural Marketing Service. Online. Available at: <http://www.ams.usda.gov/AMSv1.0/farmersmarkets> (accessed 15 October 2012).

US Department of Agriculture, Agricultural Marketing Service (USDA AMS) (2012b) *Farmers Market Growth*, Washington, DC: US Department of Agriculture, Agricultural Marketing Service. Online. Available at: <http://www.ams.usda.gov/AMSv1.0/ams.fetchTemplateData.do?template=TemplateS&leftNav=WholesaleandFarmersMarkets&page=WFMFarmersMarketGrowth&description=Farmers%20Market%20Growth&acct=frmrdirmkt> (accessed 9 October 2012).

Varner, T., and Otto, D. (2008) "Factors affecting sales at farmers' markets: an Iowa study", *Review of Agricultural Economics*, 30(1): 176–89.

Walker, J.L., Holben, D.H., Kropf, M.L., Holcomb Jr., J.P., and Anderson, H. (2007) "Household food insecurity is inversely associated with social capital and health in females from Special Supplemental Nutrition Program for women, infants, and children households in Appalachian Ohio", *Journal of the American Dietetic Association*, 107(11): 1989–93.

15 Attracting retirees as a rural wealth creation strategy

Richard J. Reeder and Faqir S. Bagi[1]

Baby boomers – individuals born between 1946 and 1964, have been described as "the largest and most affluent generation in American history" (Clement 2004: 1). As they have begun retiring in large numbers, both in the United States and in other developed countries, migrating retirees have attracted increased attention as a vehicle for rural development (Brown and Glasgow 2008; Jauhiainen 2009). State and local strategies designed to attract retirees may be able to tap into this significant source of wealth (Reeder 1998; Skelley 2004). These strategies are particularly relevant in the rural United States, which has been characterized by net in-migration of retirees over the last fifty years (Brown and Glasgow 2008: 21). This chapter examines how retiree attraction fits into the wealth creation framework, identifying the forms of wealth that retiree attraction enhances, which rural communities are best suited to attracting retirees, and how communities can avoid potential pitfalls.

Background

Retiree attraction may be viewed as a consumption-based development strategy in the sense that individuals (retirees) come into the community and consume local goods and services, thereby stimulating the local economy. This contrasts with export-based approaches involving mining, timber, agriculture, and manufacturing industries. In addition to retiree attraction, other amenity-based development approaches, such as those that emphasize recreation and tourism, belong to the consumption-based category. Also within this category are strategies involving communities that specialize as centers that sell goods and services to consumers from surrounding areas or as bedroom communities that attract individuals who live in these communities but work in a nearby central city or suburb. Consumption-based industries have had a distinct advantage over export-based industries in the United States in recent years, because they do not have to compete with lower-cost competition overseas.

Rural (nonmetropolitan) areas in the United States first began attracting retirees in significant numbers in the 1970s. USDA's Economic Research Service (ERS) identified 515 rural retirement destination counties – those whose older (age 60 and over) population grew by more than 15 percent during the 1970s as

a result of net in-migration (Bender et al. 1985). Using the same 15 percent definition, the number of rural retirement counties declined to only 190 in the 1980s
(Reeder 1998, 4), presumably due to the economic difficulties that led to greater
rural out-migration (and hence less net in-migration) during the decade. The
improved rural economy during the 1990s was reflected in an increase to 277
rural retirement counties during that decade.[2] The 2000s were expected to be a
bellweather decade for rural retirement counties, thanks to the arrival of substantial numbers of baby boomer retirees (Cromartie and Nelson 2009). But with two
recessions and a financial crisis, the 2000s have in some ways paralleled the
1980s in terms of rural economic difficulties, and have been associated with
greater rural out-migration, nationwide. Hence, the number of retirement counties could decline when the ERS updates its county classifications for the 2000s.
However, 84 percent of counties classified as rural retirement counties during the
1990s continued to benefit from population growth during the 2000s, which
compares favorably with 69 percent of recreation counties (Johnson 2012, 4). Hence,
states and localities are likely to continue to attempt to attract retirees.

Potential effects on financial, physical, and human capital

In-migrating retirees (excluding those that move only short distances, such as to
move into a smaller house) tend to have above-average incomes and educations
(Skelley 2004, 212; Brown and Glasgow 2008, 39). This "self-selection" process
is one of the main reasons that migrating retirees (hereafter referred to simply as
retirees) are considered a desirable target for economic and community development strategies. The financial wealth they bring can be shared with others in
their destination community when they spend money locally, or contribute to
local charities and invest in local businesses.[3]

Retirees are also often thought to add more to the local tax base than to local
government spending, because retiree households have little need for local
schools – the costliest of local government services. However, retirees may
demand more from some types of government services, such as libraries, park
recreation services, public transportation, or police and fire protection. In theory,
this could result in greater physical capital accumulation in the form of buildings
and equipment used on these government functions. Complicating this picture
are the in-migrating workers who fill some of the new jobs created by the spending of retirees. Studies of retiree impacts suggest that for each retirement household, about one new worker is required (Serow 2003, 899).[4] These workers tend
to be younger and may have lower incomes than the retirees, hence they can add
more to local government costs (including schools) than to the local tax base.[5]
The impacts on local governments and communities are therefore not so clear-cut
and depend on the characteristics of the retirees and laborers attracted to the
communities (Serow 2003; Reeder 1998).

Much of the enhanced physical wealth is expected to come in the form of new
and improved housing, infrastructure, and commercial construction, such as for
housing and health services thought to be particularly important to retirees.

While growth of such physical wealth is always expected to accompany substantial population growth, in-migrating retirees tend to have relatively high incomes; hence in theory they are expected to demand more in goods and services, and consequently lead to greater expansion of physical wealth in retiree attraction places than in other growing places.[6]

Retirees can contribute to their communities by applying their higher than average educations (human capital), not only as volunteers to local churches, schools, and other such organizations[7] but also by providing useful technical expertise to rural communities that might otherwise lack it.[8] Retirees are also increasingly seeking part-time employment upon retirement, yielding additional income for the community (Norris 2012, 1). In addition, retirees can contribute to human capital indirectly by stimulating economic and employment growth that allows local residents to work more and invest in their educations. The presence of retirees can also lead to a wider array of health services, which in turn can lead to improved health in the community (see note 6).

Nationwide data show that retirement counties scored significantly higher in private physical wealth (indicated by higher median housing values) and human capital (indicated by higher average levels of educational attainment and lower age-adjusted mortality rates) (Table 15.1). Moreover, trends over the last twenty years indicate retiree counties have shown more improvement in these measures than non-retirement counties. Of particular interest is that median housing values in retirement counties grew more rapidly, in constant 2005 dollars, than those in non-retirement counties in the 2000s, even though by the end of the decade, the housing bubble – believed to be particularly present in retirement counties – had already burst as of 2006.[9] Although such economic statistics are suggestive, they cannot in themselves prove that retiree attraction benefits rural wealth, so caution should be taken in interpreting these trends.[10]

One of the chief selling points of retiree attraction is that it may help to diversify a rural economy. For example, a small town is extremely vulnerable if it relies too heavily on one crop or one or two large mining or manufacturing plants. Adding retirees to the mix helps to protect against short-term collapses due to bad weather, price fluctuations, technological change, or increased global competition affecting particular industries. However, with the recent difficulties associated with the collapse of housing prices and the so-called "great recession", communities that relied heavily on housing, tourism, and retiree attraction have been subject to their own form of economic instability.

The average rural retirement county unemployment rate rose from 4.9 percent in 2000 to 10.5 percent in 2010 – this was greater than the rise from 4.6 to 8.9 percent unemployment for rural non-retirement counties (Table 15.1). The most negatively affected were retirement counties in the Southeast, West, and Midwest, as shown in Figure 15.1. These instability problems are also apparent in rural retirement counties' greater decline in real median incomes during the 2000s (–5.3 percent versus –1.8 percent for non-retirement counties).[11]

In addition, new housing construction appears to have dropped significantly in many rural retiree-attraction counties during the latter half of the 2000s. A study

Table 15.1 Selected indicators and trends for rural retirement and non-retirement counties

Indicator[1]	Retirement county[2]	Non-retirement county[2]
Median housing value[3]	*constant dollars*	
2007–2011	145,501	93,170
Change	*percent*	
1989 to 1999[6]	27.3	25.6
1999 to 2007–2011	37.2	23.4
Higher education[3,4]	*percent*	
2007–2011	18.7	16.5
Change	*percentage points*	
1990 to 2000	5.9	5.1
2000 to 2007–2011	2.9	2.3
Mortality rate[5]	*per 100,000*	
2008	826.9	871.0
Change		
1990 to 2000	−58.8	−25.8
2000 to 2008[6]	−60.7	−51.3
Unemployment rate	*percent*	
2010	10.5	8.9
Change	*percentage points*	
1990 to 2000	−2.4	−1.7
2000 to 2010	5.6	4.3
Median income	*constant dollars*	
2010[6]	35,817	35,537
Change	*percent*	
1989 to 1999[6]	21.1	17.7
1999 to 2010	−5.3	−1.8

Source: USDA-Economic Research Service, using data from the Department of Commerce/Bureau of the Census and the Department of Health and Human Services/Center for Disease Control.

Notes:
[1] Averages (simple means) are used unless otherwise indicated.
[2] ERS 2004 retirement destination county typology based on population changes in the 1990s.
[3] A five-year average is used, covering the years 2007–2011.
[4] Percentage of educated adults (age 25 and over) with bachelor's or higher college degree.
[5] Age-adjusted deaths per 100,000 population.
[6] For this year/period, the difference between retirement and non-retirement county means was not statistically significant. Otherwise, the differences in means were significant.

of two such counties (Routt County, Colorado and Rabun County, Georgia), found new residential building permits dropped about 85–90 percent from 2005 to 2010 (Nelson 2012).[12] Moreover, some developers have experienced bankruptcies and selloffs of properties, including some large-scale nationwide firms specializing in retiree housing projects.[13] A similar wave of bankruptcies afflicted retirement developments in Arizona, California, and Florida in the 1980s (Bergsman 1987).

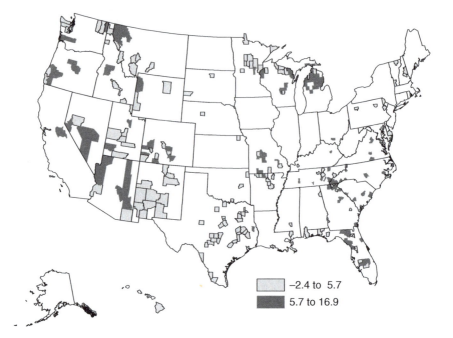

Figure 15.1 Nonmetro retirement counties, change in the unemployment rate, 2000–2010

When developers go bankrupt, local governments and taxpayers must often pay the cost of completing the roads and water systems in such developments; banks and other local institutions can also be ill affected (Raitz et al. 1984).

Another aspect that particularly concerns the retiree attraction strategy involves the implications of the future aging of baby boomer retirees and how that might place a significant financial burden on their host communities. The main concern is that their declining health will end up costing the communities more money for health services. Several offsetting factors tend to lessen this concern. Most of these costs presumably will be covered by private insurance of the retirees and by Medicare and Medicaid, and hence local communities will not bear much of the costs. An influx of medical workers and others who assist older, incapacitated retirees would add to local tax revenues to pay for any additional costs, though there is some concern that there might not be enough competent medical workers to provide quality service in rural areas (Kaye 2012). Another offsetting factor is that many retirees, upon suffering significant health deterioration, might leave the area to be closer to loved ones. Finally, after forty or more years when most of the boomers will have moved away or died, there will be an adjustment process for the community. Whether this is a severe problem or not will depend on future economic and demographic trends affecting the area. Hence there is uncertainty about what will happen over the long run.

Potential effects on natural, social, political, and cultural capital

During the 1990s, the population of rural retirement counties grew by an average of 25 percent, compared with only 5 percent for rural non-retirement counties. Although these growth rates declined considerably during the 2000s, retirement counties continued to grow more rapidly than other rural counties, adding another 10 percent to their population, on average.[14] When retiree attraction leads to rapid population growth, this has the potential to change the physical landscape of the community radically, affecting the natural environment as well as the rural character of the community. The influx of new people can also affect how well the community functions socially, and it can alter the political and cultural makeup of the community. It therefore may have implications for natural, social, cultural, and political capital.

Growth-related environmental concerns include water pollution (associated with residential septic tanks or increased use of lawn chemicals), problems with growth of local landfills, loss of natural terrain and wildlife to development, and introduction of non-native species. These problems tend to be more severe where the natural environment is more vulnerable – for example, where water supplies are limited and more subject to pollution from overflowing septic tanks, and where retirees and/or the in-migrating workers are located close to vulnerable wildlife populations (Reeder et al. 1993: 135–36). These environmental concerns can lead to increased spending on environmental infrastructure (Skelley 2004: 217).[15]

Offsetting some of these natural wealth concerns is the observation that retirees are sometimes active in groups attempting to preserve the natural wealth of the area. This is not unexpected, since many are attracted to these areas principally because of the quality of local natural amenities. In addition, some retirement developments are designed to minimize land fragmentation, preserving significant open space and natural buffers. Consequently, this form of development can be less problematic, environmentally, than where retirees more diffusely inhabit a region.

The implications for social capital are also mixed.[16] Retirees often contribute significantly to social capital by joining local churches and other organizations, and sometimes starting new social organizations. Some researchers have expressed concern that retirees may not socialize enough with other residents, reducing community social cohesion. One study using interviews of retirees in several case study communities across the country found that retirees had more social connections and participation in their communities than expected (Glasgow and Arguillas 2008). This was due partly to the finding that a significant number had at least some friends and family in the community, and partly to the tendency for many of these retirees to be, at least initially, fairly active socially, participating with various local organizations.[17] Another study, examining amenity-based development (which includes retiree attraction), found that these places tended to have more turnover in young adult population, with higher percentages of young adults both leaving and coming into the community compared with places without this form of development. This finding led the authors to be concerned that these places could suffer from less inclusiveness of these younger populations (Winkler et al. 2011).

Retirees can also have mixed effects on local political capital. On the positive side, they can bring with them social connections to the outer world that they can use to improve local conditions (Brown and Glasgow 2008: 159–60). They may also start new political groups aimed at constructive change to address local problems that had been ignored in the past. This, however, can in some cases result in political displacement of existing local power elites, which may make it more challenging for some communities to find political solutions to important issues (Brown and Glasgow 2008: 170–74).

One such potential political conflict that has attracted significant research attention involves local schools. As noted previously, retirees tend to have no direct interest in schools, hence one might expect them to be less supportive of efforts to increase school funding than other residents. Past research provides evidence of this occurring in some places (Reeder et al. 1993). More recent research in Tennessee found that, over a forty-year period, in-migration of seniors was not correlated negatively with county-level school spending per pupil (Lambert et al. 2009). On the other hand, this research found that counties with high in-migration of seniors were "less likely to translate increased fiscal capacity to fund education" than other counties. Here, a problem related to social capital appears to have made it more difficult for retirement communities to make use of their enhanced financial capital to address an issue related to human capital – a good example of how different forms of wealth interrelate.

The above discussion documents just one example of a variety of potential "we–they" political conflicts that could occur between retirees and longer-term residents (Skelley 2004). Such conflicts sometimes arise from the different situations in which retirees find themselves – for instance, they may live in a separate enclave with different problems from those living in town. With more time on their hands, they may also find it easier to become politically active and push for changes in how things are done. They may therefore become viewed as a threat of displacing the traditional power elites in a community (Brown and Glasgow 2008: 170–73). Another political threat is that the local government might be "captured" by retirement developers that come to exert substantial influence on local government boards (Skelley 2004: 219).

Retirees from different parts of the country may have different preferences for public services and different attitudes towards taxes than long-term residents. If they come from urban areas, they may have problems with agricultural noises and smells, and they may oppose informal tradition allowing neighbors to hunt on their land. They may prefer different architectural styles, and follow different religions. This may add to the cultural diversity of the locality and may help local development over the long run (e.g., it may help the community attract firms seeking a place where employees have access to a diverse array of cultural activities). However, it may also create cultural conflicts, threatening to displace the local culture (Brown and Glasgow 2008: 168–70). A large influx of retirees and other amenity-seeking individuals could also change the rural character of the community, altering the "sense of place", which in theory can reduce residents' "buy in" into efforts to improve the community.

What attracts retirees to rural areas?

Brown and Glasgow (2008: 107–10), found that most retirees they surveyed cited two main reasons for choosing a rural place to retire: (1) rural quality of life and (2) environmental considerations, including amenities and recreational opportunities.[18] Another 50 percent cited having family connections to the area as important. Economic considerations, such as affordability and employment conditions, also made a difference, but for only about 10 percent. Their logistic statistical model, furthermore, found that retirement county classification was positively affected by a county being recreation-dependent, and not agricultural-dependent, and that once a county began attracting retirees, it was more likely to keep attracting retirees, i.e., it was a self-sustaining process. This is consistent with the common explanation that "word of mouth" is important in directing retirees to retirement destinations.

Poudyal et al. (2008) examined a wide array of specific man-made and natural amenities and tested to determine which significantly affected retiree attraction in the United States during the 1990s. Among the statistically significant man-made amenities were proximity to national parks, and the presence of state parks, fishing camps, sports, and golf courses. Natural amenities that significantly added to retiree in-migration included average annual temperature and sunlight, the share of the county in forest, crop, and pasture land, and water, and miles of scenic rivers within the county. Among the other factors significantly enhancing retiree attraction were presence of hospitals, airports, proximity to highways and to metropolitan areas, percentage of population of retirement age, percentage of seasonal housing, lower property taxes, and lighter population density.[19]

Cromartie and Nelson (2009: 19) found that boomers "are increasingly drawn to areas with a combination of scenic amenities, recreation or cultural opportunities, and reasonable housing costs". They found that seasonal housing was a "particularly strong indicator" for attracting retirees. They also noted that "modern telecommunications technology and increased airport accessibility" have made it easier to work and move permanently to more remote second-home locations, consequently nonmetro retirement destinations are expected to become more dispersed geographically and less concentrated around metro areas. Cromartie and Nelson (2009) also found that among the most important factors affecting migration of the young-old (ages 50–65), is percentage of couples with no children. Interestingly, that study found that adjacency to metropolitan areas was only statistically significant in attracting retirees in their 60s, and even for these retirees, it was not among the most important factors explaining retiree attraction.

Cromartie and Nelson used their analysis of 1990s migration patterns to project trends for the next two decades, estimating that the largest increase in nonmetro population among the 55–75-year-old age group would be in the South. However, in the 2010s, the Northeast would receive the largest percentage increase in this age group (32 percent), followed by the West (31 percent), South (26 percent), and Midwest (21 percent). This regional pattern suggests that interest in tapping this important source of wealth may be more widely spread, geographically, than in the past.

Building on Cromartie and Nelson's data and model, Pender and Dinterman (Chapter 17) investigated spatial relationships in retiree attraction and found that a county's ability to attract retirees is affected by conditions in surrounding counties. This is consistent with the view that retirees may first identify a region of interest, and then narrow down their choice to an individual place with access to that region's amenities.

This collective research on factors affecting retiree migration provides a good starting point for rural communities to examine their situation and determine if they have what it takes to attract retirees. Moreover, it points to several general strategies for increasing retiree attraction by enhancing or building upon various forms of local wealth.

For example, promoting a place's natural amenities, and making efforts to preserve the natural environment and provide more access to natural amenities, could have the potential to attract more retirees. Efforts to preserve the rural character of the community (including small-town physical and social characteristics) could also help maintain the rural quality of life that many retirees seek. Communities might also consider building or enhancing the physical capital that might add to local attractiveness to retirees, including senior centers, tourist information centers, health facilities, and local recreation facilities. The use of marketing methods that attempt to re-establish ties to former residents and family members, emphasizing the social and cultural aspects of the community, could work in some places that lack significant natural amenities. Marketing efforts might also target nearby metropolitan areas to attract people looking for a quick, inexpensive rural recreation getaway and those interested in establishing a second home that might ultimately be converted into a retirement home. In addition, rural communities might benefit from collaborating on a regional retiree attraction strategy that advertises the various amenities and residential opportunities available within the region.

Although considerable research has been devoted to estimating the economic impacts of retiree attraction in the United States, little if any research is available on the cost effectiveness of employing specific methods for attracting retirees. Nevertheless, many of these methods have been adopted by state retiree attraction initiatives dating back to the 1980s (Reeder 1998). Alabama's Advantage for Retirees program, for example, included the 1989 "Alabama Reunion", inviting former state residents to come back and visit, at which time they were provided with information encouraging them to consider retiring in Alabama. Participating localities were provided with planning and technical assistance manuals to assess their situations, and financial assistance to help pay for locally produced promotional materials advertising their most attractive local assets. The state conducted a comprehensive marketing campaign in national media outlets, and provided brochures distributed at welcome centers on major highways. And to add to the quality of the amenities, it financed the construction of a series of highly acclaimed golf courses – the Robert Trent Jones Golf Trail – around which were constructed retirement housing developments to tempt visiting golfers into staying on as retirees (Reeder 1998: 14–15).

In many states, however, local communities are pretty much left to their own devices in attracting (or retaining) retirees. Community self-help models, such as that developed by the state of Washington, can help guide a community to conduct an assessment of its situation (including its assets and liabilities for attracting retirees), providing suggestions for how a local strategy might be devised and implemented to attract retirees (Severinghouse 1990). In the late 1980s, Lee Fisher, a consultant who helped twenty or so communities with their strategies, claimed that this was a relatively inexpensive and productive approach, including some notable success stories – such as Chewelah, Washington (Fisher 1989).

Policy inferences using the wealth creation framework

Local context is important in determining where retirees are most likely to go. For communities interested in pursuing retiree attraction as a development strategy, the first thing they must do, therefore, is to assess what potential they have for attracting retirees, based on their local characteristics. Local context can also help communities decide whether the effects of retiree attraction would be consistent with local goals and values. For example, if a community has suffered from long-term population decline, lacks job opportunities, or lacks fiscal capacity to fund basic public services, retiree attraction might fit well with the community's needs. If, however, the community has already experienced much population growth in recent years and is having growth-related strains on its environment, then retiree attraction might not fit so well to its local needs.

The local context may also indicate how a community might best go about designing a retirement strategy. For example, if the locality's most desirable amenity is an attractive lake, then the strategy might logically build on this natural asset by making lakefront property available for development or providing public access to the lake, with man-made amenities, like piers, to enhance the recreation experience.

It is also important to understand *how various local assets interrelate* when designing such a strategy. Retiree attraction can add significantly to local financial assets, but it can create problems for some other forms of local assets, such as human capital, if retirees oppose spending increases for public schools. Even some seemingly harmless assets, such as retirees volunteering to work in libraries and schools, might have unanticipated negative impacts on other local assets – in this case, some young workers could be displaced by these volunteers (Brown and Glasgow 2008: 174). Young workers may also be displaced by rising home values and rents, forcing them to move elsewhere. Furthermore, if retirees do not socialize much with other local residents, this may make it easier for conflicts to occur between retirees and other residents which could diminish local social, political, and cultural capital.[20]

To minimize these potentially adverse effects, communities might devise mechanisms to reach out to retirees and bring them more into contact with local activities. For example, they might encourage retirees to participate in local schools as substitute teachers or teacher's aids, or to participate in other local organizations. And to reduce long-term residents' potential adverse reactions to retirees, communities might devise methods to spread the benefits of this kind of development to the community at large, such as by using impact fees on new home sales to help finance local schools or affordable housing to help residents deal with increased housing prices. Retirement villages might also be induced into allowing long-term residents to use some of their development's resources and facilities, such as fishing ponds, golf courses, or meeting halls, to make more friends in the community.

We have discussed how retiree attraction can help *diversify a community's assets*, particularly if the local economy is heavily dependent on one or two firms or on one or two agricultural crops. But for places that have already become heavily dependent on tourism and recreation, adding retiree attraction to the mix might not help much in economic diversification. In such cases, communities might look to other strategies to diversify their economies. They might also consider employing policies aimed at lessening the severity of local housing fluctuations, such as by slowing down on the issuance of building permits during boom periods or requiring infrastructure to be built prior to allowing housing developments to expand.

The employment of *non-locally owned assets* can become an issue in retirement communities, especially when retirees move into large-scaled planned retirement developments owned by outsiders.[21] These non-local developers can make retiree attraction easier for a community by their taking on most of the burden of marketing to potential retirees. However, they will also garner much of the financial benefits in terms of income from home sales, and if the market crashes during recessions and housing busts, such developers may go bankrupt and leave local governments to pick up the pieces, at significant cost to the local taxpayer.

To avoid these financial problems and the social problems related to segregation of retirees from non-retirees, some communities may discourage large-scale retirement developments through zoning regulations, preferring that retirees build their own houses on vacant lots within the community or in the surrounding countryside. If retirees follow this pattern, this can produce more financial wealth for local residents selling the land directly to the retirees, and produce fewer problems in times of economic difficulties. However, the burden of marketing the area to retirees would under this scenario shift to the local community. And when retirees more diffusely locate within the area, this can add to the costs of providing services to them and have more negative environmental implications. Recognizing these tradeoffs in advance can help a community decide which of these paths – local versus non-local ownership – they wish to take.

Understanding *which dynamic process the community is taking* is important for undertaking retiree attraction strategies. For example, if the development process is systematically converting attractive natural landscape, such as forests, streams, and beaches, into built-up housing developments, there may come a time when retiree attraction is no longer sustainable, as the very amenity that attracted the retirees has diminished significantly. Monitoring what is happening to the quality of the local amenities can help a community detect when such an unsustainable trend is underway, so that the community can take actions to address these problems. More generally, monitoring the views of both retirees and non-retirees in the community might help to identify and address evolving difficulties that might otherwise lead to a decline in the attraction potential of the community and a decline in various forms of local wealth.

Conclusion

Retiree attraction is a way in which many rural communities might be able to create substantial wealth in the coming years as the baby boom generation retires. Many states and localities have already established policies aimed at attracting retirees. Although the cost effectiveness of these policies has not been firmly established, available research suggests that, to be successful, it helps if rural communities possess the natural and/or man-made amenities that attract retirees. Other characteristics, such as proximity to metro areas, may also be helpful. Data from the 1990s and 2000s suggest that those places that have succeeded in attracting retirees have generally added significantly to their financial, physical, and human capital, even during the more recent and difficult economic times, which have disproportionately affected such places. Nevertheless, rural communities might benefit significantly from using the lens of the wealth creation framework when designing their retiree attraction strategies.

Notes

1 The views expressed are those of the authors and should not be attributed to the US Department of Agriculture or to the Economic Research Service.
2 One reason for the long-term decline in the number of rural (nonmetro) retirement counties has been the conversion of many nonmetro counties into metro counties over this same time period – about 40 percent of the decline in the number of retirement counties during the 1980s was due to metro reclassification (Brown and Glasgow 2008). Retirement counties are particularly likely to become metropolitan due to their relatively high rates of population growth. Considering these shifts in metropolitan status, we calculated that the retirement county share of total US nonmetropolitan counties declined from 21 percent in the 1970s to 8 percent in the 1980s, then rose to 12 percent in the 1990s.
3 A case study by Serow and Haas (1992) documented how retirees added to local bank and brokerage accounts. Although that study of western North Carolina was not very representative because of the relatively high incomes of the retirees locating there (Serow 2003: 899), Hamilton (2010) cites another study, this one in Mexico (Otero 1997), showing an increase in financial services, such as banks and investment brokerages, resulting from in-migration of American retirees.

4 Most retiree impact studies use input-output models to estimate expected economic effects from retiree migration in particular places or regions. A recent exception is a study (Lambert et al. 2007) that used regression analysis to estimate the impact of the net migration of retirement-age populations from 1995 to 2000 on county employment and business establishment growth, 2000 to 2004 in the Southeastern United States, controlling for other variables such as economic and demographic structure, labor market characteristics, community governance, fiscal policy, and physical and natural amenities. That study found positive impacts on both employment and business growth, but only in nonmetropolitan counties. It also concluded that retiree attraction had the most economic effects on nonmetro counties with moderate population densities and access to urban centers, and that retiree attraction did not explain the economic growth of the most rapidly growing nonmetro counties. However, this model did not account for pre-retirement effects, such as when a person buys a seasonal residence with the intention of retiring there several years later. In such cases, much of the economic impact associated with housing construction occurs prior to retirement.

5 A good source for supply and demand effects of in-migrants is *Lost Landscapes and Failed Economies* by Thomas Power (1996).

6 Evidence that these effects are in fact occurring comes from a recent econometric analysis of US counties. Poudyal et al. (2008) found that local housing values and hospitals per thousand persons were endogenous variables in relation to retiree in-migration, implying that these physical wealth factors affect retiree in-migration while at the same time they are also affected (enhanced) by such in-migration. Hamilton (2010) cited the Otero (1997) Mexican case study indicating that attracting American retirees contributed to local physical wealth in the form of new business growth, including newly opened restaurants and expansion of mail, transportation, and medical services.

7 Glasgow and Arguillas (2008) found that retiree in-migrants were relatively active in their communities as volunteers, and participants in services in social clubs, and that this formal integration with the community was beneficial to the retirees' health, thus adding even more to local human capital.

8 Brown and Glasgow (2008: 159–60) found in interviews with community leaders in four case study communities across the country that in-migrating retirees were considered to be valuable community assets, providing talent, experience, and professional and technical expertise.

9 Unfortunately, only five-year averages are available for the final year in this series, meaning we cannot show how low housing values got at their lowest point. Were we able to do this, we may have found a smaller difference in the decade's growth in housing values between retirement and non-retirement counties, comparable to that of the 1990s.

10 Another reason for caution is that the data source for home values and education changed in the 2000s – the American Community Survey (ACS) data used to reflect conditions in 2007–2011 employs different survey techniques and defines residences somewhat differently than the decennial census data used for earlier periods covered in this table.

11 The unemployment data were obtained from the Bureau of Labor Statistics, Local Area Unemployment Statistics. The income data were from the Bureau of the Census.

12 Routt was not classified as a retirement county based on its experience in the 1990s alone, but it has become older more recently. Nelson's study estimated that its population over 55 years of age increased more than 250 percent from 1990 to 2010. Hence this county is expected to become classified as a retirement county when the next ERS county classifications are determined.

13 An example of this phenomenon is Sunrise Senior Living, which managed more than three hundred facilities, many in the Northeast United States, but was forced to sell off properties, eliminating most of its real estate development team, and was later acquired by the Health Care REIT based in Ohio (Heath 2012).

14 During the 2000s, rural non-retirement counties averaged only 0.2 percent population growth.
15 Abrams et al. (2012) offers a good review article on the international literature concerning the environmental implications of amenity migration, such as retiree migration.
16 For a review of the international literature on social as well as economic implications of amenity migration such as retiree attraction, see Gosnell and Abrams (2009).
17 Another reason for this finding might be that this study examined places where retirees did not live in planned retirement developments, so they were probably more diffusely mixed in with other residents in their communities.
18 Many experts believe that exposure to a high-amenity place via tourism can later lead to retiring in that place; however, Brown and Glasgow (2008) question this conclusion.
19 Another study (Oehmke et al. 2007) found that the presence of health facilities might actually be a problem for attracting retirees, in that it positively attracted the "old old" (ages 70+) while it detracted from migration of the "young old" (ages 65–69), which presumably are the preferred targets of retiree attraction strategies. This study used more recent migration data than the Poudyal et al. study, but it focused exclusively on data from Michigan, so it may not be very generalizable to the rest of the country.
20 A similar situation may arise when the workers attracted by the jobs created by retiree in-migration do not socialize readily with long-term residents. For example, recent research examining rural amenity-based development that attracts baby boomers shows that some of these places attract significant numbers of Hispanic workers, who tend to live in separate residential locations, raising questions about community integration and fragmentation (Nelson et al. 2009).
21 South Carolina's state retiree attraction strategy makes explicit use of private retirement community developers, providing free land as an incentive, and has argued that this has produced a significant amount of economic stimulus for the state (Reeder 1998).

References

Abrams, J.B., Gosnell, H., Gill, N.J., and Klepeis, P.J. (2012) "Re-creating the rural, reconstructing nature: an international literature review of the environmental implications of amenity migration", *Conservation and Society*, 10(3): 270–84.
Bender, L.D., Green, B.L., Hady, T.F., Kuehn, J.A., Nelson, M.K., et al. (1985) *The Diverse Social and Economic Structure of Nonmetropolitan America*, Rural Development Research Report 49, Washington, DC: US Department of Agriculture, Economic Research Service.
Bergsman, S. (1987) "The rush to build – or overbuild – for retirees", *Barron's*, 67: 64.
Brown, D.L., and Glasgow, N. (2008) *Rural Retirement Migration*, Springer Series on Demographic Methods and Population Analysis 21, Dordrecht: Springer.
Clement, D. (2004) "Is gray the new gold? The elderly are often portrayed as an economic burden, but many see seniors as a target market", *Fedgazette*, 1 May.
Cromartie, J., and Nelson, P. (2009) *Baby Boom Migration and its Impact on Rural America*, Economic Research Report No. 79, Washington, DC: US Department of Agriculture, Economic Research Service.
Fisher, L.A. (1989) *The Art of Retirement: An Economic Development Program for Rural and Distressed Areas*, Belleview, WA: Team Washington Project.
Glasgow, N., and Arguillas, M. (2008) "Social integration and health of older in-migrants to rural retirement destinations", in D. Brown and N. Glasgow (eds.), *Rural Retirement Migration*, Springer Series on Demographic Methods and Population Analysis, 21, Dordrecht: Springer.

Gosnell, H., and Abrams, J. (2009) "Amenity migration: diverse conceptualizations of drivers, socioeconomic dimensions, and emerging challenges", *GeoJournal*, 76(4): 303–22.

Hamilton, K.L. (2010) "Impact of retirement populations on local jobs and wages", *Economic Development Quarterly*, 24(2): 110–25.

Heath, T. (2012) "Sunrise Senior Living sold to health-care company for $845 million", *Washington Post*, 22 August. Online. Available at: <http://www.washingtonpost.com/business/economy/sunrise-senior-living-sold-to-health-care-company-for-845-million/2012/08/22/a654e830-ec94-11e1-a80b-9f898562d010_story.html> (accessed 20 November 2012).

Jauhiainen, J.S. (2009) "Will the retiring baby boomers return to rural periphery?", *Journal of Rural Studies*, 25: 25–34.

Johnson, K.M. (2012) *Rural Demographic Change in the New Century: Slower Growth, Increased Diversity*, Issue Brief 44, Carsey Institute, Durham, NH: University of New Hampshire.

Kaye, L. (2012) "The Boomers have arrived: preparing to meet the needs of our aging population", *Health Workforce News*, July. Online. Available at: <http://www.hwic.org/news/july12/kaye.php> (accessed 20 November 2012).

Lambert, D.M., Clark, C.D., Wilcox, M.D., and Park, W.M. (2007) "Do migrating seniors affect business establishment and job growth? An empirical look at southeastern nonmetropolitan counties, 2000–2004", *Review of Regional Studies*, 37(2): 251–78.

Lambert, D.M., Clark, C.D., Wilcox, M.D., and Park, W.M. (2009) "Public education financing trends and the Gray Peril hypothesis", *Growth and Change*, 40(4): 619–48.

Nelson, P.B. (2012) "Linked migration and changing rural economies in the United States", Charles M. Tiebout Lecture presented at the 46th Annual Pacific Northwest Regional Economic Conference, Seattle, WA, 17 and 18 May.

Nelson, P.B., Lee, A.W., and Nelson, L. (2009) "Linking Baby Boomer and Hispanic migration streams into rural America – a multi-scaled approach", *Population, Space and Place*, 15: 277–93.

Norris, F. (2012) "The number of those working past 65 is at a record high", *New York Times*, Business Day Economy, 18 May. Online. Available at: <http://www.nytimes.com/2012/05/19/business/economy/number-of-those-working-past-65-is-at-a-record-high.html> (accessed 20 November 2012).

Oehmke, J.F., Tsukamoto, S., and Post, L. (2007) "Can health care services attract retirees and contribute to the economic sustainability of rural places?", *Agricultural and Resource Economics Review*, 36(1): 95–106.

Otero, L.M.Y. (1997) "U.S. retired persons in Mexico", *American Behavioral Scientist*, 40: 914–22.

Poudyal, N.C., Hodges, D.G., and Cordell, H. K. (2008) "The role of natural resource amenities in attracting retirees: implications for economic growth policy", *Ecological Economics*, 68: 240–48.

Power, T.M. (1996) *Lost Landscapes and Failed Economies: The Search for a Value of Place*, Washington, DC: Island Press.

Raitz, K.B., Ulack, R., and Leinbach, T.R. (1984) *Appalachia, a Regional Geography*, Boulder, CO: Westview Press.

Reeder, R. (1998) *Retiree-Attraction Policies for Rural Developent*, Agriculture Information Bulletin 741, Washington, DC: US Department of Agriculture, Economic Research Service.

Reeder, R.J., Schneider, M.J., and Green, B.L. (1993) "Attracting retirees as a development strategy", in D.L. Barkley (ed.), *Economic Adaptation: Alternatives for Nonmetropolitan Areas*, Boulder, CO: Westview Press, pp. 127–44.

Serow, W.J. (2003) "Economic consequences of retiree concentrations: a review of North American studies", *Gerontologist*, 43(6): 897–903.

Serow, W.J., and Haas, W.H., III (1992) "Measuring the economic impact of retirement migration: the case of western North Carolina", *Journal of Applied Gerontology*, 11: 200–15.

Severinghouse, J.B. (1990) *Economic Expansion Using Retiree Income: A Workbook for Rural Washington Communities*, Rural Economic Assistance Project, Pullman, WA: Washington State University.

Skelley, B.D. (2004) "Retiree-attraction policies: challenges for local governance in rural regions", *Public Administration and Management*, 9(3): 212–23.

Winkler, R., Golding, S., and Cheng, C. (2011) "Boom or bust? How migration impacts population composition in different types of natural resource dependent communities in the rural US", in L. Kulcsar and K. Curtis (eds.), *International Handbook of Rural Demography*, Springer Series on Demographic Methods and Population Analysis, New York: Springer.

16 Casino development as a rural wealth creation strategy

John L. Pender[1]

Introduction

Since the late 1980s casino development has exploded in the United States. In 1988, the year Congress passed the Indian Gaming Regulatory Act (IGRA), casino gambling was legal in only two states – Nevada and Atlantic City, New Jersey. Since then, casinos have expanded into thirty-six additional states. Commercial non-Indian casino gaming revenues increased more than five-fold from $6.8 billion in 1988[2] to $35.6 billion in 2011 (American Gaming Association (AGA) 2012); while tribal casino revenues have increased to $27.2 billion (National Indian Gaming Commission (NIGC) 2012).

Tribal casinos have developed on Indian reservations and trust lands throughout the country (Figure 16.1). Commercial casinos include land-based casinos in Nevada and a few states that have legalized casinos in particular cities; boat casinos allowed on several rivers or outside state jurisdiction in ocean waters; and racetrack casinos in several states.

Most commercial casinos are in or near large urban areas (Table 16.1). By contrast, most tribal casinos are in rural areas because most Indian reservations are in rural areas. Nevertheless, the largest tribal casinos, such as Foxwoods and the Mohegan Sun in Connecticut, are located close to large urban areas.

In this chapter I consider the potential for casino development as a rural development option, based on a review of the literature on casinos. I discuss the factors that have contributed to or hindered casino development; the roles of local actors in this development; the economic and social impacts of this development; and the impacts on wealth.

Factors affecting casino development

Many factors have affected casino development, including the historical context, laws and regulations related to gambling, changes in social norms and consumer preferences, changes in technologies, access to markets and infrastructure, local institutions, and local assets and amenities. Some of these factors have affected the supply of casino gambling (e.g., laws and regulations), some have affected the demand for casino gambling (e.g., changes in consumer preferences), and some have affected both (e.g., changes in technologies).

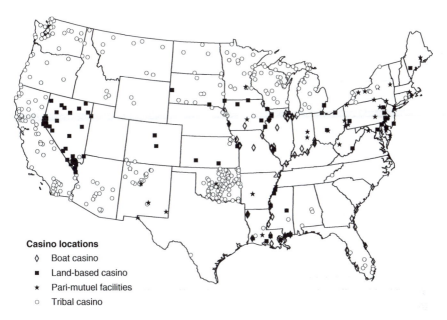

Casino locations

◊   Boat casino

■   Land-based casino

★   Pari-mutuel facilities

○   Tribal casino

Figure 16.1 Casino locations in the continental United States, 2012

Source: American Casino Guide website (<http://www.americancasinoguide.com>) and 500 Nations Native American website (<http://www.500nations.com>).

Table 16.1 Locations of casinos in the United States

Item	Tribal casinos	Commercial casinos			All casinos
		Land-based	Boat	Racetrack	
Number[1]	398	303	79	51	831
Location[2]	*Percent by casino type[3]*				
Urban center	33.7	63.0	65.8	80.4	50.3
Large rural town	21.9	9.2	13.9	15.7	16.1
Small rural town	18.1	9.2	6.3	3.9	12.9
Isolated rural area	26.4	18.5	13.9	0.0	20.7

Sources: American Casino Guide website (<http://www.americancasinoguide.com>) and 500 Nations Native American website (<http://www.500nations.com>).

Notes:

[1] The number of casinos shown in this table is less than the number identified by AGA (2012). This may be because AGA (2012) includes small gaming operations in card rooms, bars, and clubs that are not included in the websites used to construct this table.

[2] These location types are a four-category classification of ZIP Code Tabulation Areas based on rural urban commuting area (RUCA) codes (see <http://depts.washington.edu/uwruca/ruca-maps.php>). For a definition and explanation of the RUCA codes, see <http://www.ers.usda.gov/data-products/rural-urban-commuting-area-codes/documentation.aspx>.

[3] Percentages may not add to 100.0 due to rounding.

Historical context

In the early twentieth century, virtually all forms of gambling were prohibited in the United States (Rose 1991). That began to change during the Great Depression in the 1930s, as some states legalized some forms of gambling to boost economic activity and tax revenues. Nevada legalized most forms of gambling in 1931 and several states legalized racetrack betting during the 1930s. Massachusetts decriminalized bingo for charitable purposes in 1931, and by the 1950s bingo was legal in eleven states. Voter opposition to taxes led to a revival of state lotteries beginning in 1964, when New Hampshire became the first state to establish a state lottery. Since then, forty-three states and the District of Columbia have established lotteries.

Prior to the 1970s, Nevada's casino industry was viewed as a "pariah" industry (Eadington 1999), but this began to change after Nevada's Corporate Gaming Act of 1969 allowed publicly traded corporations to establish casinos. In 1976, New Jersey's voters approved casino gambling in Atlantic City to revitalize the city. By the mid-1980s, well-known corporations were operating casinos in both states. These changes, along with expansion of other forms of gambling, helped to increase the acceptability of casino gambling and set the stage for the more rapid expansion that occurred after the legal changes that came later in the 1980s.

Legal and regulatory changes

The biggest change in the legal context for casino gambling came as the result of a 1987 Supreme Court decision – *California v. Cabazon Band of Mission Indians* (480 U.S. 202 (1987)). That decision ruled that states could not regulate commercial gaming conducted by Indian tribes on their reservations as long as gambling was not prohibited as a criminal activity by the state.

In response to this Supreme Court ruling, Congress passed the IGRA, establishing a regulatory framework to govern Indian gaming. The IGRA defined three classes of Indian gaming. Class I games include social games for prizes of minimal value and traditional forms of Indian gaming, which are subject to tribal regulation only. Class II games include bingo and similar games not played against the house. They are regulated by tribal governments and the National Indian Gaming Commission (NIGC). Class III games include all other games played against the house, including slot machines, banked card games, casino games such as craps and roulette, pari-mutuel betting, and lotteries. Indian tribes are allowed to conduct Class III games in states that permit such games for any purpose by any person, subject to tribal–state compacts that specify the size, scope, and types of gaming allowed, and other agreements between the tribe and the state. The IGRA allowed tribes to sue states in federal court for failing to negotiate compacts "in good faith". However, in *Seminole Tribe of Florida v. Florida* (517 U.S. 44 (1996)), a federal court found that this provision violated the Eleventh Amendment's guarantee of state sovereign immunity (National Gambling Impact Study Commission (NGISC) 1999). This court decision strengthened the ability of states to inhibit Indian casino development or to extract concessions from tribes. Nevertheless, more than 240 tribes have successfully negotiated compacts,[3] some of these after tribes first opened Class III casinos without a compact.

Following passage of the IGRA, several states passed laws allowing non-Indian commercial casinos, often with strict limitations. South Dakota authorized low-stakes gambling in the mining town of Deadwood in 1989; riverboat casinos were legalized in Iowa, Illinois, Mississippi, Louisiana, Missouri, and Indiana between 1989 and 1993; urban land-based casinos were legalized in New Orleans in 1992 and Detroit in 1996; and racetrack casinos were authorized in several states (Wenz 2008b). Restrictions on gambling have generally been reduced over time. By 2012, non-Indian land-based or boat casinos were legal in fifteen states and racetrack casinos were legal in thirteen states (AGA 2012).

Changes in social norms and consumer preferences

Public acceptance of casino gambling has increased as gambling in general has spread, contributing as well as responding to changes in legal restrictions on gambling (Eadington 1999). As publicly traded corporations became increasingly involved in casinos, the stigma linking casinos to organized crime diminished. The percentage of American adults who had gambled in a casino in the previous year nearly tripled from only 10 percent in 1975 to 29 percent in 1998, while participation in state lotteries increased from 24 to 52 percent (Gerstein et al. 1999).

Since the late 1990s, participation in casino gambling and attitudes about its acceptability appear to have stabilized. The share of adults participating in casino gambling has remained fairly stable since the late 1990s, generally ranging between 25 and 30 percent; while the share of adults that consider casino gambling an acceptable form of entertainment has also remained around 80 percent since 2000 (AGA various years).

Technological change

Technological change has also played an important role in development of the casino industry. Electronic gaming machines have replaced traditional mechanical slot machines. Electronic machines enable casinos to offer many more options, including the ability to play multiple games, select multiple denominations, and have progressive jackpots on a single machine (Gros and Legato 2010). Class II electronic bingo games, common in many tribal casinos because they do not require approval of a tribal–state compact, have been developed that are quite similar in customer experience to Class III electronic games. In some casinos, electronic machines are networked and can be programmed to allow cooperative or competitive play among groups. Coins in slot machines have been replaced by tickets or players' club cards, reducing costs and facilitating transactions. Casinos can use the data collected through use of players' club cards to target their marketing efforts to different categories of customer. Besides their large and growing presence in casinos, electronic gaming machines now operate in many locations besides casinos in six states (AGA 2012), such as in bars, truck stops, and convenience stores.

Also affecting demand for casinos is development of the Internet, which has facilitated off-track betting and high-stakes bingo in casinos and some tribal bingo parlors, and the rapid growth of online gambling. After the first online gambling website appeared in the mid-1990s, online gambling revenues in the United States grew to more than $4 billion by 2010 (Stewart 2011). Although most of this gambling is illegal under the Unlawful Internet Gambling Enforcement Act (UIGEA) of 2006, preventing US residents from accessing websites based in other countries has proven difficult (Stewart 2011).

Access to markets and infrastructure

Casino development has likely proceeded further in places with better access to cities where large numbers of potential customers live. Cookson (2010) found that development of tribal casinos was significantly more likely closer to a large city. The local population level also affects demand for casinos. Evans and Topoleski (2002, p. 65) found that tribal casinos were more likely to be located in counties with larger populations within 50 miles of the tribal headquarters. Wenz (2008b) found that both commercial and tribal casinos were more common in counties with larger populations.

Pender and Cornelius (2012) investigated factors associated with the growth in gaming employment between 2001 and 2007 in tribal areas that had a casino in 2001, and whether a casino started up between 2001 and 2007 in tribal areas that did not have a casino in 2001. Consistent with other studies, they found that both the likelihood of a casino starting up and growth in casino employment were greater in reservation counties with larger populations (Table 16.2).[4] They also found faster employment growth associated with shorter driving time to the

Table 16.2 Factors associated with changes in Native American gaming employment, 2001–2008, and startup of casinos – statistically significant factors

Explanatory variable	*Reservation counties with tribal casino in 2001*	*Reservation counties without tribal casino in 2001*
	Change in gaming employment, 2001–2007 (OLS model)	*Startup of a tribal casino, 2001–2007 (probit model)*
Gaming employment in 2001	−0.2102** (0.0427)	NA
Population in 2000 (1,000 persons)	1.732** (0.397)	0.0121* (0.0058)
Driving time to nearest city of 1 mil. (min.)	−0.5936* (0.2984)	−0.0025 (0.0014)
Road density (miles/square mile)	−360.7* (179.5)	1.616 (1.662)
Number of observations	209	215
R^2/pseudo R^2	0.6916	0.3197

Source: Pender and Cornelius (2012).

Notes: *, ** indicate statistical significance at 5 percent and 1 percent levels, respectively. Standard errors are in parentheses.

nearest large city, reflecting both proximity to cities and highway development. However, greater local road density was associated with less growth in casino employment, perhaps reflecting higher land costs in more dense cities.

Local institutions

Institutions include formal laws and regulations, informal rules and norms, and enforcement mechanisms operating at all levels (North 1990). Indian tribal laws and norms are an example of local institutions relevant to the development of casinos. For example, the Navajo Nation prohibited casinos until 2004, when it completed its first tribal gaming compact with New Mexico. Casino development was opposed by some Navajos for various reasons, including traditional concerns about gambling and the enslavement that it can cause (Schwartz 2012).

One study of the influence of tribal institutions on the development of casinos found that tribal governments whose political boundaries span multiple states had a substantially higher probability of operating a tribal casino (Cookson 2010). Cookson argued that the ability of such tribes to induce competition among multiple states increases their ability to negotiate tribal–state compacts success- fully. Cookson also found that tribal reservations for which Public Law 280 pro- vides criminal and civil jurisdiction to state courts had a much higher probability of operating a tribal casino. He argued that this was because state courts provide more predictable contract enforcement than tribal courts, reducing the costs of casino investment.

Local amenities and assets

As a form of recreation and tourism, casinos may be more likely to attract cus- tomers in locations with favorable natural amenities. This issue has not been much addressed in the literature, although Wenz (2008b) and Calcagno et al. (2010) found a strong association between commercial casino adoption and access to a river, and Wenz (2008b) also found strong associations between both commercial and tribal casinos and coastal access. However, the location of casi- nos near rivers and coasts reflects legal requirements in some states. Pender and Cornelius (2012) found that natural amenities, as measured by the natural amen- ity scale developed by the USDA Economic Research Service, had statistically insignificant associations with both the growth of tribal gaming employment and startups of new tribal casinos.

Other kinds of local wealth endowments may also affect the supply of or demand for casino development in particular communities. Human capital endowments may affect the ability of a local tribe to start up and operate a casino, while the age composition or education of the local population may affect local gambling demand. Gerstein et al. (1999) found that a smaller percentage of peo- ple aged 65 or older had gambled in the previous year. Using multivariate analy- sis of the same data as Gerstein et al. (1999), Zimmerman (2011) also found that older adults were less likely to have gambled in the previous year, but gambled with greater frequency if they did gamble. By contrast, Evans and Topoleski

(2002) found that counties with a larger elderly share of the population were more likely to have adopted tribal gaming by 2000, while Pender and Cornelius (2012) found that the elderly share of the population had statistically insignificant associations with the startup or growth of tribal casinos.

Considering education, Gerstein et al. (1999) found that college-educated adults had a lower likelihood of being at risk, problem, or pathological gamblers than less educated adults. Similarly, Zimmerman (2011) found that adults with more schooling had a lower frequency of gambling in the past year than less educated adults. However, Pender and Cornelius (2012) found no statistically significant association between high school graduation rates and startup or growth of tribal casinos.

Local financial capital endowments may affect casino development, particularly for Indian tribes in rural locations less attractive to investment by large casino companies. However, Pender and Cornelius (2012) found that the presence of a community development financial institution had no statistically significant effect on startup or employment growth of tribal casinos.

Social capital and cultural norms can also affect the demand for casinos or the willingness and ability of a community to invest in casinos. For example, Baptists and other conservative Christians often oppose legalization of casinos. Consistent with this, Wenz (2008b) found that counties with a greater proportion of fundamentalist Christians were less likely to have a tribal casino. However, Calcagno et al. (2010) found the surprising result that casinos tended to be adopted earlier in states with a larger Baptist share of the population.[5]

Roles of local actors in casino development

Commercial casinos are owned and operated by private companies and individuals, many of which are large publicly traded corporations. In 2005, more than three hundred public companies were involved in the gaming industry (AGA 2009). In rural areas, some of these may be local entrepreneurs, but in larger markets, specialized casino and entertainment companies dominate.

Tribal casinos are owned and sometimes operated by tribal governments (AGA 2009). However, it is more common for tribes to contract commercial casino companies to operate their casinos. The IGRA requires that the management fees paid to such contractors do not exceed 30 percent of the net revenues of the casino, unless the tribe requests a higher fee of up to 40 percent of net revenues (with adequate justification). Net revenues from Class II and III games can be used only (1) to fund tribal government operations or programs; (2) to provide for the general welfare of the Indian tribe and its members; (3) to promote tribal economic development; (4) to donate to charitable organizations; or (5) to help fund operations of local government agencies. Per capita payments to members of an Indian tribe are only allowed if the tribe has an approved plan to use adequate revenues to achieve the purposes in the preceding sentence.

State governments have primary responsibility for regulating and taxing commercial casinos, and must approve tribal–state compacts for Class III tribal gaming. Local county governments have little authority over the operation of tribal casinos, but more authority over commercial casinos in some states. Their authority varies across states and has changed over time. In Nevada, local county sheriff offices had the authority to license and tax casinos when they were legalized in 1931 (Dunstan 1997). The role of the state increased over time because of concerns about organized crime and the threat of federal prohibition of casinos. Local governments now have concurrent authority with the state of Nevada to license and regulate casinos; both jurisdictions must approve casino licenses, and local governments can prohibit or restrict gambling within their jurisdiction. There was local control and local taxation of gaming in Montana until 1989, when the state put all regulation and revenue collection from gaming under a single state entity (Dunstan 1997). In several states – such as Colorado, Illinois, Indiana, Missouri, and South Dakota – all licensing, revenue collection, and regulatory control is vested in state gaming control agencies (Dunstan 1997). In other states – such as Iowa, Louisiana, and Mississippi – local governments have the option to collect particular taxes from casinos (Dunstan 1997). Local governments often have zoning authority to restrict the location of casinos, even when they do not have authority to prohibit or tax casinos.

Other local actors, such as casino owners and operators, business associations and owners, religious groups, and other local stakeholders, can influence casino development by influencing local and state laws and regulations related to casinos. An example is a campaign to ban development of an off-reservation casino by the Menominee Indian Tribe in Kenosha, Wisconsin in 1998 (Pavalko 1999). A referendum against the casino was advocated by local religious leaders and others concerned about the impacts that the casino would have on the quality of life in the community. Most state and local political leaders and even much of the business community did not take a public position on the casino. Economic conditions (low unemployment and a booming economy) did not favor adoption of the casino, but key local groups, especially organized labor, supported it because of the claimed benefits for employment and agreement by the Menominee tribe to support workers' rights to join unions and bargain collectively (Pavalko 1999). The proponents of the casino had significantly more financial resources than the opponents, and this, together with the support of organized labor and the perception that the casino would address a need for jobs, may have been pivotal in defeating the referendum to stop the casino development (Pavalko 1999).

Impacts of casinos

In this section, we review literature on economic and social impacts of casinos. There is little information on the environmental impacts of casinos, which are probably similar to the environmental impacts of other tourist activities that attract a large number of visitors to a community.

Economic impacts

In 1996, Congress established the National Gambling Impact Study Commission (NGISC) to investigate the economic and social impacts of gambling in the

United States. Based on a review of literature, several commissioned studies, and testimony from hundreds of people, the NGISC concluded that there was insufficient evidence to reach a consensus on the impacts of gambling (NGISC 1999). Here we focus on the findings of several analytical studies on these issues, mostly published after the NGISC report.

Population

Two studies investigated the impacts of casinos on local population, and both found positive effects. Rephann et al. (1997) found that population grew more in casino counties than matched non-casino counties. Evans and Topoleski (2002) found that population in counties with an Indian casino was larger four or more years after a casino opened.

Employment and unemployment

Several studies investigated employment impacts of casinos; all found positive impacts of some types of casinos. Rephann et al. (1997) found that employment grew more in casino counties, especially in services. Gerstein et al. (1999) found that unemployment was lower in communities close to a casino, and Taylor et al. (2000) found that this was true for both Indian and non-Indian casinos. Evans and Topoleski (2002) found that total employment and the employment/adults ratio was greater four or more years after an Indian casino opened in a county, and that the employment/adults ratio was slightly higher after opening a casino in a nearby county. They found that the percentage impacts on population and total employment were larger in less densely populated rural communities, but that the impacts on the share of adults employed and the unemployment rate were larger in more densely populated communities. Reagan and Gitter (2007) found that the probability of Indian tribal members being employed was not significantly affected by casinos in Metropolitan Service Areas (MSAs), but was higher in non-MSAs with Indian casinos nearby. Cotti (2008) found that total employment was greater after a casino opened, with larger impacts on the entertainment and hospitality industries. Wenz (2008a) found that total employment grew faster in counties that had an Indian casino compared with matched counties without a casino, but insignificant impacts of non-Indian casinos.

Earnings and income

Numerous studies have investigated impacts of casinos on earnings and income per capita, with most finding positive results. Rephann et al. (1997) found that earnings and income per capita grew more in counties with casinos, particularly in the service sector. Gerstein et al. (1999) found statistically insignificant impacts of casinos on overall net earnings or income per capita, but they found increased earnings in some industries (hotels/lodging, recreation/amusement, and construction) and reduced earnings in others (restaurants/bars). Taylor et al.

(2000) found that Indian casinos had a positive impact on both net earnings and income per capita, while non-Indian casinos did not. Using household-level data, Reagan and Gitter (2007) found that tribal gaming increased household income per capita both in MSAs and non-MSAs, but by a greater percentage in MSAs. Cotti (2008) found that casinos have statistically insignificant impacts on total earnings per worker at the county level, but increased earnings per worker in the entertainment and hospitality industries. Wenz (2008a) found that both Indian and non-Indian casinos had statistically insignificant impacts on growth in median household income. Anderson (2011) found that per capita income grew more and that family and child poverty rates declined more on reservations that opened a casino compared with non-Navajo reservations without a casino.

Property values

Several studies have found positive impacts of casinos on property values. Buck et al. (1991) found that real estate values were substantially higher than predicted in southern New Jersey and Atlantic City eight years after casinos opened in Atlantic City. Wenz (2007) found that a casino in a Census Bureau Public Use Microdata Area (PUMA) increased housing values by 2 percent, while a casino in a neighboring PUMA increased housing values by 6 percent. The larger impact in neighboring regions may be due to crime or other negative social impacts being greater close to casinos. Wiley and Walker (2011) found that commercial property sales prices in Detroit increased with casino revenues, especially close to the casinos.

Tax revenues

Casinos may influence state and local tax revenues through many mechanisms. Sales and gambling taxes collected directly from casinos tend to increase tax revenues. However, the net impact of casinos on tax revenues depends on how much other competing activities are displaced and the relative tax rates on competing activities. Indian casinos, which are not subject to state or local taxes, are more likely than commercial casinos to have negative revenue effects if they substitute for other taxable activities. However, casinos may attract tourists and other visitors to a region, possibly resulting in increased business and tax revenues for nearby businesses. Furthermore, to the extent that casinos increase income or property values, they may increase income or property tax revenues.

Several studies have investigated some of these possibilities. Steinnes (1998) found statistically insignificant impacts of Indian casinos on the growth in revenue from the state lottery and charitable gaming in Minnesota counties. By contrast, Siegel and Anders (2001), Elliott and Navin (2002), and Fink and Rork (2003) found a significant negative effect of casinos on lottery revenues. However, the results of both Elliott and Navin (2002) and Fink and Rork (2003) imply that the total net impact of casinos on state revenues is positive. Walker and Jackson (2008) found that increases in the net revenue per capita of commercial casinos in a state were associated with reduced business for state lotteries and dog racing, but increased volume of horse racing. Larger Indian casinos were also associated with reduced lottery revenues and increased horse racing, but surprisingly with increased commercial casino revenues. These results suggest that the impacts of casinos on other gambling are complex and context dependent.

Some studies have investigated the link between casinos and state revenues directly. Anders et al. (1998) found that Transaction Privilege Tax revenue in Arizona[6] declined soon after tribal–state gaming compacts were signed, with declines from several sectors, including amusements, hotel/motel, retail, and restaurants/bars. Siegel and Anders (1999) found that greater riverboat revenues in Missouri were associated with reduced sales tax revenue from other amusement and recreation services besides riverboats. Walker and Jackson (2011) found that each dollar of casino revenue in a state was associated with a loss of $1.44 of state revenue.

Overall, there is substantial evidence that casinos reduce revenues from other forms of gambling – especially state lotteries – and some other economic activities. However, the net impact on state and local revenues is not clear.

Social impacts

Casinos may have many social impacts. Much attention has been paid in the literature to the "social costs" of casinos, such as impacts on problem and pathological gambling, crime, bankruptcy, family problems, illness, suicide, costs of social services, regulatory costs, and other costs (Grinols and Mustard 2001). Social impacts may also include social benefits, such as reductions in crime or other problems due to improved economic outcomes resulting from casinos (Taylor et al. 2000).

Problem and pathological gambling

Based on their review of the literature, Grinols and Mustard (2001) argued that the social costs are caused primarily by problem and pathological (PP) gambling.[7] There is debate about the extent to which expansion of casinos contributes to PP gambling. A recent review of the literature found that gambling availability has a small but significant impact on the prevalence of problem gambling (Williams et al. 2012). However, there has been a general worldwide downward trend in problem gambling since the late 1990s, despite continued expansion of casinos and other gambling opportunities. This suggests that populations are adapting over time to increased gambling availability (LaPlante and Shaffer 2007), reducing the impact of casino expansion on PP gambling.

Crime

Numerous studies have investigated impacts of casinos on crime, with mixed results. Buck et al. (1991) found that Atlantic City casinos increased crime rates in New Jersey. Rephann et al. (1997) found no statistically significant differences in crime rates between counties with one casino and matched counties without casinos, though they did find higher crime rates (mainly larceny) in some multi-casino counties. Gerstein et al. (1999) found small and statistically insignificant differences in crime rates between casino and non-casino counties. Taylor et al. (2000) found significant increases in auto thefts and robberies near commercial casinos but decreases in these crimes near an Indian casino. They hypothesize that the different impacts of Indian casinos could be due to the use of casino revenues by tribal governments to pay for additional police protection and other services, and to the improvement in economic conditions in these communities. Evans and Topoleski (2002) found that violent crimes, auto thefts, and larceny were higher in casino counties four or more years after opening an Indian casino.

One of the most cited studies of casino impacts on crime is Grinols and Mustard (2006). Using county-level data on crime rates in all US counties from 1977 to 1996, they found that rates of several types of violent crime (aggravated assault, rape, and robbery) and property crimes (larceny, burglary, and auto theft) were substantially higher four years after a casino opened, and that these impacts grew over time after a casino opened. Based on these results, they estimated that about 8 percent of the crime in casino counties in 1996 was attributable to casinos, costing an average of $75 per year per adult in these counties.

Grinols and Mustard's (2006) results have been criticized by Walker (2008a) and debated subsequently by these authors (Grinols and Mustard 2008a, 2008b; Walker 2008b). An important issue in this debate concerns the crime rate used by Grinols and Mustard, i.e., the total number of crimes committed in casino counties divided by the county population. This rate does not consider that some crimes are likely committed against visitors, and thus likely overstates the likelihood that local residents are victims of crime. Other criticisms of Grinols and Mustard (2006) include concerns about the quality of the Uniform Crime Reports data that they used, the lack of a measure of the scale of casino activity, and potential omitted variables that could be correlated with casino adoption (Walker 2008a). Reece (2010) addressed these concerns in a study of the impact of commercial casinos on crime rates in Indiana counties, and found that casino activity was associated with reduced rates of all crimes investigated (larceny, burglary, auto theft, assault, robbery, and rape), except burglary (casino openings were associated with increased burglaries). Casino openings were found to contribute to increased number of hotel rooms within three years, and a greater number of hotel rooms was also associated with lower crime rates for most crimes, possibly due to the effects of growth in the hospitality industry on local employment, which may increase the opportunity cost of crime.

Bankruptcy

Numerous studies have investigated the impacts of casinos on bankruptcy rates, with mixed results. Gerstein et al. (1999) found statistically insignificant impacts of casinos on both business and non-business bankruptcy rates in their sample of casino and non-casino counties. Using data for the same counties studied by Gerstein et al. (1999), De la Viña and Bernstein (2002) also found statistically insignificant impacts of casinos on personal bankruptcy rates. Barron et al. (2002) found a positive impact of casino revenues on personal bankruptcies in the following year. Evans and Topoleski (2002) found that bankruptcy rates were increased in casino counties and nearby counties four years after an Indian casino opens. Thalheimer and Ali (2004) found that access to casinos in Illinois, Iowa, Missouri, and Mississippi had a statistically insignificant impact on bankruptcy rates. Edmiston (2006) found higher personal bankruptcy rates in counties closer to a casino. Boardman and Perry (2007) found a statistically insignificant impact of casinos on bankruptcy in Kentucky counties. Garrett and Nichols (2008) found mixed and mostly statistically insignificant impacts of in-state casinos on state-level bankruptcy rates, but found that visits to destination casinos in Mississippi (but not in Las Vegas or New Jersey) contributed to higher bankruptcy rates. Goss et al. (2009) found that casinos have a large impact on bankruptcies initially but that these impacts decline through the sixth year before increasing again. Daraban and Thies (2011) found that personal bankruptcy rates are significantly higher in Federal Judicial Districts where more is bet on casino or pari-mutuel gambling.

Overall, six of the ten studies reviewed found positive impacts of casinos on bankruptcy rates. All of the studies that found statistically insignificant impacts were sub-national in scope; their smaller sample size may account for their findings. Only one study – Garrett and Nichols (2008) – investigated the impact of casinos on bankruptcies at the place of residence of casino customers, rather than near the location of the casino. In general, the impacts of casinos on the residential communities of casino customers have been little studied.

Wealth impacts

Casinos may affect wealth through many mechanisms. By affecting employment and income, casinos may affect the wealth of households and businesses through their consumption, savings, and investment decisions. By affecting government revenues, they can affect the wealth of communities through the savings and investment decisions of state, tribal, and local governments. Casinos may affect the rate of depreciation of physical infrastructure or other capital stocks by contributing to increased usage and congestion, or increase the demand for social services and thus deplete the financial capital of local governments and community service agencies. The IGRA requires that revenues from tribal gaming be used for social and economic development purposes, which could include investments in physical, human, cultural, or other forms of capital. Casinos can affect the physical and financial wealth of households or businesses by affecting property values or by contributing to bankruptcy, as some of the studies cited above have shown. They may affect human capital if they affect the health and education of people as a result of changes in labor market conditions or problem gambling. Casinos may affect the level of trust and social capital in a community by affecting crime rates or by contributing to conflict over the distribution of benefits and costs resulting from casino activity. They may influence the distribution of political power by affecting the availability of financial resources that organizations such as tribal governments have to influence the political process. To the extent that local or regional economies become dependent upon casino revenue, they may be vulnerable to negative shocks affecting the market, such as changes in policies in nearby states or regions that lead to increased competition. Such risks could undermine the benefits of casinos for wealth creation unless the revenues are used to help diversify the local economy.

Little peer-reviewed research investigates the wealth impacts of casinos directly, although the literature already cited implies that significant wealth impacts are likely. A few studies have discussed impacts of gaming on particular types of wealth. For example, Cornell et al. (1998) reported how five Indian tribes used gaming revenue to fund investments in social infrastructure, including investments in education, vocational training, health and human services, language and cultural programs, housing and other physical assets, land reacquisition and land management, business investments, public safety, and other economic and social development. Grant et al. (2003) reported similar types of investments by gaming tribes in Oklahoma.

Although some Indian tribes are investing gambling revenues in education, educational attainment can also be affected by changes in the labor market that affect the demand for education. For example, Kim (2006) found that casinos increased employment rates and wages of Indians, and that young Indian adults responded by dropping out of high school at higher rates and reducing college enrollment rates.

Griswold and Nichols (2006) investigated the impacts of casino gambling on social capital, using data on six dimensions of social capital – trust, civic, volunteerism, group participation, giving, and meeting obligations of family and friends. They found that the introduction of a nearby casino was associated with a reduction in the overall social capital index, and among the six dimensions studied, with a reduction in the index for meeting obligations.

Other research has documented impacts on particular social, cultural, or political assets in particular case studies. Gonzales (2003) described how the dramatic increase in financial wealth of some tribes resulting from casino revenues has undermined social cohesion and contributed to displacement of some tribal members. In Deadwood, South Dakota, most gaming tax revenues have been used for historic restoration and preservation, building upon the historic cultural heritage of the community (Blevins and Jensen 1998). By contrast, in Colorado most of the funds targeted for historic preservation go to the state rather than the gaming communities (Blevins and Jensen 1998).

Conclusion

Based on this review of the literature, the factors affecting casino development, the local actors involved, and the impacts of casino development are summarized in Figure 16.2, which adapts the conceptual framework for wealth creation introduced by Pender and Ratner in Chapter 2.[8]

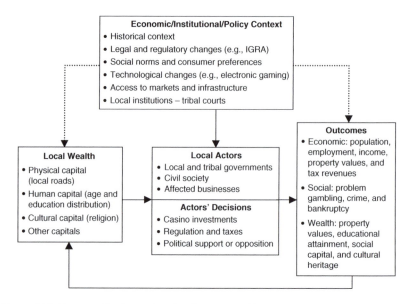

Figure 16.2 Factors affecting casino development and outcomes

The explosion of casino development in the past few decades was conditioned by the historical context of casino gambling, enabled by changes in the legal and regulatory context, and driven largely by consumer demand for gambling. Technological changes facilitated casino development, but are also fostering competition for casinos through online gambling. Other factors affecting the location of casino development include access to large urban markets, local institutions, local human capital (local population level and the age structure of the population), and local cultural norms. The key actors in this development have included casino corporations; and tribal, state, and local governments – with less influence of state and local governments on development of tribal than commercial casinos.

There is substantial evidence of positive economic impacts of casinos, particularly on employment, but also on population, earnings and income per capita, and property values. Some of these impacts appear to be larger (in percentage terms) in more rural communities and in Indian communities, because the potential for casinos to displace other businesses may be less in such contexts. One reason that impacts on income per capita are not as large as impacts on employment and earnings per capita is that by increasing employment and earnings, casinos help to reduce some kinds of government transfer payments associated with economic distress. Impacts on tax revenues appear to be more uncertain, in part because of the substitution effects of casinos, particularly for state lottery revenues. The potential for losses in state and local tax revenues appears to be greater for Indian casinos, since they do not contribute directly to these revenues and may displace other taxable activities.

There are many social costs of casino development, due largely to impacts on problem and pathological gambling. There is substantial evidence that casinos contribute to problems related to crime and bankruptcies, though findings of such impacts are not universal. In general, larger-scale studies are more likely to have found statistically significant impacts than smaller ones.

Casinos can also have social benefits as well as costs, resulting from improvements in economic opportunities and conditions. There is still much debate about whether the social benefits of casino development exceed the social costs. Given that many of the costs and benefits are context dependent, it is likely that the social net benefits are also context dependent. Studies of how the balance of costs and benefits vary across different contexts are rare.

One way of assessing whether casino development is affecting well-being in communities is by assessing the impacts on wealth, broadly conceived. Unfortunately, the available research on wealth impacts of casinos is limited and the findings are only suggestive. Still, they suggest that casinos may be having substantial impacts on many types of wealth, including property values, social capital, and others. However, such impacts appear to be largely context dependent. Much remains to be learned about how casinos influence wealth in general and in rural communities in particular.

Notes

1 The views expressed are those of the author and should not be attributed to the US Department of Agriculture or to the Economic Research Service.
2 Sources for 1988 gaming revenue: <http://gaming.unlv.edu/abstract/nvstate_1988. html>; <http://gaming.unlv.edu/abstract/ac_main.html>.
3 See <http://www.nigc.gov/Reading_Room/Compacts.aspx>.
4 Table 16.2 reports only the statistically significant results of factors associated with growth in gaming employment or startup of new casinos in counties with tribal reservations and other trust lands eligible for tribal gaming. Other factors investigated by Pender and Cornelius (2012) included median household income in 2000, the share of adults with a high school diploma in 2000, the share of adults not working in 1999, the Native American share of the population in 2000, the presence of a community development financial institution, the presence of a Native American or minority business enterprise center, the natural amenity index for the county (<http://www.ers.usda.gov/data-products/natural-amenities-scale.aspx>), and state-level fixed effects.
5 Calcagno et al. (2010) argue that the surprising positive association of Baptists with early state-level adoption of casinos may be picking up a particular effect of early adoption in Mississippi and Louisiana.
6 The Transaction Privilege Tax is the major source of revenue in Arizona, which does not have a sales tax.
7 In its fourth *Diagnostic and Statistical Manual of Mental Disorders* (*DSM-IV*), the American Psychiatric Association classifies pathological gambling as an impulse control disorder and defines ten criteria to diagnose the disorder, representing three dimensions: damage or disruption, loss of control, and dependence (NGISC 1999, pp. 4–1). "Problem gambling" is defined as falling below the threshold for five of the ten criteria.
8 Solid arrows indicate the relationships discussed in this chapter. Dashed arrows indicate types of relationships postulated in the conceptual framework of Chapter 2, but not discussed in the literature reviewed on casino development.

References

American Gaming Association (AGA) (2009) "U.S. commercial casino industry: facts at your fingertips". Online. Available at: <http://www.americangaming.org/files/aga/uploads/docs/facts_at_your_fingertips_12022010.pdf> (accessed 20 December 2012).

American Gaming Association (AGA) (2012) "State of the states: the AGA survey of casino entertainment". Online. Available at: <http://www.americangaming.org/industry-resources/research/state-states> (accessed 1 December 2012).

Anders, G.C., Siegel, D., and Yacoub, M. (1998) "Does Indian casino gambling reduce state revenues? Evidence from Arizona", *Contemporary Economic Policy*, 16: 347–55.

Anderson, R. (2011) "Tribal casino impacts on American Indians well-being: evidence from reservation-level census data", *Contemporary Economic Policy*, 31(2): 291–300, DOI: 10.1111/j.1465–7287.2011.00300.x.

Barron, J.M., Staten, M.E., and Wilshusen, S.M. (2002) "The impact of casino gambling on personal bankruptcy filing rates", *Contemporary Economic Policy*, 20(4): 440–55.

Blevins, A., and Jensen, K. (1998) "Gambling as a community development quick fix", *Annals of the American Academy of Political and Social Science*, 556: 109–23.

Boardman, B., and Perry, J.J. (2007) "Access to gambling and declaring personal bankruptcy", *Journal of Socio-economics*, 36: 789–801.

Buck, A.J., Deutsch, J., Hakim, S., Spiegel, U., and Weinblatt, J. (1991) "A Von Thünen model of crime, casinos and property values in New Jersey", *Urban Studies*, 28(5): 673–86.

Calcagno, P.T., Walker, D.M., and Jackson, J.D. (2010) "Determinants of the probability and timing of commercial casino legalization in the United States", *Public Choice*, 142: 69–90.

Cookson, J.A. (2010) "Institutions and casinos on American Indian reservations: an empirical analysis of the location of Indian casinos", *Journal of Law and Economics*, 53(4): 651–87.

Cornell, S.E., Kalt, J.P., Krepps, M.K., and Taylor, J.B. (1998) *American Indian Gaming Policy and its Socio-economic Effects*, Report to the National Gambling Impact Study Commission, Cambridge, MA: The Economics Resource Group.

Cotti, C. (2008) "The effect of casinos on local labor markets: a county level analysis", *Journal of Gambling Business and Economics*, 2(2): 17–41.

Daraban, B., and Thies, C.F. (2011) "Estimating the effects of casinos and of lotteries on bankruptcy: a panel data set approach", *Journal of Gambling Studies*, 27: 145–54.

De la Viña, L., and Bernstein, D. (2002) "The impact of gambling on personal bankruptcy rates", *Journal of Socio-Economics*, 31: 503–9.

Dunstan, R. (1997) "Gambling in California". CRB–97–003. Online. Available at: <http://www.library.ca.gov/crb/97/03/crb97003.html#toc> (accessed 17 December 2012).

Eadington, W.R. (1999) "The economics of casino gambling", *Journal of Economic Perspectives*, 13(3): 173–92.

Edmiston, K.D. (2006) "A new perspective on rising nonbusiness bankruptcy filing rates: analyzing the regional factors", *Federal Reserve Bank of Kansas City Economic Review*, 2nd quarter: 55–83.

Elliott, D.S., and Navin, J.C. (2002) "Has riverboat gambling reduced state lottery revenue?", *Public Finance Review*, 30(3): 235–47.

Evans, W.N., and Topoleski, J.H. (2002) "The social and economic impact of Native American casinos", NBER Working Paper No. 9198, Cambridge, MA: National Bureau of Economic Research.

Fink, S., and Rork, J. (2003) "The importance of self-selection in casino cannibalization of state lotteries", *Economics Bulletin*, 8(1): 1–8.

Garrett, T.A., and Nichols, M.W. (2008) "Do casinos export bankruptcy?", *Journal of Socio-economics*, 37: 1481–94.

Gerstein, D., Murphy, S., Toce, M., Hoffman, J., Palmer, A., et al. (1999) "Gambling impact and behavior study", Report to the National Gambling Impact Study Commission, National Opinion Research Center, University of Chicago.

Gonzales, A.A. (2003) "Gaming and displacement: winners and losers in American Indian casino development", *International Social Science Journal*, 175: 123–33.

Goss, E., Morse, E.A., and Deskins, J. (2009) "Have casinos contributed to rising bankruptcy rates?", *International Advances in Economic Research*, 15: 456–69.

Grant, K.W., Spilde, K.A., and Taylor, J.B. (2003) "Social and economic consequences of Indian gaming in Oklahoma", Joint Occasional Papers on Native Affairs, Harvard Project on American Indian Economic Development, Harvard University.

Grinols, E.L., and Mustard, D.B. (2001) "Business profitability versus social profitability: evaluating industries with externalities, the case of casinos", *Managerial and Decision Economics*, 22: 143–62.

Grinols, E.L., and Mustard, D.B. (2006) "Casinos, crime, and community costs", *Review of Economics and Statistics*, 88(1): 28–45.

Grinols, E.L., and Mustard, D.B. (2008a) "Correctly critiquing casino-crime causality", *Econ Journal Watch*, 5(1): 21–31.

Grinols, E.L., and Mustard, D.B. (2008b) "Connecting casinos and crime: more corrections of Walker", *Econ Journal Watch*, 5(2): 156–62.

Griswold, M.T., and Nichols, M.W. (2006) "Social capital and casino gambling in U.S. communities", *Social Indicators Research*, 77: 369–94.

Gros, R., and Legato, F. (2010) "Ten years of innovation: marketing and game technology during the first decade of G2E". Online. Available at: <http://www.americangaming.org/industry-resources/research/white-papers> (accessed 10 December 2012).

Kim, W. (2006) "The economic impacts of American Indian casinos", PhD dissertation, University of Maryland, Department of Economics, College Park.

LaPlante, D.A., and Shaffer, H.J. (2007) "Understanding the influence of gambling opportunities: expanding exposure models to include adaptation", *American Journal of Orthopsychiatry*, 77(4): 616–23.

National Gambling Impact Study Commission (NGISC) (1999) *Final Report*. Online. Available at: <http://govinfo.library.unt.edu/ngisc/reports/fullrpt.html> (accessed 1 December 2012).

National Indian Gaming Commission (NIGC) (2012) "Gaming revenues 2007–2011". Online. Available at: <http://www.nigc.gov/Gaming_Revenue_Reports.aspx> (accessed 1 December 2012).

North, D. (1990) *Institutions, Institutional Change and Economic Performance*, Cambridge: Cambridge University Press.

Pavalko, R.M. (1999) "A case study of a casino campaign: testing the Dombrink-Thompson model", *Journal of Gambling Studies*, 15(3): 247–64.

Pender, J., and Cornelius, F. (2012) "Economic factors affecting the development of Indian gaming since 2001", paper presented at the Southern Regional Science Association annual meeting, Charlotte, NC, 22–24 March.

Reagan, P.B. and Gitter, R.J. (2007) "Is gaming the optimal strategy? The impact of gaming facilities on the income and employment of American Indians", *Economics Letters*, 95: 428–32.

Reece, W.S. (2010) "Casinos, hotels, and crime", *Contemporary Economic Policy*, 28(2): 145–61.

Rephann, T.J., Dalton, M., Stair, A., and Isserman, A. (1997) "Casino gambling as an economic development strategy", *Tourism Economics*, 3(2): 161–83.

Rose, I.N. (1991) "The rise and fall of the Third Wave: gambling will be outlawed in forty years", in W.R. Eadington and J.A. Cornelius (eds.), *Gambling and Public Policy*, Reno, NV: Institute for the Study of Gambling & Commercial Gaming, University of Nevada.

Schwartz, M.T. (2012) "Fire Rock: Navajo prohibitions against gambling", *Ethnohistory*, 59(3): 515–40.

Siegel, D., and Anders, G. (1999) "Public policy and the displacement effects of casinos: a case study of riverboat gambling in Missouri", *Journal of Gambling Studies*, 15(2): 105–21.

Siegel, D., and Anders, G. (2001) "The impact of Indian casinos on state lotteries: a case study of Arizona", *Public Finance Review*, 29(2): 139–47.

Steinnes, D.N. (1998) "Have Native American casinos diminished other gambling in Minnesota? An economics answer based on accessibility", *Journal of Regional Analysis and Policy*, 28(1): 18–32.

Stewart, D.O. (2011) "Online gambling five years after UIGEA". Online. Available at: <http://www.americangaming.org/industry-resources/research/white-papers> (accessed 12 December 2012).

Taylor, J.B., Krepps, M.B., and Wang, P. (2000) "The national evidence on the socioeconomic impacts of American Indian gaming on non-Indian communities". Online. Available at: <http://www.northforkrancheria.com/files/Taylor%20Kreps%2020002.pdf> (accessed 1 December 2012).

Thalheimer, R., and Ali, M.M. (2004) "The relationship of pari-mutuel wagering and casino gaming to personal bankruptcy", *Contemporary Economic Policy*, 22(3): 420–32.

Walker, D.M. (2008a) "Do casinos really cause crime?", *Econ Journal Watch*, 5(1): 4–20.

Walker, D.M. (2008b) "The diluted economics of casinos and crime: a rejoinder to Grinols and Mustard's reply", *Econ Journal Watch*, 5(2): 148–55.

Walker, D.M., and Jackson, J.D. (2008) "Do U.S. gambling industries cannibalize each other?", *Public Finance Review*, 36(3): 308–33.

Walker, D.M., and Jackson, J.D. (2011) "The effect of legalized gambling on state government revenue", *Contemporary Economic Policy*, 29(1): 101–14.

Wenz, M. (2007) "The impact of casino gambling on housing markets: a hedonic approach", *Journal of Gambling Business and Economics*, 1(2): 101–20.

Wenz, M. (2008a) "Matching estimation, casino gambling and the quality of life", *Annals of Regional Science*, 42: 235–49.

Wenz, M. (2008b) "The spatial evolution of casino gambling", *Cityscape*, 10(3): 203–27.

Wiley, J.A., and Walker, D.M. (2011) "Casino revenues and retail property values: the Detroit case", *Journal of Real Estate and Financial Economics*, 42(1): 99–114.

Williams, R.J., West, B.L., and Simpson, R.I. (2012) "Prevention of problem gambling: a comprehensive review of the evidence and identified best practices", report prepared for the Ontario Problem Gambling Research Centre and the Ontario Ministry of Health and Long Term Care. Online. Available at: <https://www.uleth.ca/dspace/bitstream/handle/10133/3121/2012-PREVENTION-OPGRC.pdf?sequence=3> (accessed 13 January 2013).

Zimmerman, J. (2011) "Casino gambling as an income-based leisure activity: evidence from the gambling impact and behavior study", *Journal of Business & Economics Research*, 1(12): 49–58.

Part IV

Synthesis and conclusions

17 Developing a typology of wealth creation approaches and contexts

Hypotheses and an example for the case of attracting retirees

John L. Pender and Robert Dinterman[1]

Introduction

As argued by Pender et al. in Chapter 1 and Pender and Ratner in Chapter 2, achieving broadly shared and sustainable rural prosperity requires economic development strategies to build upon and build up rural wealth, broadly defined, and that are well suited to the spatial and temporal context in which these strategies are pursued. The case studies of wealth creation strategies presented in Part III of this book demonstrate the importance of local context and wealth endowments in determining the prospects of different strategies. It is clear that there is no "one-size-fits-all" approach to achieving successful rural wealth creation. Going beyond this truism to provide useful information and practical guidance to policy makers and development practitioners still presents a considerable challenge to rural development researchers, however.

Part of the challenge is to produce generalizable knowledge – specifically, lessons that extend beyond a particular local context – while still recognizing that the lessons of rural development rarely apply everywhere. Developing a typology of wealth creation approaches and contexts – that is, conducting research on "what works where" with regard to rural development strategies – could help to address this challenge. Without attempting to discover what works in every situation, research could shed light on the types of strategies that have potential in particular types of situations, offering guidance to policy makers, local community leaders, and others about their options without prescribing which option is best.

In terms of the conceptual framework for rural wealth creation presented by Pender and Ratner in Figure 2.1 of this book, in this chapter we propose a typology of rural economic development strategies, summarizing sets of actors' decisions represented in the center box of that figure. We draw on the literature and the case studies presented in this book to begin to develop such a typology. We then suggest a method for identifying and mapping the places in which one particular strategy – attracting retirees – has potential, considering the contextual factors and asset types represented in the top and left boxes in Figure 2.1. This typology and example do not address other relationships shown in Figure 2.1, such as the outcomes of pursing a particular strategy or how those outcomes lead to changes in rural wealth stocks over time. However, they can provide the basis for further research on those issues, taking such contexts and strategy options into account. We conclude with some observations about how this approach could be extended and used to guide a program of applied research on rural wealth creation.

Toward a typology of rural wealth creation approaches and contexts

In Chapter 10 of this book, Steven C. Deller argues that rural community economic development policy has proceeded through various waves in the past several decades. First-wave approaches focused on recruiting large industrial firms, or "smoke-stack chasing", as critics have characterized the approach. The prototypical policy approach to achieve this was the Mississippi Balance Agriculture with Industry (BAWI) Act enacted in the 1930s, which sought to attract industrial firms to Mississippi through availability of cheap labor, land, and tax breaks. This approach dominated community economic development policy for decades, and continues to be widely pursued today. The second wave of development policy emphasized retention and growth of existing (mostly small and medium-sized) businesses and entrepreneurship. Policies associated with this approach focused on increasing investment capital for local firms, development of business incubators, and provision of technical assistance, revolving funds, and tax increment financing. Third-wave policies focus on increasing competitiveness and public–private partnerships. Development of regional clusters to achieve agglomeration economies and competitiveness, as advocated by Michael Porter (1990), are associated with this wave. Policies associated with this wave emphasize integrating fragmented programs into a coherent set of policies for regions to be able to innovate and be competitive.

Drabenstott (2006) offered a similar classification of eras of regional economic development, distinguishing the eras of industrial recruiting (prevalent from the 1950s to early 1980s), cost competition (early 1980s to early 1990s), and regional competitiveness (early 1990s to present). The first and third eras described by Drabenstott correspond to the first and third waves described by Deller. Drabenstott's second era is somewhat different than Deller's second wave – focusing on industry consolidation and cost cutting rather than retention and growth of local businesses. However, both authors argue that current thinking emphasizes the local specificity of development strategies, specifically, that "one-size-fits-all" approaches do not work.

Pender et al. (2012) also argued that rural economic development strategies need to be suited to local contexts. They identified four "traditional" and four "nontraditional" strategies. The traditional strategies that they discussed include industrial recruitment, developing as a regional commercial or government center, developing as a bedroom community, and developing based upon natural or other amenities that can attract tourists and new residents. The nontraditional strategies include promoting small businesses and entrepreneurship, regional cluster-based development, rural innovation and knowledge-based development, and attracting the creative class. These strategies are not all mutually exclusive.

There is potential overlap among these strategies, and rural regions and communities may choose to pursue more than one of these strategies simultaneously. For example, development of biofuels processing could occur as part of a broader cluster strategy to promote bio-industries that add value to traditional agriculture in an agricultural region.

The economic strategies discussed by Pender et al. (2012) build on the waves discussed by Deller, including first-wave industrial recruitment, second-wave emphasis on small business development and entrepreneurship, and third-wave emphasis on regional clusters, innovation, and knowledge. These strategies are not synonymous with the waves, which are broad changes in policies and approaches that followed from changes in conceptual thinking. Rather, the strategies discussed by Pender et al. are more of a set of options that rural communities may consider today. These also include other strategies that may have potential to contribute to rural wealth creation in particular contexts and that have been discussed in the literatures on rural economic development and regional science. Development of regional centers of commerce based on scale economies and transport cost advantages is one of the predictions of central place theory, and many rural areas have developed in a way broadly consistent with this theory (Shaffer et al. 2004). Many other rural communities have developed as bedroom communities as a result of proximity to larger metropolitan areas, particularly as urban and suburban populations have grown and development of roads and other transportation options made this more feasible (Heimlich and Anderson 2001). Amenity-based development – including development as recreational centers and as destinations for tourists and retirees – is one of the dominant patterns among more successful rural communities in recent decades (McGranahan 1999; Deller et al. 2001). Linked to amenity-based development and entrepreneurship is attraction of the "creative class" – workers in occupations that specialize in creative tasks. McGranahan et al. (2011) showed that outdoor amenities attract more of the creative class in rural communities and that this is associated with greater economic growth, especially where this occurs in an entrepreneurial context.

The typology of rural economic development strategies proposed by Pender et al. (2012) excludes some important traditional strategies in rural areas. For example, strategies based on use of natural resources, such as agriculture, forestry, mining, and renewable energy development, are neglected. Some strategies focusing on meeting local consumption demand, such as local foods production, are also not emphasized. The typology that we propose incorporates these additional strategies.

Our proposed typology of rural economic development strategies is summarized in Table 17.1. The strategies can be grouped according to which contextual factors or local assets are most essential to the strategy. For example, agriculture, forestry, mining, and renewable energy development are all examples of natural resource-based strategies. Industrial recruitment can be considered largely a labor-based strategy, emphasizing the availability of low-cost labor to attract manufacturing or other labor-intensive industry; though other factors also

Table 17.1 Typology of rural economic development strategies and hypotheses about key contextual factors and assets

Type of strategy	Strategy	Key contextual factors and assets
Resource-based	Agriculture	Natural capital (land and water availability, land quality, climate), physical capital (irrigation and transport infrastructure), human capital (farm management, low-cost labor)
	Forestry	Natural capital (natural forests, climate, land availability), physical capital (transport infrastructure)
	Mining	Natural capital (mineral resource), physical capital (transport and waste disposal infrastructure), human capital (available labor), social capital (social support)
	Biofuels processing	Natural capital (for feedstock production, water for processing), physical capital (transport infrastructure), social capital (social support)
	Wind and solar energy	Natural capital (resource potential, available land), physical capital (electricity infrastructure)
Low input cost-based	Industrial recruitment	Human capital (low cost labor), physical capital (infrastructure), social capital (social support)
Location-based	Regional center	Central location, transportation advantages, physical capital (infrastructure)
	Bedroom community	Proximity to urban/suburban areas, physical capital (infrastructure)
	Local foods production/ marketing	Proximity to urban/suburban areas, same factors as for agriculture
Amenity-based	Recreation and tourism	Natural and/or cultural capital (amenities), physical capital (transport infrastructure, accommodations), access to urban areas
	Attracting retirees	Natural and/or cultural capital (amenities), physical capital (infrastructure, housing), access to urban areas and services
Knowledge- and innovation-based	Small business entrepreneurship	Access to urban areas, physical capital (infrastructure), human capital (training and technical assistance, education level), natural capital (amenities), financial capital
	Attracting creative class	Natural and/or cultural capital (amenities), access to urban areas and services, physical capital (infrastructure)
	Cluster strategies	Access to urban areas, intellectual capital (universities or other research centers), physical capital (infrastructure), presence of interrelated enterprises

matter, such as the availability of low-cost land, infrastructure, financing, and tax breaks. Strategies focused on locational advantages, such as proximity to large urban markets or central locations with transport cost advantages, include development as regional centers or bedroom communities, and local foods production. Development of recreation and tourism and attracting retirees are examples of amenity-based strategies; such strategies typically depend on the availability of natural, cultural, or other amenities that can attract visitors and migrants, as well as other assets and services. As a form of tourism development, casino development can also be considered an amenity-based strategy. Promoting entrepreneurship, cluster strategies, and attracting the creative class are examples of knowledge- and innovation-based strategies.

The chapters in Part III of this book provide examples of several of these strategies, including resource-based development related to energy production (Chapter 11); amenity-based development linked to Federal forest land (Chapter 12); attracting retirees (Chapter 15) and casino development (as an example of tourist development) (Chapter 16); entrepreneurship (Chapter 13); and local food systems (Chapter 14). The reviews of literature and empirical work conducted by the authors of several of these chapters reveal some of the contextual factors and assets that are important in determining the potential of these strategies.

For the energy industries discussed by Weber et al. in Chapter 11, access to the relevant resources (natural gas deposits and wind potential) is of primary importance, of course. Other local factors – such as state policies in support of or restricting development; access to labor, public infrastructure, water, waste treatment and disposal facilities; and trust between local residents and the industry (social capital) – are important for natural gas extraction. Wind energy development depends upon access to land and electrical transmission lines, as well as upon the wind potential. Local social capital as it relates to organized public support or opposition can also be important for siting wind turbines.

In Chapter 13, Low reviews the literature on how different types of wealth affect entrepreneurship and provides new empirical estimates of the influence of indicators of five types of wealth – financial, physical, human, intellectual, and natural capital – on six indicators of entrepreneurship (self-employment rates, establishment rates, and establishment birth rates in innovative sectors and in all sectors). She finds that each of the wealth type indicators is positively associated with at least one indicator of entrepreneurship, with the natural capital indicator (natural amenities index) positively associated with all of the entrepreneurship indicators and human capital (percentage of adults with a college degree) positively associated with all but one entrepreneurship indicator. Physical capital (infrastructure index, based on indicators of highway expenditures, commercial air traffic, and broadband Internet) is positively associated with birth rates of all establishments and of innovative establishments. Financial capital (bank deposits per capita) is also positively associated with births of all establishments and innovative establishments, but negatively associated with the total and innovative nonemployer self-employment rates.[2] Intellectual capital (patents per capita) is positively associated with the total and innovative nonemployer self-employment rates, but negatively associated with the establishment rate.[3] Most of these findings are consistent with other literature. Low also cites recent research showing the importance of cultural capital for entrepreneurship.

In Chapter 15, Reeder and Bagi review the literature related to migration of retirees to rural areas, and find that several types of assets and contextual factors have been shown to attract retirees. Among the most important are natural amenities, and recreational and cultural opportunities. Availability of low-cost housing, seasonal housing, hospitals, highways, airports, telecommunications, social connections, lower property taxes, and lower population density were other factors found to be associated with greater immigration of retirees in the literature.

In Chapter 16, Pender reviews the literature related to casino development. He finds that casino development has been affected by changes in the legal and regulatory context, changes in social norms and consumer preferences with regard to gambling, technological change, access to markets and infrastructure, and some local assets. Among the location-specific factors, proximity to large urban markets and large local populations, and local institutions and cultural norms appear to be the most important determinants of where this option has potential.

Mapping domains of rural development strategies – the case of attracting retirees

The typology of rural economic development strategies summarized in Table 17.1 offers some hypotheses about local contextual factors and assets that affect the potential of particular strategies. These hypotheses can be useful to help guide further research on these strategies, yet do not provide specific guidance to decision makers about where these strategies are likely to have economic potential. In this section, we illustrate an approach that could help identify and map locations that have potential for particular development strategies, using econometric analysis of the factors determining where such strategies are currently being pursued. The approach we propose could also be used to help guide applied research into why areas that are predicted to have potential for particular strategies have not yet pursued such strategies, or why some areas are pursuing strategies to a greater extent than would be expected, given their predicted potential.

As an example, we focus on identifying areas that have potential for attracting retiree immigrants. As argued by Reeder and Bagi in Chapter 15 of this book, rural retirement destination communities generally have had more favorable economic outcomes than other rural communities, and have substantial potential for creating multiple forms of wealth. This potential is likely to increase as the Baby Boom generation retires, given the tendency for older people to move to rural areas (Figure 17.1). Based on an econometric model of migration by different age cohorts, Cromartie and Nelson (2009) predicted that the non-metro population between ages 55 and 75 could increase by 30 percent by 2020.

This is not to argue that rural communities that have potential for attracting retirees should seek to do so. There are potential drawbacks of this development strategy, as discussed by Reeder and Bagi, and many others in the literature.

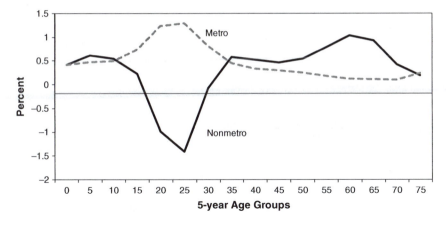

Figure 17.1 Average annual net migration rates by age, 1980–2000

Source: Cromartie and Nelson (2009).

Whether to pursue such a strategy, even where potential exists, is a decision for local decision makers to make, based upon their own priorities and constraints. The main point of mapping the locations that have potential for this or any other development strategy is to help local decision makers identify and consider their development options, and to guide further applied research to help in that process.

The current approach used by the US Department of Agriculture Economic Research Service (ERS) to classify retirement destination counties is based on actual historical migration rates, with counties classified as retirement destination counties if they had a net migration rate (NMR) of people age 60 and older of at least 15 percent over a ten-year inter-census period (Cook and Mizer 1994).[4] While this classification is useful, it has the drawback that it is not predictive. There may be places that have strong potential to attract retirees even though they had low net migration rates of retirees in the past, while other places may be attracting more retirees than would be expected based on the factors found to predict net migration rates. Identifying such contrasting types of situations could help guide research into the reasons for these divergences, and opportunities for regions and communities that may be underperforming in attracting retirees compared with their potential.

To predict migration by retirees and near retirees, we estimated three models of county-level NMR of people between age 50 and 69 in 1990, for the period 1990 to 2000. The models estimated included (1) ordinary least squares (OLS) regression, (2) the spatial error model (SEM), and (3) the simultaneous autoregressive (SAR) model. The models and the explanatory variables are described in the Appendix. The explanatory variables in the models included almost all of the explanatory variables used by McGranahan (2008), Poudyal et al. (2008), and

Cromartie and Nelson (2009) to predict net migration rates. These include indicators of natural and recreational amenities; access to urban areas, infrastructure, and health care; employment and housing market factors; property tax rates; poverty rates; crime rates; industrial structure; and demographic characteristics.

The regression model results are reported in Table 17.2. To save space, we report only coefficients for variables that are statistically significant at the 10 percent level or less.[5] The fourth column of Table 17.2 provides a measure of how much of the explained variance is accounted for by particular factors in the OLS model.[6] The ten variables that account for the largest share of the variance in migration include (in decreasing order of importance): the percentage of houses that were occupied seasonally in 1990 (positive association with migration (+)); the mean temperature in January (+); the elderly percentage of the population in 1990 (+); the percentage of workers employed in agriculture (–) or in mining (–) in 1989; the mean humidity in July (–); the percentage of households that were married couples with no children in 1990 (+); the share of land that was public land in 1992 (+); the number of golf courses per capita in the 1990s (+); and the South Atlantic region (+).

The signs of all of these coefficients are consistent with effects found in previous literature. The strong positive effect of seasonal housing suggests that recreational areas that attract seasonal visitors are more likely to become retirement destinations (Cromartie and Nelson 2009). The positive impact of the elderly share of the population may reflect the effect of social networks or other linkages that make it easier to attract retirees once they begin to be attracted to a location; consistent with path dependency in retiree attraction as argued by Brown et al. (2011). Of course, there could be other reasons for a positive association between the elderly share of the population and subsequent retirement migration, such as unobserved factors that cause certain locations to be persistently more successful in attracting retirees (e.g., marketing efforts by retirement communities). Not surprisingly, climate factors are important determinants of retiree migration, particularly higher temperatures in the winter and lower humidity in the summer. It is interesting that other natural amenities commonly thought to be important, such as access to coasts or to inland water bodies, do not appear to be as important as climate factors.

The OLS model (as well as the spatial models) predicts fairly well the general patterns of retiree migration, including migration to traditional retirement destinations such as the Southwest, Florida, the northern Great Lakes region, the Ozark Mountains, and the Great Smoky Mountains (Figures 17.2 and 17.3). Most of these regions have been retirement destinations since the 1950s or 1960s (Johnson et al. 2005). Of course, the model does not predict perfectly; it explains about 55 percent of the variance in net migration rates of retirees and near retirees during the 1990s. The residuals from the model exhibit some spatial patterns, with the model under-predicting migration (positive residuals) to parts of the Southwest, Florida, and some other regions, and over-predicting migration (negative residuals) to some other regions, including the Sierra Nevada region of California and parts of other regions (Figure 17.4).

Table 17.2 Determinants of net migration of retirees and near retirees (age 50–69 in 1990), 1990–2000

Variable	OLS	SEM	SAR	Explanatory power in OLS model[1]
Unemployment rate, 1989	-0.2528** (0.0888)	-0.1388 (0.0869)	-0.3476*** (0.0845)	0.21
Employment change, 1990–1993	0.1731*** (0.0384)	0.0996** (0.0358)	0.1472*** (0.0364)	0.52
Median home value, 1990	1.76e (7 9.61e–8)	4.44e–7*** (1.07e–7)	3.53e–7*** (9.10e–8)	0.09
Percent seasonal housing, 1990	0.3791*** (0.0234)	0.3811*** (0.0227)	0.3456*** (0.0222)	6.78
Rural metro dummy	0.01080 (0.00727)	0.00870 (0.00677)	0.01071 (0.00688)	0.06
Nonmetro non-adjacent dummy	0.00043 (0.00651)	-0.00212 (0.00622)	0.00030 (0.00616)	0.00
Nonmetro adjacent dummy	0.00883 (0.00607)	0.00426 (0.00564)	0.00776 (0.00574)	0.05
Population density, 1990	-8.49e–6** (2.68e–6)	-3.37e–6 (2.58e–6)	-6.02e–6* (2.54e–6)	0.26
Population density squared, 1990	1.19e–10** (4.44e–11)	3.34e–11 (4.22e–11)	7.80e–11 (4.21e–11)	0.18
Percent urban, 1990	-0.01915* (0.00975)	-0.03116*** (0.00917)	-0.02625** (0.00923)	0.10
Percent married no children, 1990	0.4805*** (0.0719)	0.4628*** (0.0700)	0.4778*** (0.0681)	1.15
Percent foreign born, 1990	-0.0113 (0.0785)	0.1169 (0.0791)	-0.0388 (0.0744)	0.00
South Atlantic dummy	0.04299*** (0.00667)	0.00982 (0.01070)	0.01839** (0.00642)	1.07
East South Central dummy	0.01334 (0.00693)	0.00757 (0.00947)	0.01088 (0.00655)	0.10
West South Central dummy	-0.03679*** (0.00677)	-0.02868** (0.01086)	-0.02753*** (0.00644)	0.76
Percent of land in forest, 1992	0.000406 (0.000253)	0.000563* (0.000271)	0.000211 (0.000240)	0.07
Percent of land in forest squared, 1992	-6.63e–6 (2.62e–6)	-5.98e–6* (2.77e–6)	-4.40e–6 (2.48e–6)	0.17
January mean temperature z score	0.03898*** (0.00316)	0.03027*** (0.00758)	0.02153*** (0.00319)	3.93
January mean days of sunshine z score	0.00433* (0.00221)	0.01281*** (0.00387)	0.00350 (0.00211)	0.10
July mean temperature z score	-0.00286 (0.00239)	-0.00600 (0.00319)	-0.00500* (0.00227)	0.04
July mean humidity z score	-0.02013*** (0.00285)	-0.00827 (0.00481)	-0.01310*** (0.00275)	1.28
Topography scale z score	-0.00465* (0.00223)	0.00462 (0.00240)	-0.00009 (0.00211)	0.11
Distance to large airport, 2005	-6.07e–5* (3.01e–5)	-1.46e–4*** (3.98e–5)	-4.57e–5 (2.86e–5)	0.10
Rural roads acres, 1992	1.65e–6*** (2.77e–7)	9.54e–7*** (2.73e–7)	1.29e–6*** (2.63e–7)	0.92
Number of natural resource-based attractions, 1990s	-0.00475 (0.00258)	-0.00978*** (0.00246)	-0.00991*** (0.00245)	0.09
Golf courses per capita, 1990s	94.73*** (14.70)	72.61*** (13.73)	89.46*** (13.91)	1.07

(Continued)

Table 17.2 (Continued)

Variable	OLS	SEM	SAR	Explanatory power in OLS model[1]
All crime occurrences per capita, 1994	-3.718*** (0.998)	-4.487*** (0.926)	-4.240*** (0.944)	0.36
Poverty rate, 1989	0.1658*** (0.0448)	0.1339*** (0.0435)	0.1863*** (0.0425)	0.35
Percent of population with a college degree, 1989	-0.00395*** (0.00075)	-0.00455*** (0.00075)	-0.00433*** (0.00071)	0.72
Percent employed in agriculture, 1989	-0.00348*** (0.00039)	-0.00411*** (0.00038)	-0.00345*** (0.00037)	2.04
Percent employed in mining, 1989	-0.00403*** (0.00050)	-0.00330*** (0.00048)	-0.00375*** (0.00047)	1.70
Percent employed in manufacturing, 1989	-0.00104*** (0.00027)	-0.00137*** (0.00027)	-0.00127*** (0.00025)	0.39
Percent employed in business services, 1989	0.003259*** (0.001265)	0.00291*** (0.00118)	0.00293* (0.00120)	0.17
Percent employed in recreation, 1989	0.00301*** (0.00073)	0.00232** (0.00071)	0.00230*** (0.00070)	0.43
Active MDs per capita, 1990	2.765 (1.552)	2.779 (1.448)	2.294 (1.469)	0.08
Percent of population age 62 and over, 1990	0.5123*** (0.0537)	0.5215*** (0.0537)	0.4152*** (0.0514)	2.35
Black percent of population, 1990	-0.00070*** (0.00018)	-0.00094*** (0.00020)	-0.00050** (0.00017)	0.38
Hispanic percent of population, 1990	-0.00042 (0.00023)	-0.00092*** (0.00032)	-0.00047* (0.00022)	0.08
Percent of employees commuting out, 1990	0.000244* (0.000112)	0.00016 (0.00011)	0.00014 (0.00011)	0.12
Cropland percent of land, 1992	-0.000390*** (0.000108)	-5.01e-5 (1.16e-4)	-0.000305** (0.000102)	0.34
Pastureland percent of land, 1992	0.000675*** (0.000180)	0.000490* (0.000205)	0.000046 (0.000175)	0.36
Public land percent of land, 1992	0.000799*** (0.000123)	-7.46e-5 (1.33e-4)	0.000186 (0.000118)	1.10
Property taxes per household, 1992	-2.04e-5*** (4.62e-6)	-1.66e-5*** (4.60e-6)	-1.80e-5*** (4.38e-6)	0.50
Intercept	-0.2002*** (0.0313)	-0.1514*** (0.0358)	-0.1828*** (0.0296)	
λ		0.9252*** (0.0217)		
ρ			0.6142*** (0.03544)	
Adjusted R-squared	0.5526	0.6129	0.5965	

Notes: Statistical significance levels: *** = 0.001, ** = 0.01, * = 0.05. Standard errors in parentheses.
[1] Explanatory power of variables = $\eta^2/R^2 \times 100$.

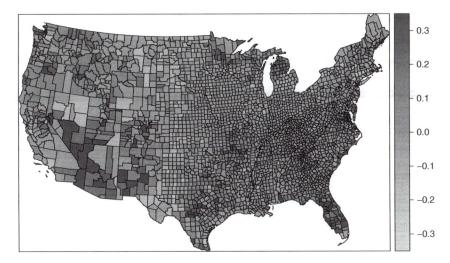

Figure 17.2 Annual net migration rate of retirees and near retirees (age 50–69 in 1990), 1990–2000

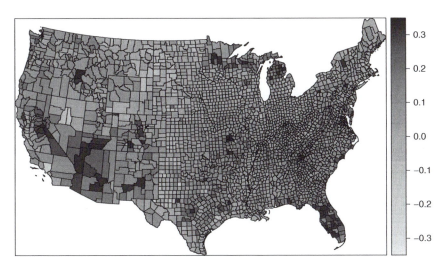

Figure 17.3 Predicted (using OLS model) annual net migration rate of retirees and near retirees, 1990–2000

The spatial models (SEM and SAR) address this spatial autocorrelation issue. The results of the spatial models are qualitatively quite similar to the OLS model results, with similar signs and magnitudes of the statistically significant coefficients in almost all cases. Although the SEM and SAR models both have somewhat higher explanatory power than the OLS model, the spatial pattern of residuals from these models is very similar to that in the OLS model.[7]

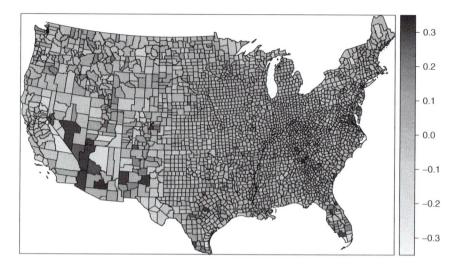

Figure 17.4 Residuals (from OLS model) of annual net migration rate of retirees and
near retirees, 1990–2000

Expanding the classification of retirement destination counties to consider the
potential for attracting retirees, we use both actual and predicted migration rates
to classify counties into three categories: (1) low potential and low actual net
migration of people near or at retirement age, with both predicted and actual NMR
over ten years of less than 15 percent; (2) retirement attraction "underachievers",
with predicted NMR greater than or equal to 15 percent, but actual NMR less than
predicted; and (3) retirement attraction "overachievers", with actual NMR
greater than or equal to 15 percent, but predicted NMR less than actual. Figure
17.5 shows these three classes on a scatter plot of predicted and actual NMRs,
using the results of the OLS model for predicted NMRs. The current ERS
classification of retirement destination counties is represented by the set of observations above the horizontal dashed line at an actual NMR of 15 percent. Our
classification includes most of those observations as retiree attraction overachievers (shown as black triangles in Figure 17.5). However, some of the counties
with NMRs greater than 15 percent during the 1990s are predicted to have even
higher NMR than they achieved. These counties are included in the class of
underachievers (shown with gray squares in Figure 17.5). Other underachievers
had actual NMRs of less than 15 percent and predicted NMRs of greater than
15 percent (in the lower right quadrant of Figure 17.5); these counties appear to
be even further below their potential to attract retirees.

A map of these classes using the OLS results to predict migration rates illustrates some interesting patterns (Figure 17.6). Most counties are classified as
low-low, with both relatively low actual and predicted NMRs. Retiree attraction
underachievers and overachievers are found in many of the same regions, including

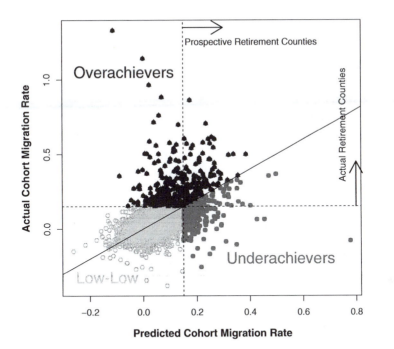

Figure 17.5 Scatter plot of typology of retiree attraction counties, using OLS model results

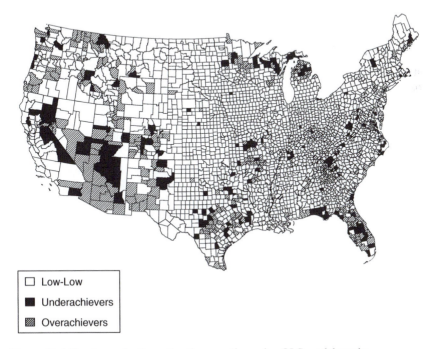

Figure 17.6 Typology of retiree attraction counties, using OLS model results

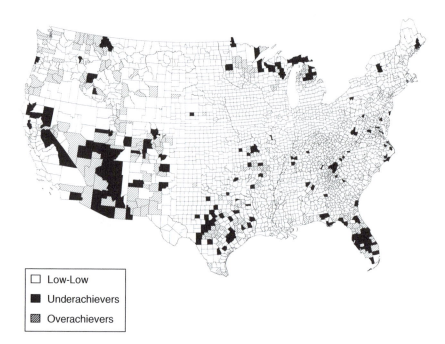

Legend:
- □ Low-Low
- ■ Underachievers
- ▨ Overachievers

Figure 17.7 Typology of retiree attraction counties, using SAR model results

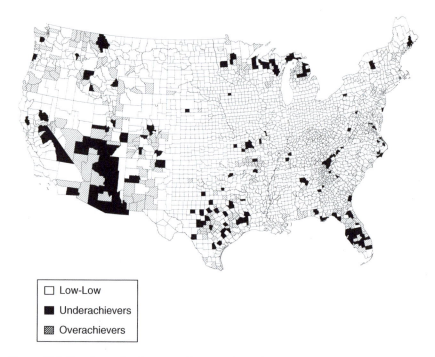

Legend:
- □ Low-Low
- ■ Underachievers
- ▨ Overachievers

Figure 17.8 Typology of retiree attraction counties, using SEM model results

parts of the Southwest, Texas, Florida, the Ozark Mountains, Appalachia, and the northern Great Lakes regions. Substantial numbers of overachievers are also found in the Pacific Northwest and Rocky Mountain regions. Substantial numbers of underachievers are found in the Sierra Nevada region of California. Maps of the classes using the spatial models reveal similar patterns (Figures 17.7 and 17.8).

Conclusion

It is obvious that no "one-size-fits-all" approach to achieving rural wealth creation can be successful in all contexts. What is less obvious is "what works where", i.e., what approaches have potential in which contexts. Although much applied research has been conducted on particular rural economic development approaches and strategies, research identifying and assessing the menu of development options that rural communities can choose from is relatively rare. To make informed decisions about rural wealth creation strategies, rural policy makers and other decision makers need less advocacy for or against particular options, and more information about the range of feasible options available and the potential impacts in their particular context.

To help researchers begin to provide such information, we have proposed a typology of rural economic development strategies and offered some hypotheses about key contextual factors and asset endowments that may determine where these strategies have the most potential. This typology and these hypotheses could form the basis of a large program of applied research. As shown by several chapters in this book, a substantial amount is already known about the factors affecting particular strategies and the impacts of those strategies. However, less is generally known about the relationships between rural economic development strategies and the multiple types of rural wealth discussed in this book, considering how multiple forms of wealth influence development strategies and vice versa. Furthermore, there are few examples of research that go beyond estimating econometric relationships or presenting case study findings to attempt to identify and map locations having potential for particular strategies.

We have presented an example of a methodology for identifying and mapping locations with potential for one particular rural economic development strategy: attracting retirees. Our methodology extends the current method used by ERS to identify retirement destination counties by incorporating information on predicted migration rates of retirees and near retirees, in addition to information on actual migration rates. We showed that a substantial number of "underachievers" appear to have potential to attract large numbers of retirees, based on the factors found in previous literature significantly to predict actual migration rates, including natural and recreational amenities; labor and housing market conditions; access to urban areas, infrastructure, and health care services; crime, poverty, and tax rates; demographic and other factors. Many such underachievers are located close to other counties that were more successful in attracting retirees in the 1990s in traditional retirement destination regions such as the Southwest and Florida. Others are in other locations, such as the Sierra Nevada region of California.

Case study research comparing such underachievers with otherwise similar overachievers could help to identify key factors that account for different outcomes. It could also be interesting to compare underachievers that are attracting relatively large numbers of retirees (e.g., those above the threshold of actual migration to be classified by ERS as retirement destination counties) with similar counties that are attracting fewer retirees (e.g., those below the ERS threshold). Among the factors that may be important but difficult to include in an econometric analysis is the extent to which communities are interested in pursuing this development option. It is important to emphasize that our results are not prescriptive; we are not arguing that counties that have potential to attract retirees should pursue this option. That is a decision that only local decision makers can make based upon their preferences, available options, and constraints. The point of this mapping exercise is to identify locations that may have potential for this option, both to assist local decision makers in identifying their options and as a catalyst for further applied research on this topic.

Beyond stimulating more research on retirement migration, we hope that the typology and methods discussed in this chapter may stimulate applied research on other rural economic development strategies as well. The methods that we used to identify locations that may have underexploited potential to attract retirees could be used to identify locations with potential for other options. Once the potential for multiple development options has been identified and mapped, such maps could be used to provide information to rural communities in any location about the range of options available to them. Further research on the impacts of different options in particular types of contexts could also be used to predict potential impacts in similar contexts elsewhere. Such an approach to applied research could progressively build up a knowledge base about the potentials of alternative economic development options to contribute to sustainable wealth creation and prosperity in the diverse contexts of rural America.

Appendix: data and regression models

The data used in the econometric analysis and their sources are summarized in Table 17.A1. The data sources include those cited by McGranahan (2008), Poudyal et al. (2008), and Cromartie and Nelson (2009). Almost all explanatory variables were for the early 1990s or just before 1990. Exceptions include data on recreational amenities from the National Outdoor Recreation Supply Information System (NORSIS). The codebook for NORSIS is dated 1997 but it is not clear what year some of the variables represent. The variables for distance to a large airport and to the nearest interstate highway were based on geographic analysis of 2005 data by Christiane von Reichert, Professor of Geography, University of Montana. We regard these data to be reasonable proxies for the variables as they would have been at the beginning of the study period in 1990.

Table 17.A1 Data summary and sources

Variable	Mean	Std. Dev.	Minimum	Maximum	Data source[1]
Net migration rate, 1990–2000, ages 50–69 in 1990	0.057446	0.118347	−0.38136	1.331298	Voss et al. (2004)
Unemployment rate, 1989	0.066504	0.030675	0	0.305341	Census (1990)
Employment change, 1990–1993	0.014617	0.039547	−0.12794	1.803207	BEA-REIS
Median home value, 1990	53,374.92	32,914.23	14,999	500,001	Census (1990)
Percent seasonal housing, 1990	0.056489	0.093564	0	0.753937	Census (1990)
Rural metro dummy	0.08328	0.276349	0	1	Cromartie and Nelson (2009)
Nonmetro adjacent dummy	0.322143	0.467373	0	1	Cromartie and Nelson (2009)
Nonmetro non-adjacent dummy	0.41091	0.492078	0	1	Cromartie and Nelson (2009)
Population density, 1990	226.9495	1711.103	0.165827	68,156.91	Census (1990)
Population density squared, 1990	2,97,8434	9.08E+07	0.027499	4.65E+09	Census (1990)
Share urban, 1990	0.364436	0.29803	0	1	Census (1990)
Share married no children, 1990	0.327992	0.041487	0.130493	0.512093	Census (1990)
Percent foreign born, 1990	0.022056	0.035815	0	0.451485	Census (1990)
South Atlantic dummy	0.186249	0.389371	0	1	Cromartie and Nelson (2009)
East South Central dummy	0.117172	0.321678	0	1	Cromartie and Nelson (2009)
West South Central dummy	0.152034	0.359111	0	1	Cromartie and Nelson (2009)
Percent of land in forest, 1992	36.6564	30.30448	0	97.28653	NRI (1992)
Percent of land in forest squared, 1992	2,261.757	2,531.849	0	9,464.67	NRI (1992)
January mean temperature z score	0.003542	0.996081	−2.62742	2.84074	ERS
January mean days of sunshine z score	0.001854	0.997559	−3.11652	3.44725	ERS
July mean temperature z score	0.001465	0.995927	−2.85779	6.50064	ERS
July mean humidity z score	−0.00816	0.999538	−1.64342	2.87475	ERS
Topography scale z score	0.000512	0.999613	−1.19466	1.83868	ERS
Water area z score	0.030486	0.969983	−2.35103	2.37209	ERS

(Continued)

Table 17.A1 (Continued)

Variable	Mean	Std. Dev.	Minimum	Maximum	Data source[1]
Wild and scenic river miles, 1992	2.084893	20.16021	0	640	USDA-FS, USDI-NPS, and BLM
Coastal dummy	0.105875	0.31396	0	1	NORSIS (1997)
Distance to large airport (≥375,000 embarkations), 2005	106.3331	75.01705	10	510	FAA
Distance to nearest interstate highway, 2005	29.051	24.48046	10	190	FHWA
Rural roads acres, 1992	8,695.416	6,281.416	0	90,000	NRI (1992)
State park dummy	0.483215	0.499799	0	1	NORSIS (1997)
No. of natural resource-based attractions, 1990s	0.137508	0.776932	0	28	NORSIS (1997)
No. of entertainment, amusement and sports attractions, 1990s	0.196256	1.257933	0	37	NORSIS (1997)
No. of historical and cultural attractions, 1990s	0.194965	0.889475	0	17	NORSIS (1997)
No. of fishing camps, 1990s	1.096837	1.821813	0	24	NORSIS (1997)
Golf courses per capita, 1990s	8.07E−05	0.000109	0	0.002522	NORSIS (1997)
All crime occurrences per capita, 1994	0.000462	0.00203	0	0.065002	FBI-UCR
Poverty rate, 1989	0.162448	0.077604	0	0.617855	Census (1990)
College enrollment per capita, 1990	0.02019	0.057109	0	0.578417	Census (1990)
Percent of population with a college degree, 1990	8.575009	4.119564	1.825193	38.48048	Census (1990)
Percent employed in agriculture, 1989	7.591824	8.791976	0	68.69159	Census (1990)
Percent employed in mining, 1989	1.760174	3.962949	0	42.18643	Census (1990)
Percent employed in manufacturing, 1989	18.568	10.55035	0	53.67465	Census (1990)

Table 17.A1 (Continued)

Variable	Mean	Std. Dev.	Minimum	Maximum	Data source[1]
Percent employed in business services, 1989	5.098915	2.029635	0	17.32714	Census (1990)
Percent employed in recreation, 1989	7.294962	3.125355	0.808081	33.54509	Census (1990)
Active MDs per capita, 1990	0.001022	0.001286	0	0.026623	HRSA-ARF
Proportion of population age 62 and over, 1990	0.177973	0.04872	0.017007	0.402975	Census (1990)
Black percent of population, 1990	8.639352	14.38099	0	86.23598	Census (1990)
Hispanic percent of population, 1990	4.481688	11.1105	0	97.21605	Census (1990)
Percent of employees commuting out, 1990	28.29681	18.55113	−225.94	88.44728	Census (1990)
Cropland percent of land, 1992	26.23885	25.50918	0	93.17889	NRI (1992)
Pastureland percent of land, 1992	9.823083	10.87477	0	71.80599	NRI (1992)
Public land percent of land, 1992	13.54552	19.6555	0	98.48812	NRI (1992)
Property taxes per household, 1992	559.0539	432.9772	22.91248	7,242.991	COG (1992)

Note: [1]Sources of data: Census (1990) – 1990 Population Census; BEA-REIS – Bureau of Economic Analysis Regional Economic Information System; NRI (1992) – 1992 Natural Resource Inventory; ERS – USDA Economic Research Service natural amenities data; USDA-FS, USDI-NPS, and BLM – Forest Service, National Park Service, and Bureau of Land Management; FAA – Federal Aviation Administration; FHWA – Federal Highway Administration; NORSIS – National Outdoor Recreation Supply Information System; FBI-UCR – Federal Bureau of Investigation, Uniform Crime Report; HRSA-ARF – Health Resources Services Administration, Area Resource File; COG – Census Bureau, Census of Governments.

The specifications of the regression models are:

1   OLS: $y = X\beta + e$
2   SAR: $y = \rho Wy + X\beta + e$
3   SEM: $y = X\beta + u, u = \lambda Wu + e$

where y is the net migration rate, X is the vector of explanatory variables, e is an error term assumed to be independently and identically distributed across counties, W is a spatial weights matrix, and ρ and λ are parameters that determine spatial effects in the SAR and SEM models. If ρ and λ equal 0, these spatial models reduce to the OLS model.

We used a distance-based spatial weights matrix to account for similarity in climates across distances and driving proximity in neighboring counties that may influence retiree migration. We considered this type of matrix to be more appropriate than weight matrices based on adjacency (e.g., Queen or Rook contiguity matrices) because of differences in the areas of counties across the United States. The weights matrix was calculated by selecting all counties whose centroids are within a certain distance of the county centroid. The distance was selected to provide the strongest rejection of the null hypothesis of no spatial autocorrelation (in the OLS model) using a Moran's I test. The distance selected was 175 miles, i.e., all counties whose centroids were within 175 miles of the centroid of a particular county were regarded as neighbors in the weights matrix.

The Moran's I test statistic for the OLS model (Moran's I standard deviate = 29.0) indicates a strong rejection of the null hypothesis of no spatial autocorrelation. Both the SAR and SEM model results also imply rejection of OLS, since ρ and λ are statistically significantly different from 0. To test for which model fits the data best, we used spatial Lagrange Multiplier (LM) tests suggested by Anselin et al. (1996). The tests assume:

$$y = \rho Wy + X\beta + u$$

There are two tests used. The first test is LMerror and holds the null hypothesis that $\lambda = 0$ in the presence of the nuisance parameter ρ. The second test is the LMlag and holds the null hypothesis that $\rho = 0$ in the presence of the nuisance parameter λ. If both tests fail to reject the null hypothesis, then the tests give evidence that OLS is the best model. If the null hypothesis of the LMerror (LMlag) is rejected and the LMlag (LMerror) is not rejected, the best model is SEM (SAR). If the null hypothesis is rejected in both cases, it is not possible to identify which model is best based upon these test statistics. Using robust LM statistics, both null hypotheses were rejected (robust LMerror test statistic of 266 and robust LMlag test statistic of 63, both significant at 1 percent level). Hence, we cannot say which of the two spatial models is better.

Notes

1 The views expressed are those of the authors and should not be attributed to the US Department of Agriculture or to the Economic Research Service.

2 Low argues that the negative association between bank deposits and self-employment may be because self-employed people lack access to bank credit, and may need access to alternative sources of microfinance.
3 Low suggests that the negative association between intellectual capital and establishment rates may be because patents are associated with larger firms in nonmetropolitan areas.
4 Cohort net migration for a county is estimated as the cohort population for a county in 2000 minus the cohort population for a county in 1990, plus the expected deaths for that cohort over the decade from 1990 to 2000. The net migration rate is net migration divided by the cohort population for that county in 1990, and the annual net migration rate is the net migration rate divided by 10 (since the period studied is ten years).
5 The full results are available from the authors upon request.
6 Specifically, the fourth column reports $\eta^2/R^2 \times 100$, where η^2 is the sum of squares for a particular variable from an analysis of variance divided by the total sum of squares. For a model with independent explanatory variables, the sum of η^2 equals R^2. With correlated explanatory variables, this sum will generally be less than R^2 (Philip Ender, UCLA Statistical Consulting Group, personal communication). Nevertheless, this ratio still provides a useful indicator of the effect size of particular variables in a multiple regression.
7 The correlation between the residuals in the OLS model and the residuals in the SEM model is 0.958 and the correlation between the residuals in the OLS model and the residuals in the SAR model is 0.966.

References

Anselin, L., Bera, A., Florax, R., and Yoon, M. (1996) "Simple diagnostic tests for spatial dependence", *Regional Science and Urban Economics*, 26(1): 77–104.

Brown, D.L., Bolender, B., Kulcsar, L., Glasgow, N., and Sanders, S. (2011) "Intercounty variability of net migration at older ages as a path-dependent process", *Rural Sociology*, 76(1): 44–73.

Cook, P.J., and Mizer, K.L. (1994) *The Revised ERS County Typology: An Overview*, Rural Development Research Report No. 89, US Department of Agriculture, Economic Research Service.

Cromartie, J., and Nelson, P. (2009) *Baby Boom Migration and its Impact on Rural America*, Economic Research Report No. 79, Washington, DC: US Department of Agriculture, Economic Research Service.

Deller, S., Tsai, T.-H., Marcouiller, D., and English, D. (2001) "The role of amenities and quality of life in rural economic growth", *American Journal of Agricultural Economics*, 83(2): 352–65.

Drabenstott, M. (2006) "Rethinking Federal policy for regional economic development", *Federal Reserve Bank of Kansas City Economic Review*, 1st quarter: 115–42.

Heimlich, R., and Anderson, W. (2001) *Development at the Urban Fringe and Beyond: Impacts on Agriculture and Rural Land*, Agricultural Economic Report No. 803, Washington, DC: US Department of Agriculture, Economic Research Service.

Johnson, K., Voss, P., Hammer, R., Fuguitt, G., and McNiven, S. (2005) "Temporal and spatial variation in age-specific net migration in the United States", *Demography*, 42(4): 791–812.

McGranahan, D. (1999) *Natural Amenities Drive Rural Population Change*, Agricultural Economic Report No. 781, Washington, DC: US Department of Agriculture, Economic Research Service.

McGranahan, D. (2008) "Landscape influence on recent rural migration in the U.S.", *Landscape and Urban Planning*, 85: 228–40.

McGranahan, D., Wojan, T., and Lambert, D. (2011) "The rural growth trifecta: outdoor amenities, creative class and entrepreneurial context", *Journal of Economic Geography*, 11(3): 529–57.

Pender, J., Marré, A., and Reeder, R. (2012) *Rural Wealth Creation: Concepts, Strategies, and Measures*, Economic Research Report No. 131, Washington, DC: US Department of Agriculture, Economic Research Service.

Porter, M. (1990) *The Competitive Advantage of Nations*, New York: Free Press.

Poudyal, N., Hodges, D., and Cordell, H. (2008) "The role of natural resource amenities in attracting retirees: implications for economic growth policy", *Ecological Economics*, 68(1): 240–48.

Shaffer, R., Deller, S., and Marcouiller, D. (2004) *Community Economics: Linking Theory and Practice*, Ames, IA: Blackwell.

Voss, P.R., McNiven, S., Hammer, R.B., Johnson, K.M., and Fuguitt, G.V. (2004) "Country-specific net migration by five-year age groups, Hispanic origin, race and sex 1990–2000", Working Paper 2004–24, Center for Demography and Ecology, University of Wisconsin-Madison.

18 Rural wealth creation

Conclusions and implications

*John L. Pender, Bruce A. Weber,
Thomas G. Johnson, and
J. Matthew Fannin[1]*

Introduction

As indicated in Chapter 1, the main objective of this book is to synthesize and contribute to knowledge about rural wealth creation, how rural wealth can be measured, and strategies for creating and maintaining rural wealth that contribute to lasting and broadly shared rural prosperity. The contributors to this book have pursued this objective by defining wealth concepts and introducing a conceptual framework for rural wealth creation and an accounting framework for measuring wealth in Part I of the book; providing six case studies measuring multiple kinds of wealth at different geographic scales in Part II; providing a historical overview of community economic development strategies and their relationship to rural wealth creation, and six case studies of rural wealth creation strategies in Part III; and introducing a typology of rural wealth creation strategies in Chapter 17 that draws on these case studies and demonstrates an approach to mapping locations having potential to pursue one particular strategy. In this final chapter, we seek to synthesize the main themes and lessons from the preceding chapters and to suggest implications and the way forward for applied research on this topic.

Measuring rural wealth

As is evident in Chapters 2 and 3 and the case studies presented in Part II, there are many types of wealth in rural areas, and measuring and comparing different types of wealth presents considerable challenges. Conceptually, wealth as a set of stocks of assets must be distinguished from the flows of goods and services that depend on wealth, such as monetary income and consumption of non-monetary goods and services. Pender and Ratner provided examples of eight different types of wealth in Chapter 2 and some of the flows of goods and services to which these contribute. In Chapter 3, Johnson et al. elaborated further on these concepts, and illustrated conceptually how a wealth accounting system could track changes in wealth stocks over time, based on initial stocks, inflows such as income and natural growth, and outflows such as consumption and depreciation.

Several of the chapters in Part II provided examples of measuring wealth of different types and their dynamics, and demonstrated some of the challenges.

In Chapter 5, Marré estimated household marketable net worth (including physical and financial assets) and the dynamics of net worth, using household panel survey data. One of the challenges of using this approach to measure rural wealth creation is the lack of such data at a detailed geographic level, making it difficult to learn about wealth dynamics in particular rural communities or regions. Another challenge is the fact that such data focus only on marketable wealth, ignoring non-marketed and intangible forms of wealth such as human and social capital. These data also focus only on private household wealth and exclude public forms of wealth, such as infrastructure and knowledge generated by publicly funded research. Hence, the understanding of wealth dynamics using such household survey data is inevitably incomplete, although a useful starting point for a more complete accounting of wealth.

It is possible to use data from household surveys and censuses to estimate some other kinds of wealth, such as the value of human capital. In Chapter 4, Marré and Pender applied the method of Arrow et al. (2012) to estimate the value of human capital due to formal educational attainment in rural communities in Oregon, using data from the Population Census and the American Community Survey. They combined these data with estimates of the value of residential, commercial, and industrial real estate in these communities from the Oregon Department of Revenue. As Marré and Pender pointed out, these two categories of wealth likely include the vast bulk of the wealth of these communities, considering that Arrow et al. (2012) estimated that human capital accounts for more than 90 percent of the wealth of the United States, and the fact that some of the value of non-marketed forms of wealth such as natural amenities will be reflected in property values.

In Chapter 8, Ghadimi, Harris, and Warner demonstrated another approach to measuring the value of non-marketed wealth. They estimated the value of natural capital that provides ecosystem services at the county level in West Virginia, using geographic land cover data and published estimates of the annual value of ecosystem services provided by different land cover types. Inevitably, their approach requires untested assumptions about the future time path of ecosystem services and the choice of social discount rate to estimate the net present value of these future flows. The dependence on untested assumptions is a threat to the validity of such wealth estimates, as it is to other studies estimating the value of comprehensive wealth at national and other scales (Arrow et al. 2012; World Bank 2006, 2011; UNU-IHDP and UNEP 2012).

When feasible and based on defensible assumptions, estimating wealth in monetary value terms has considerable advantages. This enables comparisons across different types of wealth, facilitating consideration of tradeoffs occurring during the process of development. Unless all types of wealth are moving in the same direction, it is not possible to say whether aggregate wealth (and well-being) is increasing or decreasing if different types of wealth are measured in different units. For the case of the Oregon communities, Marré and Pender did find that the values of human capital and property moved in the same direction on average in the 1990s and 2000s, although this masks variations occurring across communities. Similarly, comparisons of the overall wealth of one region or group of people with another at a given point can be facilitated by monetary valuation of different forms of wealth. For example, Ghadimi et al. (Chapter 8) provided estimates of housing values as well as values of natural capital across counties in West Virginia; comparisons of aggregates of these values could be used to estimate which counties were wealthier in terms of the aggregated wealth.

Valuing all forms of wealth is not always feasible or necessary, however. How wealth should be measured depends on the purposes of measuring it. For example, in Chapter 6, Ratner and Levy described quantitative and qualitative indicators of seven different types of wealth selected by coordinators of four community development networks participating in a Ford Foundation initiative on rural wealth creation in central Appalachia. They argued that the process of selecting indicators helps practitioners to plan their activities to best serve project objectives and provide accountability for measurable results. They also argued that use of indicators selected by practitioners, rather than externally imposed indicators, helps to ensure that the practitioners can and will use the indicators to improve their practices, internalizing measurement in their ongoing operations. Such self-selected indicators may be very useful for the purpose of improving project management and internal learning, but are likely to be less useful in drawing lessons across different projects or networks or for evaluating their impacts.

Even for the purpose of establishing a comprehensive wealth accounting framework, it is not necessary to value all forms of wealth, as Johnson et al. point out in Chapter 3. Wealth accounts can be kept in quantitative non-monetary terms, and this provides the basis for monetary valuation if that is feasible.

An important concern raised by Johnson et al. with regard to wealth measurement is the potential problem of double-counting wealth. As they point out, this potential is greater when valuing wealth in monetary terms. For example, adding an estimate of the value of natural amenities to land values would involve double-counting, since part of the value of natural amenities is likely to be reflected in land values. On the other hand, undercounting of total wealth is also possible when there are complementarities between different types of wealth. For example, the returns to investments in human capital are generally higher in economies with good infrastructure. If one were to account for wealth by adding the expected net present value of returns to human capital to the net present value of returns to investment in infrastructure, without accounting for the positive interactions between these investments, one would underestimate the wealth represented by these combined investments. In general, total wealth may be greater than or less than the sum of individual wealth components if there are interactions between different types of wealth in their contributions to well-being.

The interactions among different types of wealth represent an opportunity as well as a challenge for measuring wealth. They are an opportunity because the interrelationships between different types of wealth can sometimes be used to estimate indirectly the value of types of wealth that are difficult to measure directly. For example, hedonic price analysis can be used to estimate contributions of natural, social, and cultural capital to property values. Such interactions also represent a challenge and opportunity for regions and communities seeking to create and maintain wealth that contributes to lasting prosperity. Taking such interactions into account requires coordination of investments in diverse types of assets, which is a challenge for local planning processes, but to the extent this can be achieved, the returns to investments can be increased.

Two other important measurement issues highlighted by Johnson et al. are the need to distinguish and measure people-based wealth (the wealth owned by the residents of a region) from place-based wealth (the wealth physically located within a region), and the need to incorporate public as well as private wealth in both measures. Johnson et al. defined people- and place-based wealth and showed conceptually how they can be measured, and included the role of public wealth in this. In Chapter 7, Fannin and Honadle applied Johnson et al.'s framework to measure the people- and place-based public wealth of Lincoln Parish, Louisiana. Fannin and Honadle's example illustrates how these two measures of wealth can differ (greater place-based than people-based wealth in the example), and they used these differences to highlight implications for the development prospects of this parish. In general, regions with greater place-based wealth than people-based wealth are more dependent on the external owners of assets for decisions that influence their development prospects (two state universities in this example).

The same issue affects many natural resource dependent communities, such as agriculture and forest dependent communities in Alabama (discussed by Bailey and Majumdar in Chapter 9) and forest dependent communities in Oregon (discussed by Chen and Weber in Chapter 12). In Chapter 9, Bailey and Majumdar estimated absentee ownership of land in fifty counties of Alabama, and found that more than 60 percent of forest land and more than 40 percent of agricultural land was owned by absentees from outside the county, with more than one-third of absentee-owned land the property of people from outside the state. They showed that absentee land ownership is associated with lower per capita incomes, lower educational attainment, and a higher percentage of students receiving free or reduced price meals; and argued that absentee land ownership is an obstacle to local wealth generation in rural Alabama. Although they did not estimate the total people-based or place-based wealth of these counties, it is likely that the place-based wealth of many of these counties is greater than the people-based wealth as a result of absentee land ownership.

In Chapter 12, Chen and Weber pointed out that much of the land in rural Oregon is forest land owned and managed by the Federal government. Many rural communities have long been heavily dependent on this place-based wealth for their livelihoods, and are vulnerable to changes in Federal policies concerning management of this land, such as the Northwest Forest Plan, which reduced timber harvests from Federal forests beginning in 1994. Chen and Weber showed that decisions about the management of this externally owned natural capital stock had significant impacts on the property wealth, human capital (total population), and incomes of rural communities close to the Federal forest land and lumber mill towns; with negative impacts initially on mill towns and logging dependent communities but positive impacts on other forest adjacent communities not dependent on logging. Their findings emphasize the complex distributional impacts that such a policy change can have on communities that are dependent on public lands. A similar situation exists in many Western states.

Even when most of the wealth is locally owned, changes in policies or economic circumstances can have complex distributional impacts at the local level. For example, in Chapter 11, Weber, Brown, and Pender discussed the natural gas and wind energy booms that have occurred in many rural areas in the past decade, and estimated the impacts on farm households' wealth of payments made by energy companies for access to natural gas, oil, and land for wind projects. They estimated that $2.3 billion in energy payments were made to farms in 2011 and that these payments increased farm households' wealth by $7.7 billion, mainly due to increased land values. As these wealth impacts are tied primarily to land ownership, Weber et al. argued that the benefits of these payments are unequally distributed and could undermine social capital in rural communities. Unfortunately, data on the distribution of wealth in rural areas is quite limited and more available for farm households than for other rural households. Thus, investigating the impacts of policies or other changes on the distribution of wealth in rural areas represents a considerable challenge.

Although wealth measurement is beset by many challenges, incremental progress can be achieved as conceptual and empirical bases for wealth measurement advance. Having a sound accounting framework, as proposed by Johnson et al. in Chapter 3, should accelerate the achievement of this goal by highlighting the types of indicators needed.

Strategies for rural wealth creation

Many strategies are possible for pursuing rural wealth creation and sustainable and broadly shared rural prosperity. As emphasized by Deller in Chapter 10 and Pender and Dinterman in Chapter 17, no strategy is suited to all contexts, and multiple strategies may be effective in particular contexts. Pender and Dinterman drew upon the waves of development policy described by Deller and prior work by Pender et al. (2012) to develop a typology of rural economic development strategies and hypotheses about key contextual factors and assets that determine the potential for these strategies. These strategies can be classified according to the main assets or contextual factors that they are based on, including natural resource based strategies such as agriculture, forestry, mining, and renewable energy production; low input (mainly labor and land) cost strategies such as industrial recruitment; strategies based on locational advantages such as developing as a regional commercial center or bedroom community, or production and marketing of local foods; amenity-based strategies such as recreation, tourism, and attracting retirees; and knowledge- and innovation-based strategies such as promoting small business entrepreneurship, attracting the creative class, and cluster strategies. Although much literature exists on each of these strategies and although each strategy is being pursued in a significant number of rural communities, little research has sought to identify where and under what conditions these strategies are likely to be successful, or how decision makers can compare the potential implications of pursuing alternative or joint strategies.

In Chapter 2, Pender and Ratner offered several hypotheses about rural wealth creation, based on their conceptual framework and the example of ethanol development. The case studies of particular wealth creation strategies in Part III of this book provide further insights about some of these hypotheses.

Wealth creation is highly context dependent

Several of the case studies in Part III of this book shed light on the roles that particular contextual factors and local assets play in determining the potential for particular wealth creation strategies. In Chapter 11, Weber et al. discussed the key contextual factors and assets that contributed to the recent booms in shale gas and wind energy production. Among the most important factors have been energy policies, technological developments, and changes in the prices of energy relative to inputs. Beyond such general factors, local endowments of various assets have had a large role in determining the locations where development has occurred; including, of course, the relevant natural resources (shale gas deposits and wind potential), but also including physical assets such as transportation, waste disposal and electricity infrastructure, and local social support for the activity.

In Chapter 13, Low reviewed the literature on factors influencing rural entrepreneurship and provided new econometric estimates of the impacts of several types of rural wealth on various indicators of rural entrepreneurship. She found that each of the wealth indicators is positively associated with at least one indicator of entrepreneurship; with the natural capital, human capital, and physical capital indicators positively associated with several entrepreneurship indicators. Financial and intellectual capitals have more mixed impacts.

In Chapter 16, Pender found that casino development has been affected by changes in the legal and regulatory context, changes in social norms and consumer preferences with regard to gambling, technological change, access to markets and infrastructure, and some local assets. Among the location-specific factors, proximity to large urban markets and large local populations, and local institutions and cultural norms appear to be the most important determinants of where this option has potential.

In Chapter 15, Reeder and Bagi found that several types of assets and contextual factors have been shown to attract retirees in the literature, including natural amenities, recreational and cultural opportunities, availability of low-cost housing, seasonal housing, hospitals, highways, airports, telecommunications, social connections, lower property taxes, and lower population density. These findings are supported by the empirical analysis of Pender and Dinterman (Chapter 17), who found that the most important factors include indicators of natural and recreational amenities and social connections.

These case studies demonstrate the critical role of local context and asset endowments in determining the potential for various rural wealth creation strategies. Little research is yet available that attempts to identify and map the domains in which particular strategies have potential. In Chapter 17, Pender and Dinterman demonstrated an approach to doing this based on econometric analysis of the determinants of retirement migration. They showed that most rural counties appear to have low potential to attract retirees, but among those that have high potential many have attracted fewer retirees than would be expected, given their geographic characteristics and asset endowments. Such retiree attraction "underachievers" can be found in many traditional retirement destination regions, but also in some other regions, such as the Sierra Nevada region of California. Such a mapping exercise does not say that local decision makers in such regions should pursue a strategy focused on attracting retirees, but it can help to identify options for them to consider. Similar efforts to map the potential for other wealth creation strategies could help to provide a set of options to most rural communities.

Interrelationships among assets are important

Little empirical research, including the studies in this book, formally investigates asset interrelationships, such as whether and in what contexts different types of wealth act as complements or substitutes in contributing to income and well-being. Nevertheless, different types of interrelationships are discussed in many of the chapters.

In Chapter 14, Jablonski described how farmers draw on the physical capital (facilities) and human capital (production and marketing knowledge) in farmers' markets to build social capital (relationships among farmers and customers) and generate financial capital (earnings that can be saved and invested). Reeder and Bagi (Chapter 15) discussed how natural amenities and physical capital infrastructure can attract human capital in the form of migrant retirees to rural communities, contributing to those communities' ability to invest in further development of their assets and attract more retirees.

Several chapters discuss how rural development strategies often involve converting one type of wealth into others. In Chapter 7, Fannin and Honadle explain how privately owned financial capital is converted via the tax system into publicly owned physical infrastructure or publicly financed investments in human capital (education). Weber et al. discuss in Chapter 11 how natural capital in the form of energy resources is converted into financial and physical capital. In Chapter 16, Pender discusses how financial capital earned by casinos has been used in some cases to finance investments in other forms of capital, including physical infrastructure and schools, education and training programs, and preservation of cultural traditions.

Investments in wealth are risky, but investments in multiple forms may reduce risk

Some of the case studies in the book provide insights relative to Pender and Ratner's third hypothesis. Weber et al.'s discussion in Chapter 11 of the development of shale gas and wind energy illustrates some of the risks involved with an energy boom fostered in part by high energy prices and policy incentives. As shale gas production has rapidly expanded, prices have already fallen dramatically, potentially threatening the viability of some wells and associated economic activity. Wind energy faces a risk that the federal renewable electricity production tax credit may not be renewed, although it was extended for a year by the Taxpayer Relief Act of 2012 (H.R. 6, Sec. 407). Reeder and Bagi discuss how pursuing a strategy of attracting retirees can help to diversify the economy of many rural communities and thus help to reduce risks, though this may not be the case in communities already heavily dependent on this strategy.

Investments in locally owned assets can increase local benefits, but may involve tradeoffs

As discussed previously, a few chapters discuss how dependence on externally owned assets can increase the vulnerability of rural communities, such as agricultural and forest dependent communities in Alabama (Chapter 9) and logging dependent communities in Oregon (Chapter 12). This is the converse of Pender and Ratner's hypothesis. In her review of the literature on the impacts of local farmers' markets, Jablonski (Chapter 14) found several studies that support the positive impacts of these markets on local incomes and different types of local wealth, although the evidence on such impacts is quite limited and subject to substantial weaknesses, as she emphasized.

Wealth creation is a dynamic process with multiple possible pathways

Some rural development strategies have potential to contribute to broad-based wealth creation, with increases in many types of assets occurring simultaneously. Reeder and Bagi discussed improvements in several types of wealth – especially financial, physical, and human capital – that can occur as a result of attracting retirees to rural areas. Similarly, Jablonski discussed improvements in financial, social, human, and natural capital that may be occurring as a result of development of farmers' markets. As the authors of both of these chapters pointed out, however, evidence on these impacts is limited, and such broad-based wealth improvement is not assured.

Tradeoffs in impacts on different forms of capital are also likely for several of the other development strategies discussed in this book. For example, investments in shale gas development have contributed to depletion and pollution of natural water supplies in some cases (Weber et al., Chapter 11). Protection of Federal forests (natural capital) in Oregon has reduced growth in property values in rural mill towns (Chen and Weber, Chapter 12). Attraction of retirees (human capital) to rural areas may contribute to damage to natural and physical capital due to population growth (Reeder and Bagi, Chapter 15). Development of casinos (accumulation of physical and financial capital) can contribute to losses in human capital (reduced educational attainment) and social capital (social conflict resulting from unequal distribution of benefits) (Pender, Chapter 16).

Overall, the case studies in this book support the hypotheses about rural wealth creation proposed by Pender and Ratner in Chapter 2. However, the evidence on these issues is still very limited. Much more research is needed on these topics, as well as on the issues of measurement discussed previously. In the next section of this chapter we elaborate on the implications of our findings, focusing primarily on research implications, consistent with the objectives of this book.

Implications

Researchers are sometimes criticized for always recommending more research. Those readers harboring such an opinion will not be disappointed by the implications that we draw from the lessons of this book. In this case, however, we feel justified in focusing on research implications and not policy implications, because the primary objective of this work has been to take stock of (and add to) available knowledge related to rural wealth creation, in order to build a foundation for future research on this under-researched topic. Given the findings discussed above with regard to some of our key hypotheses, such as the context dependence of rural wealth creation and the need to understand interrelationships among different types of assets – both issues that have been little addressed in the literature – it would be foolish to offer bold policy implications in the light of the current state of knowledge on this topic.

This caveat notwithstanding, there are some implications that rural policy makers and development practitioners may find useful. One is that serious attention must be paid to the issue of how rural development policies and programs affect rural wealth, broadly defined. As the theoretical literature has shown, sustainable improvements in well-being require improvements in multiple forms of comprehensive wealth (Arrow et al. 2012). It is not sufficient to know how an intervention has affected employment or income to say whether well-being has improved or sustainable development has occurred. Yet the dominant focus of many policy makers and development practitioners – when they consider the outcomes of interventions – is usually on employment and income.

Learning how policies and programs affect rural wealth and well-being would benefit from substantial new commitments by development funders, data collection agencies, and the research community. The impacts of most rural development interventions, even on employment and income, are not well known. A commitment to collecting the necessary data to evaluate impacts would support research clarifying the concepts that are to be measured, and demonstrating the methods to be used.

Besides efforts to assess the impacts of particular rural development interventions, data on rural wealth, broadly defined, are needed to be able to assess and compare progress in people's well-being. Wealth is arguably just as important for well-being as current income, yet data on wealth are less available. Data on some tangible forms of household private wealth are routinely collected and reported by large national surveys, but as noted earlier, these exclude many important intangible forms of wealth, such as human and social capital, and exclude public capital. Furthermore, these data are not available at a disaggregated geographic level, so they are difficult to use to assess the dynamics or distribution of rural wealth other than in broad aggregations, as investigated by Marré in Chapter 5.

Although research on rural wealth creation is hampered by the lack of available public data on wealth, new research could contribute a great deal to knowledge about rural wealth creation using existing data sources, combined with targeted primary data collection efforts. There is a need for additional research on how to conceptualize and measure the different types of wealth. Johnson et al. have provided a template for applied research on wealth measurement with their wealth accounting framework in Chapter 3. Research is needed on how to measure the different elements of their extended SAM framework, distinguishing place-based and people-based wealth and public and private wealth. Fannin and Honadle have provided a start on this type of research with their demonstration of how to measure place-based versus people-based public wealth using publicly available data in Chapter 7. Bailey and Majumdar (Chapter 9) demonstrated that publicly available data on land ownership can be used to investigate impacts of absentee ownership of assets. The same type of data would provide a starting point for research estimating differences between private people- and place-based wealth of counties in the United States.

Substantial progress in wealth measurement is possible using existing data sources and focusing on what are likely to be the most important types of wealth for well-being. For example, Marré and Pender (Chapter 4) demonstrated that the value of human capital can be estimated at the community level using data from the Population Census and the American Community Survey, and combined with publicly available data on property values to estimate the vast bulk of the comprehensive wealth of rural towns in Oregon. This builds on the recent work of Mumford (2012), who applied the methods of Arrow et al. (2012) to estimate the value of human capital and other components of comprehensive wealth for all US states. Further research along these lines could yield greatly expanded information about major components of wealth of rural communities elsewhere in the United States. Researchers can also draw upon available spatial data infrastructures to estimate rural wealth at various scales, as argued and illustrated by Ghadimi et al. in Chapter 8. Such geographically detailed information can be especially (but not only) useful for estimating natural capital stocks.

Much more research is needed on when and how to aggregate different types of wealth in terms of monetary values or other common units. As pointed out earlier, double-counting or undercounting is a serious concern when adding together different types of wealth, if the levels of these different types of wealth affect each other. Whether and in what contexts the different types of rural wealth are complements or substitutes in their contributions to well-being is a critical unaddressed question in the literature. This question underlies the debate about weak versus strong sustainability of economic development. If different types of assets are sufficiently substitutable, sustainability can be achieved by maintaining the aggregate value of wealth (weak sustainability perspective) (Stiglitz et al. 2009). On the other hand, some forms of wealth, such as ecosystems that provide basic life-support functions, may be essential and not substitutable (strong sustainability perspective). Empirical research investigating the extent of substitutability among different types of rural wealth would be very valuable for addressing these issues.

To the extent that there are interactions among different types of wealth, researchers can use this fact to help measure the value of non-marketable forms of wealth. The underlying theory and methods for doing this are well established in the literature on hedonic price analysis, and can be built upon to improve understanding about the wealth of rural areas.

There is also a need for research on how different forms of wealth interact, whether simultaneously or inter-temporally, to determine the feasibility and outcomes of different rural wealth creation strategies. Empirical research on the determinants of particular wealth creation strategies, such as that cited by Weber et al. (Chapter 11), Low (Chapter 13), Reeder and Bagi (Chapter 15), and Pender (Chapter 16), usually investigates the independent impact of each factor, without investigating the interaction effects of factors. More research is needed on how the different types of wealth interact with each other and with contextual factors to influence the potential of different strategies.

Understanding interactions between different types of wealth is also important in identifying resiliency of regions to external shocks such as natural disasters. Johnson et al. (Chapter 3) proposed a method for adjusting regional wealth based on stochastic events. Understanding how these interactions operate to impact the rate of change of wealth stocks in natural disasters would add to the depth of understanding of the economic consequences of these events beyond simple economic flows. Further, an understanding of the interactions can provide greater insight into best practices for wealth investments for increasing regional resiliency from these stochastic events.

Empirical research is greatly needed that goes beyond identifying factors that have a statistically significant influence on the potential of wealth creation strategies, to identify places where these strategies may have unexploited potential for success. Pender and Dinterman (Chapter 17) have demonstrated an approach to doing this for the strategy of attracting retirees. If similar research were conducted on a large number of wealth creation strategies and their domains of high potential mapped, overlays of these domains could be used to provide valuable information to decision makers concerning the options that appear to have potential in any location.

Beyond mapping locations that have economic potential for particular strategies, it would be useful to conduct case study research comparing locations that have similar predicted potentials for a given strategy but different uptake of those strategies. Such case studies could reveal new insights about the influence of less readily measurable factors, such as the priorities and efforts of local communities themselves. Such research could improve knowledge about the central box in the conceptual framework presented by Pender and Ratner in Chapter 2: the local decision makers and their key decision rules and decisions influencing rural wealth creation.

Empirical research is also greatly needed on the impacts of different rural wealth creation strategies on economic, social, and environmental outcomes; especially on the dynamics of different types of wealth. The case studies in Part III have revealed the dearth of information about wealth impacts of any of the strategies studied, despite quite large literatures in some cases. The potential for such research is of course affected by the limited availability of data measuring wealth at local levels, but as noted earlier, much can still be accomplished with available data. An example of what is possible is provided by Chen and Weber's study (Chapter 12), in which they estimated the impacts of forest and logging dependence in the wake of the Northwest Forest Plan on changes in property wealth as well as on changes in income and population in rural Oregon communities. Their approach could be augmented with estimates of changes in the value of human capital, such as estimated by Marré and Pender (Chapter 4), or other types of wealth to obtain a broader perspective on the wealth impacts of that policy.

It is not just the community aggregate levels of different forms of wealth that may determine the outcomes of different wealth creation strategies. There is good reason to expect that the distribution of different forms of wealth critically affects both the level of development in particular places and the effect of different strategies. There is evidence that income inequality affects regional growth and that the relationship between inequality and growth varies across regions (Atems 2013). But there has been no research to our knowledge on the effect of wealth inequality on rural or regional development. This is in part because of the lack of locality-specific data on wealth distribution. Nevertheless, given the increased inequality in the distribution of net worth among metro and nonmetro households in the United States during the past decade noted by Marré in Chapter 5, and the available data used in that analysis, there appears to be an opportunity for fruitful research on how inequality in some types of wealth affects regional economic, social, and environmental outcomes and sustainability in this country.

There are conceptual links between inequality in the distribution of different forms of capital and regional sustainability that bear further exploration if distributional data can be developed. Neumayer (2011), for example, outlines a framework in which he links inequalities in the distribution of various forms of capital (particularly human, financial, and political capital) with "unsustainability", which he defines as inadequate savings and investments in several forms of capital (human, social, physical), and degradation of critical forms of natural capital (natural resources that absorb pollution and provide environmental amenities). Neumayer posits a vicious cycle in which greater inequality in income and human capital (education and health) leads to more built capital (better educated and healthier people are more productive and have more income; richer people save and invest more than poorer people) but less human capital (poorer people have less money to invest in education), less social capital (the "social fabric" gets frayed), and less natural capital (the rich consume and pollute more and resist public policies that protect the environment). More built capital and less human, social, and natural capital are hypothesized to generate inequalities in income and in financial, political, human, and social capitals.

Wealth impacts can also be investigated using available household survey data, such as the Agricultural Resource Management Survey data used by Weber et al. (Chapter 11) to estimate impacts of energy payments on the net worth of farm households. Similar national survey data are unfortunately not available for nonfarm rural households. Targeted survey efforts focusing on rural nonfarm households in particular regions or states could help to address knowledge gaps about the wealth impacts of particular strategies on these households.

Research is also needed on wealth creation in urban as well as rural areas, and in other countries. The dearth of information about multiple types of wealth, their interactions and dynamics in processes of development extends to these other domains as well. Empirical research on these issues is more advanced in some developing countries; inspired by the influential Sustainable Livelihoods Framework of the United Kingdom's Department for International Development (Carney 1998).[2] Nevertheless, the information available on these issues in other countries is still quite fragmented and limited. Research on multiple types of wealth and asset-based livelihood strategies in urban areas is even more rare.

As explained in Chapter 1, our focus in this book has been on wealth creation in rural areas. In focusing on rural areas, we are not suggesting that rural wealth creation can occur independently of urban development or that what happens in urban places is unimportant. Indeed, rural economic, social, and environmental well-being is tightly linked to the health of urban and global society, markets, and policies, and the study of rural wealth creation will be richer if done within the context of the larger urban system of which rural places are a part. By focusing on rural areas, we seek to highlight the unique and complex and relatively neglected geography of rural America and call attention to the contribution that rural people and places make to the larger economy and society.

Notes

1   The views expressed are those of the authors and should not be attributed to the US Department of Agriculture or to the Economic Research Service.
2   See, for example, Adato and Meinzen-Dick (2002); Jansen et al. (2006); Babulo et al. (2008); and Ansoms and McKay (2010).

References

Adato, M., and Meinzen-Dick, R. (2002) *Assessing the Impact of Agricultural Research on Poverty Using the Sustainable Livelihoods Framework*, Washington, DC: International Food Policy Research Institute.

Ansoms, A., and McKay, A. (2010) "A quantitative analysis of poverty and livelihood profiles: the case of rural Rwanda", *Food Policy*, 35(6): 584–98.

Arrow, K.J., Dasgupta, P., Goulder, L.H., Mumford, K.J., and Oleson, K. (2012) "Sustainability and the measurement of wealth", *Environment and Development Economics*, 17: 317–53.

Atems, B. (2013) "A note on differential effects of income inequality: empirical evidence using U.S. county-level data", *Journal of Regional Science*, 54(4): 656–71, DOI: 10.1111:jors.12053.

Babulo, B., Muys, B., Nega, F., Tollens, E., Nyssen, J., Deckers, J., and Mathijs, E. (2008) "Household livelihood strategies and forest dependence in the highlands of Tigray, Northern Ethiopia", *Agricultural Systems*, 98(2): 147–55.

Carney, D. (1998) "Implementing the sustainable livelihoods approach", in D. Carney (ed.), *Sustainable Rural Livelihoods: What Contribution Can We Make?*, London: Department for International Development.

Jansen, H.G., Pender, J., Damon, A., Wielemaker, W., and Schipper, R. (2006) "Policies for sustainable development in the hillside areas of Honduras: a quantitative livelihoods approach", *Agricultural Economics*, 34(2): 141–53.

Mumford, K.J. (2012) "Measuring inclusive wealth at the state level in the United States", in UNU-IHDP and UNEP, *Inclusive Wealth Report 2012: Measuring Progress toward Sustainability*, Cambridge: Cambridge University Press.

Neumayer, E. (2011) *Sustainability and Inequality in Human Development*, United Nations Development Programme Human Development Reports, Research Paper 2011/04.

Pender, J., Marré, A., and Reeder, R. (2012) *Rural Wealth Creation: Concepts, Strategies and Measures*, Economic Research Report No. 131, Washington, DC: US Department of Agriculture Economic Research Service.

Stiglitz, J.E., Sen, A., and Fitoussi, J.-P. (2009) *Report by the Commission on the Measurement of Economic Performance and Social Progress*. Online. Available at: <http://www.stiglitz-sen-fitoussi.fr/en/index.htm> (accessed 1 March 2012).

United Nations University International Human Dimensions Programme on Global Environmental Change (UNU-IHDP) and United Nations Environment Programme (UNEP) (2012) *Inclusive Wealth Report 2012: Measuring Progress Toward Sustainability*, Cambridge: Cambridge University Press.

World Bank (2006) *Where is the Wealth of Nations? Measuring Capital for the 21st Century*, Washington, DC: World Bank.

World Bank (2011) *The Changing Wealth of Nations. Measuring Sustainable Development in the New Millennium*, Washington, DC: World Bank.

Index